The Cambridge Guide to
Research in Language Teaching and Learning

THE CAMBRIDGE GUIDES SERIES

Authoritative, comprehensive and accessible guides, addressing both the theoretical and the practical aspects of key topics in second language teaching and learning.

For more information on these titles, please visit: www.cambridge.org/elt

Other titles in this series:

The Cambridge Guide to Blended Learning for Language Teaching
Edited by Michael McCarthy

The Cambridge Guide to Second Language Assessment
Edited by Christine Coombe, Peter Davidson, Barry O'Sullivan and Stephen Stoynoff

The Cambridge Guide to Pedagogy and Practice in Second Language Teaching
Edited by Anne Burns and Jack C. Richards

The Cambridge Guide to Second Language Teacher Education
Edited by Anne Burns and Jack C. Richards

The Cambridge Guide to Teaching English to Speakers of Other Languages
Edited by Ronald Carter and David Nunan

The Cambridge Guide to Research in Language Teaching and Learning

Edited by
James Dean Brown
Christine Coombe

CAMBRIDGE
UNIVERSITY PRESS

University Printing House, Cambridge CB2 8BS, United Kingdom

Cambridge University Press is part of the University of Cambridge.

It furthers the University's mission by disseminating knowledge in the pursuit of education, learning and research at the highest international levels of excellence.

www.cambridge.org
Information on this title: www.cambridge.org/9781107485556

© Cambridge University Press 2015

This publication is in copyright. Subject to statutory exception
and to the provisions of relevant collective licensing agreements,
no reproduction of any part may take place without the written
permission of Cambridge University Press.

First published 2015

Printed and bound in Italy by Rotolito Lombarda S.p.A.

A catalogue record for this publication is available from the British Library

Library of Congress Cataloguing in Publication data
The Cambridge guide to research in language teaching and learning /
edited by James Dean Brown ; Christine Coombe.
    pages cm. – (The Cambridge Guides series)
Includes index.
ISBN 978-1-107-48555-6 (pbk.)
1. Language and languages – Study and teaching – Research. 2. Language acquisition – Research. 3. Language teachers – Training of – Research.
I. Brown, James Dean, editor. II. Coombe, Christine A. (Christine Anne), 1962– editor.
P118.2.C355   2015
418.0071 – dc23   2015008287

ISBN 978-1-107-48555-6 Paperback
ISBN 978-1-316-50641-7 Apple iBook
ISBN 978-1-316-50643-1 eBooks.com ebook
ISBN 978-1-316-50640-0 Google ebook
ISBN 978-1-316-50642-4 Kindle ebook

Cambridge University Press has no responsibility for the persistence or accuracy of URLs for external or third-party internet websites referred to in this publication, and does not guarantee that any content on such websites is, or will remain, accurate or appropriate.

CONTENTS

Acknowledgements			*page* viii
Introduction		Research in Language Teaching and Learning *James Dean Brown and Christine Coombe*	xiii

Section 1		**Primary Considerations**	1
Chapter	1	Teacher Research Engagement: Primary Motivators and Obstacles *Christine Coombe and Dean Sheetz*	3
Chapter	2	Critiquing the Research of Others *Eric Dwyer and Benjamin Baez*	11
Chapter	3	Applying for Research Funding and Grants *Ahmar Mahboob*	19
Chapter	4	Using Research in the Language Classroom *Andy Curtis*	27

Section 2		**Getting Ready**	35
Section 2A		*Preliminary Decisions*	37
Chapter	5	Framing and Defining Your Research Project *Liying Cheng*	39
Chapter	6	Deciding Upon a Research Methodology *James Dean Brown*	46

Section 2B		*Choosing a Research Method*	53
Chapter	7	Essentials of Quantitative Research for Classroom Teachers *Thom Hudson*	55
Chapter	8	Qualitative Research *Keith Richards*	61
Chapter	9	Research Paradigms in Second Language Research *Peter Stanfield*	68
Chapter	10	Mixed Methods Research *James Dean Brown*	78

Section 2C		*Choosing a Research Type*	85
Chapter	11	Critical Research in TESOL and Language Education *Salah Troudi*	89

v

Chapter	12	Action Research *Anne Burns*	99
Chapter	13	Teacher Research *Simon Borg*	105
Chapter	14	Case-study Research *Patricia A. Duff and Tim Anderson*	112
Chapter	15	Corpus Research *Jesse Egbert, Shelley Staples and Douglas Biber*	119
Chapter	16	Conversation Analysis *John Hellermann*	127
Chapter	17	Discourse Analysis *Brian Paltridge*	134
Chapter	18	Replication Research in Quantitative Research *Graeme Porte*	140
Chapter	19	Ethnography *David M. Palfreyman*	146
Chapter	20	Narrative Inquiry *Lauren Stephenson and Barbara Harold*	155

Section 3	**Doing the Research**	**165**
Section 3A	***Preliminary Steps***	***167***

Chapter	21	Doing a Literature Review and Creating Your Research Niche *Ali Shehadeh*	169
Chapter	22	Ethics in Research *Magdalena Kubanyiova*	176
Chapter	23	Human Subjects Review *Dudley W. Reynolds*	183
Chapter	24	Creating Effective Research Questions *Deena Boraie and Atta Gebril*	190
Chapter	25	Sampling and What it Means *John McE. Davis*	198

Section 3B	***Data Gathering***	***207***

Chapter	26	Conducting Interviews *Gabriele Kasper*	209
Chapter	27	Constructing Questionnaires *Christine Coombe and Peter Davidson*	217
Chapter	28	Conducting Focus Groups *Sena C. Pierce*	224
Chapter	29	Using Introspective Methods *Sheryl V. Taylor and Donna Sobel*	231

Chapter	**30**	Designing and Using Rubrics *Larry Davis*	238
Chapter	**31**	Conducting Diary Studies *Kathleen M. Bailey*	247
Chapter	**32**	Analyzing Your Data Statistically *Matthew A. Robby and Christina Gitsaki*	253
Section 3C		**Reporting Findings**	**263**
Chapter	**33**	Presenting Your Research *Andy Curtis*	265
Chapter	**34**	Publishing Your Research *Paul Kei Matsuda*	272
Section 4		**Research Contexts**	**279**
Chapter	**35**	Using Research in Language-program Evaluation *Janet Orr and Deon Edwards-Kerr*	281
Chapter	**36**	"It's like crossing a desert": An Oasis of Language Teacher Research Across Six Continents *Thomas S. C. Farrell*	288
Index			299

ACKNOWLEDGEMENTS

THE CO-EDITORS

This book is dedicated to our research students at the University of Hawai'i at Manoa, Dubai Men's College and the University of Exeter.

We would very much like to thank all the contributors to this book for their fine chapters and for their cheerful cooperation throughout the entire process of producing this book. Thanks are also extended to the anonymous reviewers for their helpful comments and suggestions.

James Dean Brown
Christine Coombe

THE CO-EDITORS AND THE PUBLISHERS

The authors and publishers acknowledge the following sources of copyright material and are grateful for the permissions granted. While every effort has been made, it has not always been possible to identify the sources of all the material used, or to trace all copyright holders. If any omissions are brought to our notice, we will be happy to include the appropriate acknowledgements on reprinting and in the next update to the digital edition, as applicable.

Text on p. 3 from 'Research and Teaching: Changing Relationships in a Changing Context' by Angela Brew in *Studies in Higher Education*, 24, pp. 291–301, Copyright © 1999 by Routledge, Published by Routledge/Taylor & Francis Group; Text on p. 6 from 'Conditions for Teacher Research' by Simon Borg in *English Teaching Forum*, 44, pp. 22–27, 2006, Published by Bureau of Education and Cultural Affairs, United States Department of State; Text on pp. 7–9 from 'Research Education as an Objective for Teacher Learning' by Simon Borg in *The Role of Research in Teacher Training* by B. Beaven & S. Borg (Eds.), 2003, Published by IATEFL Publications; Text on p. 7 from 'Teaching Idea sources and Work Conditions in an ESL Program' by Graham Crookes & Lowell Arakaki in *TESOL Journal*, 8, pp. 15–19, Spring 1999, Copyright © 1999 by TESOL International Association, Published by John Wiley & Sons; Text on p. 11 from 'Eleven Theses on Feuerbach' by Karl Marx in *Marx/Engels Selected Works* by Engels, Volume 1, 1969, Published by Progress Publishers; Text on p. 12 from *The Cambridge Advanced Learner's Dictionary, Fourth Edition*, available online at dictionary.cambridge.org, Copyright © 2013 by Cambridge University Press, Reproduced with permission; Text on p. 12 from *Scientific Research in Education* by Richard J. Shavelson & Lisa Towne (Eds.), Copyright © 2002 by the National Academy of Sciences. All rights reserved, Published by National Academy Press; Text on p. 27 from *The Management of a Student Research Project, Third Edition* by Keith Howard and John A. Sharp, Copyright © 2002 by John A. Sharp, John Peters, and Keith Howard. All rights reserved, Published by Gower Publishing Company; Text on p. 28 from the *Introduction to Designing and Conducting Research* by Clifford J. Drew, 1980, Published by Mosby/Elsevier;

Text on p. 28 from *Doing Your Research Project: A Guide for First-Time Researchers in Education and Social Science, Fourth Edition* by Judith Bell, 2005, Copyright © 2002 by Judith Bell, Published by Open University Press; Text on p. 28 from 'The Quest for Meaning in Educational Research' by Deborah Court in *Academic Exchange Quarterly*, 8, pp. 1–7, Fall 2004, Published by Rapid Intellect Group; Text on p. 28 from *Second Language Classrooms: Research on Teaching and Learning* by Craig Chaudron, Copyright © 1988 by Cambridge University Press, Published by Cambridge University Press; Text on pp. 28, 31, 32 from 'Research Issues: Some Guidelines for Conducting Quantitative and Qualitative Research in TESOL' by Carol A. Chapelle and Patricia A. Duff in *TESOL Quarterly*, 37, pp. 157–178, Spring 2003, Copyright © 2003 by TESOL International Association, Published by John Wiley & Sons; Text on p. 30 from 'Quantitative Versus Qualitative?' by Janet Beavin Bavelas in *Social Approaches to Communication* by Wendy Leeds-Hurwitz (Ed.), Copyright © 1995 by the Guilford Press, Published by Guilford Press; Blackwell Publishing Ltd., for the adapted figure on p. 47, from 'Research Methods of Applied Linguistics: Scope, Characteristics, and Standards' by J. D. Brown in *The Handbook of Applied Linguistics* edited by Alan Davies and Catherine Elder, Copyright © 2004 by Blackwell Publishing Ltd, Reproduced with permission of Blackwell Publishing Ltd; Text on pp. 49, 79–80 from *Mixed Method Research for TESOL* by James D. Brown, Copyright © 2014 by James D. Brown, Published by Edinburgh University Press; Text on p. 57 from *By Design: Planning Research on Higher Education* by Richard J. Light, Judith D. Singer, and John B. Willett, Copyright © 1990 by the President and Fellows of Harvard College. All rights reserved, Published by Harvard University Press; Text on p. 61 from 'Introduction: The Discipline and Practice of Qualitative Research' in *The SAGE Handbook of Qualitative Research, Fourth Edition* by Norman K. Denzin and Yvonna L. Lincoln, Copyright © 2011 by Sage Publications, Inc., Published by Sage Publications; Text on p. 64 from *Ways with Words: Language, Life, and Work in Communities and Classrooms* by Shirley B. Heath, Copyright © 1983 by Cambridge University Press, Published by Cambridge University Press; Text on p. 78 from 'Toward a Definition of Mixed Methods Research' by R. Burke Johnson, Anthony J. Onwuegbuzie, and Lisa A. Turner in *Journal of Mixed Methods Research*, 1, pp. 112–133, April 2007, Copyright © 2007 by Sage Publications, Inc., Published by Sage Publications; Excerpt on p. 80 from 'The Validity Issue in Mixed Research' by Anthony J. Onwuegbuzie and R. Burke Johnson in *Research in the Schools*, 13, pp. 48–63, Spring 2006, Copyright © 2006 by the Mid-South Educational Research Association, Published by the Mid-South Educational Research Association; Text on p. 81 from *The Delphi Method: Techniques and Applications* by Murray Turnoff and Harold Linstone, Copyright © 2002 by Murray Turnoff and Harold Linstone, Published by the New Jersey Institute of Technology; Text on p. 82 from 'Utilization-Focused Evaluation for Program Development: Investigating the Need for Teaching Experience within the Bachelor of Arts Program in Second Language Studies' by Sena Pierce in *Second Language Studies*, 30, pp. 43–107, 2012, Published by the University of Hawaii; Text on p. 90 from 'Critical Approaches to Research in Practice' by Michael Collins in *Educational Research in Practice* by Joanna Swann and John Pratt (Eds.), Copyright © 2007 by Joanna Swann and John Pratt, Published by Continuum; Text on p. 92 from 'Chapter 33 – Reflection on Action Research' by Salah Troudi in *Proceedings of the 13th TESOL Arabia Conference: Best Practice in English Language Teaching* by Adel Jendi, Christine Coombe, and Salah Troudi, 2008, Published by TESOL Arabia; Text on pp. 93–94 from 'Critical Classroom Discourse Analysis' by B. Kumaravadivelu in *TESOL Quarterly*, 33, pp. 453–484, Autumn 1999, Copyright © 1999 by TESOL International Association, Published by John Wiley & Sons; Text on p. 94 from *Doing Critical Ethnography, Qualitative Research Methods Series*, Volume 26 by Jim Thomas, Copyright © 1993 by Sage Publications, Inc., Published by Sage Publications; Text on p. 95 from 'Forms of Ideology–Critique: A Pedagogical Perspective' by Nicholas C. Burbules in *International Journal of Qualitative Studies in Education*, 5, pp. 7–17, January 1992, Copyright © 1992 by Routledge, Published by Routledge/Taylor

Francis Group; Text on p. 99 from *The SAGE Handbook of Action Research: Participative Inquiry and Practice, First Edition* by Peter Reason and Hilary Bradbury, 2001, Published by Sage Publications; Text on p. 121 from *Longman Grammar of Spoken and Written English* by Douglas Biber, Stig Johansson, Geoffrey Leech, Susan Conrad, and Edward Finegan, Copyright © 1999 by Pearson Education Limited, Published by Pearson Education Limited; Text on p. 142 from *Replication Research in Applied Linguistics* by Graeme Porte, Copyright © 2012 by Cambridge University Press, Published by Cambridge University Press; Text on p. 142 from *Experimental and Quasi-Experimental Designs for Research* by Donald T. Campbell and Julian Stanley, Copyright © 1963 by Houghton Mifflin Company, Published by Houghton Mifflin Harcourt; Text on p. 143 from *Publication Manual of the American Psychological Association, Sixth Edition* by the American Psychological Association, 2010, Published by the American Psychological Association; Text on p. 144 from 'Focus article: Replication in Second Language Writing Research' by Graeme Porte and Keith Richards in *Journal of Second Language Writing*, 21, pp. 284–293, September 2012, Copyright © 2012 Elsevier Inc., All rights reserved, Published by Elsevier; Text on p. 151 from *Ethnographic Fieldwork: A Beginner's Guide* by Jan Blommaert and Doug Jie, Copyright © 2010 by Jan Blommaert and Dong Jie, Published by Multilingual Matters; Text on p. 155 from 'Narrative Methodologies: Subjects, Silences, Rereadings and Analyses' by Liz Stanley and Bogusia Temple in Qualitative Research, 8, pp. 275–281, July 2008, Copyright © 2008 by Sage Publications, Published by Sage Publications; Text on pp. 155, 158 from 'Teacher Development in a Global Profession: An Autoethnography' by A. Suresh Canagarajah in *TESOL Quarterly*, 46, pp. 258–279, June 2012, Copyright © 2012 by TESOL International Association, Published by John Wiley & Sons; Text on p. 157 from 'Autoethnography: An Overview' by Carolyn Ellis, Tony E. Adams, and Arthur P. Bochner in *Forum: Qualitative Social Research*, 12, Art. 10, January 2011, 2014, Published by Forum Qualitative Sozialforschung; Text on p. 158 from 'Personal Ethnography' by Lyall Crawford in *Communication Monographs*, 63, pp. 158–168, June 2, 1996, Copyright © 1996 by Routledge, Published by Routledge/Taylor & Francis Group; Text on p. 159 from *The Ethnographic Self: Fieldwork and the Representation of Identity* by Amanda Coffey, Copyright © 1999 by Amanda Coffey, Published by Sage Publications; Text on p. 161 from 'Life History's History: Subjects Foretold' by W. Tierney in *Qualitative Inquiry*, 4, pp. 49–70, March 1998, Copyright © 1998 by Sage Publications, Published by Sage Publications; Text on pp. 171, 173 from *Second Language Research: Methodology and Design (Second Language Acquisition Research)* by Alison Mackey and Susan M. Gass, Copyright © 2005 by Lawrence Erlbaum Associates, Inc., Published by Routledge/Taylor & Francis Group; Text on p. 173 from 'Quantitative Methods: Concepts, Frameworks, and Issues' by Sebastian M. Rasinger in *Research Methods in Linguistics* by Lia Litosseliti (Ed.), Copyright © 2010 by Lia Litosseliti and contributors, Published by Continuum; Text on p. 180 from *Collaborative Action Research for English Language Teachers (Cambridge Language Teaching Library)* by Ann Burns, Copyright © 1999 by Cambridge University Press, Published by Cambridge University Press; Text on p. 184 from *Recommendations on Good Practice in Applied Linguistics* by The British Association for Applied Linguistics, 2006, Published by the British Association for Applied Linguistics; Text on p. 192 from *Research Design: Qualitative, Quantitative, and Mixed Methods Approaches, Third Edition* by John W. Creswell, Copyright © 2009 by Sage Publications, Inc., Published by Sage Publications; Text on p. 193 from *Educational Research: Quantitative, Qualitative and Mixed Approaches, Fourth Edition* by Robert Burke Johnson and Larry B. Christensen, Copyright © 2009 by Sage Publications, Inc., Published by Sage Publications; Text on p. 198 from *Research in Applied Linguistics: Becoming a Discerning Consumer, Second Edition* by Fred L. Perry, Jr., Copyright © 2011 by Taylor and Francis, Published by Routledge/Taylor & Francis Group; Text on p. 200 from 'Sampling: Quantitative Methods' by James Dean Brown in *The Encyclopedia of Applied Linguistics* by Carol A. Chapelle (Ed.), Copyright © 2013 Blackwell Publishing Ltd, All rights reserved, Published by

John Wiley & Sons; Text on p. 200 from 'Survey Research' by E. Wagner in *Continuum Companion to Research Methods in Applied Linguistics (Continuum Companions)* by Brian Paltridge and Aek Phakiti (Eds.), Copyright © 2010 by Brian Paltridge and Aek Phakiti, Published by Continuum; Text on p. 200 from *The Research Manual: Design and Statistics for Applied Linguistics* by Evelyn Hatch and Anne Lazaraton, 1991, Published by Newbury House; Text on p. 203 from 'Relationship between English Learning Motivation Types and Self-identity Changes among Chinese Students' by Gao Yihong, Zhao Yuan, Cheng Ying, and Zhou Yan in *TESOL Quarterly*, 41, pp. 133–155, March 2007, Copyright © 2007 by TESOL International Association, Published by John Wiley & Sons; Text on p. 203 from *Research Methods in Applied Linguistics: Quantitative, Qualitative, and Mixed Methodologies* by Zoltán Dörnyei, 2007, Published by Oxford University Press; Text on p. 213 from 'Learning how to ask: Native Metacommunicative Competence and Incompetence of Fieldworkers' by Charles L. Briggs in *Language in Society*, 13, pp. 1–28, March 1984, Copyright © 1984 by Cambridge University Press, Published by Cambridge University Press; Text on p. 224 from *Focus Groups: A Practical Guide for Applied Research, Fourth Edition* by Richard A. Krueger and Mary Anne Casey, Copyright © 2009 by Sage Publications, Inc., Published by Sage Publications; Text on p. 225 from 'Where to begin? Grappling with how to use participant interaction in focus group design' by J. A. Belzile and G. Öberg in *Qualitative Research*, 12, pp. 459–472, March 2012, Copyright © 2012 by Sage Publications, Published by Sage Publications; Text on p. 225 from *The Focused Interview: A Manual of Problems and Procedures, Second Edition* by Robert K. Merton, Marjorie Fiske, and Patricia L. Kendall, 1990, Copyright © 1956, 1990 by The Free Press, A Division of Macmillan, Inc. and Introduction Copyright © 1990 by Robert K. Merton, Published by Free Press; Text on p. 244 from *Developing, Using, and Analyzing Rubrics in Language Assessment with Case Studies in Asian and Pacific Languages* by James Dean Brown, Copyright © 2012 by James Dean Brown, Published by the University of Hawaii; Text on pp. 247, 248 from *Exploring Second Language Classroom Research: A Comprehensive Guide* by David Nunan and Kathleen M. Bailey, Copyright © 2009 by Heinle, Cengage Learning, Published by Heinle Cengage Learning; Text on p. 250 from 'On Becoming a Language Teacher: Insights from Diary Studies' by Carol Numrich in *TESOL Quarterly*, 30, pp. 131–151, Spring 1996, Copyright © 1996 by TESOL International Association, Published by John Wiley & Sons; Text on p. 267 from 'Negotiating the Swamp: The Opportunity and Challenge of Reflexivity in Research Practice' by L. Finlay in *Qualitative Research*, 2, pp. 209–230, August 2002, Copyright © 2002 by Sage Publications, Published by Sage Publications; Text on pp. 267–268 from 'Presenting Your Research' by Lindsey L. Cohen, Laurie A. Greco, and Sarah R. Martin in *The Portable Mentor: Expert Guide to a Successful Career in Psychology* by Mitchell J. Prinstein (Ed.), Copyright © 2013 by Springer Science+Business Media New York, Published by Springer; Text on pp. 267–268 from *Nursing Research: Principles and Methods, Eighth Edition* by Denise F. Polit and Cheryl Tatano Beck, Copyright © 2004 by Lippincott Williams & Wilkins and Wolters Kluwer Business, Published by Lippincott Williams & Wilkins; Text on p. 268 from 'How to present your research well', http://openwetware.org/wiki/How_to_present_your_research_well; Text on p. 268 from 'Typical Problems', http://openwetware.org/wiki/How_to_present_your_research_well; Text on p. 269 from 'Paralanguage' by David Abercrombie in *International Journal of Language & Communication Disorders*, 3, pp. 55–59, April 1968, Copyright © 1968 by the Royal College of Speech & Language Therapists, Published by John Wiley & Sons; Text on p. 269 from *How to do Things with Words* by J. L. Austin, Copyright © 1962 by Oxford University Press, Published by Oxford University Press; Text on p. 281 from 'Toward a Methodology of ESL Program Evaluation' by Alan Beretta in *TESOL Quarterly*, 20, pp. 144–155, March 1986, Copyright © 1986 by the TESOL International Association, Published by John Wiley & Sons; Text on p. 283 from *Language Program Evaluation: Theory and Practice (Cambridge Applied Linguistics)* by

Brian K. Lynch, Copyright © 1996 by Cambridge University Press, Published by Cambridge University Press; Text on p. 283 from *Program Evaluation in Language Education (Research and Practice in Applied Linguistics)* by Richard Kiely and Pauline Rea-Dickins, Copyright © 2005 by Richard Kiely and Pauline Rea-Dickins, Published by Palgrave Macmillan; Text on p. 285 from *The Logic Model Guidebook: Better Strategies for Great Results* by Lisa Wyatt Knowlton and Cynthia C. Phillips, Copyright © 2009 by Sage Publications, Inc., Published by Sage Publications.

INTRODUCTION

Research in Language Teaching and Learning

James Dean Brown and Christine Coombe

WHAT IS RESEARCH IN LANGUAGE TEACHING AND LEARNING?

Within the field of language teaching and learning, research is many things. In the early 1980s, research in our field meant linguistic analysis, case studies, or statistical studies, but in the past three decades, the variety of research types has proliferated greatly. We have seen new developments in quantitative research methods, and much expansion in the options available in qualitative research methods, as well as the appearance of mixed methods studies.

Quantitative research methods, which were limited in our field to simple statistical analyses, have proliferated into at least four categories of studies – descriptive studies, exploratory studies, quasi-experimental studies, and experimental studies – each of which can also be subdivided into three to six substantially different forms of analysis (see Figure 6.5 in Chapter 6). Quantitative research methods are well-represented in this book but especially in Chapters 7, 18, 25, and 32.

Similarly, qualitative research methods, which were limited to simple case studies or linguistic analyses, have proliferated into at least: action research, case studies, conversation analyses, corpus research, critical research, diary studies, discourse analyses, ethnographies, interviews, introspection methods, narrative inquiries, open-ended questionnaires, and teacher inquiries. These are discussed in Chapters 11–17, 19–20, 26, and 28–31, but elsewhere as well.

Chapter 10 deals with the relatively new mixed methods research (MMR), which only emerged as a recognized research paradigm at the beginning of this century. Given its flexibility and power as a research methodology, we are confident that it will continue to grow in importance in our field.

As editors, we do not take any explicit stance in this volume regarding the superiority of any particular type of research over any other. Indeed, all of the approaches found in this book provide legitimate and useful research avenues that readers may decide to follow either in their reading, or in their own research efforts. Certainly, the chapters occasionally present opposing, overlapping, and conflicting views and approaches. But, rather than seeing this as a problem for the book, we take it to be a way of empowering readers so they can make fully informed choices about their own research interests.

The proliferation of research options described above makes it difficult to define the notion of research in such a way that it fits all of the various types of research in our field (and all the types described in this book), yet is precise enough to be meaningful. A broad yet meaningful definition was suggested by Donald Freeman (an expert in the field of teacher research): "any principled inquiry." For the purposes of this book, we will use the slightly modified version of that definition that appeared in Brown (2004: 478): "any systematic and principled inquiry in applied linguistics. I have added the word *systematic* because to me research must not only be *principled*, but also orderly, methodical, precise, and well organized, all of which are listed as synonyms for *systematic* in my computer's dictionary."

What is "Research Literacy"?

In the Introduction to Coombe et al. (2012), the authors addressed the issues involved in the notion "assessment literacy", which is a topic with a large and well-developed literature backing it up (also see Brown, 2013). We began to wonder if any work has been done about a parallel concept that might be called "research literacy". As also pointed out in Brown (2013), there has certainly been plenty of work on statistical literacy in terms of the background and skills needed to comprehend and apply:

- The *statistical language and tools* needed for adults to be completely numerate (Garfield and Ben-Zvi, 2007; Rumsey, 2002)
- The *statistical reasoning* needed to interpret statistical evidence (Garfield, 2002)
- The *statistical thinking* used by professional statisticians including: a) why certain research designs are used; b) why specific statistics are chosen; c) what assumptions underlie each statistic; and d) what limitations there are to the inferences that can be made (Chance, 2002; Pfannkuch and Wild, 2004; Wild and Pfannkuch, 1999).

In addition, several books on how to read educational research have appeared over the years (e.g., Bracey, 2006; Vierra and Pollock, 1992). In applied linguistics, a few articles (e.g., Brown, 1991/1995, 1992) and books (e.g., Brown, 1988; Porte, 2010) have appeared designed to help language teachers read research. However, all of these books and articles have focused entirely on quantitative research. We were in search of a much broader notion of research literacy that would fit the diversity of research methods in language teaching and learning. Shank and Brown (2007) fits that bill by covering research literacy related to qualitative, quantitative, and mixed methods research. However, we discovered little else in the general literature on research literacy, and nothing specifically designed for professionals in language teaching and learning. Since helping readers develop research literacy was one of the primary purposes of this book (see p. xv), we decided to explore here the notion of research literacy, with specific reference to the language teaching and learning context.

According to Shank and Brown (2007), research literacy also requires the abilities to read a wide variety of different types of research, to read critically, and to use the information that the research contains. In other words, readers need to be good consumers of research, who can efficiently and effectively find whatever information they need to use and be critical in the process. As a result, research literacy requires that research literate readers:

- Be skillful
- Recognize that research operates with an established set of ideas
- Understand how research is generated, and
- Realize that the research paper or article is the fundamental way that research is reported in the education field.

Stiggins (2007: 2) discusses the skills required to be assessment literate. Drawing on those ideas and our own experiences with research, especially in developing this book, we came up with a similar list of the skills necessary for language teaching professionals (teachers, administrators, curriculum developers, and even researchers) to be considered research literate in language teaching and learning. These are the ability to:

- Understand what data-gathering strategies can be used to collect dependable and valid information for research;
- Recognize well-formulated research questions and how they differ for qualitative, quantitative, and mixed method research;
- Know how data can be analyzed in various research traditions in order to address such research questions adequately;
- Recognize sound research interpretations that are justified by research results;
- Understand the general differences between sound and unsound research, and read critically;
- Communicate effectively with others about research results that they have read;
- Use research and research results to maximize the effectiveness of language teaching and learning.

The language teaching and learning profession is different from other humanities in that it is based on a substantial and ever-growing empirical research literature. Thus the skills involved in research literacy have become essential to language teachers, who need access to that research, but also need to be able to judge its dependability and the adequacy of its research questions, analyses, results, and interpretations. Perhaps more importantly, the professionalization of each of us as individuals, and of the field more generally, depends on our ability to communicate research results and use those results to improve our language teaching and our students' language learning.

THE PURPOSE OF THIS BOOK

The Cambridge Guide to Research in Language Teaching and Learning covers 36 core areas of second language research in one volume and, in the process, offers up-to-date information from experts in the field about a wide variety of types of research. It does so in considerable depth, but without getting bogged down in the minutiae of any particular research method. The book is aimed at an audience that we call "students of research" – that is, pre-service or in-service language teachers interested in research methods, as well as those studying research methods in Bachelor, MA, or PhD graduate programs around the world.

The goals of this book are to provide those students of research with:

- A comprehensive overview of research methods in second language teaching and learning;
- In-depth, easy-to-understand overviews of a variety of approaches to research;
- Theoretical background in key issues associated with such research methods;
- Practical advice on how to improve their effectiveness in any research they may conduct;
- The basic knowledge and research-literacy skills needed to be critical consumers of such research;
- Suggested readings and resources for further study in all the areas of research covered;
- A foundation for discussion of the issues involved in research in language teaching and learning.

THE ORGANIZATION OF THIS BOOK

The overall organization of this book is meant to help readers see the connections between and among the chapters. The book includes four main sections (and subsections) as follows:

1. Primary Considerations;
2. Getting Ready (including Preliminary Decisions, Choosing a Research Method, and Choosing a Research Type);
3. Doing the Research (including Preliminary Steps, Data Gathering, and Reporting Findings);
4. Research Contexts.

PRIMARY CONSIDERATIONS

Section 1 of this book addresses the primary considerations that researchers should ponder as they set up a research project. **Christine Coombe** and **Dean Sheetz** begin by explaining the practical value of research to teachers, especially in terms of using research to make teachers more effective in their classrooms, and some of the obstacles to teacher research engagement. **Eric Dwyer** and **Benjamin Baez** discuss strategies for critiquing the research of other researchers by providing two sets of guidelines and explaining how such guidelines can be used to help read research critically, in order to understand the internal logic of the study as well as its social, historical, political, and cultural underpinnings. **Ahmar Mahboob** explores the issues involved in applying for grants including: identifying sources of funding; applying for the grant; and securing the funding. He also provides guidelines and a checklist for writing an effective proposal, along with an annotated model. **Andy Curtis** focuses on using research in language classrooms by discussing: definitions of "research"; the importance of research in classrooms; quantitative, qualitative, and mixed methods research (and subjectivity versus objectivity); and seven steps in classroom action research.

GETTING READY

Section 2 covers a number of issues that need to be considered before starting a research project. This section includes three subsections on *Preliminary Decisions*, *Choosing a Research Method*, and *Choosing a Research Type*.

The first subsection of Section 2 on *Preliminary Decisions* considers choices that generally need to be made before conducting a research project. **Liying Cheng** considers the topics of framing and defining research in terms of how research problems are defined, where research problems come from, what the components of research problems are, how framing and defining a research project is a cyclical process, and what the five main steps are in research. **James Dean Brown** describes three general research paradigms (quantitative, qualitative, and mixed-methods research) in terms of what types of research fit into each, how the three paradigms are related, and what the eight basic steps are in deciding on a general research methodology.

The second subsection of Section 2 on *Choosing a Research Method* zeros in on the issues involved in choosing a specific research method, with four chapters that examine in detail the three paradigms that researchers typically work within: quantitative, qualitative, or mixed methods. **Thom Hudson** discusses quantitative research and how it systematically uses numerical data to address research questions; shows the importance of variables and attending to internal and external validity; and outlines the many quantitative approaches and methods available. **Keith Richards** explains qualitative research in terms of various definitions; highlights five characteristics of qualitative research; gives an overview of how qualitative research developed; and explains the key issues of "respondent validation," "triangulation," and "thick description." **Peter Stanfield** considers second language research paradigms generally from ontological and epistemological perspectives, and explains how they lead to a tripartite hermeneutic model, especially with regard to experimental, interpretative, critical, and pragmatic strategies. **James Dean Brown** explains how mixed methods research (MMR) combines qualitative and quantitative methods into a third stronger paradigm by: defining MMR; explaining how the nine types of *legitimation* enhance MMR; and showing how convergence, divergence, elaboration, clarification, exemplification, and interaction strengthen MMR.

The third subsection of Section 2 on *Choosing a Research Type* covers the issues involved in choosing a specific research type within the more global quantitative, qualitative, or mixed methods paradigms. **Salah Troudi** examines "critical research," a type of qualitative interpretive research with a critical research question and agenda (e.g., to challenge and change current practices), by discussing the variety of such studies and providing a demonstration of how critical research can be applied. **Anne Burns** defines "action research" (AR), and looks at developments in AR, criticisms and constraints of AR, how AR is conceptualized, AR's different forms, its main features, and links between complexity theory and AR. **Simon Borg** defines "teacher research," and explains the types of resources available, the barriers teacher/researchers face, and actions that school leaders can take to promote teacher research and create a productive teacher research environment. **Patricia A. Duff** and **Tim Anderson** define "case study research"; trace developments in the area; stress the importance of narratives as data; explain the crucial elements and steps involved; explore single versus multiple-case studies; and describe sampling strategies that are often used. **Jesse Egbert**, **Shelley Staples**, and **Douglas Biber** define "corpus research"; describe a variety of free online corpora; explain developments in corpus-based research; argue for the usefulness of learner corpora; describe classroom uses of corpora; suggest ways for teachers to do corpus research; and provide examples of the sorts of research questions that can be answered. **John Hellermann** defines "conversation analysis" (CA); describes transcription processes; covers developments; argues that CA has made an impact (by using naturalistic data, viewing language as co-constructed, and maintaining an agnostic attitude toward learner identity); and suggests ways to apply CA in classrooms. **Brian Paltridge** defines "discourse analysis" (DA); describes developments (in terms of DA's relationships to pragmatics, structure of texts, genre analysis, critical DA, multimodal DA, identity, CA, classroom DA, and corpus-assisted DA); and discusses the implications of DA for cross-cultural communication and language teaching/learning. **Graeme Porte** defines "quantitative replication research"; laments the scarcity of replication research and the consequences of that scarcity; describes three types of replication studies (exact, approximate, and conceptual); discusses its background; clarifies what can/should be replicated; and explores obstacles to replication research faced by social scientists. **David M. Palfreyman** defines "ethnographic research"; describes its characteristics; provides example studies; explains various types of ethnographic data; lays out the general steps involved in ethnographic research; and discusses recent developments in online contexts and critical ethnography. **Lauren Stephenson** and **Barbara Harold** define "narrative inquiry"; then focus in on one type of narrative inquiry called *autoethnography* (which they describe in terms of its special uses and characteristics); and finally describe the stages and steps involved in doing narrative inquiry research as well as potential challenges.

DOING THE RESEARCH

Section 3 addresses what is involved in actually doing the research. This section includes three subsections on *Preliminary Steps*, *Data Gathering,* and *Reporting Findings.*

In the first subsection of Section 3, the chapters cover the preliminary steps that need to be taken in a research project. **Ali Shehadeh** covers the process of writing a literature review by discussing: the purposes and organization of a good literature review; the importance of creating a niche for the study; the four advantages of reviewing the literature; and a practical list of dos and don'ts. **Magdalena Kubanyiova** writes about research ethics, including respect for persons; beneficence; justice; informed consent; anonymity; confidentiality; risk/benefit ratio; macroethical and microethical principles; and practical guidelines for doing ethical research when power is unequal in multilingual/multicultural and digital settings. **Dudley W. Reynolds** explores human subjects review, including legal, ethical, and institutional issues; macroethical and microethical considerations; principles that should govern research; the researcher's responsibility to informants; professional organization guidelines; human subjects review boards; and currently debated ethics issues. **Deena Boraie** and **Atta Gebril** discuss what research questions (RQs) are; what their purpose is; where RQs should be in a report; the ideal number of RQs; RQs and hypotheses; ordering RQs; and differences between quantitative, qualitative, and mixed methods RQs (with examples of well-written RQs of all three types). **John McE. Davis** defines "sampling" and related terms; introduces "generalization," "external validity," and "representativeness"; describes two types of sampling; discusses probability sampling; warns that nonprobability sampling limits generalizability; explains the steps involved; and discusses sample size issues.

The second subsection of Section 3 covers the issues involved in gathering data in a research project. **Gabriele Kasper** discusses researcher interviews, covering: survey interviews; structured interviews; qualitative interviews; semi-structured interviews; ethnographic interviews; life history interviews; sociolinguistic interviews; oral proficiency interviews; the role of interviews in research; and representation of interview data. **Christine Coombe** and **Peter Davidson** describe questionnaire construction by explaining: the different types of questionnaires; the usefulness of questionnaire research; the qualities of good questionnaires; questionnaire design and formatting; response rates; suggestions for writing, administering, and analyzing questionnaires; and ethical principles. **Sena C. Pierce** describes the characteristics, benefits, and limitations of focus groups; looks at the issues involved in focus-group methodology; discusses common practices in using focus groups; and shows the value of combining focus groups with other research methods. **Sheryl V. Taylor** and **Donna Sobel** describe introspective methods including: the goals of introspective research; its history, guiding principles, and key concepts (like verbal reporting, stimulated recall or retrospection, interviews, and diary studies); important considerations in conducting introspective research; and a classification scheme for eliciting introspective data. **Larry Davis** explores the use of rubrics; identifies three types; discusses their importance, and the advantages and disadvantages of different types; matches rubrics to research uses; examines approaches to building rubrics; gives an example rubric research project (and how the author dealt with problems); and discusses currently active rubric research areas. **Kathleen M. Bailey** addresses diary studies by discussing various ways that diary studies have been applied in theoretical and practical second language acquisition research, and providing practical advice for keeping and using a teaching journal. **Matthew A. Robby** and **Christina Gitsaki** examine statistical data analysis by: discussing hypothesis testing; identifying and measuring variables; preparing data for statistical analysis; screening data for statistical analysis; deciding on statistical tests; and providing advice on what should be included in selecting and reporting on statistical procedures.

The third subsection of Section 3 covers reporting findings after the research project has been conducted. **Andy Curtis** covers the issues involved in presenting research by discussing the benefits of presenting research; the importance of visual support; the value of professional presentations; the controversial issue of presentation as salesmanship; and the importance of experienced presenters writing about the issues involved. **Paul Kei Matsuda** writes about publishing research, including the importance of publishing, and the steps involved (choosing an appropriate journal, submitting the manuscript, waiting for a response, dealing with the initial decision, and what to do after acceptance).

RESEARCH CONTEXTS

Section 4 is about research done in specific contexts. **Janet Orr** and **Deon Edwards-Kerr** address research in language program evaluation contexts, covering: research methods and program evaluation; contextual factors that influence research strategies; key issues in choosing research methods; example evaluations; and the value of contextually relevant research methods. **Thomas S. C. Farrell** summarizes language teacher research across six continents, including 68 studies about teacher/researcher views of their own teaching practices, by considering: the methods used; the results; key teacher reflections; as well as the types of researchers and the settings in which they work.

References

Bracey, G. W. (2006). *Reading educational research: How to avoid getting statistically snookered*. Portsmouth, NH: Heinemann.

Brown, J. D. (1988). *Understanding research in second language learning: A teacher's guide to statistics and research design*. Cambridge: Cambridge University.

Brown, J. D. (1991). Statistics as a foreign language – Part 1: What to look for in reading statistical language studies. *TESOL Quarterly*, 25(4), 569–586.

Brown, J. D. (1992). Statistics as a foreign language – Part 2: More things to look for in reading statistical language studies. *TESOL Quarterly*, 26(4), 629–664.

Brown, J. D. (1995). Statistics as a foreign language: What to look for in reading statistical language studies. In H. Douglas Brown & S. T. Gonzo (Eds.), *Readings in Second Language Acquisition* (pp. 15–35). Englewood Cliffs, NJ: Prentice Hall. Reprinted and adapted by permission from the original article.

Brown, J. D. (2004). *Research methods for applied linguistics: Scope, characteristics, and standards*. In A. Davies & C. Elder (Eds.), *The handbook of applied linguistics* (pp. 476–500). Oxford: Blackwell.

Brown, J. D. (2013). Teaching statistics in language testing courses. *Language Assessment Quarterly*, 10(3), 351–369.

Carter, R., & Nunan, D. (2001). *The Cambridge guide to teaching English to speakers of other languages*. Cambridge: Cambridge University.

Chance, B. L. (2002). Components of statistical thinking and implications for instruction and assessment. *Journal of Statistics Education*, 10(3). Retrieved from http://www.amstat.org/publications/jse/v10n3/chance.html

Coombe, C., Davidson, P., Stoynoff, S., & O'Sullivan, B. (2012). *The Cambridge guide to second language assessment*. Cambridge: Cambridge University.

Garfield, J., & Ben-Zvi, D. (2007). How students learn statistics revisited: A current review of research on teaching and learning statistics. *International Statistical Review*, 75, 372–396.

Garfield. J. (2002). The challenge of developing statistical reasoning. *Journal of Statistics Education*, 10(3). Retrieved from http://www.amstat.org/publications/jse/v10n3/garfield.html

Pfannkuch, M., & Wild, C. (2004). Towards an understanding of statistical thinking. In D. Ben-Zvi & J. Garfield (Eds.), *The challenge of developing statistical literacy, reasoning and thinking* (pp. 17–46). New York: Kluwer Academic.

Porte, G. K. (2010). *Appraising research in second language learning: A practical approach to critical analysis of quantitative research* (2nd ed.). Amsterdam: John Benjamins.

Rumsey, D. J. (2002). Statistical literacy as a goal for introductory statistics courses. *Journal of Statistics Education*, 10(3). Retrieved from http://www.amstat.org/publications/jse/v10n3/rumsey2.html

Shank, G., & Brown, L. (2007). *Exploring educational research literacy*. New York: Routledge.

Stiggins, R. (2007). Conquering the formative assessment frontier. In J. McMillan (Ed.), *Formative classroom assessment*. New York: Colombia University Teachers College.

Vierra, A., & Pollock, J. (1992). *Reading educational research*. Scottsdale, AZ: Gorsuch Scarisbrick.

Wild, C. J., & Pfannkuch, M. (1999). Statistical thinking in empirical enquiry. *International Statistical Review*, 67, 223–265.

SECTION I

PRIMARY CONSIDERATIONS

In Section 1, this book addresses primary considerations that researchers should ponder before setting up a research project. The four chapters in this section examine why we read and do research, how we critique the research of others, how we get funding and grants to support our research, and how research can be used to improve classroom teaching and learning.

Chapter 1 sets out to explain the practical value of research to teachers, especially in terms of using research to make teachers more effective in their classrooms. To do so, the chapter explores basic concepts like "scholarship," "practice," and "research." The authors also discuss the benefits of doing research, the various obstacles that teachers face to getting involved in research, as well as motivations and strategies for getting around such obstacles.

Chapter 2 focuses on critiquing the research of other researchers. The chapter defines research and discusses two sets of guidelines: one set for scientific research and the other set for submitting research papers. The authors then reflect on how such guidelines can be used to help read research critically 'against' the text and get underneath the text in order to understand not only the internal logic of the study, but also the social, historical, political, and cultural bases for the text.

Chapter 3 addresses the issues involved in applying for grants and other funding to support research. Those issues include identifying sources of funding, applying for the grant, and actually securing funding to support research. The author also provides guidelines for writing an effective research grant proposal with an annotated model of a successful proposal and a checklist of items to consider when writing and submitting such a proposal.

Chapter 4 thoroughly examines definitions for the concept of research. The author then considers why research is important in language classrooms from a variety of perspectives, and discusses the distinction between quantitative and qualitative research (and mixed methods research) as well as the notions involved in subjectivity versus objectivity. The chapter ends by discussing the seven steps involved in one type of classroom research called "action research."

Editors' Note

We would like to make it clear that this volume does not explicitly take a stance regarding any specific type of research and that the chapters might sometimes present opposing, overlapping, and conflicting views and approaches. This is because our aim is not to convince readers of the "rightness" of a particular view or set of views, but to empower them to make informed choices about their own research.

Editors' Preview Questions

We will begin each section with questions that you might want to consider before reading the chapters involved. In addition, one way to review the chapters after finishing them would be to revisit these questions. You may be surprised at how your answers have changed and expanded.

1. What do you think are your primary motivations for reading and doing second language research? What obstacles do you face in reading research? What obstacles do you face in doing research? (see Chapter 1)

2. Do you know how to read research critically? What criteria do you apply in judging the quality of a research study? (see Chapter 2)

3. Would you like to get funding for your research? Where and how should you apply for funding? (see Chapter 3)

4. What problems do you and your students have in your classrooms? What types of research might help you find solutions to those problems? (see Chapter 4)

CHAPTER 1

Teacher Research Engagement: Primary Motivators and Obstacles

Christine Coombe and Dean Sheetz

INTRODUCTION

Research is an ambiguous term which means many different things to different people: people conduct research under differing circumstances, with differing objectives and from different philosophical viewpoints. What we hope to do in this chapter is to clarify what research means on a practical basis for teachers, and give some ideas about how teachers can use research as a tool to increase their classroom effectiveness.

Typically, when a group of educators is asked what research is, they list characteristics associated with an objectivist[1] (positivist) view of research, such as scientific, objective, experimental, statistical, generalizable, etc. (Borg, 2003). However, the basic assumptions and requirements of practice are difficult to fulfill when doing research on the day-to-day activities of the classroom. For this reason, a more fluid, context-driven approach to research has increasingly come to dominate educational research – constructionism[2]. Constructionism, however, is also problematic with regard to research into day-to-day classroom activities: in terms of the reality of the practicing educator, both objectivist and constructionist views on research have practical flaws and no practices have so far emerged which allow researchers to easily mitigate or overcome them. To gain help with this problem, it is necessary to take a step back and look at where research fits into the bigger picture of teaching, practice, and individual scholarship.

BACKGROUND

SCHOLARSHIP

Angela Brew (1999: 297) defined scholarship as "the interpretation of what is already known." It is very similar to learning, which she went on to characterize as "the generation of personally useful knowledge" (p. 299). Looking at learning and scholarship as similar things leads to a conception of the teacher's role as facilitating, modeling, and promoting scholarship. Scholarship, however, does not need a teacher. It can be seen as an activity which takes as input material from many types of sources in many different forms. Whether those sources are oral, written, visual, experiential, or experimental is immaterial. Scholarship is the act of interpreting the meaning and value of source material and molding it into a form which is personally useful to the scholar. The act of scholarship is independent of age or level. With this general definition, a first-grade pupil is just as much a scholar as a graduate student; the local barber as the professor whose hair he cuts.

The idea of scholarship as being an act of generating personally useful knowledge leads us to the next concept to be discussed here: practice. Practice is another part of the map in which research is situated.

PRACTICE

Practice, in general, is applying what is known to personal situations. However, practice also brings with it the risk of encountering the unknown. Therefore practice is an activity where both the known – addressable through scholarship – and the unknown – addressable through research – must be dealt with at the personal level. Of course, this once again begs the question of what research is, as few people outside of academia will claim that they do research as part of their daily practice.

We would argue that the question of practical application of research should be of some concern to academics. While academics would like to be able to make claims about the eventual practical application of what they do, evidence of the connection between academic research and its application in practice is limited (Hemsley-Brown and Sharp, 2003). Or, to put it into the terms which are being developed in this paper, there is a breakdown in scholarship where research is not being converted into personally useful knowledge outside of academia.

In addition, what is "unknown" is difficult to pin down. Despite the growth in the amount of data and information available, and the consequent increase in our abilities to search through that data and information, it can still be amazingly difficult to determine whether something that is unknown to one individual is unknown to all individuals, and thus whether it is a subject for scholarship (as defined above) or research. Also, even if one person's unknown is another person's known, the opportunity or ability to communicate that knowledge may be problematic. This leads us to a discussion of the role of the teacher.

TEACHING

Teaching is a form of practice. However, it is unique in many ways. First of all, the heart of the practice of teaching is the facilitation of scholarship or "the deliberate act of helping learners to develop understanding and skills" (Ball and Forzani, 2007: 530). But it is slightly more than just facilitation, as teachers are frequently called upon to make decisions about the elements that comprise scholarship for the students. In other words, they must make decisions about what personally useful understanding and skills the students must develop within the context of their class. Thus, the second unique thing about teaching is that it always includes two or more fields of practice: teaching plus one or more content fields.

This observation is in sharp contrast to the common conception that teaching primarily requires common sense rather than some deep knowledge or skill set related to a practical discipline (Ball and Forzani, 2007). In reality, good teaching requires the knowledge of a practitioner along with an extra skill set that the average practitioner need not necessarily have. However, like many types of practice, teaching knowledge and skills are hard to arrive at through scholarship alone. There is a certain amount of practical experience required with the application of teaching principles before they become personally useful knowledge. In other words: you can't really learn how to teach until after you've taught. Thus teachers require a certain amount of hands-on research of teaching before arriving at scholarship.

RESEARCH

Research is how we explore the unknown. Under this loose conception, everyone does research. Brew (1999: 299) provides a stricter guideline with, "Research ... has as its primary purpose the generation of socially useful knowledge." Notice the major difference between scholarship/learning (personally useful knowledge) and research (socially useful knowledge). Scholarship is for the good of the scholar. Research is for the good of a greater group.

As researchers, we also desire a certain systematic approach – as opposed to trial and error. Our definition then becomes: research is the systematic exploration of the unknown for a socially useful purpose. Research informs both practice and scholarship. Scholarship informs practice and depends on research for new knowledge. Practice reveals needs for scholarship and for research (Figure 1.1). Teaching is a special form of practice where the practice is promoting scholarship.

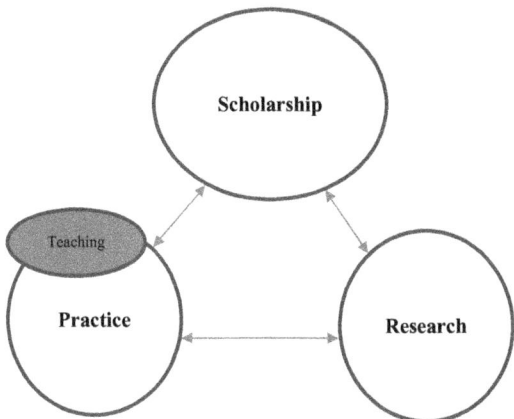

Figure 1.1 The Interdependence of Scholarship, Research and Practice

RESEARCH ON THIS TOPIC

In the field of FL (foreign language) and SL (second language) education, teachers have traditionally been seen as subjects or consumers of research done by others. In the last decade, however, educators have developed a vision of good professional development that focuses on issues teachers deem important in their work, that respects and builds on the knowledge and expertise that teachers already have, and that nurtures and supports teachers' intellectual leadership capacity (Corcoran, 1995; Little, 1993). An activity that addresses all three of these criteria is teacher research.

WHAT IS SECOND LANGUAGE CLASSROOM RESEARCH?

Foreign/Second language classroom research is quite simply research that is carried out in the language classroom for the purpose of answering important questions about the learning and teaching of languages (Nunan, 1990: 1). This kind of research derives its data from either genuine language classrooms or experimental laboratory settings that are set up for the purpose of research.

THE TEACHER AS RESEARCHER

Borg (2006: 22, quoting Cochran-Smith and Lytle, 1999: 22) refers to teacher research as "all forms of practitioner enquiry that involve systematic, intentional, and self-critical inquiry about one's work." The teacher-researcher is engaged in research to improve practice. As stated above, all teachers have to engage in a practical sort of research as part of the scholarship of teaching. However, the teacher-researcher goes beyond basic personal knowledge in pursuit of more advanced understanding. The knowledge gained is socially useful in that it contributes to the greater good of the group being taught. The reward for teacher research is an overall increase in the level of scholarship for the teacher's pupils.

PRACTICAL APPLICATIONS
THE BENEFITS OF DOING RESEARCH

Advocates of teacher research cite its many advantages and describe it as a valuable form of professional development. Zeichner (1999) favors teacher research as it allows teachers to become better at what they do and to find their voice (Rainey, 2000). In addition, it helps teachers become more flexible and open to new ideas. A third advantage is that it narrows the gap between teachers' aspirations and realization. Zeichner (1999) went on to state that teacher inquiry heightens the quality of student learning and stimulates positive changes in the culture and productivity of schools. Teacher research also raises the status of the teaching profession in society. A final advantage is that teacher research produces knowledge about teaching and learning that is useful to teachers, policy makers, academic researchers, and teacher educators.

The literature clearly shows that teachers who have carried out research often report significant changes to their understanding of teaching (Richards and Farrell, 2005). Studies also have found that teachers who engaged in research have experienced professional and personal growth and a decrease in feelings of frustration and isolation (Goswami and Stillman, 1987; Maloy and Jones, 1987; Noffke, 1997; Oja and Pine, 1987). Research by Boudah and Knight (1996) reported positive effects from participation in teacher research in terms of improved teacher attitudes toward research, increased feelings of self-efficacy related to low-achieving students, and increases in positive interactions with students. Finally, teacher research processes may also help to create a positive school culture – one that is supportive of teacher reflection and experimentation (Francis, Hirsch, and Rowland, 1994).

For many of us, improving our practice is the primary reason or motivation for involvement in research projects. We are interested in research because it encourages us to reflect on our practice.

THE OBSTACLES THAT HINDER TEACHER RESEARCH ENGAGEMENT

Despite widespread agreement on its importance, research is often a much-neglected area in teaching practice. There are a number of possible reasons for this neglect, one of which deals with problems of terminology (McGee, 2007). McGee feels that one reason why teachers often fear research is that the terminology used in association with research philosophies is often confusing, contradictory, and not easily accessible to the average practitioner. For example, Khun's term 'paradigm' (1970) has been widely used and cited in the social sciences, and he suggests various meanings of paradigm, such as a set of symbolic generalizations – shared commitments to models of shared values about theory and science in general. However, Seliger and Shohamy (1989) use the term 'parameters' to refer to similar ideas in association with conceptual frameworks. Moreover, terms such as 'parameter' and 'paradigm' are also often used in SL research to refer generally to research methods or strategies.

Borg (2003) points to a number of factors that hinder teachers' research efforts and engagement. He cites the following as the major inhibitors to teachers successfully engaging in research:

- inaccessibility;
- lack of local relevance;
- lack of narrative;
- lack of ownership;
- lack of credibility;
- pressure;
- implied inadequacy;
- self-image;
- lack of recognition;
- lack of technical knowledge.

Borg notes that teachers often feel that research is inaccessible to them (p. 1). Their belief is that researchers often write for other researchers rather than for the teachers they are trying to help. This results in much of the published research not being accessible conceptually or linguistically to the teachers.

Another reason for lack of teacher engagement in research is the feeling that much of the research does not relate to the teachers own teaching/learning contexts. There is empirical evidence to suggest that teachers are most convinced by research that is: a) specific; b) contextualized; c) observable; and d) testable (Borg, 2003: 2). Research conducted by researchers often lacks specificity and does not enable teachers to relate it to their own contexts. As a result, teachers are less likely to be convinced of its relevance and therefore less inclined to read it.

Lack of ownership in the research process is cited as another major inhibitor of teacher research engagement. When teachers are not involved in the research process from the outset, the process can come across as a top-down one in which teachers feel no ownership. The absence of any sense of ownership can result in a lack of interest or even feelings of negativity on the part of the teachers.

When the previous three factors (relevance, narrative and ownership) are absent, this results in the general lack of credibility which research often has in the eyes of teachers. Teachers often feel that researchers – because of their lack of classroom experience – don't have the credibility to make decisions and recommendations for classroom practice. Such sentiments are based on the belief that researchers live in an ivory tower which is far removed from the classroom and have no real knowledge about what happens in the classroom on a day-to-day basis. This sentiment is reflected in research conducted by Crookes and Arakaki which found that "many participants articulated a strong, stereotypical image of researchers as living in an ivory tower and tended to feel that only working teachers could have credible opinions about good teaching" (Crookes and Arakaki, 1999: 16). This sentiment was echoed by others (for example, Goswami and Stillman, 1987, and Mouhanna, 2009).

Another major factor cited by teachers which limits their research engagement is time pressure or time constraints. Many teachers simply feel that they don't have time for research as they are too busy coping with the daily demands of their jobs.

Implied inadequacy is yet another reason why teachers do not conduct research. In fact, it is believed that classroom research in particular takes place to find solutions to problems that exist in the classroom and the very idea of doing research is an admission of a problem. As Borg (2003: 5) puts it, "the suggestion that teachers engage in research, by implying they are inadequate in some way, can in fact be construed as a threat to their competence. When such attitudes prevail, research is seen as an undesirable activity to engage in."

Another obstacle to teacher research involvement is teacher self-image. According to Gurney (1989), teachers see themselves as "knowledge implementers" or those that put into practice the ideas created by others. Researchers are often viewed as "knowledge generators." The belief that "there's nothing worth studying in my classroom and why would anyone want to hear about it?" contributes to feelings of low teacher self-image.

A feeling that academics don't take teacher research seriously is another factor that discourages teachers from conducting research. These stereotypic beliefs stem from popular generalizations about what research is. There is "Research" with a capital R, which is used to refer to empirical studies, with control and experimental groups, such as those reported on in journals like *TESOL Quarterly*. There is also "research" with a small r, to designate the studies and projects that are often carried out by classroom teachers without training in skills needed to conduct research such as statistical analyses (LoCastro, 2000). Teachers' efforts to contribute to the knowledge base in the field are often undervalued if such a view of research exists in their institutional contexts. Others simply feel they lack the technical knowledge required to effectively carry out research on their own practice – for example, they may lack knowledge about research design or data analysis techniques.

RESEARCH ON TEACHER MOTIVATORS AND OBSTACLES TO RESEARCH INVOLVEMENT

Despite the prevalence of research studies highlighting the importance of research in teachers' careers, there is substantially less focus on teachers' beliefs about the factors which encourage and/or inhibit teacher research. In a study by Kennedy (1997), teachers found that much of the research out there lacked authority, was often irrelevant, and did not address teachers' concerns. Another finding pointed to the fact that research findings in general were often too difficult for teachers to understand.

In a study by Mouhanna (2009), teachers in an intensive English program in the Gulf were asked to identify motivating factors as well as obstacles for conducting research in their contexts. His findings indicate that most teachers were motivated by intrinsic factors to conduct research. More specifically, teachers reported that their main motivations for conducting research were self-managed professional development, to improve the teaching situation, and to solve practical problems in their own classrooms. Those same teachers reported that the main obstacles they faced when involving themselves in research were overcoming time constraints and a workplace culture that didn't encourage research.

Conclusion

Some important points emerge in the discussion above about the primary motivators and obstacles that teachers face when they engage in research. Probably the most important is that there are often very good, concrete reasons why teachers do not involve themselves in research. These factors must not be ignored. Rather, as Borg (2003: 6) puts it, "they can provide direction for research education initiatives which are grounded in the real psychological, emotional, and contextual challenges teachers face vis à vis research."

Discussion Questions

1. What is your personal conception of research? Is it similar to the concept of research presented here?

2. Do you do research into your teaching practice? If yes, what obstacles to research have you encountered? If no, what is preventing you from doing research?

3. What benefits do you think doing research into your teaching practice could bring to you personally?

4. If you started a research project, what kind of support do you think you would get from those around you?

5. If you could do one research project right now, what would you like to research and how would you go about doing the research?

References

Ball, D. L., & Forzani, F. M. (2007). What makes education research "educational"? *Educational Researcher*, 36(9), 529–540.

Borg, S. (2003). "Research education" as an objective for teacher learning. In B. Beaven & S. Borg (Eds.), *The role of research in teacher training* (pp. 41–48). Whitstable, Kent: IATEFL.

Borg, S. (2006). Conditions for teacher research. *English Teaching Forum*, 42, 22–27.

Boudah, D. J., & Knight, S. L. (1996). *Participatory research and development* (Technical Report to the Office of Special Education Programs, U. S. Department of Education). College, TX: Texas A & M University.

Brew, A. (1999). Research and teaching: Changing relationships in a changing context. *Studies in Higher Education*, 24(3), 291–301.

Corcoran, T. (1995). *Helping teachers develop well: Transforming professional development.* Madison, WI: Center for Policy Research in Education.

Crookes, G., & Arakaki, L. (1999). Teaching idea sources and work conditions in an ESL program. *TESOL Journal*, 8(1), 15–19.

Francis, S., Hirsch, S., & Rowland, E. (1994). Improving school culture through study groups. *Journal of Staff Development*, 13, 12–15.

Goswami, D., & Stillman, P. (1987). *Reclaiming the classroom: Teacher research as an agency for change*. Upper Montclair, NJ: Boynton Cook.

Gurney, M. (1989). Implementer or innovator: A teacher's challenge to the restrictive paradigm of traditional research. In P. Lomax (Ed.), *The management of change* (pp. 13–28). Clevedon: Multilingual Matters.

Hemsley-Brown, J., & Sharp, C. (2003). The use of research to improve professional practice: A systematic review of the literature. *Oxford Review of Education*, 29(4), 449–471.

Kennedy, M. (1997). The connection between research and practice. *Educational Researcher*, 26(7), 4–12.

Khun, T. (1970). *The structure of scientific revolutions*. Chicago: The University of Chicago Press.

Little, J. W. (1993). Teacher professional development in a climate of educational reform. *Educational Evaluation and Policy Analysis*, 15(2), 129–151.

LoCastro, V. (2000). Teachers helping themselves: Classroom research and action research. *The Language Teacher*, 18(2), 4–7.

Maloy, R., & Jones, B. (1987). Teachers, partnerships, and school improvement. *Journal of Research and Development*, 20, 19–24.

McGee, A. (2007). Developing good research practices. In S. Midraj, A. Jendli, & A. Sellami (Eds.), *Research in ELT contexts* (pp. 163–184). Dubai: TESOL Arabia Publications.

Mouhanna, M. (2009). Teacher research in EFL: Beliefs and practices. *UGRU Journal*, 8, 1–26.

Noffke, S. (1997). Professional, personal, and political dimensions of action research. *Review of Research in Education*, 22, 305–343.

Nunan, D. (1990). *Second language classroom research*. ERIC Digest: Clearinghouse on Languages and Literature. Washington, DC: Center for Applied Linguistics.

Oja, S., & Pine, G. (1987). Collaborative action research: Teachers' stages of development and school context. *Peabody Journal of Education*, 64, 96–116.

Rainey, I. (2000). Action research and the English as a foreign language practitioner: Time to take stock. *Educational Action Research*, 8(1), 65–91.

Richards, J. C., & Farrell, T. S. C. (2005). *Professional development for language teachers*. Cambridge: Cambridge University Press.

Seliger, H. W., & Shohamy, E. (1989). *Second language research methods*. London: Oxford University Press.

Zeichner, K. (1999). *Teacher research as a professional development activity for P–12 educators*. Washington, DC: U.S. Department of Education.

Notes

[1] The objectivist/positivist philosophy holds that things exist as meaningful entities independently of consciousness and knowledge can be acquired through experience. Knowledge is transferred from the outside to inside the learner.

[2] The constructionist view is that there is no one objective truth waiting to be discovered. Meaning is created (or constructed) by engaging with world around us. The teacher's job is to guide the learner in constructing knowledge.

CHAPTER 2

Critiquing the Research of Others

Eric Dwyer and Benjamin Baez

INTRODUCTION

Karl Marx (1959: 243) wrote, "The philosophers have only interpreted the world, in various ways: the point, however, is to change it." Similarly, we want to ask here whether our conventional ideas about second language research prevent us from critically engaging and transforming the context in which that research will be used. Like Marx, we believe that to be critical is to think about and strive for social change. More precisely, we want to ask how it is possible to be critical in terms of the way we conduct second language research and the ways that we read it.

Perhaps you consider yourself a language teacher. You might aspire to be a researcher, a scholar, or an advocate. No matter what your aspiration is, you'll be watching conference presentations, attending workshops, and reading news and journal articles, all in efforts to craft your art, which you describe as language teaching and promotion of language acquisition. In other words, you end up asking yourself, "What helps me (or anyone) become a better language teacher or conversationalist of how people learn languages?" As you build upon your own answers to this question, you may find that there are other overarching issues emerging from teaching and conversing, leading to ponderings and debates about the responsibilities one has when teaching language, how it affects children and minorities – those often not allowed to speak for themselves – as well as those who ultimately benefit from language teaching and research.

With respect to those who have sought effective teaching techniques, ways to learn a new language, and the implications thereof, many have committed to sharing their inquiries with those who follow them in various expert texts on language acquisition and teaching. As suggested before, these texts entail research articles and conference presentations, offered by those we endow with academic expertise for conveying such knowledge. This chapter serves as a contemplation of how one might approach these texts. We'll discuss the ways in which colleagues and self-ascribed experts have often advised others regarding ways to approach these texts when reading them, but our main task is to offer ways of "reading against these texts" so as to situate them in the cultural and historical contexts that they represent more or less explicitly. This reading, we think, will force us to focus on the people whose lives are affected by these texts – mostly students and teachers – as well as the ethical responsibilities experts should have when purporting to impart knowledge about people who often have little say about the creation of academic texts and how they are used (for more on ethical issues, see Chapters 22 and 23).

Before examining the importance of our language texts and of reading them, we should also examine the context about which and in which these texts take place: in education and schooling, in learning language, and in the teaching of it, none of which necessarily entail reference to academic expertise. These are the contexts in which we live, we work, and we learn. We are left with our own lived experiences and ways of dealing with them that work only in the moment. These experiences are not invalid; in fact, hunches from them usually spark sound research. However, our experiences in teaching and learning every day, as well as the need to reproduce them across time and space and with multiple audiences, compel us to think about more than just simple solutions that work in the moment. Thus, without research and techniques for conducting it, we believe we are left only with our hunches, which, if effective, are so only in the moment. Research ostensibly offers us ways of moving beyond the moment.

Research on this Topic

"Research" by most accounts has a simple definition: "A detailed study of a subject, especially in order to discover (new) information or reach a (new) understanding" (*Cambridge Advanced Learner's Dictionary*, 2013). This definition in itself excludes neither the everyday experiences we discussed before, nor the expertise of teachers or students who live them. Nevertheless, when viewing the institutional structures subtending research enterprises, we see that research entails something other than ordinary experiences, and it is not seen as conducted by ordinary teachers and students, who are often only its objects. Indeed, when one attends to the definitions of research put forth by, say, the National Research Council (NRC), the research arm of the National Academy of Sciences, we see that education research should somehow be scientific; in other words, it requires a rigorous, systematic, and objective set of procedures. In its 2002 report, *Scientific Research in Education,* we are told that – to be deemed scientific – the research "must allow direct, empirical investigation of an important question, account for the context in which the study is carried out, align with a conceptual framework, reflect careful and thorough reasoning, and disclose results to encourage debate in the scientific community" (Shavelson and Towne, 2002: 6). To call education research scientific is to say that it conforms to the six guiding principles of all scientific research:

- it poses significant questions that can be investigated empirically;
- it links research to relevant theory;
- it uses methods that permit direct investigation of questions;
- it offers a coherent and explicit chain of reasoning;
- it is replicable and generalizable across studies; and
- it discloses research to encourage professional scrutiny and critique.

The NRC's definition of scientific research, which also entails a way of reading it and critiquing it, makes it clear that the world of the everyday and the world of research are different. These ideas about science clearly distinguish (a) the producer of knowledge from (b) its objects and its users: students and teachers. The latter, while participating regularly in the studied phenomena, may be considered unqualified to engage in the debate about this knowledge; in other words, the opinions about the value of this knowledge – its critical evaluation – are given only by the community of scientists.

We will have occasion to revisit this logic, but for now it is important to say that this kind of inquiry is what seems to be privileged in venues seeking the prestige conferred on scientific knowledge, and it is what we see privileged in academic journals like *TESOL Quarterly*, which has been in existence for approximately 50 years. Thus, from a very important perspective, a perspective privileging the primacy of scientific knowledge over and perhaps against the (unscientific?) experiential knowledge gained by us in learning and teaching, critiquing research entails reading research in the way espoused by the NRC, by those deemed the scientific community, and by those seeking to align themselves with that community so as to gain its recognition.

PRACTICAL APPLICATIONS

If one picks up a research article, one wants to believe its contents. In arriving at that belief, we are socialized in the academy to examine research by cross-matching an article's contents against goals espoused by experts like the NRC. If the evidence and the methods used to obtain it are deemed reliable by those making use of them, we may try its techniques in classrooms. But if the methods are deemed faulty, then our tendency might be to consider the study meaningless.

In line with the philosophy of science we see in the NRC's definition of scientific research, several authors (e.g., Rodgers, 1997; State University of New York Institute of Technology, 2003; Oncology Nursing Society, 2002) have offered checklists for readers of research articles. These checklists are likely similar to what reviewers have in mind as they examine articles submitted for publication. One illustration is worthy of note. The American Educational Research Association (AERA) (2012) offers guidelines for submitting research papers to be presented at its annual conferences, which is not dissimilar from formats implemented in the preponderance of classically published language education articles. Below we have summarized these guidelines and attempted to include what we see are the conventional kinds of questions associated with them:

OBJECTIVES OR PURPOSES

- Are the objectives or purposes significant?
- Are they relevant?
- Is the author clear with respect to any underlying story that prompted the research?

THEORETICAL FRAMEWORK

- Is the literature review balanced?
- Is the literature review critical?
- Is the literature review current?
- Does the literature review ultimately support research questions or hypotheses?

METHODS, TECHNIQUES, OR MODES OF INQUIRY

- Does the theoretical framework clearly define concepts and variables?
- Is there a logical link between research questions or hypotheses and methods?
- Does the methodology clearly address validity and reliability?
- Has the researcher included an appropriate subject size?

DATA SOURCES, EVIDENCE, OBJECTIVES, OR MATERIALS

- Are the instruments clearly described?
- Are data collection procedures clearly described?
- Is there a clear logical link connecting research questions and hypotheses to methods and subsequently to procedures?
- Are the researchers' roles in the data addressed?
- Are the subjects appropriately protected?
- Can readers replicate this study?

RESULTS, SUBSTANTIATED CONCLUSIONS, WARRANTS FOR ARGUMENTS, OR POINTS OF VIEW

- Is the data analysis clear?
- Is there a clear logical link connecting research questions and hypotheses to methods and to procedures and then results?
- Do the results make statistical sense?
- Are there sufficient examples? Is triangulation addressed?
- Does the author address issues of bias?

SCIENTIFIC OR SCHOLARLY SIGNIFICANCE OF THE STUDY OF WORK

- Does the reflection of the results refer to the theoretical framework?
- Does the reflection of the results refer to the literature review and previous findings?
- Does the reflection of the results refer to the underlying story?
- Does the author address limitations?
- Does the author address generalizations?

SPECIFICATIONS

- Does the article conform appropriately to conventions of formality or publisher specifications – for example, the *APA Manual,* or *The Chicago Manual of Style*?

In reading a paper under this logic, one might notice the inherently recursive nature of the process suggested: that one begins with a purpose well justified in a literature review, which can prompt the drawing of research questions and hypotheses. This then begets a methodology, which directly recalls the research questions or hypotheses but may also recall previously conducted methodology. Experimental tasks and procedures similarly refer to all previously indicated emphases: methodology, research questions, earlier studies, and the initial motivation for the study. Likewise, the results must logically link to procedures, methods, and previous literature. Finally, one's conclusions must logically link all these components, placing these results into the context already established in terms of any theoretical framework, previous studies, and the underlying story that prompted the author's study in the first place.

The recursive nature of approaching research from the experts' points of view allows readers to ask, at the most fundamental, this question: Does the work closely mimic what we imagine to be scientifically valid? In other words, does it fulfill the goals elicited by experts like those of the NRC? The *desideratum* here appears to be the scientific validity and reliability of the research enterprise in the eyes of its experts. In working through this logic, one's attention is driven to the researcher's methods and the rigor with which they are conducted. This has its usefulness, for if we are training researchers – even those who will be ethically responsible to their participants and not just to the research enterprise – we will have to teach them this logic of the academy. They will have to learn it, even if they must ultimately question it.

But there are other questions we may ask about this logic. First, does the scientific logic seem overly focused on what can be measured, and does this then privilege measurement over meaning? We know that living is complicated, irreducible to the cold logic of scientific precision. Such precision, for example, requires us to consider such things as statistical significance over practical significance; it requires us to obscure the messiness of actual living in favor of manipulation of variables that lend themselves to measurement; it requires us to ignore the outlier, which is something that cannot, and should not, be possible in actual classrooms or other learning situations.

More fundamentally, we can ask, is this research committed to goals that might run counter to those of students and teachers? Privileged by this scientific logic is the research enterprise itself, not necessarily the people who are or will be affected by it, not the agendas of the people conducting this research or the institutions that support it, and certainly not the ethical responsibility that comes with making claims that may have an impact on the lives of people who will have little say in the matter. For example, a key text in our field, Porte's (2002) thoroughly crafted *Appraising Research in Second Language Learning,* is committed to methodological purity by offering step-by-step guidelines for conducting second language research. Like many such texts, however, it does not address critical questions about which research is privileged, by whom, and for whom. Indeed, we are concerned that much of education research is overly committed not only to maintaining its expertise but also to supporting those seeking funding and recognition by those with the purse strings, who are often committed to their own interests and not necessarily those of actual students and teachers.

Not privileged within such logic are the social and political contexts in which all of this takes place. The articles coming closest to matching this scientific logic tend to be accepted at face value by reviewers and readers alike when they may have problematic assumptions, and may be supporting ideas that are actually detrimental to the lives being represented in these texts. For example, many of us believe strongly that high-stakes testing is highly detrimental to learning and teaching in context, and yet numerous studies obscure the fact that their overriding concern is the maintenance of such testing (we will allude here to the particularly insidious examples of studies promoting parental involvement in schools for racial minorities but which on close reading are concerned only with promoting their test scores). It is in these ways that we propose a need to *read against* these texts.

BEYOND THE SCIENTIFIC CRITIQUE: WE DON'T JUST WANT YOU READING

"Reading against" a text means to us a critical examination not only of the internal logic of research texts (both in terms of their adherence to what we imagine to be scientific and of the rhetorical strategies they use) but also of the historical and socio-political contexts of which they are more or less explicit. This is difficult, for we are socialized from early on in schools that scientific texts are privileged because they aspire to objectivity and truth. We have faced resistance from our students in trying to encourage such critical examination, but we have developed some strategies that have emerged out of experiences. By only requiring readers to go through the checklists ostensibly put forth as entailing critical reading of scientific rigor, we have inadvertently fostered readers who tick off whether a text meets this or that standard. But this kind of reading fails to engage the material and, as a consequence, ends up privileging measurement over meaning. It is not enough, therefore, to judge a text simply for the accuracy of the social realities it espouses or assumes or for the rigor of the methods it uses. We must have readers be critical in a more fundamental way. We strive for another vision of research and how one might read it, one that follows Paris and Winograd's (1990) argument that skepticism during reading can advance the likelihood that readers will remember the article in the first place, whether they warmly receive it or not, and one that asserts that research, or the reading of it, is not simply valid for the experts but for those who must live out its consequences.

We insist that future researchers and readers of research go beyond just reading passively what experts tell them. They must engage the text critically to uncover its underlying logic, assumptions, and institutional bases of support, which are often inexplicit. In other words, to understand an article and reflect on its meaningfulness does not necessarily mean that one has reflected deeply about a text. Nor does it mean that we dismiss such texts out of hand. It means only that we subject all texts to a critical analysis. Thinking critically requires asking how and to what extent a text addresses its own political assumptions, as well as those that dictate how we live and work. To be critical of the kinds of texts with which we are concerned means more than simply offering judgments about their scientific validity, and it means more than simply being negative or contrarian. It requires understanding how crucial texts are to the ways the world can be seen and to the ways the world can reach us. It is to see these texts as being as political as the ones that come to us from formal political government, and thus to treat them with the kind of skepticism we attribute to other texts in the world.

Such consideration is important because research texts can be tricky. They may be more or less explicit about where they come from, what motivates them, and which ideologies they further and of which they are representative. To read critically, we stress, is to get underneath what is read in order to understand the social, political, and cultural underpinnings of the text. While we do not wish to diminish the value of critiquing a project for its scientific rigor, we want to assert that in-the-moment experiences are not just given sound attention but used to judge the value of the research. Readers and authors both bring with them assumptions and presuppositions before ever opening a book or turning on a laptop.

This kind of reading is not easy. Thus, as we conclude our missive, we would like to offer what we find to be useful ways of having our students read against the texts we assign them. The following questions offer initial stages for students to move beyond passive reading and toward a more critical role in what will come to be what they learn:

- What are the author's assumptions about the social institutions being discussed?
- What are the implications of these assumptions for policy making, and what would be gained or lost by buying into them?
- What is the nature of the world assumed by the author?
- What assumptions does the author make *a priori* to writing?
- What is at stake in the author's argument, for the author and for you?
- Who (or what) is the author arguing for and against?
- How does the author construct and articulate his or her arguments?
- How is the author (or text) positioned in relation to others you have read?
- How does the author (or text) fit or not fit in relation to your own thought and practice?
- What effects or consequences are potentially raised politically as a result of this article?
- What are the ramifications of abiding or not abiding by the logic espoused by the author?
- What questions did you find yourself asking after reading?

We find these questions useful for beginning a conversation that never ends, for our tendency is always to accept the experts' words at face value. Indeed, some of us don't even think of experts as having words, which many of us will concede are and can be manipulated to further political agendas. Expertise is deemed extra-lingual, in a sense, and when heavily masked by statistics, it might not even register as language at all. But language it is, and, as language, it has socio-political contexts and effects we might worry about rather than assume as non-existent.

CONCLUSION

The premise of scientific research seems to be that an idea leads logically to the next, that questions lead to methods, that methods lead to answers, and so forth. But those of us in the so-called real world know that such is rarely the case, that we cannot make sense of all our experiences. Some things don't make sense, and sometimes what makes sense is not always describable in the methodical ways suggested by research studies. Our lived experiences are often muddled. More questions are raised than answered. Muckiness is what we have. Research should be deemed no less mucky, and we should worry about research that assumes otherwise. Lending attention to the less-than-clean allows us to expand our considerations for as many people as possible. Thus, advancing critical analysis allows us to consider politically the people whom research could affect most, either positively or negatively, but who are often reduced merely to "data" abstracted from the very material contexts in which they live.

We believe readers are not passive, nor should they be. To read passively is to abdicate our responsibility for living and engaging in the world, a world often made sense of through academic texts, and a world that teachers and students know first-hand but are not trusted to give adequate account. Research texts greatly affect our world and the ways we live. Reading them, therefore, should be critical. Talburt (2002) suggests that we think about research not for its veracity but for how it opens up new lines of thought. We can't agree more. We must let go of the idea of the all-knowing researcher, which ultimately forces us to focus simply on methods, and allow ourselves the freedom to ask questions and to engage with others in a discussion that presents the possibility of seeing our world differently. The world can be transformed only when it is seen differently than before. It is in this way that critical research is the most practical thing we offer to higher education. And to end where we started, the point of research following Marx, is not simply to interpret the world, but to change it.

Discussion Questions

1. Should the language education profession be satisfied with so-called scientific-based research? Why or why not?

2. Consider a recent academic article you have read. To what extent do you think it remains within a so-called scientific framework? And now, given the arguments offered in this chapter, to what extent would the meaning the article had for you now change?

3. Imagine that this article was part of the blogosphere and you could give the authors immediate feedback on it. Given the ideas espoused in this chapter, what would you say to the authors?

4. The origin of research methodology and the critics' concerns emerge from a western cultural foundation. How do you think such rhetoric may be received in other parts of the world?

5. Now, read against us; that is, critique our chapter. By this we mean, do you buy our arguments? What are our assumptions? What do we take for granted? What social change, if any, do we seek to promote? What are the ethical considerations of such change? Are there winners and losers in the change we envision?

References

American Educational Research Association (2012). Retrieved from http://www.aera.net/AnnualMeetingsOtherEvents/AnnualMeeting2012Details/2012PresenterandParticipantInformation/tabid/12375/Default.aspx#paper

Cambridge Advanced Learner's Dictionary, (4th ed.) (2013) available online at http://dictionary.cambridge.org.

Marx, K. (1959). Theses on Feuerbach. In L. S. Feuer, *Marx & Engels: Basic writings on politics & philosophy* (pp. 243–245). New York: Anchor Books.

Oncology Nursing Society (2002). Did you know critique criteria? Supplement to the March/April *Clinical Journal of Oncology Nursing*, 5, 2. Retrieved from http://pcs.mgh.harvard.edu/CCPD/Nursing_Research/Research_Critique_Criteria.asp

Paris, S. G., & Winograd, P. (1990). How metacognition can promote academic learning and instruction. In B. F. Jones & L. Idol (Eds.), *Dimensions of thinking and cognitive instruction* (pp. 15–51). Hillsdale, NJ: Lawrence Erlbaum Associates.

Porte, G. K. (2002). *Appraising research in second language learning: A practical approach to critical analysis of quantitative research.* Amsterdam: John Benjamins Publishing.

Rodgers, B. L. (1997). Guidelines for critique of research reports. Retrieved from http://www.uwm.edu/People/brodg/Handout/critique.htm

Shavelson, R. J., & Towne, L. (Eds.), (2002). *Scientific research in education.* Washington: National Academy Press.

State University of New York Institute of Technology (2003). Format for qualitative critique. Retrieved from http://www.tele.sunyit.edu/qualcritique_format.html

Talburt, S. (2002). *Verify data.* Paper presented at the Annual Meeting of the Association for the Study of Higher Education, Sacramento, CA.

CHAPTER 3

Applying for Research Funding and Grants

Ahmar Mahboob

INTRODUCTION

Regardless of which stage of our academic careers we might be at, identifying, applying for, and securing research funding is a crucial part of our work. This is perhaps even truer today than it was in the past. In today's world of economic belt-tightening and limited budgets, it is crucial to be able to secure funds in order to carry out our projects. In addition, building a track record of writing successful grant applications is also a key measure in our professional performance, and it can play a pivotal role in promotion and other applications.

This chapter will help you in identifying some of the key things that you need to consider in writing a research-oriented grant application. It includes an annotated model of a successful grant application and a checklist that you can use as you develop your proposal for submission. Given the nature and the purpose of this chapter, I will not provide a literature review on the topic. Instead, I have provided a list of resources that you may want to consult at the end of the chapter.

BACKGROUND

Writing a grant application is a lengthy process. It starts with searching for and identifying the right type of grant for your project. As you search and apply for grants, you will note that there are a number of different types of grants; it is important for you to select and apply for the one that is most appropriate for your project and context. For example, grants can be categorized based on whether they are teaching-oriented or research-oriented; there are grants for students, for early career researchers, and for those who are more advanced in their career. There are grants that are available locally – from one's department, or faculty, or university – and grants that are offered by private organizations, communities, trusts, and corporations; and there are grants that are offered by various governmental organizations. Each grant has a specific set of guidelines and eligibility criteria (including, in some cases, citizenship status) and you need to find grants that best suit your project needs and profile.

Once you have identified a potential grant, look at the list of projects that the funding agency has supported in the past. This will help you in gauging whether this is the right funding option for you. You should then look at any forms or guidelines that are available and take notes on the kind of information that you will need to complete this application. You should also check to see if the funding agency has provided any sample proposals. If they have, do read these carefully and pay special attention to what information is included in the model, how the application is structured, and what language is used in the different parts of the application.

Then, when you are drafting your application, adopt a similar style and language. If you identify multiple potential grants for your project, you should consider applying for more than one grant. This increases your chances of securing funding for your project, in the eventuality that your preferred source for the grant does not work out. Of course, in doing so, you do need to make sure that you qualify for the grant on offer, have modified your grant application to suit the particular agency you are applying for, and have provided all the information that is requested for each of the grants. Do remember that while there is no guarantee that a well-drafted application will be funded, applications that do not meet the guidelines will not be considered. Therefore, read the guidelines very carefully and make sure that you address each of the requirements in the best way that you can.

Identifying and writing a successful grant application requires that you do your homework before you start drafting your application. You need to take on a structured and organized approach to working on your research grant application. The following process works reasonably well in most scenarios:

- Identify a grant and make sure that you are eligible.
- Take detailed notes about what information is needed and organize these notes to start drafting.
- Draft the application.
- Let the application sit for a few days.
- Revise and edit the application.
- Share and discuss the application with a colleague.
- Revise, proofread, and submit the application.

As with most things academic, the more time you invest in doing your preparatory work, the better the chances of your success. Putting together a quick application is likely to impact the quality of the proposal and is therefore not advisable.

PRACTICAL APPLICATIONS

A grant application is a type of persuasive writing – you need to be able to persuade and convince the reviewers and the funding body that your project is worth supporting. To write a convincing grant application, you need to be able to create a strong case for: why the project needs to be undertaken; what specific issues you will be addressing; why you are the right person to do it; what type of data will be collected: how, when, and where the data collection will take place; how the data will be analyzed; how ethical issues will be handled; and how the findings will be disseminated.

To convince the grant reviewers of the importance of your project, you need to show how your project addresses a key gap or an issue in your field. This can be done by either referring to the current literature on the topic and/or highlighting the practical implications of the work. When you refer to other peoples' work, do remember that you are doing so in order to build a case for your own project – therefore, remember to keep the focus of the proposal on your own research. Refer to the work of others uniquely for the purposes of creating a niche for your own project. In referring to other research, you should also be careful not to critique it unnecessarily: there is a fine line between making critical references to other people's work to justify your own project and simply criticizing it. You never know who will be reviewing your proposal and you don't want to risk alienating them by making inappropriate comments.

You will also need to convince the reviewers of your own expertise in the particular area you are planning to work on so that they can see why you are the right person to undertake this project – this can be done by referring to your own work, providing details about any relevant training or prior engagement related to the topic of your project, and/or by including names and contact details of referees.

Your grant proposal needs to include specific details about your research methodology and analytical framework. In drafting this section, do provide as many details as you can. The reviewers need to know that you have thought your methodology through. In looking at this section of your grant application, the reviewers are keen to gauge whether the nature and amount of data that you will collect will be appropriate to meet your project goals. They will also consider if the analytical tools that you are planning to adopt are aligned with the data collected and the research questions. It is therefore crucial that you have a clear alignment between your research goals, your methodology, and your analytical framework. Reviewers will also consider any ethical concerns that may pertain to your research methodology. Furthermore, the funding agency may need formal ethics approval from your institution before the research funding is released. Finally, it is useful to provide some indications of what you plan to do once you have completed the project – for example, where you plan to present and/or publish your work.

In order to see how the advice given above is realized in an actual grant application, I have included an annotated model of a successful research grant application that Lia Kamhi-Stein and I submitted to TIRF in 2003 (Table 3.1). Our TIRF grant application had six sections: a) Cover page; b) Project summary (limited to 250 words); c) Detailed proposal (limited to six single spaced pages); d) Detailed budget (limited to two pages); e) Referees for each of us; and f) CVs of each of us (limited to two pages). Given space constraints, I will focus on the detailed proposal section of the application here. In annotating the text below, I will highlight the key things that Lia and I were trying to achieve in each part of the text. In the interest of saving space, I have replaced some of the actual text with comments in square brackets "[ ]" or removed the information "XXX."

The annotated proposal shows how a successful grant proposal was structured, using references to current research (at the time that proposal was written) to create a niche for the proposed project and then filling this niche by setting up a unique project. Throughout the text, we used formal language and were careful about explaining terms and concepts that were unique to the project. We kept referring to how our own personal and professional contexts would aid this study.

You will notice that the introductory section of the grant application served a number of purposes: it introduced the topic, provided background information, referred to some key literature and identified a gap in this literature, stated the purpose of the project, listed the key research questions, introduced the methodology, and outlined some of the benefits of the project. Providing this kind of detailed introduction is essential because it helps the reviewer to get a broad picture of what is being proposed, and why, and how it will be achieved. By providing this kind of introduction, the authors increase the likelihood that the reviewers – who may or may not be from their discipline (and who will most certainly be pressed for time) – will understand the nature of the project and why it is important.

ANNOTATION	TEXT
Setting up the project (background)	**Statement of Research Issues** Over the last few years, there has been a growing interest in issues related to non-native English-speaking (NNES) professionals. [*More background*].
Identifying what has been done Pointing out what is missing from current work	As will be explained in the Theoretical Background section below, research on NNES professionals has focused on a variety of topics, including the advantages and disadvantages of being NNES professionals, the perceptions of NNES professionals about their status in the TESOL field, the self-perceived language needs of NNES professionals, and NNES professionals and their professional preparation. However, missing from the literature are investigations designed to understand the relationship between NNES teachers' English language proficiency and the levels of competence required for effective curriculum delivery in English.
Purpose of the study Specific purpose of the project Defining technical terms (threshold hypothesis)	This study, designed to fill this gap in the literature, is grounded on the premise that English language proficiency will influence curriculum delivery in English. The study will investigate the contribution of second language (L2) proficiency to curriculum delivery in terms of the threshold hypothesis of language proficiency. The main idea underlying this concept is that teachers will not be able to teach effectively in English until they have developed a certain level of proficiency in it, although the threshold level may vary from classroom task to classroom task and teacher to teacher.
List of questions	The study is designed to answer the following question: What is the relationship between NNES teachers' level of proficiency in English and their curriculum delivery in English? Specifically, what is the relationship between the teachers' curriculum delivery in English, when teaching in two classes with different linguistic demands, and the teachers' proficiency in English?
Broad description of methodology Expected outcome/ benefit of the project	To answer the question, this investigation will rely on a case study approach. Specifically, the study will focus on selected NNES professionals teaching two different grade levels in English in two kinds of settings: English as a foreign language (EFL) and post-colonial settings. The study will integrate qualitative and quantitative techniques designed to create reliable and detailed case studies. In turn, it is expected that the case studies will allow the identification of a threshold level of English language competence required for effective curriculum delivery in English at different instructional levels.
Identifying the main sources of literature	**Theoretical Background** This study is informed by research in three areas: NNES professionals, second language acquisition (SLA), and world Englishes (WE). It is a known fact that most teachers of English to speakers of other languages around the world are NNES professionals (Kachru, 1996). However, interest in issues related to these professionals is only recent.
Discussion of key research on NNES professionals	Initial research on issues related to NNES professionals focused on the advantages and disadvantages of being NNES professionals (see for example, [*references*]). [*Discussion of one area of related research*]

(ctd.)

ANNOTATION	TEXT
Discussion of another key research on NNES professionals	The self-perceived language needs of NNES professionals is another area of research that has received attention within the literature. Several studies have identified pronunciation (see for example, [*references*]), writing, vocabulary (including idioms and slang), and cultural knowledge as areas of perceived difficulty ([*references*]), and grammar and reading as areas of strength ([*references*]). However, research in this area has shown that lack of English proficiency does not have a negative effect on the teachers' perceptions about their instructional practices ([*references*]).
Relating current research to project goals	[*Discussion of additional areas of related research; identifying gaps in the literature; including references to the authors' work to indicate their expertise in the area*]
Identifying two ways in which the proposed project will fill the gap in the literature.	This study will contribute to the literature in two central ways. First, the proposed study fills a gap in SLA and WE research by looking at the interface between the language proficiency of instructors teaching in settings where English is a foreign language and an institutionalized language and the teachers' curriculum delivery in English. Second, while there has been increased interest in issues related to NNES teachers, missing from the literature is research designed to assess how NNES teachers' language proficiency affects curriculum delivery in English.
The research methodology includes a number of sub-sections	**Research Methodology**
	Setting and Participants
Location of study Rationale for the selection of these locations	Data for this study will be collected in three countries, Pakistan, S. Korea, and Argentina. These three countries were selected for two reasons. First, the countries fall on different ends of the continuum of English language use and recognition. [*Details elaborating this rationale*]
Showing why the researchers are the right ones to work in this context	Second, the principal investigators are natives of two of the countries in which the study will be conducted (and they have English language teaching/learning/teacher education experiences in all three of these countries).
Specific details about the participants and rationale for selecting them	In each of these countries, three public high schools located in a middle-class neighborhood in a large city will be identified. Moreover, within each school, two English language instructors, each instructor teaching two grade levels (preferably 9 and 12) and each instructor having different degrees of experience – one experienced and the other a novice – will be selected. By selecting language instructors teaching two different grade levels, with different linguistic demands, and being at the two ends of the experience spectrum, it will be possible to develop an in-depth understanding of how curriculum delivery in English is affected by the teachers' English language proficiency. [*Additional details about methodology/rationale*]

(continued overleaf)

(ctd.)

ANNOTATION	TEXT
Specific information about the nature of data collected (4 types)	**Data Collection and Analysis** The NNES teachers' case studies will be developed by collecting data from different sources. These will include: [*List of data to be collected*]
Process of analysing data	Individual teachers' case studies will be created by integrating quantitative data (scores on the essays, the summaries, oral interviews, and the beliefs' inventories) and qualitative data (content analysis of the videotaped lessons, the essays, and the teachers' and the administrators' oral interviews). [*Details about the analytical approach, with citations to relevant research*]
Uniqueness of the project	**Statement of Implications of Research** The findings of this qualitative study, while they are not meant to be generalized, will have a substantial impact in a number of areas. Research focusing on the language threshold has been limited to the field of L2 reading. To the researchers' knowledge, this study will be the first one designed to provide information on the relationship between teachers' language proficiency and their instructional practices. Therefore, the findings will open up a new area of investigation.
Benefits of the project for future research	Second, this study will provide much needed baseline data from which future research studies can draw. It is expected that larger, quantitative studies will be able to rely on the information provided in this investigation. Third, the results of this study will contribute to the field of TESOL teacher preparation. TESOL teacher education programs in the United States do not require their students to take any language courses. Instead, they use the TOEFL or other standardized tests to measure prospective students' language abilities at the time of admission and then consider those sufficient for teacher preparation and language teaching purposes. Therefore, the results of the proposed study will provide in-depth information that can be used when TESOL MA programs consider making curricular decisions about the role of language instruction language TESOL teacher preparation programs. Finally, the results of this study will help NNES teachers develop a better understanding of how language proficiency affects their instructional practices. Therefore, teachers and prospective teachers may use the findings to focus on their own language skills.
Practical applications of the research	
Benefit to practitioners	
Identifying key collaborators who are not part of the project, but will contribute	**Role and Expertise of all Consultants** This investigation will be conducted in three different countries. While the two principal investigators were born and raised in Argentina and Pakistan respectively, two of the countries where the study will be conducted, they will rely on consultants who reside in the three countries where the study will be conducted. [*Names and details about the consultants*]
Stating that agreement with the consultants is in place	All of the consultants have agreed to provide local assistance as needed.

ANNOTATION	TEXT
(ctd.)	
Details about the role and contribution of the consultants	Specifically, they will help in the identification of the schools and the teachers and in the data collection process. Additionally, XXX will provide Korean language assistance as needed. They will also provide staff support.
Detailed timeline of the project	**Timetable** [*Schedule of activities*]
Identifying how the findings of the project will be disseminated	**Plans for Dissemination** Plans for dissemination include: a) presentations at professional conferences such as XXX; b) manuscripts to be submitted to XXX; c) a book proposal to be submitted to potential publishers. [*Details about the projected outcomes*]
Specifying how research ethics will be maintained	**Brief Explanation of how Principles of Research Ethics will be Upheld** Principles of research ethics will be upheld by adhering to ethical and legal standards as outlined by *TESOL Quarterly*. Specifically, informed consent will be obtained from all participants. [*Details about what information will be included in the informed consent forms*]

Table 3.1 An Annotated Model of a Successful Research Grant

Conclusion

This chapter provided a number of suggestions about how to write a research grant application. Below, I am including a checklist based on the various aspects that were discussed in this chapter. You may want to use this checklist as you draft and submit your research applications.

- Do I meet the eligibility criteria for the grant?
- Does this grant fund projects like mine?
- Have I provided all the details that they ask for?
- Have I looked at sample applications for this grant, if available?
- Have I used clear, formal and field specific language in my proposal?
- Have I identified a unique gap in the area that my project will address?
- Have I shown the theoretical and/or practical benefits of my project?
- Are my references current?
- Have I stressed the main points of the project?
- Have I described the research methodology in detail?
- Have I discussed the analytical approach that I will use to analyze the data?
- Have I identified how ethical issues will be handled?
- Have I articulated why I am the best person to work on this project?
- Have I shared my application with a colleague and received feedback?
- Have I proofread and edited my proposal?

Finally, in concluding, we need to remember that writing a successful grant application takes time. A good grant application satisfies the what, why, who, how, when, and where questions about the proposed project in sufficient detail. It needs to convince the reviewers that the proposed project is indeed one that needs to be carried out and that the authors of the proposal are the most suitable ones to be carrying it out. To achieve this, the authors of the grant proposal need to use appropriate formal and field-specific language. Their linguistic choices should reflect confidence and expertise and they should not be afraid to use technical language. However, it is a good idea to define any specialized terms to the reviewers – as the reviewers may or may not share your sub-specialty. To achieve the right balance between the technical aspects and the tenor of the application requires some effort and it is not uncommon for a good proposal to go through a number of drafts. It takes time to draft and edit a good proposal – and this is time worth investing. Good luck!

Discussion Questions

1. What are some of the things that you need to look for as you search for a funding opportunity?
2. What information should you include in the introductory section of your grant proposal?
3. What are some of the key things that you need to consider in writing up your research methodology?
4. What style and register of language should you use in drafting your grant proposal?
5. Why is it important to let your grant application sit for a while before revising it?

References

Given the nature of this chapter, I have not included any in-text references, but here is a list of selected references that I have found useful in my own work.

Aldridge, J., & Derrington, A. M. (2012). *The research funding toolkit*. London: Sage Publications.

Bonnici, L. (2008). *A guide to applying for funding for research, travel, and language study for linguistics graduate students*. Retrieved from http://linguistics.ucdavis.edu/pics-and pdfs/Funding%20Guide%20for%20Research,%20Travel,%20Lg%20Study%20Revised.pdf

Chapin, P. G. (2004). *Research projects and research proposals: A guide for scientists seeking funding*. Cambridge: Cambridge University Press.

Clarke, C. (2007). *Grant proposal makeover: Transform your request from no to yes*. San Francisco: Jossey-Bass.

Harris, D. (2007). *The complete guide to writing effective and award-winning grants*. Ocala, FL: Atlantic Publishers.

Kenneth, H. T. (2004). *Grant writing in higher education: A step-by-step guide*. Boston: Allyn and Bacon.

Locke, L. F., Spirduso, W. W., & Silverman, S. J. (2007). *Proposals that work: A guide for planning dissertations and grant proposals* (5th ed.). Newbury Park, CA: Sage.

Przeworski, A., & Salomon, F. (1995). *The art of writing proposals: Some candid suggestions for applicants to social science research council competitions*. Retrieved from http://fellowships.ssrc.org/art_of_writing_proposals/

CHAPTER 4

Using Research in the Language Classroom

Andy Curtis

INTRODUCTION

Definitions of research are far fewer than might be expected, given the thousands of research papers published every year, in all the different academic disciplines and domains of scholarly knowledge. Even published research papers that focus on doing research do not necessarily include a definition. For example, the paper by Chapelle and Duff, published in 2003 in *TESOL Quarterly,* and titled *Research Issues: Some guidelines for conducting quantitative and qualitative research in TESOL* (pp. 157–178), did not include any definitions of research.

One reason for this conspicuous absence might be that research writers assume that their readers already know what research is, as they are, by definition, part of the research community if they are reading a research paper. However, another possible reason is that how research is defined depends on what kind of research is being carried out, for what purpose(s) and by whom, as well as where, and even when the research is being carried out.

For language educators, meaning is often sought in the origins of words, and according to Harper (2012), "research" comes from the 1530s Old French word *recercher*, meaning to seek out or to search closely, which in the 1570s came to mean the act of searching closely. Building on that idea, Curtis has presented research as re-search (see, for example, Curtis, 1999), to emphasize the act of looking again.

This looking again and looking more closely can have at least three different foci, looking to see: a) what has always been there, but that was not noticed before; b) what is there now, that was not there before; and c) what is not there now, that was there before. In the case of educational research, the "there" could be the classroom, the school, or any of the places and spaces within which the teaching and learning being researched is taking place.

According to Howard and Sharp (2002: 2), research is "seeking through methodical processes to add to one's own body of knowledge and, hopefully, to that of others, by the discovery of non-trivial facts and insights." Although useful, one of the limitations of

Howard and Sharp's definition is the question of what is "non-trivial." How is it decided – by whom, when, where, and how – what is and what is not trivial or important? Many years earlier, connecting definition and purpose, Drew (1980: 4) stated that "research is a systematic way of asking questions, a systematic method of enquiry" and that "research is conducted to solve problems and to expand knowledge."

Drew's definition, which considerably pre-dates but which concurs with Howard and Sharps' notion of contributing to a body of knowledge, could be expanded to include research as a systemic way of answering questions, as well as asking them. The names or linguistic labels applied to objects, or in this case, to research methods, are important, especially for language educators. However, as Bell (2005: 2) points out: "It is the systematic approach that is important in the conduct of your [research] projects, not the title of 'research', 'investigation', 'enquiry', or 'study.'" Therefore, in spite of the different definitions of research, and the different kinds of research, there are a few essential characteristics, as noted above, that distinguish this kind of activity from others in the language classroom.

It is also worth noting that, in the same way that "Research practices evolve as new issues and questions emerge and as new methods and tools are developed to address them" (Chapelle and Duff, 2003: 157), what constitutes a language classroom has also been changing. For decades, and even centuries, a classroom was defined in terms of a physical structure, typically with students at desks, and with a teacher at the front of the classroom. However, with the advent of the Internet and other Web-based technologies, students and teachers can now be almost anywhere in time and space, interacting synchronously or asynchronously via computers, and increasingly via smaller and smaller handheld devices, such as cellular telephones.

Background

Why research in the language classroom is important

Why undertake language research? This is a valid question for language educators, as many are already busy with preparing, teaching, marking, and the myriad of other roles and responsibilities of language teachers. For a fortunate few, their main duties are to formulate research questions or hypotheses, design data-gathering tools and instruments, then gather and analyze data that will enable them to propose answers or to test hypotheses. However, these days most language researchers are also language teachers, and vice versa.

For this reason, the question asked by Court (2004: 1) is relevant: "Why, collectively, do we perform educational research?" Court presents three answers to her own question: "We want to learn about effective programs and teaching methods to help students learn. We want to discover relationships between variables in educational settings to plan interventions. We want to understand cultural contexts of schools to create schools that embody justice and reduce prejudice and inequality" (p. 1). If we look at the early work in this area, such as that carried out by Craig Chaudron, we can see that the answers to the question of why we do research have broadened over time. For example, Chaudron in the introduction to his book, *Second Language Classrooms: Research on Teaching and Learning* (1998: 1), stated that: "The fundamental goal of most such research has, of course, been to determine which variables best, or more frequently, lead to academic achievement." However, Chaudron (1998: 1) did also note that: "The range of applications of classroom-based research is broad, and the number of factors and issues seems endless."

These three answers from Court (2004) identify thee major sets of reasons for carrying out research in language education. These are: first, to assess or to measure and maximize the effectiveness of the teaching and learning taking place; second, to uncover and unpack the complex relationships between, for example, teaching and testing, the first language and the target language, the teaching materials and the teaching methods, and many other relationships; third, to enable and support the creation of teaching and learning environments that enable all teachers and learners to engage in meaningful, pedagogical activity and interaction. Following on from Court's three answers, a fourth one – specifically related to language research – is that language educators in language classrooms are best placed to carry out this kind of research as they are the experts in their own particular teaching and learning contexts. Such goals may seem, at best, over-ambitious, or even completely unattainable within certain contextual constraints. However, in relation to the use of research in the language classroom, any research which does not have any intention of improving and enhancing the teaching and learning taking place, has no place in the classroom.

For Court (2004: 1), "we do educational research as part of a quest for meaning", in relation to personal meaning – i.e., "the researcher's quest for meaning through research" – and contextual meaning – i.e., "meaning in relation to linguistics and culture" – which are shared through communication with the research community, by presenting and/or publishing our work. Although Court is referring to educational research in general, the answers she gives to her question apply equally well to research in language education.

Personal interest can also be one of the main reasons why language educators decide to carry out language research. As Court notes, "we investigate topics about which we are curious or passionate" (p. 1) as well as the research requirements of certain academic positions, in which, for example, publishing research papers is necessary for initial hiring, continued academic employment, tenure, promotion, etc.

Whatever our reasons for engaging in language research, Court concludes that: "In terms of the conduct of our research, it means care, honesty, rigor, time and patience, with our methods of data collection and analysis, our interpretations and our language" (p. 6), with her latter point having particular significance for language teachers and language researchers.

RESEARCH ON THIS TOPIC

It could be claimed that one of the most important issues in research, applied to the language classroom, but also in research in all environments that entail interpersonal interaction – such as classrooms – is the question of quantitative versus qualitative methods and approaches. However, as Bavelas (1995: 50) points out: "The quantitative-qualitative debate could now be described, not entirely whimsically, as a series of concatenated false dichotomies, having expanded in scale and complexity to the status of (equally false) isomorphisms.[1]" Bavelas emphasizes "false dichotomies" – which implies the existence of clear differences and unequivocal distinctions. Such black-and-white versions of reality tend to polarize, and emphasize differences rather than similarities – as a result of which Bavelas (and others) prefer continua to dichotomies, "as each of these [dichotomies] is, at the very least likely to be a continuum rather than a dichotomy and is even more likely to be a complex combination of several continua" (p. 49).

However, even with the acceptance of a continuum between the hypothetically pure quantitative language research at one of the far ends, and the equally hypothetical purely qualitative language research at the other, the relative strengths and weaknesses of both sets of research methods are still being debated. In response to this dichotomous division, the use of mixed methods research, with elements of both, is now commonly advocated and used (for a definition of mixed methods research and more information, see Chapter 10). Furthermore, there are certain criteria that apply to both approaches. For example, Chapelle and Duff (2003: 158) state that, regardless of whether quantitative or qualitative research is being carried out in the language classroom, "an overriding theme is that researchers should be explicit about the research contexts, populations, procedures, analyses, and basis for interpretations."

Within the "false dichotomy" of quantitative versus qualitative approaches, Bavelas (1995: 51) describes the tension between empirical and non-empirical as "one of the most extreme isomorphisms," and notes that, "Sometimes a quantitative approach is equated with empirical research whereas qualitative research is treated as non-empirical." However, as Bavelas explains, all approaches that make use of some kind of data are empirical, which are different from conclusions "based on intuition, authority, faith, or some other means of knowing, without recourse to data."

Bavelas also challenges the "false dichotomy" of subjective versus objective, and suggests that, "In a research context, the best working definition of objective is intersubjective agreement," in the sense of two or more subjects (people or parties) agreeing with the result. Bavelas contrasted this with "Measurements on which people cannot agree well" which "might be called subjective." However, Bavelas also notes that, "All measurement is subjective in the sense of requiring some human interference" (p. 52).

All this implies that within research of this kind, and especially research in language classrooms, pressure to conform to any of the either/or dichotomies should be resisted. Instead the strengths of different approaches and different kinds of data collected in different ways should be maximized, while at the same time, employing and combining them in ways that minimize their individual limitations.

PRACTICAL APPLICATIONS

The practical applications of research in the language classroom are, in many ways, unlimited, as almost every aspect of language teaching and learning can be researched, from the development of a curriculum or a course and the creation of teaching and learning materials, to the evaluation, assessment, and testing of teaching and learning outcomes. The research can be focused on the learners or on the teachers, or on both parties, or it can be focused on other stakeholders in the language education process, such as government agencies, publishers, parents, or the myriad of other parties. The research can also be focused on the processes, rather than the parties involved, or on any aspect of the language teaching and learning environment.

However, a significant amount of the research carried out in language classrooms by language teachers and students follows the steps of what is called action research (Curtis, 1999). The most commonly followed steps are:

1. Identify a change;
2. Observe the present situation;
3. Plan different possible interventions;
4. Carry out the intervention;
5. Observe the effects of the intervention;
6. Evaluate results against original goals; and
7. Publish/share findings.

Most of these steps can involve the gathering of and the analysis of data of some kind. In the first step, the teacher-researcher (TR) identifies some aspect of what is happening – or not happening – in their classroom that they would like to change. For example, the TR might want to encourage and enable students to produce more of the target language orally in class. For the action research to be focused, the change needs to be quite specific, otherwise the scale and scope of the change will become overwhelming. For example, if a TR wanted to improve or increase students' motivation to learn English, although such a goal may be highly desirable, it is not as amenable to action research as something more focused, and less all encompassing.

In the second step, the TR carefully observes the present situation in class. In the example of more target language spoken by the learners, the TR would make notes, and record how much target language is currently being spoken (if any). There are many ways to note and record the present situation – for example, using audio recordings, video recordings, or for the TR to keep a teaching journal or diary, with entries focused on this aspect of the classroom activity.

Steps three, four, five and six all relate to planning and carrying out some kind of intervention, then observing and evaluating the effects of the intervention. In the example above, the TR could plan a number of ways to bring about more in-class oral production of the target language – for example, using pair-work and small group work, using poems and songs, music and movies, etc.

A common problem here is what is sometimes called "premature evaluation" (Curtis, 1999), in which TRs evaluate *before* they observe. For example, if the students tended to revert to using their first language when put into small groups, then that should be the observation noted by the TR (e.g., in his/her journal entry). However, if the TR wrote in his/her diary: "Putting students into small groups didn't work", then that would be an evaluation, not an observation, and some sort of data should be provided to support the statement.

This is an important point, as teachers are often so used to giving corrective feedback in class, that they can easily forget that observing and evaluating are two quite different activities. So steps five and six need to be carried out carefully and separately. There is not universal agreement on the seventh and last step – publish/share findings – as some researchers and writers feel that it is not essential for teachers to publish their work. However, for others, the sharing of the research process, findings, and outcomes are an important part of building professional communities of reflective teacher-practitioners and classroom-based researchers.

Conclusion

As Chapelle and Duff (2003: 159) noted, "Quantitative research has played an important role in TESOL for a long time" and it is likely that this will continue. However, the use of qualitative methods, such as case study research and ethnographic studies, as well as mixed methods research, is likely to continue to grow, due to the complex nature of different instructional settings and contexts. Within classroom-based language research there is also likely to be an increase in the use of critical approaches, defined by Chapelle and Duff, in relation to ethnography, as follows: "Research approaches that use the qualifier *critical* differ from *descriptive* or *interpretive* approaches, which historically adopted a more detached, objective, value-free orientation to knowledge." (p. 172)

Chapelle and Duff go on to explain that, "Critical approaches align themselves with the post-Enlightenment philosophical tradition of situating research in its social context to consider how knowledge is shaped by the values of human agents and communities, implicated in power differences, and favorable for democratizing relationships and institutions" (p. 173). What this means for classroom-based language research is that students may assume a more important role in such research in the future, in which this kind of research is done with students, not to them, so that the students play a more active role and benefit from the findings of the research. For example, as noted above, this kind of research should have some intention of improving the quantity and quality of teaching and learning. However, historically, students have generally played a passive role in classroom-based research, as the targets, recipients, or consumers of the teaching methods and materials used and produced by teachers and materials publishers. As a result, a great deal of data is generated by students – for example, when they complete questionnaires or give interviews – but the students themselves are rarely involved in the research, beyond generating data for the researchers.

An analogous situation used to be common in the days when fulltime, professional education researchers, often trained in the scientific method used in the natural sciences since the 1600s, but with little or no training in teaching, gathered data from the backs of classrooms, with minimal interaction with teachers or students. With the growth of action research, exploratory practice, and other teacher-directed research methods, the power gradually shifted from the fulltime, professional education researchers to teacher-researchers, which is alluded to in the reference above to "power differences, and favorable for democratizing relationships and institutions" (Chapelle and Duff, 2003: 172–173).

Therefore, the next stage in this process of democratizing relationships in language education research is likely to be learners taking on more active roles, and becoming more than just data-generating subjects. In the future, then, students may, for example, play a role in deciding where the classroom-based research is focused. They may help to formulate the research questions or hypotheses, or decide how the research outcomes are applied in the classroom. It is also possible that, if this democratizing process continued, other stakeholders, such as parents, employers, and others, could also be invited to participate more actively in this kind of research.

However, what may not change in the future is the ongoing need to be wary of the kinds of "false dichotomies" challenged by Bavelas (1995), which was also alluded to by Chapelle and Duff (2003: 171): "A critical approach questions the traditional separation of theory and method, interpretation and data, subjective and objective, and ethics and science, and particularly the treatment of the second term in each pair as constituting valid research."

Discussion Questions

1. How would you define research and/or classroom research in your particular teaching/learning context?

2. If you are required, or are planning, to carry out research in your teaching/learning context, what kind(s) of research do/will you do and why?

3. If you are required to carry out research in your teaching/learning context, is most of it more towards the quantitative or qualitative end of the continuum and why?

4. If you could help bring about one change in your language classroom, what would that be, and how would you plan to research it?

References

Bell, J. (2005). *Doing your research project: A guide for first-time researchers in education and social science.* Buckingham, England: Open University Press.

Bavelas, J. B. (1995). Quantitative versus qualitative? In W. Leeds-Hurwitz (Ed.), *Social approaches to communication* (pp. 49–62). New York, NY: Guilford Press.

Chapelle, C. A., & Duff, P. A. (Eds.). (2003). Research issues: Some guidelines for conducting quantitative and qualitative research in TESOL. *TESOL Quarterly*, 37(1), 157–178.

Chaudron, C. (1998). *Second language classrooms: Research on teaching and learning.* Cambridge, England: Cambridge University Press.

Court, D. (2004). The quest for meaning in educational research. *Academic Exchange Quarterly*, 8(3), 1–7.

Curtis, A. (1999). Re-visioning our roles: Teachers as experts, researchers and reflective practitioners. *ThaiTESOL Bulletin*, 12(2), 24–32.

Drew, C. J. (1980). *Introduction to designing and conducting research*. St. Louis, MO: Mosby.

Harper, D. (2012). *Online etymological dictionary*. Retrieved from http://www.etymonline.com/

Howard, K., & Sharp, J. A. (2002). *The management of a student research project*. Aldershot, England: Gower.

Note

[1] An isomorphism is similarity in organisms of different ancestry, resulting from evolutionary convergence.

SECTION 2

GETTING READY

SECTION 2A

PRELIMINARY DECISIONS

In Section 2, Getting Ready, the chapters are about the issues involved in getting ready to do research, and thus, they examine ideas that need to be considered before starting a research project. It is organized into three sections on: A) Preliminary Decisions; B) Choosing a Research Method; and C) Choosing a Research Type.

In section 2A, the chapters cover the preliminary decisions that need to be made in a research project. While there are only two chapters, they are important ones about framing and defining your research project and deciding upon a research methodology.

Chapter 5 is about framing and defining research. The chapter argues that research is based on processes of systematic collection and logical analysis of data for purposes that the researcher defines. The author also explains how research problems are defined; where research problems come from; what the components of research problems are; and how framing and defining a research project is a non-linear, cyclical process. The chapter expands on each of those issues and, in the process, describes five main steps in the research process.

Chapter 6 explains three general research paradigms: quantitative, qualitative, and mixed methods research in terms of the types of research that fall into each category and how the three paradigms are related. The chapter then describes the processes of deciding on a research methodology in eight basic steps: find a research problem; search the literature; read and take notes; learn as much as you can; write tentative research questions; talk with other researchers; seek expert advice; and repeat the process from the first step (because of the cyclical nature of selecting a research methodology).

Editors' Preview Questions

Once again, we will begin this section with questions that you might want to consider before reading the chapters in this section. And again, one way to review the section after finishing it is to revisit these questions.

1. What problems do you face in your teaching? What problems do your students have in learning English? What research could you conduct to solve some of these problems? What would the steps be between noticing a problem and deciding on a research topic? (see Chapter 5)

2. Would the research you are thinking about in question 1 be better addressed using quantitative, qualitative, or mixed methods? What steps would you take in deciding which to use? (see Chapter 6)

CHAPTER 5

Framing and Defining your Research Project

Liying Cheng

INTRODUCTION

Research is the systematic process of collecting and logically analyzing data – i.e., evidence-based – for the purpose defined by the researcher (McMillan and Schumacher, 2010). It is a systematic process, which requires the researcher to follow certain procedures in conducting the research and to report the procedures used. There are two main stages in this process: the process of collecting the data and the process of analyzing the data. However, it is common that researchers tend to focus more on the process of collecting the data than the process of analyzing it. For this reason, it is essential that while framing and defining a research project, researchers spend sufficient time on both aspects. Further, researchers will need both to justify their rationale and to detail the procedures they follow.

A research project is a study into a research problem or problems derived from certain theories and hypotheses. A research problem can take the form of a statement that identifies the phenomenon to be studied. Such statements need to be clear, focused, concise, complex and arguable questions around which a researcher centers his or her research. But where do these questions come from? How do we know that these questions are important to ask and answer? When a research project is driven by a certain theory – for example, Gardner's socio-cultural model of motivation (Gardner, 2006) – the project is influenced by the existing research studies in this area. Such a research project is explanatory in nature – the researcher is testing a theory in a new research context. On the other hand, when a research project is driven by a hypothesis or a teacher's observation of his or her instructional context – for example, the fact that students tend not to read the reading passages prior to answering reading comprehension questions in a language testing situation (Cheng and Gao, 2002) – the project is exploratory in nature and designed to test the hypothesis by collecting and analyzing data systematically.

It is worthwhile to note that research projects conducted in language teaching and learning are rarely dichotomous (either explanatory or exploratory), but rather on a continuum in terms of the nature of the research involved. Irrespectively, in either case mentioned above, a researcher will need to identify an existing research problem in order to frame and define a research project. Defining a research problem is the first and foremost step in framing and defining a research project. "The research problem is the issue, controversy or concern that initiates the study" (McMillan and Schumacher, 2010: 47). The research problem is usually included in the introduction section of a research report or article and provides the foundation for the contribution of the study. It identifies why an evidence-based inquiry is important and indicates the reasons for the researcher's choice of a particular area of inquiry.

SOURCES OF RESEARCH PROBLEMS

A research problem implies the possibility of empirical investigation of data collection and analysis. The sources of the research problem could be any of the following or a combination of the following. There are sources of research problems other than the list presented below, but the following are applicable to the language teaching and learning situation:

- observations, interests, and experiences of the researcher;
- application of theory;
- clarification of contradictory findings and/or confirmation of findings;
- extension of the study to different participants;
- extension of the study using different methods;
- development of more effective interventions.

For classroom teachers and educators, the research problem is likely to come first of all from our own observations of the classroom environment. Maybe we consistently notice certain student behaviors that stimulate our interests and/or hypotheses of further inquiries – for example, we might want to know more about how our students deal with reading comprehension in the classroom, based on our previous engagement and experience teaching reading comprehension or invigilating reading comprehension tests.

A second possible origin of a research problem could be a desire to apply theory in our own classrooms. For example, if you wished to identify your students' motivation in your own classroom, you could adopt Gardner's social-cultural theory and apply it in your own situation. A third, possible source is the clarification of contradictory findings that you have read or heard about at conferences and professional development events. For example, you may have read or heard evidence which both supports and refutes an instructional strategy such as process writing in certain classroom contexts (Kroll, 1990). You have a sense it may or may not work in your classroom so you decide to try it out with your students and to systematically collect and analyze the data in order to draw conclusions from it. The same process would apply to the confirmation of findings.

Replication, the next possible source of research problem on the list, is one of the most useful sources of research problems for classroom teachers and educators. This would involve, as mentioned above, the clarifying and confirming of findings of previous studies, with you obtaining the information about a particular research study – for example process writing – and wishing to investigate whether this instructional strategy works in your classroom. You would adopt the research design used by the researcher(s) of the study; employ their research instrument(s), and their ways of analyzing the data in order to compare the findings of the previous study with similar and different findings from your own study. There is nothing inherently good or bad about similar or different findings except you would need to understand or interpret why this instructional strategy worked in the context of the previous original study but not in your context, or vice versa. The teaching and learning context plays a key role in the success of an instructional strategy, and carrying out a research study is to seek to understand, using systematically collected evidence, why certain instructional strategies work or not.

There are other sources of research problems related to replication, i.e., a project to extend a study to different participants, or to use different methods. A replication study repeats, exactly or approximately, a previous study to discover if its findings are reliable and/or can be generalized to other participants and circumstances (see Porte, 2012 for a detailed discussion of replication studies). For example, you can choose to conduct a study by collecting data from a different set of participants; if the previous study is conducted in a university setting, you can do your research project in a school setting. Alternatively, if a previous study is conducted in the North American context, you can do the research in an Asian, South American, or African context. In either of the cases, you would need to modify the research instrument(s) to suit your research context, and you might also need to translate the instrument(s) into the language that your students/participants function predominantly in. You would also need to justify your reasons for changing the context since certain contextual differences – for example, the age of the participants – could be crucial to the validity of your study. You can also choose to use a different research method from the previous study – for example to use a qualitative method rather than a quantitative method, or vice versa. The philosophical underpinning of different methods – for example quantitative and qualitative methodology – is dealt with elsewhere in this book by other contributors. In many cases, the choice of research methodology is also based on your own belief and skills. It is possible that a mixed methods design may be more appropriate as such a research design can provide a better fit to understand the complex teaching and learning context (Johnson and Onwuegbuzie, 2004).

A final possible source of research problems is in the development of more effective interventions. This is a common source for teachers and educators as we are constantly exploring the ways in which effective intervention can improve our instruction and enhance our student learning.

The above sources of research problems help us to identity the why and, in some ways, the how of our research study, and thus complete the first essential step in framing and defining a research project.

COMPONENTS OF A RESEARCH PROBLEM

A research problem has three major components: context, purpose and significance (see Figure 5.1). The *context* is the background that places the research problem within the framework of a larger area of research. For example, a researcher might state that Ontario secondary schools have seen the greatest increase of English as a second language (ESL) students, yet teachers and support programs for these ESL students in Ontario schools have declined by 30% over the past five years. Meanwhile, large-scale achievement testing has increasingly been used to measure student competency and ensure system accountability. The confluence of the increased number of second language students with decreased provision and the expanding testing framework has created a new and largely unanticipated educational problem: alarmingly high failure rates for these students (Cheng, Klinger, and Zheng, 2007). This example context frames the research problem within which the researchers can start to pose research questions.

The significance of a research problem is determined by the extent to which it contributes to current knowledge and/or practice in education. For example, theory-driven studies should be linked closely to existing knowledge and theory and also to practice-driven studies. For practice-driven studies, it is essential that the research problem be situated in

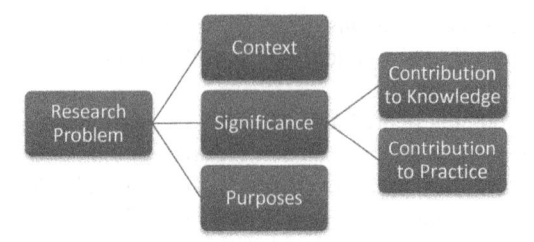

Figure 5.1 Components of a Research Problem

the actual classroom or educational contexts. In either case, significance is the essential justification for the research project, i.e., why the research project should be done and what the project is contributing to. The purpose is a statement that indicates in a more specific manner what is being investigated, and what we hope to achieve by it. For example, the purpose of the Ontario study is to explore the factors that contribute to or impede ESL students' academic success in Ontario secondary schools. Purpose statements can be similar to research questions. Research questions are more specific and are often framed in a question format – for example, what is the relationship between the test-takers' background (gender, parents' education, and home language) and their in-school and after-school literacy activities? Research questions help researchers focus their research by providing a path through the research process. The specificity of a well-developed research question helps researchers work toward supporting a specific and arguable research focus (Onwuegbuzie and Leech, 2006).

Research on This Topic

The significance of the research problem is the rationale for a research project. A research problem is significant when it contributes to the development of theory, knowledge, or practice. After you have defined the significance of your research problem, i.e., you have clearly established in what ways your study is important and is likely to make a contribution to language teaching and learning, the next step is to formulate a research design and choose the appropriate methods for your systematic data collection and analysis procedures. The process that can support you to do so is to conduct a review of the relevant literature. A review of the relevant literature can help you to establish the important link between existing knowledge and your research problem, and it can also help you to choose the appropriate methods for your research project. McMillan (2008) lists six specific purposes for conducting a literature review:

- redefining the research problem;
- establishing a conceptual or theoretical framework;
- developing significance;
- identifying methodological limitations;
- identifying contradictory findings;
- developing a research hypothesis.

In our current information age, there is a vast amount of information on any particular topic. Where do you start to conduct a review of the literature? The best place to begin is by identifying your field of study, i.e., the professional association(s) you belong to, the conference(s) you attend and present at, and the journals that are associated with your professional association(s). Considering the massive amount of information available to most of us electronically online, you will also need to make sure that you know about the quality of the sources of the literature. It is important to understand the fundamental difference between the primary and secondary sources. A primary source is the one that reports original data, and this could be an article, a technical report, or a book chapter. The most accessible primary source for research data on language teaching and learning is the journals that publish empirical studies (studies that collect and analyze original data), e.g., *TESOL Quarterly*, *Language Assessment Quarterly*, and *Language Learning*. The way to identify a primary source is to ask the following questions about a research study:

- Have data been collected?
- Is there a design, methods, or methodology section?
- Is there a section on findings or results?

In contrast to a primary source, a secondary source summarizes, reviews, analyzes, or discusses primary sources of information. There are three major secondary sources of research literature. They are: a) annual reviews and yearbooks – for example, the *Annual Review of Applied Linguistics*; b) academic and professional books – for example, *Cambridge Guide to Second Language Assessment* (Coombe, O'Sullivan, Davidson, and Stoynoff, 2012); c) reference books – for example, *Encyclopedia of Language and Education, Vol. 7: Language Testing and Assessment* (Shohamy and Hornberger, 2008), and *Handbook of Research in Second Language Teaching and Learning* (Hinkel, 2011). In addition to the above, ERIC Digests[1] are excellent secondary sources of literature. They are useful short reports that synthesize research ideas about contemporary language education issues.

Five main steps are essential in conducting a review of the literature. They are as follows:

1. Identify topic and key words;
2. Identify databases;
3. Conduct the searches;
4. Identify sources as primary and secondary sources;
5. Evaluate and analyze.

The goal of conducting the literature review is not simply to find some sources of literature, but to find the most appropriate and reliable sources that can help you to both establish the significance of your research project, and also to design your research methods, be they quantitative, qualitative, or mixed methods. The conducting of the literature review is another key aspect in framing and defining your research project. Without this essential aspect of literature review, you will not be able to know whether your research project is worthwhile to carry out. After you have evaluated and analyzed the literature, you will need to write up a literature review. This summarizes and synthesizes the existing research studies. Simply put, the summarizing of the literature is the "what" of the existing research, and the synthesizing is the "so what" – i.e., the link between the existing research studies and your research project and the research gap that you are going to address in your project.

PRACTICAL APPLICATIONS

The process of framing and defining your research project is not linear but cyclical in nature: you may need to go through all the processes several times before you are ready to conduct your study. Even when you have completed your data collection and data analysis, you may still need to conduct a further review of the literature and refocus your research problem. In fact, many researchers keep an on-line alert with major databases and journals so they get updated information frequently.

You may find the following checklist – which is a summary of the discussions above – a useful self-assessment guide in this process.

1. Clarify the source(s) of your research problem:
   - observations, interests, and experiences of the researcher
   - application of theory
   - clarification of contradictory findings and/or confirmation of findings
   - replication
   - extension of the study to different participants
   - extension of the study using different methods
   - development of more effective interventions

2. Identify the components of your research problem – its context, purpose, and significance. It is a useful strategy to start your research project by stating, in one sentence, your research purpose: "My study aims to …"

3. Conduct the literature review and check to see whether you have achieved the following or aspects of the following:
   - redefining the research problem
   - establishing a conceptual or theoretical framework
   - developing significance
   - identifying methodological limitations
   - identifying contradictory findings
   - developing a research hypothesis

Going through this checklist will help to ensure the quality of your research project. The process can also help you in understanding and interpreting your data later on in the research process.

CONCLUSION

McMillan and Schumacher (2010: 2) point out that "the times we live in are truly amazing in terms of the possibilities for educational research!" As educators, our day-to-day classroom teaching and learning provides the best scenario for us to explore, examine, and systematically investigate the research problems close to our heart. Furthermore, we are in the best possible position to conduct the research since we know our context and our students better than any outside researchers could do. Taking sufficient time to frame and define our research project using the step-by-step processes mentioned above will help us to improve our practice, the strength of research evidence, and the quality of our results.

Discussion Questions

1. What is the fundamental difference between a research study and an inquisitive activity we conduct in our classroom?

2. What are the potential sources of your research problem?

3. What are the major components of your research problem?

4. What is the importance of conducting a review of the literature in framing and defining a research project?

5. What are the steps of conducting a review of the literature?

References

Cheng, L., & Gao, L. (2002). Passage dependence in standardized reading comprehension: Exploring the College English Test. *Asian Journal of English Language Teaching*, 12, 161–178.

Cheng, L., Klinger, D., & Zheng, Y. (2007). The challenges of the Ontario Secondary School Literacy Test for second language students. *Language Testing*, 24, 185–208.

Coombe, C., O'Sullivan, B., Davidson, P., & Stoynoff, S. (Eds.), (2012). *The Cambridge guide to second language assessment.* Cambridge: Cambridge University Press.

Gardner, R. C. (2006). The socio-educational model of second language acquisition: A research paradigm. *EUROSLA Yearbook*, 6, 237–260.

Hinkel, E. (2011). *Handbook of research in second language teaching and learning*, Volume II. New York, Routledge.

Johnson, R. B., & Onwuegbuzie, A. J. (2004). Mixed methods research: A research paradigm whose time has come. *Educational Researcher*, 33, 14–26.

Kroll, B. (Ed.) (1990). *Second language writing: Research insights for the classroom.* Cambridge: Cambridge University Press.

McMillan, J. H. (2008). *Educational research: Fundamentals for the consumer* (5th ed.). New York: Longman.

McMillan, J. H., & Schumacher, S. (2010). *Research in education: Evidence-based inquiry* (7th ed.). New York: Pearson.

Onwuegbuzie, A. J. & Leech, N. (2006). Linking research questions to mixed methods data analysis procedures. *The Qualitative Report*, 11(3), 474–498.

Porte, G. (2012). *Replication research in applied linguistics.* Cambridge: Cambridge University Press.

Shohamy, E. & Hornberger, N. H. (Eds.), (2008) *Encyclopedia of language and education, Vol. 7: Language testing and assessment* (2nd ed.). New York: Springer Science & Business Media.

Note

[1] The Education Resources Information Center (ERIC) is an online library of education research and information, sponsored by the Institute of Education Sciences (IES) of the U.S. Department of Education.

CHAPTER 6

Deciding Upon a Research Methodology

James Dean Brown

INTRODUCTION

Skimming through this book will quickly reveal that research methods come in many flavors, including a wide variety of quantitative research methods and even more diverse qualitative methods. *Quantitative research methods* are those that deal with numbers, statistics, and probabilities including descriptive, correlational, means comparisons, frequency comparisons statistics, and many elaborations of those four themes. *Qualitative research methods* are those that do not deal with numbers, indeed often eschew numbers, including ethnographic, naturalistic, and action research, as well as discourse analysis, conversation analysis, and many others. In the last dozen years, another formal research method paradigm called *mixed methods research* (MMR; see Chapter 10) has emerged. This paradigm combines quantitative and qualitative methods systematically in such a way that the whole is greater than the sum of the parts and the final results are more valid, credible, and indeed, *legitimate* (to use mixed methods research terminology; see Chapter 10 for a definition).

BACKGROUND

The question that this chapter addresses is: how do researchers decide from among all of these options upon a research methodology? The problem of course is that such decisions are difficult without devoting many years to learning all of what a researcher needs to know in the quantitative, qualitative, and mixed methods research traditions. For instance, I took 11 courses at UCLA in statistical research while I was a graduate student, and I have spent much of the 30-plus years since then learning more about designing quantitative studies and analyzing and reporting the results – and that is just one of the three paradigms discussed above. Given that you may not have that much time to devote to deciding on and applying a research methodology, you will need to narrow the range of options very quickly and yet effectively.

Research on this Topic

Unfortunately, even narrowing the range of options can be challenging. Indeed, a high percentage of the questions I get from the wide range of graduate students I encounter have to do with the issue of deciding on a research methodology. The problem is that, as much as we might like it to be true, deciding on a research method within the quantitative, qualitative, or MMR paradigms is not reducible to a set of black and white choices. A number of authors (including me) have tried to reduce the decision-making in statistical analyses to trees or other forms of binary choice figures (see for example, Brown, 1988: 160–161; 1992: 63–638 and 646–650; or Hatch and Lazaraton, 1991: 543–545; also see Figure 32.1 in Chapter 32), but in my experience, in the end, such tree or binary-choice charts or tables do not work very well because there is so much grey area in these sorts of research decisions and because there are many binary choices for which both options make sense for different reasons.

Another way to make decisions about which research method to use is to simply examine all the possibilities and then chose one or more. The problem with that approach is that there are so many options that this method may prove inefficient. For example, in Brown (2004), being as yet unaware of mixed methods research, I divided research methodologies into qualitative, survey, and quantitative research methods (as shown in Figure 6.1) with a total of 11 options within those three categories ranging from case studies to experimental research.

However, with mixed methods research added and the constant adoption of new research methods from other fields, I have come to divide research into quantitative, qualitative, and mixed methods research traditions (see Figure 6.2) with many new options in those three categories, ranging: a) in qualitative research, from critical research to introspective methods (see Figure 6.3); b) in mixed methods research, from qualitative mixed to quantitative mixed (see Figure 6.4); and c) in quantitative research, from at least two options in descriptive statistical methods (e.g. descriptive statistics and cross-tabulations) to 10 options in exploratory methods (i.e. correlational, simple and multiple regression, discriminant function, logistic, cluster, factor, and confirmatory factor analyses, and implicational scaling, and structural equation modelling) to 10 options *each* in non-random assignment quasi-experimental and random assignment experimental methods (i.e., z-test, t-test, and various versions of univariate and multivariate analysis of variance designs and the covariate variations of each of those) (see Figure 6.5). So instead of the 11 options shown in Figure 6.1, there are more than 45 options described here. I'm not sure if all of this expansion means that research methods are proliferating in applied linguistics or just that my awareness of them is growing. Both are probably true.

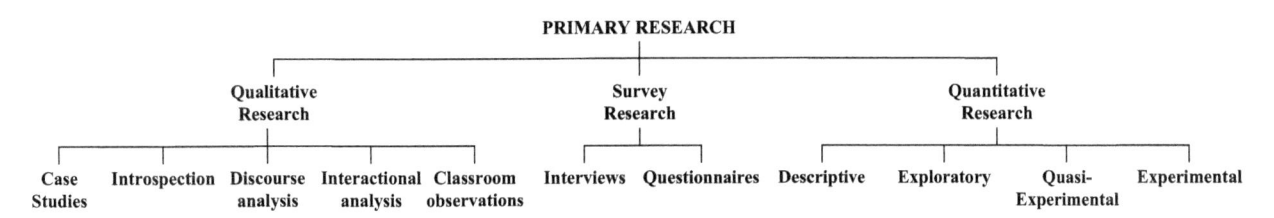

Figure 6.1 Primary Research Types (adapted from Brown, 2004: 7)

```
                        Research Traditions
        ┌───────────────────┼───────────────────┐
   Qualitative         Mixed methods        Quantitative
```

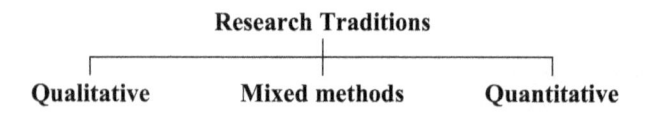

Figure 6.2 Three Research Traditions or Paradigms

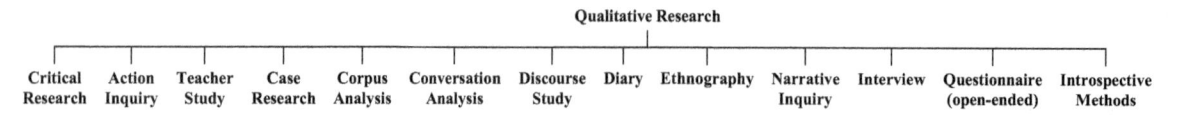

```
                                    Qualitative Research
  ┌────┬────┬────┬────┬────┬────┬────┬────┬────┬────┬────┬────┐
Critical Action Teacher Case  Corpus Conversation Discourse Diary Ethnography Narrative Interview Questionnaire Introspective
Research Inquiry Study Research Analysis Analysis Study              Inquiry            (open-ended)   Methods
```

Figure 6.3 Qualitative Research Types

```
       ┌──────────────┬──────────────┬──────────────┬──────────────┐
 Pure Qualitative  Qualitative Mixed  Pure Mixed  Quantitative Mixed  Pure Quantitative
```

Figure 6.4 A Continuum of Research Types from Pure Qualitative to Pure Quantitative (see Figure 10.1 in Chapter 10 and the associated prose discussion)

```
                          Quantitative Research
      ┌──────────────┬──────────────┬──────────────┐
 Descriptive      Exploratory    Quasi-Experimental    Experimental
```

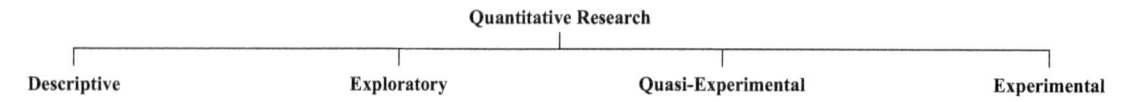

Figure 6.5 Quantitative Research Types (Brown, 2011: 1)

Clearly, there are many research methods available to researchers in applied linguistics and several ways to classify them with trees, diagrams, tables, etc. A number of recent books on this topic have offered a menu of the most prominent research method options with the goal of letting the reader choose which is most suitable for their research. For example, Brown and Rodgers (2002) covered a variety of different research options (including case study, introspection, classroom research, descriptive statistics research, correlational research, and quasi-experimental research) with lots of examples, and thus gave readers a fairly wide overview that was meant to help them make decisions about which research methodology they might want to use. The book you are presently reading offers an even broader variety of options. For instance, the table of contents offers at least two levels at which you need to be thinking about this issue: research methods and research types. These two levels are not necessarily independent of each other. Choosing a conversation analysis research type means that you will most likely be doing only qualitative analyses; whereas, if a study is a traditional pretest-posttest or treatment-control group comparison research type, that means almost inevitably that the research method will be quantitative. However, there are many other research types where the lines cannot be so neatly drawn (as explained at length in Brown, 2014), and in such cases, you may be well advised to consider using mixed methods research.

Practical Applications

This chapter has listed a large number of research options, but it makes no attempt to offer a clear-cut set of binary trees of choices that you can trace through to decide on which research method(s) to use in your study. Instead, you will find here eight steps that you can use in considering and deciding on what research method(s) you may want to use.

STEP 1 – FIND A RESEARCH PROBLEM

While you are learning to be a researcher, you should constantly be on the lookout for research problems, research questions, or research ideas that may really interest you and be ready to find such ideas in surprising places. As Brown (2014: 232) put it, "… research ideas are lying around everywhere in our professional lives. I have found research ideas at the ends of research papers in the suggestions for future research; in literature review papers where they are explicitly listed; in questions asked by my ESL or EFL students; and in teacher meetings, graduate course discussions, discussions with colleagues, and so forth." Off the top of my head, I can think of at least one study that I have done that arose from each of those sources.

For example, I remember one idea that came up in my EFL class in China. One bright student in my speaking class asked why he could understand my English when I was speaking to the class but not when I was talking with other Americans. That simple question in class led me to conduct an empirical study on reductions with a research partner, to write a number of articles that analyzed issues of fluency and connected speech, and to edit two books on connected speech – all thanks to a Chinese student's insightful question.

Another idea that I recall came up in a teacher meeting. One day I was bored out of my mind in a teacher meeting at UCLA, when one of the teachers said that he had noticed that there were two distinctly different groups of students in his class: one was made up of higher achieving students who had been placed directly into the course and the other consisted of lower achieving students who had progressed into this course from lower level courses. The study that resulted showed that there were indeed differences in achievement between these two groups called placed students and continuing students. This study was published as a chapter in the proceedings from a national conference, appears as an example study in Chapter 5 of Brown 1988, has been replicated by three other researchers, and has been cited a total of 16 times in the literature (according to Google Citation) – all thanks to a teacher's insightful observation in a meeting.

The trick of course is to constantly be on the lookout for such ideas in all of your professional interactions, to recognize these ideas when they pop up, and then to think about and analyze them so that they become research studies. The remaining steps in this list will help you accomplish all of that.

STEP 2 – SEARCH THE LITERATURE

Given that it is rare that a research idea has not occurred to others in one form or another, the next step is probably to find out what is already known about the particular idea, problem, or research question that has aroused your curiosity. One productive way to do that is to search the literature for articles, books, websites, and research studies on the topic that interests you. Of course, you can do that by going to the library and slogging through the print sources related to your issue, but in today's world, online sources can make that job much easier. My first instinct is to turn to Google Scholar, the online catalog for our university library, or the Internet more broadly, to search using key words relevant to the research idea of interest. I then scan the resulting articles, books, etc. and refine my key words and continue the search. It is also sometimes useful to keep a list of authors whose names come up a lot as citations in the articles you are finding, and then search for those names. All of this may take a few hours, but will be well worth the effort.

STEP 3 – READ AND TAKE NOTES

Once you have collected the articles, books, websites, and research studies that interest you, skim, scan, and selectively read those sources that seem the most relevant to you, especially those that are similar to what you want to do. Some people like to highlight as they skim, scan, and read; others like to take notes. I use the latter strategy because I have noticed that the act of note-taking into a computer file makes me be very selective, and at the same time gradually reveals patterns to me of what specifically my mind finds salient, interesting, and worth pursuing. I may start a research project with a vague idea or problem, but basically I have no precise notion of where the study is headed. In some way that I really don't understand, this sort of reading and note-taking usually shows me where the study is headed.

In addition to building your literature review and finding out where the study is headed, during the reading and note-taking stage, you should be paying special attention to whatever research methods the authors are using in their empirical studies of the issue. Some similar set or subset of those research methods may be exactly what you need to use in conducting your research study.

STEP 4 – LEARN AS MUCH AS YOU CAN

At the same time that all of this reading and note-taking is going on, you may find that there is a lot that you need to learn about one or more research methodologies. If you are in a graduate program, you are in an ideal position to learn the research knowledge and skills for the relevant research method(s) by taking research method courses in your academic department or in another related department – for example, in education, psychology, anthropology, etc. If you are finished with your formal studies, you may need to learn the same material and skills by buying and reading books, finding and reading research methods articles, searching online for information, etc., and by a good deal of trial and error. However, the next two steps (Steps 5 and 7) may also help in this regard especially if talking with other researchers and getting advice from experts leads you to finding more resources that you can access, consult, and digest.

STEP 5 – WRITE TENTATIVE RESEARCH QUESTIONS

At about this point, it may help you focus on what you want to do to take a stab at formulating research questions for your project if it is quantitative, or research goals or aims if it is qualitative, or some combination of the two if your research is mixed methods. You may also want to start sketching out how you think you might find answers to your research questions or address your goals or aims. You should be prepared at this point to be very flexible because you may need to change, revise, and rethink the directions of your research more than once as your research develops. You may also need to repeat Steps 2 through 5 several times.

STEP 6 – TALK WITH OTHER RESEARCHERS

I have always found it useful to talk with other researchers about any research project I am planning or conducting. Whether you turn to your professors, teaching colleagues, fellow graduate students, etc., the old adage that two heads are better than one always seems to turn out to be true. The fact that they are looking at the issues from different angles and from different knowledge bases may provide you with new ways of thinking about the issues involved, ideas for new directions to pursue, warnings about potential pitfalls, etc. – all of which is potentially valuable for finding your way to a research project and deciding on what research methods you will ultimately use. Be sure also to ask these other researchers if they know of any books or articles that will help you learn about the research topic as well as about what research method(s) they think are appropriate for that topic and what you will need to know to use those research methods. You may also want to ask them if they know of anyone who has particular expertise in the research topic or research methods involved. Importantly, you should be prepared for such a relationship to become reciprocal in the sense that you should offer to help in return if other researchers need and request it.

STEP 7 – SEEK EXPERT ADVICE

One way or the other, you will benefit by identifying expertise that you can rely on. Local experts – for example, statisticians in the Education Department or technical staff in the Computer Science Department, etc. – will be the easiest to contact and work with, but given the ubiquity of email, experts at a distance may also be a real possibility. The next step is to contact some of them. They may not be willing to help you, but nothing is gained by not asking. And you may be surprised to find that experts are human and that they will often be intrigued by others who are interested in the same academic topics and research methods that they use. If you find people like this who are willing to help you, be sure not to abuse that privilege by assuming that they will spend hours of their time showing you things you should have learned on your own, or by writing them long involved emails that would take hours to answer. If you have done your homework, you should have clear and concise questions that they can answer from their knowledge without spending hours doing it. Note that they will probably be more willing to read material that you have carefully written up and comment on it if it is presented to them in hard copy with double spacing and wide margins to accommodate their comments in the margins. And again, be sure to ask these experts if they know of any books or articles that would help you to learn more without draining their time and energy.

STEP 8 – REPEAT STEPS 1–7

I need to stress that throughout this process you will need to stay flexible. As mentioned above you may need to change, revise, and rethink the directions of your research several times as it develops, which may necessitate repeating Steps 2 through 7 several times.

Conclusion

I discussed in this chapter several approaches to deciding upon your research method(s): using the trees and diagrams approach which often doesn't help much or surveying the available options and deciding on the basis of what you learn. I then suggested eight steps that you can take in the process of focusing in on the research method(s) you will ultimately decide to use: find a research problem, search the literature, read and take notes, learn as much as you can, write tentative research questions, talk with other researchers, seek expert advice, and repeat steps 1 through 7.

Given the consistent trend in our field from a few research methods in the early days of my career to a much larger array of options today, I would not be surprised if the research methods don't continue to become more numerous and diverse in the future. That probably means that you would benefit from remaining open and willing to learn about and use new methods as they develop and suit your research purposes. This may mean trying new ways of research that develop within applied linguistics or adapting new research methods from other fields to your purposes within applied linguistics. In either case, since you are the future of research in our profession, your choices may be important not only to you but to the field at large.

Discussion Questions

1. What are the basic differences between quantitative, qualitative, and mixed methods research?

2. Why do you suppose that the trees and diagrams designed to help you select a research method do not really work?

3. What are at least five of the many qualitative research method options that you have for doing research? Which is most interesting to you?

4. What are at least five of the many quantitative research method options that you have for doing research? Which is most interesting to you?

5. If you decided to combine the favorite research methods that you listed in numbers 3 and 4 into a mixed methods study, would you prefer that it be qualitative-mixed, quantitative-mixed, or pure-mixed? In approximately what proportions would you design the study to draw on your quantitative method(s) and qualitative method(s)?

6. Where do you think you might find interesting research questions/problems in your professional life?

7. How would you go about consulting the literature to find out more about a research question/problem that interests you? Why is that important?

8. How would you go about finding and consulting with research colleagues and getting advice from experts about your research question/problem? Why is all of that important?

References

Brown, J. D. (1988). *Understanding research in second language learning: A teacher's guide to statistics and research design*. Cambridge: Cambridge University Press.

Brown, J. D. (1992). Statistics as a foreign language Part 2: More things to look for in reading statistical language studies. *TESOL Quarterly*, 26(4), 629–664.

Brown, J. D. (2001). *Using surveys in language programs*. Cambridge: Cambridge University Press.

Brown, J. D. (2004). Research methods for applied linguistics: Scope, characteristics, and standards. In A. Davies & C. Elder (Eds.), *The handbook of applied linguistics* (pp. 476–500). Oxford: Blackwell.

Brown, J. D. (2011). Quantitative research in second language studies. In E. Hinkel (Ed.), *Handbook of research in second language teaching and learning*, volume 2 (pp. 190–206). New York: Routledge.

Brown, J. D. (2014). Mixed methods research for TESOL. Edinburgh, UK: University of Edinburgh Press.

Brown, J. D., & Rodgers, T. (2002). *Doing second language research*. Oxford: Oxford University Press.

Hatch, E., & Lazaraton, A. (1991). *The research manual: Design and statistics for applied linguistics*. Rowley, MA: Newbury House.

SECTION 2B

CHOOSING A RESEARCH METHOD

In section 2B, Choosing a Research Method, the chapters cover the issues involved in choosing a research method on a fairly global level. There are four chapters that will help you understand what general paradigms researchers are currently working in: quantitative, qualitative, or mixed methods.

Chapter 7 examines quantitative research and how it systematically uses numerical data to address research questions. The chapter discusses the importance of the different types of variables. The author goes on to explain how generalizability is enhanced by attending to internal and external validity, and then discusses the many approaches to quantitative research that are available in applied linguistics. The chapter ends with discussions of null hypotheses significance testing and the practical importance of understanding quantitative research methods.

Chapter 8, on qualitative research, begins by exploring various definitions of qualitative research and in contrast with quantitative research, then settles into a discussion of five characteristics of qualitative research. After providing an overview of how qualitative research developed and became well-established, the author discusses key issues in qualitative research including respondent validation, triangulation, and thick description. The chapter also describes a number of important references that readers can read to learn more about qualitative research and discusses the practical importance of qualitative research.

Chapter 9 considers second language research paradigms generally from ontological and epistemological perspectives leading the author to posit a tripartite hermeneutic model, which further leads him to explain methodological perspectives including experimental, interpretative, critical, and pragmatic strategies. He concludes by explaining how the paradigm that a researcher chooses will strongly influence all other aspects of the process of doing research.

Chapter 10 shows how mixed methods research (MMR) can combine qualitative and quantitative research methods to create a third paradigm that adds value to the other two paradigms. The chapter begins by defining MMR, and explaining the relationships among pure qualitative, qualitative mixed, pure mixed, quantitative mixed, and pure quantitative research types. The author also discusses how the nine types of *legitimation* can be used to enhance and defend MMR, as well as how convergence, divergence, elaboration, clarification, exemplification, and interaction techniques can be used to strengthen a MMR study.

Editors' Preview Questions

1. In broad terms, are you more interested in quantitative research, qualitative research, or mixed methods research? Why?

2. What paradigms and strategies are available to you as a researcher? (see Chapter 9) How could you use quantitative research to help you to understand language learning and teaching, and to solve problems you have in the classroom and professionally? (see Chapter 7) What about qualitative research? (see Chapter 8) And, mixed methods research? (see Chapter 10)

3. What are the fundamental differences between quantitative, qualitative, and mixed methods research? What are the similarities?

CHAPTER 7

Essentials of Quantitative Research for Classroom Teachers

Thom Hudson

INTRODUCTION

Quantitative research in language studies is a systematic approach to addressing research questions with numerical data which utilizes empirical methods to assist in explaining how people learn, use, and conceptualize language. It is a systematic and disciplined process of inquiry, which involves researchers instituting control over potential sources of error during each stage of the data collection process. In order for classroom teachers to be effective consumers and producers of research, it is important for them to have a basic understanding of the quantitative research process. The literature that teachers read often includes discussions of the results from quantitative studies, and educators often use quantitative methods to see how some teaching approach affects student outcomes. This chapter focuses on issues classroom teachers may need to consider when reading or discussing research studies in their field.

BACKGROUND

Quantitative research is useful for description of numerical relationships and for examining causal relationships. It can have as its purpose either description or explanation, or both. For example, a research project could use demographic data collected during the application process for entry into a language program to describe the first language, age, educational history, ethnic background, length of residence, and other pertinent variables on potential students. On the other hand, the program might institute a research project seeking to explain how exposure to a particular type of reading instruction affects vocabulary acquisition by learners at different language proficiency levels.

In general, quantitative research is interested in one of two relationships: either how variables[1] vary together, or how groups differ in relation to defined variables. Examples of the first category are correlational studies – these examine how the values of one variable change as a second or third variable increases or decreases. In the second category are studies of, for example, how participants differ on achievement tests as a function of their first language. The two types of research interest focus on either how objects tend to go together or how they tend to be different. In quantitative research, the goal is to determine the relationship between one thing (an independent variable) and another (a dependent or outcome variable) in a population. A central concern surrounds the identification and, at times, control of variables, of which there are a number of different types in the literature. The major variable types are described below.

- *Independent variables*: the variable that identifies what causes a change in another variable. The category of interest in language education can be affected by variables such as the role of the first language, level of language proficiency, or gender on rate of learning.
- *Dependent variables*: the variable that varies as the result of changes in values of the independent variable. It is often identified as the test or instrument that is used to provide quantitative values for analysis.
- *Moderator variables*: a variable that affects the relationship between an independent variable and a dependent variable. For example, if a particular instructional approach is not effective until learners have achieved a particular level of ability, then ability level would be considered a moderator variable.
- *Confounding variables*: a variable – not included and unaccounted for – that is wholly, or in part, the explanation for an experimental result. For example, a study might find that language students who studied the most hours achieved higher proficiency. A conclusion might be that we should make students study more hours. However, it may be that those students who were the most motivated chose to study more hours. In this instance, motivation might be the causal factor rather than number of hours.
- *Control variables*: variables that are held constant in a study. For example, a researcher might hold age constant in a study, focusing on adult learners rather than also including children. In this instance, age would be a control variable.
- *Intervening variables*: variables that explain a relationship or provide a causal link between variables. They are the underlying, theoretical factors that link the operational independent and dependent variables. For example, a study might designate number of semesters spent learning a language as the independent variable, and a test of language ability as the dependent variable. The use of number of semesters spent studying is in actuality a surrogate for language knowledge – the intervening variable.

The ability to generalize is a key issue for quantitative research. This ability hinges on the concepts of internal and external validity – the generalizability of research-generated implications beyond the immediate context. There is a desire to, for example, apply findings from one study to broader samples of subjects. Internal validity is related to whether the experimental stimulus caused the observed change while external validity relates to whether the findings can be generalized to other populations and settings. Researchers have indicated several common threats to internal and external validity (Shadish, Cook, and Campbell, 2002). The most common threats are discussed below.

Threats to internal validity often relate to the verity of the causal relations that are being identified. These factors may involve subject selection, history, maturation, reliability, attrition, and instrumentation. Subject selection can affect the internal validity when a control group is not actually equivalent to a treatment group, as when intact classes are selected for a study and one group is initially different from the other. History is a threat in that events (natural disasters, wars, etc.) external to the study may affect the subjects' responses. Maturation may be a factor when studying children if the study takes place over an extended period of time and the children's developmental levels change. The reliability or consistency of the dependent variable instruments can affect whether or not an effect is found for a particular study. Attrition may affect the internal validity of a study if one particular group of subjects differentially drops out of a study – for example, when subjects with low vocabulary ability withdraw from a study of vocabulary instruction, but subjects with better vocabulary ability remain. And instrumentation may affect the validity of a study if a rater changes her or his rating criteria/severity through the rating process over time.

External threats to validity relate to how extensively the results of a study can be applied to other populations or settings. All of the threats to internal validity are also threats to external validity. Specific external threats can result from sample representativeness; interaction effects of testing; reactive effects of the experimental arrangements; carry-over of treatment effects; or irrelevant replicability effects. Sample representativeness relates to the extent to which the specific sample of subjects in the study is representative (or not) of other populations that are of interest or relevance to the study being undertaken. Interaction effects of testing may occur if a pre-test is used in the study, but because of a reaction to the pre-test, the treatment is only effective if a pre-test is given first. Reactive effects of the experimental arrangements are connected to what is sometimes called the Hawthorne Effect. Because the study subjects know that they are in an experiment, they feel special in some way and behave in ways that subjects who are not in a novel situation do not. A carry-over of treatment effects can happen if there are a number of tests and the tests themselves interact with the treatment in such a way that the results of the treatment are dependent upon the tests being given. Finally, irrelevant replicability effects can occur when a very complex treatment is given which is difficult for any other researchers to replicate. (See Shadish, Cook, and Campbell (2002) for a more extensive discussion.)

RESEARCH ON THIS TOPIC

Quantitative research methods originated in the natural sciences but are now used extensively in education and social sciences. There are many types of quantitative research including surveys, experiments, demographic reporting, etc. and they all involve the collection of data that allow the researcher to provide description or to draw inferences through different statistical tests.

Modern quantitative methods rely on research design to ensure success and to control for the threats to validity noted above. Research design thus requires careful attention to the development of the research questions, which should be clearly stated and be answerable with empirical data. Light, Singer, and Willett (1990) believe that "clearly specified research questions are the only basis for making sensible planning decisions" (p. 15). The research questions help to identify the target population, the outcome variables, predictor variables, the sample size, and the research context. In short, they control all aspects of the research design and it is essential that they are clear because they can help researchers set up the design of each study.

Campbell and Stanley (1963) early on classified experiments as "pre-experimental," "true experimental," "quasi-experimental," "correlational," and "*ex post facto*" (carried out after the fact/event) designs. They introduced the category of pre-experimental designs not because they endorse them, but because they observed that some educational research employed them although – in their opinion – they should not have. Essentially, the category involves non-controlled comparisons. They identify three such designs: a) one-shot case study; b) one-group pre-test – post-test design; and c) static-group comparison. The one-shot case study involves giving a group a treatment of some sort, and then giving a post-test and interpreting the post-test score as being due to the treatment. However, there is virtually no control and there is no comparison to make in order to interpret the meaning of the post-test score. The one-group pre-test – post-test design is similar to the one-shot case study with the difference that a pre-test is given. Differences between the two tests are then interpreted as being due to the treatment. However, Campbell and Stanley (1963) point out that any difference between the two scores could be due to any number of variables other than the treatment itself. There has been no control. Finally, they introduce the static-group comparison design in which a treatment is given to a particular group and then a post-test is given to the group that received the treatment and compared on the test to a group that did not receive the treatment. However, they point out that such a design does not account for any initial differences between the two groups. There is no way of knowing whether the groups were equivalent or not at the beginning of the study.

The true experimental designs are constructed to control for threats to internal validity. The most common of the designs will be presented here in order to demonstrate the strengths of the design family. The pre-test – post-test control group design involves the creation of two groups through random assignment from a common population. Both groups are given a pre-test. Then one group receives a treatment and after the treatment both groups are given a post-test. Since the only difference between the two groups was the treatment, any difference between the pre-test score and the post-test score is seen as being due to the treatment. Note that it is essential that the only difference between the groups is due to the treatment and not to other extraneous variables. Thus, it is important that the two groups be tested at the same time and that the control group does not experience irrelevant events during the testing. Obviously, this is a difficult feat to achieve; however, sufficient control can be implanted to minimize the effects of any unwarranted events.

The third family of designs introduced by Campbell and Stanley (1963) represents quasi-experimental designs. These designs involve research in settings in which full control over the experiment is not possible through randomization. These designs are often used with intact classes of students. Such designs require that any compared groups used in the study be tested to ensure that they are equivalent in all important respects in order to make the inferences about scores sound. One type of design involves a time series study in which several measurements are taken over time in order to establish stability of a characteristic followed by a treatment of some sort which is then followed by another number of measurements to test for change or stability.

Correlational and *ex post facto* designs generally involve contexts in which experimental treatments are not introduced. They generally involve the use of data that already exist in some form. Often data are examined in order to determine whether to proceed to an experimental study more fully.

Several types of statistical tests have been used in language studies. These tests tend to address the two issues of how variables vary together or how groups differ from one another. Some of the more common tests that have been used to compare group differences are t-tests[2], analysis of variance (ANOVA)[3], and chi-square[4]. These tests are all used to determine whether groups differ significantly from one another. T-tests are used to compare two groups to each other while ANOVA is generally used for three or more group comparisons. Chi-square is used for comparing data involving frequencies. Correlation, regression, and factor analysis are generally used to explore the relationships between different variables. They show how strongly different variables vary together.

A quick review of some prominent journals in the language teaching field shows a breadth of applications of quantitative methods. Lazaraton (2005) reviewed four applied linguistics journals over an eleven-year period (1991–2001) for the use of quantitative and qualitative research presented. The journals were *Language Learning*, *Modern Language Journal*, *Studies in Second Language Acquisition*, and *TESOL Quarterly*. She reported that of the 524 empirical articles examined, approximately 450 (86%) were quantitative. The most common statistical procedures were ANOVA, correlation, t-tests, regression and chi-square. Thus, the research applications in the language learning literature were interested both in how variables vary together and in group differences. See Plonsky (2013) for an in-depth survey from 1990 to 2010.

The statistical procedures noted above all rely on decisions that are made about the probability of a result being due to some independent variable or set of independent variables as opposed to being due to some chance factor. This decision is usually based on null hypothesis significance testing (NHST). The null hypothesis is a statement made by a researcher that there is no difference between two means: the initial assumption before any analysis is that we should not expect that there is a difference, and that it is up to the researcher to show a difference. A further issue is that – since the researcher is working with samples of a population, rather than a population – there is a chance that the sample that is selected is not from the target population about which a generalization is to be made. The statistical tests are used to determine whether there is an acceptable chance that a rejection of the null hypothesis is not in error. In language education and social sciences, the conventional acceptable probability is 95%. That is, if the researcher conducting a study finds that the two measures are different, it is acceptable that this decision is likely in error only five times out of a hundred. If this result is obtained, the study is said to have found a statistically significant difference.

While NHST is very common, it has come under criticism over the past few decades. A primary criticism that has been raised is that the finding of "statistical significant difference" does not indicate how important the difference is, its "practical significance" (Kirk, 1996). Rather, the chance of finding statistical significance is often an artifact of having a large sample size in the study. Thus, many researchers are concerned with the magnitude of an effect rather than simply finding statistical significance. This is why many journals now require researchers to report effect sizes along with significance levels.

Practical Applications

Knowledge of how quantitative research functions in second language research is important in consuming the research literature. Knowing the different variable types can help to clarify whether the research is making appropriate inferences from the study data. Carefully examining the specifics of the independent and the dependent variables provides some sense of how broadly a generalization can be made about the scope of the research findings. Likewise, understanding the types information needed to make causal inferences is valuable. The ability to recognize that an appropriate control group was not used can serve to protect the reader from many unwarranted conclusions about research outcomes.

Additionally, knowledge that quantitative research reports should include measures of effect size as well as significant difference findings allows the reader to evaluate the importance of the finding. A very small difference in magnitude can be significant if the study has a large sample size. The reader of studies needs to be able to make a decision about whether the differences that are reported are important differences.

Conclusion

To summarize, quantitative research involves the collection of numerical data and it is a fundamental type of second and foreign language research. A primary concern with quantitative research – due to the fact that there a number of different variable types – is the categorization and control of variability in order for generalizations to be sound. As noted, quantitative research involves pre-experimental, true experimental, quasi-experimental, correlational, and *ex post facto* designs. Pre-experimental designs are undesirable in that they do not control the effects of target variables. In non-experimental research – such as correlational and *ex post facto* designs – the independent variable is often not created by the researcher. Rather, in *ex post facto* research, the researcher is looking at patterns in the world with data that already exist. In experimental and quasi-experimental research, on the other hand, the independent variable is manipulated in order to demonstrate some causal relations between the independent variable and the dependent variable outcomes. In all cases, quantitative research attempts to use numerical relationships to explain outcomes.

Discussion Questions

1. What are the different types of research variables? What function does each serve?
2. How do quasi-experimental designs differ from true experimental research designs?
3. What function do research questions serve?
4. What is the difference between statistical significance and practical significance?
5. What are some criticisms of null hypothesis significance testing?

References

Campbell, D. T. & Stanley, J. C. (1963). Experimental and quasi-experimental designs for research on teaching. In N. L. Gage (Ed.), *Handbook of research on teaching* (pp. 171–246). Chicago: Rand McNally.

Kirk, R. E. (1996). Practical significance: A concept whose time has come. *Educational and Psychological Measurement*, 56, 746–759.

Lazaraton, A. (2005). Quantitative research methods. In E. Hinkle (Ed.), *Handbook of research in second language teaching and learning* (pp. 209–224). Mahwah, NJ: Lawrence Erlbaum Associates.

Light, R. J., Singer, J. D., & Willett, J. B. (1990). *By design: Planning research on higher education*. Cambridge, MA: Harvard University Press.

Plonsky, L. (2013). Study quality in SLA: An assessment of designs, analyses, and reporting practices in quantitative L2 research. *Studies in Second Language Acquisition*, 35, 655–687.

Shadish, W. R., Cook, T. D., & Campbell, D. T. (2002). *Experimental and quasi-experimental designs for generalized causal inference*. Boston: Houghton Mifflin.

Notes

[1] A variable is a characteristic or condition that can vary. It can take different categories: a general attribute (for example, a subject's first language); a level, (for example, high, intermediate, or low); or an amount, (for example, a test score).

[2] A t-test is a test of statistical significance which examines the difference between two mean scores. It indicates whether or not the difference between two groups' averages most likely reflects a "real" difference in the population from which the groups were sampled.

[3] ANOVA stands for "analysis of variance." It is a test of statistical significance, which examines the differences between three or more mean scores. (When there are only two samples the t-test can be used.)

[4] Chi-square is a statistical test of significance for categorical data. It is used to assess the "goodness of fit" between observed data with data we would expect to obtain according to a specific hypothesis.

CHAPTER 8

Qualitative Research

Keith Richards

INTRODUCTION

Qualitative research (henceforth QR) is primarily concerned with representing in textual (and sometimes visual) form an analysis of people's lived experiences in specific contexts as these are represented though their behaviour and discourse. However, as Denzin and Lincoln note in their introduction to a standard work in the field, QR is a "complex, interconnected family of terms, concepts, and assumptions" that crosscuts "disciplines, fields and subject matter" (2011: 3). It is hence not susceptible to overarching definitions, though members of the QR family share some common characteristics and draw on a distinctive set of data collection methods.

Definitions of qualitative research are conventionally expressed in terms of a contrast with quantitative research. However, a number of researchers have challenged this oppositional approach and, at a time when mixed methods research is becoming increasingly important, it seems more productive to focus on the distinctive character of QR rather than on more naïve representations.

The naïve view of QR derives from a focus on the adjective "qualitative" as distinct from "quantitative" and represents QR as research in which quantification plays little or no part. However, as a number of researchers have pointed out, some form of quantification is almost inevitable in QR (as in the claim that *many* or *most* participants subscribe to a particular view) and there is no principled way in which we can determine the existence of a cline between quantitative and qualitative research, so the representation of QR in these terms, while convenient, is potentially more confusing than illuminating. There are also approaches to the analysis of text that may be non-numerical – and could therefore be described as qualitative – but which would not normally be thought of as qualitative research. A more productive approach to understanding the nature of QR can be achieved by examining the features which are characteristic of it.

Although there are paradigmatic differences within the QR family, there is broad agreement that the social world and our knowledge of it are jointly constructed. Similarly, across the wide spectrum of what falls under the general heading of QR, a number of common characteristics can be discerned, although the extent to which these feature in any particular study will vary. These characteristics are conventionally grouped under five broad headings:

1. LOCALLY SITUATED

Qualitative researchers are interested in human participants in natural settings rather than in broader populations. This means that such research tends to focus on the social world, drawing on naturally occurring data and taking care to avoid artificially constructed situations. Given these concerns, due attention must be given to contextual factors, though the ways in which these are determined and their place in subsequent analysis will vary.

2. PARTICIPANT-ORIENTED

QR's interest in human behaviour means that it is naturally participant oriented, and this has methodological as well as relational implications. The researcher seeks to understand the social world from the participants' own perspectives rather than analyzing it in terms of researcher-imposed categories, which means that data collection must be designed to elicit these perspectives, analysis must be grounded in the data itself and representation must strive for the authentic representation of participant voices.

3. RESEARCHER-SENSITIVE

The reflexive relationship between researcher and data is important in QR. Because the researcher is directly involved in data collection and representation – usually via direct contact with participants – the place of the researcher in the research process needs to be considered. This may involve, for example, a consideration of field relations or an analysis of interactional positioning in research interviews.

4. HOLISTIC

The pursuit of an in-depth understanding of the social world implies a holistic approach in which particular aspects are studied in their context rather than being abstracted from it and studied in isolation.

5. INDUCTIVE

The holistic perspective is associated with a process of interpretation that involves immersion in the data and is characteristically exploratory in orientation, allowing for an element of flexibility as insights emerge from the data. The extent to which concepts, categories, and themes are treated as wholly emergent is a matter of debate, but while QR does not preclude the advance formulation of research questions or acquaintance with a conceptual frame, neither does it allow prior determination of categories to be used in analysis.

While other characteristics, such as a preference for small samples rather than large populations and a privileging of textual over graphic representation, may be equally common in QR – and part of a wider set of family resemblances – they are not definitional and have been omitted from the list. The five aspects identified represent not only what might be considered core elements, but also points of orientation for the researcher as part of the reflexive process of data collection and analysis.

Background

For many years – and perhaps understandably – the dominant research issues in language teaching and learning concerned the nature of language acquisition, and the cognitive perspective associated with this lent itself to the sort of experimental research that falls outside QR (experimental research being generally accepted in the literature to be associated with quantitative research). However, some researchers – recognizing that the social and interactional complexities of the language classroom and the learning process were not susceptible to the experimental or qualitative methodology – instead explored the potential of QR to generate insights into the nature of language learning and teaching as they are more broadly conceived. In doing so, they joined a wider debate in which newly emerging research paradigms challenged the dominance of traditional "scientific" approaches.

The period of the 1970s and 1980s was marked by what have been described as the "paradigm wars" in which rival claims regarding research legitimacy were played out in various ways across numerous fields, including language teaching. The passions these debates engendered are now largely spent and a more pragmatic approach has emerged in which interest is directed towards practical issues associated with research questions and procedures. While this sits comfortably with a burgeoning interest in mixed methods, it is less well aligned to the thinking associated with another significant trend: a shift to standards-based education with its emphasis on quantifiable performance.

Although QR is now well-established, there is still no general agreement on which approaches should be included under its umbrella. However, there is a general consensus that ethnography[1] is representative. Ethnography, which depends on extended exposure to the field collecting data primarily through observation and interviews, has all of the characteristics identified above (see Chapter 19 for a detailed discussion). Other traditions which might be described as essentially qualitative in their orientation and which feature in research on language learning include autoethnography, linguistic ethnography, conversation analysis (see Chapter 16) and narrative inquiry (see Chapter 20). Action research (see Chapter 12) and case study (see Chapter 14) are also often included in this list, probably because much research in these traditions has been qualitative. However, they are perfectly amenable to mixed methods research and there are signs that case study research is moving in this direction.

From a methodological perspective, the naturalistic orientation of QR means that researchers avoid data collected under artificial conditions, preferring data sources that will generate insights into the lived world of participants. As a result, interviews or observation feature prominently; though in language teaching research, audio or video recordings tend to be more widely used than field notes as representations of relevant activity. Other data sources might include journals, documents, and teaching materials.

Qualitative researchers use a range of techniques to ensure the quality of their work, but three terms have become relatively commonplace. The first of these, respondent validation (or member validation) involves the researcher presenting relevant findings to participants and seeking their views on these. This provides researchers with an opportunity to assess the correspondence between their own findings and the perceptions of participants while also giving participants the chance to respond to the representation of their voice in the research. While respondent validation can be useful, it is not essential and is not a substitute for triangulation.

The term triangulation[2] describes a method that researchers use to help them get a stronger fix on the data. Basically, it is a way of ensuring the validity of research by using more than one method to collect data on the same topic: it can involve different types of samples as well as methods of data collection. So, for example, a feature that is apparent from field notes may also be apparent in participant interviews and perhaps also in aspects of their talk. Similarly, if teams of researchers are involved, more than one researcher might have evidence of the same aspect of behavior and different researchers can be involved in coding the data. Triangulation is not a requirement of QR, however, and there is no specification as to how many perspectives are needed.

Although both respondent validation and triangulation are valuable tools, they are not a substitute for thick description. Thick description is a much misunderstood term originally proposed by Clifford Geertz, who adapted an expression used by the philosopher Gilbert Ryle. It is often used to refer merely to the richness of the description provided by a researcher, when in fact it goes beyond this. Thick description involves not only describing but interpreting actions in their social context, which in turn involves capturing as far as possible the thoughts, emotions and motivations of the relevant participants. The result should be an account detailed and specific enough to strike readers as authentic and resonant with their own experience.

Research on this Topic

Despite its somewhat rocky road to acceptance, QR is now long-established and with a substantial body of work to its name. Its relevance to language teaching and learning as situated activities has produced a body of work in journals such as *TESOL Quarterly*. Such work uses observation, recordings, and interviews to understand the way learning is constructed in classrooms and other contexts; interviews to explore relevant experiences and relationships outside the classroom; narrative inquiry to generate insights into teacher and learner histories and understandings; and – more recently – autoethnography to represent personal engagements with the learning process (for an overview of QR in language learning, see Richards, 2009).

While no single study covers this wide range of approaches, Shirley Brice Heath's *Ways with Words* has claims to being regarded as a classic study of how ethnography can be used to reveal the interconnectedness of community and language learning, and the power of the relationship between home and school to influence the nature of pedagogic engagement. A reading of Heath's study of the Trackton and Roadville communities offers not only important insights into language learning but also a sense of what it means to be a qualitative researcher and why this matters:

> These ethnographies of communication attempt to let the reader follow the children of Roadville and Trackton from their home and community experiences into their classrooms and schools. The reader will come to know these children and their teachers and will see how both groups retained some of their language and cultural habits and altered others. The influence of these mutual adjustments on an individual level often exceeded that of the major educational policy shifts and reshufflings of teachers and students which marked these times. (Heath, 1983: 7)

The literature on qualitative research methods is almost as extensive as its research outputs, though book-length treatments related to language learning are still relatively limited. Beginning researchers, especially those who are also teachers, should find Heigham and Croker's collection (2009) particularly valuable. The introduction provides an overview of the field, while the chapters are relatively short and clearly written, covering a range of approaches and data collection methods. Richards (2003) also has sections designed for novice researchers but includes more advanced treatments up to doctoral level, while Holliday (2007), not directed specifically to language learning but written by someone in the field, provides an excellent introduction, particularly useful for those working at doctoral level and above.

More general introductions to QR abound, but Silverman's *Doing Qualitative Research*, now in its fourth edition (2013), has never been surpassed. It is an authoritative and eminently readable guide relevant to all researchers. Just as authoritative is *The Sage Handbook of Qualitative Research*, also in its fourth edition. This is a standard resource on all aspects of QR and the introduction provides an excellent overview of key issues (Denzin and Lincoln, 2011).

Practical Applications

Since it is the unfathomable complexity of the social world that makes QR necessary, it is unsurprising that qualitative researchers are not given to authoritative pronouncements on how their findings can be applied. Instead, they offer insights that deepen our understanding of experience, practice, and performance within their social and interactional contexts: fresh light is thrown on taken-for-granted daily practices, hidden influences and constraints are revealed, and new connections are made. The understandings this generates can then be used to transform practice or challenge prevailing configurations. To do this, however, the research must be regarded by relevant parties as suitably rigorous.

In QR, contextual features cannot be abstracted and treated as specifiable variables that can be applied for comparative purposes; instead the researcher must find reliable ways of identifying and representing aspects of complex social and relational worlds. QR is not easy to do but it is easy to do badly: criticisms of QR relating to issues such as generalisation and replication are undermined by their failure to appreciate the distinctive contribution made by QR, but accusations of subjectivity go to its heart. All research should be rigorous, but the involvement of the researcher in the data collection and analysis process presents particular challenges for QR and considerable attention has been paid to this, including the replacement of standard terms with more appropriate equivalents in order to ensure trustworthiness. (See Lazaraton, 2003 for a discussion of evaluative criteria, with a specific focus on ethnography and conversation analysis.) In terms of reliability, the researcher needs to ensure that the process used for coding data is adequately explained, so that the reader can see how categories were determined and understand the criteria used to determine membership of them. In order to ensure validity, researchers also need to be transparent about their data set and selection procedures, avoiding "cherry picking" examples and quotations in order to disguise thin data and inadequate analysis. Procedures such as respondent validation, triangulation, and thick description can all contribute to this process, but ultimately it is the responsibility of the researcher to take whatever steps may be necessary to ensure that the research process is adequately rigorous and that there is sufficient warrant for claims arising from it.

QR also brings with it distinctive ethical challenges, not least in terms of confidentiality and anonymity, and the researcher must address these before, during, and after the research process. There is, though, a broader ethical dimension that is associated with an aspect of QR which some would claim is a core feature: the engagement of the researcher with the situation. QR may expose unacceptable practices such as institutionalized bias or prejudice, systemic disempowerment, or discrimination against particular groups, and these raise ethical issues for the researcher. Critical approaches to QR concern themselves directly with structural power asymmetries and seek to expose oppressive social practices, while other traditions – for example, emancipatory action research – position the researcher as a change agent, but all researchers must confront the ethical implications of their work and their responsibilities as moral agents. (See Chapters 22 and 23 for more detailed discussion of ethics in research.)

Conclusion

Research that potentially challenges the status quo and is wary of categorical prescription inevitably provokes the suspicion of policy-makers and politicians whose interest lies in identifying system-friendly deliverables with assessable impact. The current shift towards traditional science at the expense of QR is therefore unsurprising, but the case for QR is arguably stronger now than it has ever been.

One of the most significant developments in research generally has been the growth of mixed methods. This, coupled with growing recognition of the value of interdisciplinary research, offers exciting opportunities for qualitative researchers to forge new research relationships and to demonstrate the value of this approach in a genuinely complementary relationship. The case for QR should also be strengthened by technological developments. Increased facilities for data storage and retrieval via online access will allow greater transparency as data sets, procedures, etc. are made available. The growth of multi-modal analysis facilitated by technological innovation will serve only to strengthen this further. Both these developments will bring with them new ethical challenges but not insuperable ones.

Qualitative researchers, wrestling with the complications of the social moment, are unlikely to be seduced into accepting future scenarios, however persuasively articulated – at best we can identify straws in the wind. Nevertheless, if anything is certain it is that the complexities of the social world and of language learning will neither diminish nor become reducible to precise specification, and as long as this is the case there will be a need for qualitative research.

Discussion Questions

1. Does it matter that the findings of QR cannot be generalized to large populations? How might a deep understanding of one setting contribute to our understanding of other settings?

2. Most qualitative researchers would argue that their work cannot be replicated. How far is this true and how much is it likely to remain true in the future?

3. What might be the value of QR to the researcher as a person?

4. If a particular school is the subject of a study, is absolute anonymity a realistic prospect and if so, what are the implications of this?

5. Can qualitative research ever be neutral or is it always in some sense "interested"?

References

Denzin, N. K., & Lincoln, Y. L. (2011). Introduction: The discipline and practice of qualitative research. In N. K. Denzin & Y. L. Lincoln (Eds.), *The Sage handbook of qualitative research* (4th edition) (pp. 1–20). Thousand Oaks, CA: Sage.

Heigham, J., & Croker, R. A. (Eds.) (2009). *Qualitative research in applied linguistics*. Basingstoke, UK: Palgrave Macmillan.

Holliday, A. (2007). *Doing and writing qualitative research* (2nd ed.). London: Sage.

Heath, S. B. (1983). *Ways with words: Language, life, and work in communities and classrooms*. Cambridge: Cambridge University Press.

Lazaraton, A. (2003). Evaluative criteria for qualitative research in applied linguistics: Whose criteria and whose research? *The Modern Language Journal*, 87(1), 1–12.

Richards, K. (2003). *Qualitative inquiry in TESOL*. Basingstoke, UK: Palgrave Macmillan.

Richards, K. (2009). Trends in qualitative research in language teaching since 2000. *Language Teaching*, 40(2), 147–180.

Silverman, D. (2013). *Doing qualitative research* (4th ed.). London: Sage.

Notes

[1] The term ethnography is formed from the Greek *ethnos* "people, folk, or nation" and *grapho* meaning "I write," and it refers to the systematic study of people and cultures. The researcher observes and describes a society and culture from the point of view of the subject of the study – see the definition of ethnography in the *Cambridge Advanced Learner's Dictionary*: "a scientific description of the culture of a society by someone who has lived in it, or a book containing this."

[2] Triangulation is a procedure used to establish different perspectives on a particular phenomenon or interpretive position in order to minimize the risks of incomplete, misjudged, or misdirected interpretation. The perspectives can derive from multiple data sources, methods, researchers, or theoretical constructs.

CHAPTER 9

Research Paradigms in Second Language Research

Peter Stanfield

INTRODUCTION

The research paradigm of an academic investigation into second language learning is a statement about the philosophical and intellectual assumptions the researcher is making about the world, specifically about language, learning, and the learner. Researchers often initially approach a study from various intellectual perspectives. Some have a clear view from the outset of the kind of data they wish to collect due to their immediate professional concerns. Some will have read widely and begin with a review of the literature associated with the problem they intend to investigate. Others have an interest in a certain methodology or a predilection for a particular theoretical framework such as feminism or postcolonialism and will start their study from these deeper vantage points. At some stage, however, the researcher will need to reflect carefully on the deepest and often opaque beliefs, norms, and values that drive the research process and must state them as transparently as possible in an explication of the research paradigm of the study.

Research paradigms in the social sciences can be divided into two major types. Firstly, there are positivist paradigms adopted from the natural sciences. These regard social reality as existing independently of the unbiased observer. Such inquiry requires that abstract variables are clearly delineated so that they can be generalized to a broad population. These paradigms tend to take a somewhat simplistic and mechanistic view of the causality of social phenomena. Secondly, there are postpositive or naturalistic paradigms (Lincoln and Guba, 2000). These regard social reality as collaboratively constructed by human beings as they make sense of the world through social action. Such inquiry employs methodologies that seek to reveal the lived experiences of the language learner and regards the researcher as a co-constructor of the multiple realities that emerge from research. Rather than induce abstracted variables, studies within this paradigm seek to deduce a rich understanding of specific situations which can help us investigate other language learning contexts in new ways.

The purpose of this chapter is to briefly clarify the nature of language and the second language learner and how we might gain knowledge about them so that researchers are able to work outwards from their particular points of departure toward an understanding of the paradigmatic terrains of their studies.

PERSPECTIVES

ONTOLOGICAL PERSPECTIVE: WHAT IS THE NATURE OF LANGUAGE AND THE SECOND LANGUAGE LEARNER?

The researcher's beliefs about the ontology of the second language learner will be a primary determinant of the research paradigm of a study. Ontology is concerned with the nature of things that exist in the world and the relations between them. It is a theory of being. The fundamental nature of the human being is its "being-in-the-world-with-others" (Heidegger, 1962); that is to say, we are defined by our social relations. This is true of the second language learner, whose consciousness is reshaped through using a newly acquired language within the social relations of classrooms, libraries, cafeterias, corridors, and other places in the broader community beyond educational institutions.

The constituents of any language, its words and syntactic sense relations, break reality up into ready-made meanings or metaphors (Derrida, 2001) that enable us to carry out daily intercourse within relatively cohesive societies. The values embedded in these metaphors evolve over generations as people live out practical quotidian lives, share meanings with others principally through language, and deposit a layer of largely sub-consciousness beliefs about the world. The consciousness of the second language learner is thus inextricably linked (Ochs, 1990) to social practices (Foucault, 1977; 2002). These are accessible quite immediately through observing the surface patterning of everyday second language usage – for example, the amount of target language they use in various contexts; the structure of their linguistic errors; their ability to interject speech in a conversation, etc. However, the meaning of such behavior is less easily accessed. It can only be adequately explicated through understanding how learners, teachers, and other interlocutors interactively symbolize the world in order to meet their specific needs. This is a process Blumer (1969) has termed symbolic interactionism.

The symbols arising from social interaction emerge as language, which is the most sophisticated hermeneutic[1] (interpretative) system human beings possess (Eggins, 2004) with which to communicate their experiences to others in the world. However, linguistic symbols are not precise concepts of reality but utilitarian approximations forged in the vicissitudes of life. They are prototypical, *fuzzy* best examples against which to compare further experiences (Aitchison, 1987). For instance, we talk of *bright* and *at risk* language learners. However, these constructs encapsulate a limited, pre-selected range of the total set of characteristics pertaining to the specific individuals they conceptualize. They are merely working models of our experience that offer an immediate grasp on the infinitely more complex human reality of the second language learner.

Achieving hermeneutic utility in this manner is necessary because, whilst the human mind may have considerable powers of long-term memory it has a limited-capacity for simultaneous processing (McLaughlin, 1987). The socially constructed, prototypical symbols that constitute the linguistic constructs of any language embed implicit assumptions in our thinking by default – in order to prevent mental overload at the point of social action. If human beings were required to simultaneously process the precise and full potential of a word or syntactic structure and its interrelations with all other relevant linguistic constructs, mental processing-power would be inadequate and arrest the interaction upon which social survival depends. Human behavior is, therefore, of necessity, assumptive in action and analytic only upon reflection. As Gadamer eloquently perceives, it is the prejudices embedded in our language rather than our conscious judgments which reveal our true being (1975). This is both the strength and weakness of language; whilst it enables us to metaphorize reality and function adequately in-the-world-with-others, it hides from conscious view the full range of values upon which we operate. Hence the assumptions which drive human behavior and motivate second language learners, their teachers, and researchers, are founded on a largely subconscious layer of values or axioms we hold to be true. This "axiological" layer of consciousness requires a special approach if it is to be revealed adequately.

EPISTEMOLOGICAL PERSPECTIVE: HOW DO WE POSSESS KNOWLEDGE OF LANGUAGE AND THE SECOND LANGUAGE LEARNER?

Epistemology is concerned with the manner in which we come to understand our own being and that of other existents in the world. It is a theory of knowledge. A positivist paradigm would regard language and the language learner as distinct realities to be ascertained by the researcher as an unbiased observer. A postpositive, naturalistic, or social constructivist (Berger and Luckmann, 1966) paradigm would suggest that the consciousness of the language learner and indeed the researcher is not only formed by being-in-the-world-with-others but also contributes to the formation of social relations and reorders our understanding of the world through the social action of language acquisition and research. Ontology and epistemology thus emerge simultaneously in an interactive process. This dual emergence (Osberg and Biesta, 2008) has significance for the practice of research into second language learning.

In their outward everyday social practice, second language learners behave in patterned ways which – of necessity – gloss over the pre-fabricated metaphors inherent in the language of those institutional stakeholders who systematically arrange their learning. They follow language syllabi, attend the classroom according to an administered schedule, and are candidates for language assessments without a full understanding of the power relations that lie behind these bureaucratic processes. It is not that their world does not make sense, but rather that others make sense of it for them whilst they remain largely unaware of the assumptions that drive the decision-making processes involved. Knowledge of the language learner cannot, therefore, be directly achieved through positivistic experimental research into the outward patterns of learner behavior. It is rather to be found in the internal patterns of thought which are determined by linguistic structure and the values upon which these are founded.

A TRIPARTITE HERMENEUTIC MODEL OF KNOWLEDGE

The above discussion leads me to propose a tripartite model of knowledge of language and the language learner (see Figure 9.1). I postulate that this consists of: 1) a layer of outward nomothetic[2] patterns of language use which can quite easily be accessed through studying exhibited learner behavior; 2) a more hidden ideographic[3] stratum of internal thought processes which can be investigated through an understanding of how these arise within social interaction; and 3) a deeply hidden layer of beliefs, norms, and assumptions upon which 1 and 2 are founded. These only become apparent as learners, teachers, and researchers reflect critically about second language learning experiences.

METHODOLOGICAL PERSPECTIVES: WHAT STRATEGIES CAN WE EMPLOY TO ACCESS KNOWLEDGE ABOUT LANGUAGE AND THE LANGUAGE LEARNER?

If knowledge is formed in such a tripartite manner, it would seem reasonable to employ different strategies to gain understanding of language and the language learner. In this regard – as the model below indicates – experimental, interpretative and critical strategies each focus to different degrees on nomothetic, ideographic, and axiological strata of human knowledge. We can employ them appropriately in order to contribute to an adequate understanding of language and the language learner. In a postpositive paradigm, knowledge of

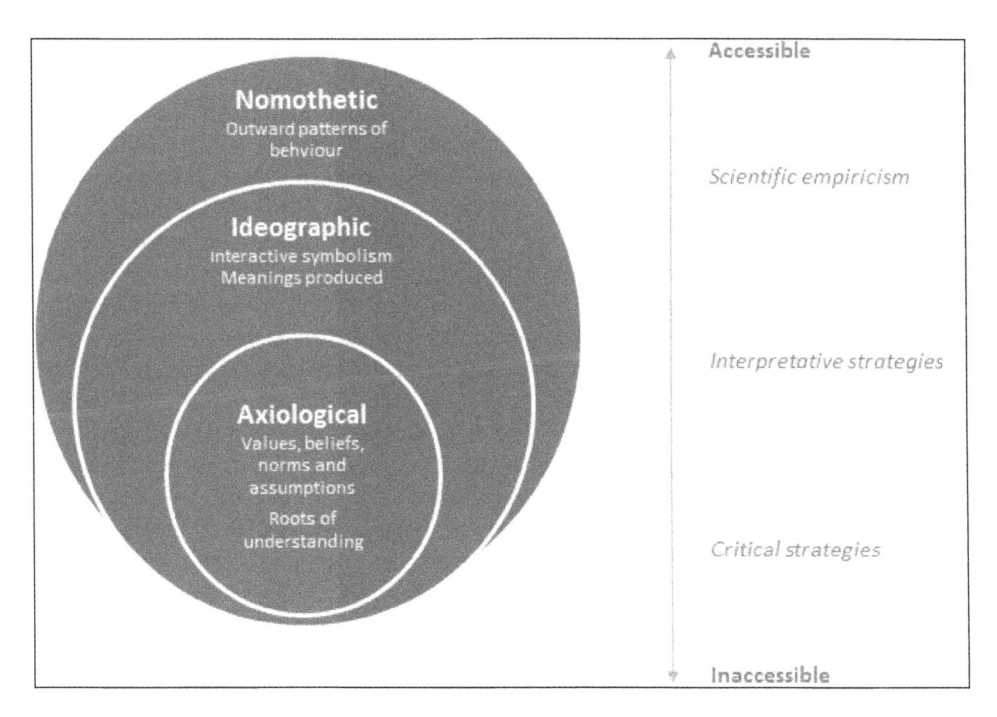

Research Paradigms in Second Language Research

Figure 9.1 Tripartite Hermeneutic of Knowledge

the world is partial, situated, constantly open to change and, at best, adequate for a set of defined needs. We gain knowledge of language and the second language learner, therefore, by unpacking the values embedded in the symbolic constructs of the language employed by learners, teachers, and researchers as they seek to meet specific needs through the social actions of learning, teaching, and researching in discrete contexts.

STRATEGIES

EXPERIMENTAL STRATEGIES

Experimental strategies provide the most immediate access to knowledge about the second language learner. Popper (1959) and Kuhn (1962) like Giddens (1979) argue that all knowledge is necessarily interpretative in nature. They include in this the scientific method as first proposed by Francis Bacon (1893) – observation, hypothesis, experimentation, and verification – none of which have a one-to-one relationship with the physical world, but interact with it through the hermeneutic processes of language as briefly described above. Nevertheless, the inductive reasoning of experimental methodology has been powerful in interpreting the physical world, and its techniques of observation and measurement are equally helpful in understanding certain aspects of second language learning. For example, systematic observation often indicates that the regularities of learner language use is at variance with teachers' assumptions about what learners do, leading to critical questioning and new insights into the divergence between thought and action in language teaching and learning (Fox, 2004).

However, as Pring (1996) points out, language learning is a social practice and of such a complex nature that the direct application of experimental research methodology is not always appropriate. It is extremely difficult, for example, to identify and maintain separation between independent and dependent variables within the complex set of social interactions under investigation in language learning. Hence comparison of pre-test and post-test scores after a planned intervention in the teaching and learning process usually offers limited understanding of the consequences of the experiment. This is because experimental inquiry requires that reality be reduced to a limited set of abstracted variables in order to establish causal relationships. Although experiments with factorial and repeated measure designs offer more detailed views of social practice (Creswell, 2003) they can never provide adequate descriptions of the language learning processes. Moreover, true experiments are required to assign participants to treatment randomly in attempts to create valid conditions for generalizability. However, educational research is always conducted in unique spatial, societal, and temporal locations which have consequences for the research participants' behavior and discourse as well as the researcher's mode of interpretation (Angen, 2000; Osberg and Biesta, 2008; Stanfield, 2013 and 2014). This necessarily militates against general statements being made about experimental outcomes in language learning research.

Although researchers have become more fully aware of these limitations, academic institutions and policy-making bodies such as university senates and ministries of education often continue to insist that the researcher approaches an investigation objectively in order to validate the inquiry. This objectivity is supposed to come from the process of describing and operationalizing variables and creating research instruments which selectively delineate parts of reality in a precise manner. However, this process depends on the fundamentally interpretative characteristics of language which is employed to describe such research designs. Both participants and researcher must necessarily approach their investigation from the axiological values laid down in previous being-in-the-world-with-others. The nearest they can come to the objectivity required in experimental research is to reflect on such values and describe them as transparently as possible in their statement of the research paradigm.

Scientific methodologies that employ statistical analysis, including quasi-experiments such as non-randomized, single-subject, and correlational designs and surveys, give insightful access to the uppermost hermeneutic layers of knowledge; nomothetic identification of the range, distribution, and frequency of the social practices of language learning and acquisition. They are a specific strategy of inquiry appropriate for understanding the outward patterning of the language learner's behavior and not the arbiter of other methodologies as is sometimes claimed. In order to penetrate the lived experiences of the language learner more deeply they must be complemented by interpretative and critical methodologies.

INTERPRETATIVE STRATEGIES

While reductionist scientific methodologies are easily understood they are often incomplete and inaccurate (Pennycook, 1989) for the purposes of language learning research. For researchers who wish to measure what they value rather than value what they can measure (MacGilchrist, Myers, and Reed, 1997) other strategies must be employed that go beyond nomothetic patterning toward an ideographic understanding of the symbolic realities of language and the language learner. Research into language education must, therefore, take cognizance of each unique learning context, making it an integral part of the explanation of the regularities explored rather than relegating it to a background sketch as is often the case with experimental research designs (Simon and Dippo, 1986).

Various interpretative strategies are used to access symbolic layers of language that shape the language learner. In the case of ethnographic studies, societal or institutional cultures and their settings are the focus, with data being collected through the observation of participants over a period of time (longitudinal studies) and the researcher taking a participant-observer role. By contrast, grounded theory – as described by Glaser and Strauss (1967) and Charmaz (2006) – focuses on specific social processes, actions, and interactions, sampling different groups in a comparative fashion. In addition, case studies concern themselves with a few individuals or a single case respectively. All these strategies seek to explain the social practice of the language learner deductively and allow relevant symbolic categories – as well as theories about them – to emerge during the research process.

Ethnography and phenomenological studies in particular, employ a participant/observer process whereby the researcher's perspective is acknowledged but held in abeyance (Henwood and Pigeon, 2003). The intention is to "make strange" second language learning practices by regarding them simultaneously from outside and within, thus penetrating the processes which construct the second language learner's consciousness. Such an approach shocks us into a realization that the apparently stable arrangements for language learning are in fact socially constructed within given power relations – and potentially highly dynamic (Silverman, 2000). Such interrogation of the obvious enables the researcher to expose the assumptions learners, teachers, and researchers make about language and language learning.

Another approach is to reverse given assumptions about power relations – for example, to ask what the language teacher's world looks like through the perspective of a language learner. Narrative research – where learners tell their language-learning stories – especially has the potential to provide significant insight into the processes through which symbolic categories arise. Baker achieves similar insights in a dramatic fashion by having her participants dress up and act like puppets, which causes them to behave in different ways, making powerful statements about how the social order is arranged and might be re-arranged (Silverman, 2000). Such "re-storying" (Clandinin and Connelly, 2004) of a participant's history in collaboration with the researcher, is an interpretative methodology that gives access to the symbolic life of the learner and would seem particularly appropriate for studying the ideographic layer of knowledge about language and the language learner.

The aim of these interpretative strategies is to understand the rules of discourse by which knowledge is encoded and acted out in society (Foucault, 2002). At their most heuristic[4], they take the researcher beyond an understanding of the matrixes of symbolic interaction, toward the values which inform them. However, it is the critical researcher who traverses directly into the hermeneutic realm of axiology.

CRITICAL STRATEGIES

If scientific research accesses nomothetic understanding of the language learning process and interpretative studies give insight into the ideographic production, appropriation, and articulation of symbolic constructs during language learning, critical methodology aims to reveal the values in which these hermeneutic layers of understanding are embedded. Considering the importance of language in structuring our lived realities, it is ironic that language teaching is often perceived as a value-free practice. On the contrary, Morgan recognizes the power of language to put people in their place (1995). This is often seen in its essence in the language classroom where teachers not only have superior control of the target language but also the institutional rights to decide on the language features to be acquired and the power to use language to control student behavior (Walsh, 1989). Critical methodology is, therefore, fundamentally political in nature, seeking to expose what Gramsci regarded as self-regulating processes of hegemony (Leszek, 1981) by which power over material, cultural, and linguistic resources is constructed and maintained. In language learning research, critical methodology, therefore, aims to unpack the assumptions about power relations which go unnoticed in the words we use (Atkinson, 2002).

Such a methodology is made necessary by the nature of language. As we have seen, a key advantage of language is the utility of its prototypical constructs in allowing us to metaphorize complex reality and articulate it with limited parallel processing capacity. However, this is also its disadvantage. If assumptive action is not regularly subjected to intellectual scrutiny, the constructs it employs begin to lose their symbolic nature; their selective orientation toward reality appears to be the *only* available reality which becomes naturalized (Fairclough, 1989) into discourse. Without analysis upon reflection, prototypical constructs rapidly become stereotypical, laden with prejudicial assumptions. As such, they are easily manipulated, both consciously and unconsciously, by the holders of power in society, allowing them to maintain social relations advantageous to themselves without exerting overt constraints. The agenda of critical language learning research is to bring to consciousness and illuminate the submerged values that determine the power relations between agents in the language learning processes (Cohen, Manion, and Morrison, 2000).

Employed by the critical researcher, interpretative strategies have therefore tended to evolve into powerful re-interpretation. In exposing the axiological strata of human interpretative processes (hermeneutics), and the values underpinning power relations, they are able not only to describe sociological phenomena as they exist but to envision new forms of being; language puts people in their place but it can also be used to change places (Morgan, 1995). In realizing that all pedagogies are underpinned by a political vision, critical research has the potential to empower second language learners to become en-languaged in radically different ways (Angen, 2000).

Two basic critical strategies may be considered here. Firstly, there is the long tradition of pragmatics which recognizes that students of a language not only learn vocabulary, syntax, and inflexions, etc. but also learn when to speak, to whom, in what tone and register, and for what reasons (Hymes, 1979). Critical pragmatics employs this understanding to show the specifics of how students and teachers become embedded in a set of hegemonic (dominant and dominating) social relations. The aim is to enable individuals to understand how they become competent practitioners of their everyday worlds in another language (Pierce, 1995). Secondly, critical researchers have turned their attention to the insights of discourse analysis, regarding communicative competence as being constructed by social practice and constitutive of it. The key aim of critical discourse analysis is to expose and illuminate structural relationships of dominance, discrimination, power, and control as manifested in language (Fairclough, 1989; Pierce, 1995). The kinds of signposts to axiological knowledge the critical analyst seeks are the contradictions between the ideals espoused by teachers and the conditions prevalent in society that deny their realization in the second language learning process. It is therefore a research strategy not only concerned with constructing different knowledge but also constructing knowledge differently (Atkinson, 2002); with changing the axiological foundation upon which language, society, and cultures are built.

PRAGMATIC STRATEGIES

If all knowledge is interpretative and constituted by three primary hermeneutic layers, nomothetic, ideographic, and axiological, then the language learning researcher is best served by employing research strategies according to the paradigmatic orientation of the inquiry, the requirements of the context and the purposes to be achieved (Cumming, 1994). This commonly leads to pragmatic methodologies (Tashakkori and Teddlie, 2003) that blend a variety of theoretical frameworks, strategies, and instruments toward an investigation of a central problem. The result is a mixed methods approach where either scientific or interpretative strategies predominate in sequential or integrated research designs (Creswell, 2003). In some cases, scientific methodology will be used to establish relationships between patterns of behavior in order to indicate phenomena for interpretative investigation. Subsequent interpretative research will go beyond this surface, nomothetic level and penetrate the ideographic knowledge of individual consciousness. In other cases, interpretative methodology may first be used to establish the existence of language learning phenomena which are then investigated experimentally in order to provide the kinds of quantitative data often required by educational policy makers. Critical elements may be added such as integral researcher/participant collaboration in setting an agenda for the research; member checking to validate the findings; and participant involvement in implementation of recommendations for changes in approaches to second language learning.

Conclusion

The research paradigm of a second language learning study is concerned with the axiological element of the hermeneutic model of knowledge put forward here – i.e., the values and assumptions upon which the research is founded. Understood in this manner, it is clear that the research paradigm will significantly influence all aspects of the research process: the researcher's choice of theoretical framework, the range of literature referenced, type of methodology, data collection, analytical processes employed, the conclusions drawn, and recommendations made. It is, therefore, crucial to the validity of research into second language learning that the research paradigm is stated in the most transparent manner feasible by making strenuous efforts to reveal the researcher's foundational values, norms, and beliefs about language, learning, and the learner.

Discussion Questions

1. What distinguishes the research paradigm of a second language learning study from its theoretical framework and methodology?

2. What are some of the main types of research paradigm that can be employed in second language learning research?

3. What key characteristics of language and the language learner should be considered when formulating the research paradigm of a second language learning study?

4. What type of research paradigm is likely to be associated with experimental strategies for second language learning research?

5. What type of research paradigm is likely to be associated with interpretative and critical research strategies?

6. What are the strengths and limitations of experimental strategies for second language learning research?

7. For what purposes might interpretative strategies be employed in second language learning research?

8. For what purposes might critical strategies be employed in second language learning research?

9. Why might it be difficult to formulate a research paradigm for a study that employs pragmatic strategies?

10. Does the postulated tripartite hermeneutic model of knowledge help clarify the nature of a research paradigm?

References

Aitchison, J. (1987). *Words in the mind: An introduction to the mental lexicon.* Oxford: Blackwell.

Angen, M. (2000). Pearls, pith and provocation. *Qualitative Health Research*, 10(3), 378–395.

Atkinson, E. (2002). The responsible anarchist: postmodernism and social change. *British Journal of Sociology of Education*, 23(1), 73–87.

Bacon, F. (1893). *The advancement of learning.* London: Cassell.

Berger, P. L., & Luckmann, T. (1967). *The social construction of reality.* Garden City, NY: Doubleday.

Blumer, H. (1969). *Symbolic interactionism.* Los Angeles: University of California Press.

Charmaz, K. (2006). *Constructing grounded theory: A practical guide through qualitative analysis.* Thousand Oak: Sage.

Clandinin, D. J., & Connelly, F. (2004). *Narrative inquiry: Experience and story in qualitative research.* Toronto: Wiley.

Cohen, L., Manion, L., & Morrison, K. (2000). *Research methods in education* (5th ed.). London: Routledge.

Creswell, J. W. (2003). *Research design: Qualitative, quantitative, and mixed methods approaches* (2nd ed.). Thousand Oaks, CA: Sage.

Cumming, A. (Ed.) (1994). Alternatives in TESOL research: Descriptive, interpretive, and ideological orientations. *TESOL Quarterly,* 28(4), 673–703.

Derrida, J. (2001). *Writing and difference.* Oxford: Routledge.

Eggins, S. (2004). *An introduction to systemic functional linguistics.* New York: Continuum.

Fairclough, N. (1989). *Language and power.* New York: Longman.

Foucault, M. (1977). *Discipline and punish: The birth of the prison.* New York: Penguin.

Foucault, M. (2002). *The archaeology of knowledge.* Oxford: Routledge.

Fox, K. (2004). *Watching the English.* London: Hodder & Stoughton.

Gadamer, H. G. (1975). *Truth and method.* New York: Continuum.

Giddens, A. (1979). *Central problems in social theory: Action, structure, and contradiction in social analysis.* Los Angeles: University of California Press.

Glaser, B., & Strauss, A. (1967). *The discovery of grounded theory: Strategies for qualitative research.* New York: Aldine.

Heidegger, M. (1962). *Being and time.* Oxford: Blackwell.

Henwood, K., & Pidgeon, N. (2003). Grounded theory in psychological research. In P. M. Camic, J. E. Rhodes, & L. Yardley. (Eds.), *Qualitative research in psychology: Expanding perspectives in methodology and design* (pp. 131–155). Washington, DC: American Psychological Association.

Hymes, D. (1979). Language in education: Forward to fundamentals. In O. K. Garnica & M. L. King (Eds.), *Language, children, and society* (pp. 1–19). Oxford: Pergamon Press.

Kuhn, T. (1962). *The structure of scientific revolutions.* Chicago: University of Chicago Press.

Leszek, K. (1981). *Main currents of Marxism, Vol. III: The breakdown.* Oxford: Oxford University Press.

Lincoln, Y. S., & Guba, E., G. (2000). Paradigmatic controversies, contradictions and emerging confluences. In N. K. Denzin & Y. S. Lincoln (Eds.), *Handbook of qualitative research* (2nd ed., pp. 163–188). Thousand Oaks, CA: Sage.

MacGilchrist B., Myers K., & Reed, J. (1997). *The intelligent school.* Thousand Oaks, CA: Sage.

McLaughlin, B. (1987). *Theories of second-language learning.* New York: Oxford University Press.

Morgan, B. (1995). Promoting and assessing critical language awareness. *TESOL Journal,* 5(2), 10–14.

Ochs, E. (1990). Indexicality and socialization. In J. Stigler, R. Shweder & G. Herdt. (Eds.), *Cultural psychology: Essays on comparative human development* (pp. 287–308). Cambridge: Cambridge University Press.

Osberg, D., & Biesta, G. (2008). The emergent curriculum: Navigating a complex course between unguided learning and planned enculturation. *Journal of Curriculum Studies*, 40(3), 313–328.

Pierce, B. (1989). Toward a pedagogy of possibility in the teaching of English internationally: People's English in South Africa. *TESOL Quarterly*, 23(3), 401–20.

Pennycook, A. (1989). The concept of method, interested knowledge, and the politics of language teaching. *TESOL Quarterly*, 23(4), 589–618.

Popper, K. (2002). *The logic of scientific discovery*. Abingdon: Routledge.

Pring, R. (2004). *Philosophy of educational research*. London: Continuum.

Silverman, D. (2000). *Doing qualitative research: A practical handbook*. London: Sage.

Simon, R. I., & Dippo, D. (1986). On critical ethnographic work. *Anthropology & Education Quarterly*, 17, 195–202.

Stanfield, P. W. (2013). *An exploration of place-based TESOL*. Saarbrücken: Lambert Academic.

Stanfield, P. W. (2014). Analyzing learner agency: A place-based approach. In P. Deters, X. Gao, E. R. Miller, & G. Vitanova. (Eds.), *Theorizing and analyzing agency in second language learning: Interdisciplinary approaches*. Abingdon, Multilingual Matters.

Tashakkori, A., & Teddlie, C. (Eds.), (2003). *Handbook of mixed methods in social and behavioral research*. Thousand Oaks, CA: Sage.

Walsh, C. A. (1989). *Pedagogy and the struggle for voice: Issues of language, power, and schooling for Puerto Ricans*. Toronto: OISE Press.

Notes

[1] Hermeneutics is derived from the Greek *hermeneuō*, meaning "translate," or "interpret." It refers to the science of interpretation of texts (originally religious texts) and in philosophy has the broader meaning of the study and interpretation of human behavior and social institutions.

[2] Nomothetic is derived from the Greek *nomos* meaning "law." It means being concerned with establishing laws or generalizations – for example, it could be said that scientific research is fundamentally law seeking or nomothetic.

[3] Idiographic is derived from the Greek *idios* meaning "own" or "private." It means relating to or dealing with what is individual, or unique and cannot be generalized. It is often opposed to nomothetics.

[4] Heuristic comes from the Greek *heuriskein* meaning to "find" or discover" and broadly speaking it means using experience to learn or improve. However, the term is widely used in the social sciences with more specific applications. In language teaching it is used to mean allowing students to learn by discovering things themselves and learning from their own experiences, rather than by telling them things.

CHAPTER 10

Mixed Methods Research

James Dean Brown

INTRODUCTION

Mixed methods research (MMR) is not qualitative research per se, nor is it quantitative research pure and simple. Formal mixed methods research, which surfaced in the literature a little over a decade ago, can be defined as:

> ... an intellectual and practical synthesis based on qualitative and quantitative research; it is the third methodological or research paradigm (along with qualitative and quantitative research). It recognizes the importance of traditional quantitative and qualitative research but also offers a powerful third paradigm choice that often will provide the most informative, complete, balanced, and useful research results. (Johnson, Onwuegbuzie, and Turner, 2007: 129)

BACKGROUND

Oddly, as new as the concept is, there are already different types of MMR, which can best be described along a continuum of research types like the one shown in Figure 10.1 (considerably simplified from Johnson, Onwuegbuzie, and Turner, 2007: 124).

Pure qualitative research is at the left end of the continuum and pure quantitative at the right end. Covering the middle are three types that can all be taken as variants of mixed methods broadly defined, including qualitative mixed, pure mixed, and quantitative mixed. Qualitative mixed research includes both qualitative and quantitative methods combined with the qualitative ones dominating, while quantitative mixed research also includes both qualitative and quantitative methods combined, but with the quantitative ones dominating. And, pure mixed research also combines qualitative and quantitative methods but with both having equal and balanced standing.

Pure Qualitative   Qualitative Mixed   Pure Mixed   Quantitative Mixed   Pure Quantitative

Figure 10.1 A Continuum of Research Types from Pure Qualitative to Pure Quantitative

Another way to look at MMR is to consider what it is not. MMR is not just a hodgepodge of qualitative and quantitative methods combined with no rhyme or reason. In fact, if a research project does not use the qualitative and quantitative methods systematically and in a complementary manner such that they reinforce each other, it is not MMR. If the research is just a collection of qualitative and quantitative research methods thrown together, it would be more appropriate to call it multi-methods research (to be said with the upper lip curled slightly in disdain).

RESEARCH ON THIS TOPIC

In looking through the language research literature, I have found many studies that claim to be MMR. MMR has clearly become a catchphrase in our field that researchers are using without really understanding what it means in other fields and what the great benefits would be if it were applied properly. Most of these studies should in reality be labeled "multi-methods research" (don't forget the lip curl).

However, I have found a few studies that I would classify as actual "qualitative dominant MMR": the Alyousef and Picard (2011) metadiscourse study of cooperative and collaborative literacy practices in the wiki group projects of business students, and the Miyazoe and Anderson (2011) paper on anonymity in blended learning. I have also identified two examples that I would categorize as "quantitative dominant MMR": Chang's (2007) study of the influences of group processes on students' autonomous beliefs and behaviors, and Phuong's (2011) study of the effectiveness of CALL for teaching listening skills to Vietnamese university EFL students. In terms of *pure* MMR, I think the Kletzien (2011) and Pierce (2012) program evaluation studies qualify – though I may be biased because both of these authors were my students.

PRACTICAL APPLICATIONS

In practical terms, researchers who want to apply MMR need to plan and carry out their investigations with the goal of enhancing the mixed nature of the study and defending the quality and value of mixing methods. Quantitative researchers enhance and defend their studies in terms of notions like reliability, validity, replication, and generalizability. Qualitative researchers are more prone to do the same in terms of the loosely analogous, parallel concepts of dependability, credibility, confirmability, and transferablility (for explanations and examples of all of these quantitative and qualitative terms, see Brown, 2001, 2004, or 2014).

Analogously, MMR investigators can enhance and defend the combination of qualitative and quantitative research methods through the overall notion of legitimation (Onwuegbuzie and Johnson: 2006), which Brown (2014: 128) defined as: "the degree to which MMR integration of qualitative and quantitative research strengthen and provide legitimacy, fidelity, authority, weight, soundness, credibility, trustworthiness, and even standing to the results and interpretations in MMR. Clearly, MMR investigators will want to think about legitimation in terms of how they can design their research to enhance it and thereby enhance the resulting meta-inferences (i.e., inferences at the MMR or integration level of study)."

Onwuegbuzie and Johnson (2006: 56–60) explain nine different subtypes of legitimation and the strategies that can be used to enhance the legitimation of MMR:

1. *Sample legitimation* can be enhanced by integrating qualitative and quantitative samples;
2. *Inside-outside legitimation* can be enhanced by adequately using insider and outsider perspectives;
3. *Weakness minimization legitimation* can be enhanced by compensating for the weaknesses in some approaches with the strengths of others;
4. *Sequential legitimation* can be enhanced by minimizing the effects of method sequencing;
5. *Conversion legitimation* can be enhanced by maximizing the effects of using both qualitative and quantitative data;
6. *Paradigmatic mixing legitimation* can be enhanced by combining and blending the traditions, standards, and belief systems that underlie qualitative and quantitative paradigms;
7. *Commensurability legitimation* can be enhanced by maximizing the benefits that accrue from switching and integrating different worldviews;
8. *Multiple validities legitimation* can be enhanced by maximizing the benefits that arise from legitimation of the separate qualitative and quantitative methods based on the use of quantitative, qualitative, and mixed validity types;
9. *Political legitimation* can be enhanced by maximizing the degree to which the consumers of the MMR value the inferences from both qualitative and quantitative methods.

Thus we know that legitimation can be enhanced and defended in an MMR study by systematically combining samples, inside-outside perspectives, and paradigms. It can also be achieved by minimizing the effects of the weaknesses in and sequencing of different research methods and maximizing the degree to which consumers value both qualitative and quantitative inferences; the effects of using both qualitative and quantitative data; integrating different worldviews; using separate qualitative and quantitative methods; and mixing validity types. Using some or all of these strategies to strengthen the legitimation of any particular MMR study will increase the soundness of any and all meta-inferences that result.

If these nine concepts seem a bit overwhelming, Brown (2014: 134) provides six key practical techniques that MMR investigators can use to plan and enhance the quality of their studies:

1. *Convergence* involves bringing multiple data sources together and showing how they provide evidence of similar conclusions. For example, a researcher who includes interviews, classroom observations, and questionnaires as data sources in an MMR study might investigate the ways the data sources agree or cross-validate each other.
2. *Divergence* requires further careful examination of any contradictions, anomalies, and/or surprises that the researcher found with the goal of investigating the degree to which they might lead to conclusions of their own, or to additional productive inquiries. For instance, the same researcher who included interviews, observations, and

questionnaires as data sources might examine the ways the data sources disagree or contradict each other.

3. *Elaboration* entails analyzing one or more data sources with the aim of using them to expand or amplify the interpretations of other data sources. For example, an MMR researcher might explore how the interview data expand the interpretation of the questionnaire data.
4. *Clarification* requires examining how some data sources may help to explain or illuminate conclusions drawn from other data sources. For instance, the same MMR researcher might investigate how the classroom observation data help to explain what was learned in the qualitative interview and quantitative questionnaire data.
5. *Exemplification* involves examining how some data sources may provide examples of inferences drawn from other data sources. For example, an MMR investigator might look in the interview data for examples in the words of the participants of some result in the quantitative questionnaire data.
6. *Interaction* entails shifting from qualitative to quantitative to qualitative, and back again, cyclically building on and including all five of the other techniques. For instance, an MMR researcher might go back and forth between the qualitative and quantitative data repeatedly looking for convergence, divergence, elaboration, clarification, exemplification, and interaction.

Again, using some or all of these techniques to strengthen an MMR study will enhance the soundness of any and all meta-inferences that result. Researchers who find themselves doing multi-methods research may want to turn their research into MMR by using some of the strategies and techniques explained in this section. One relatively simple way to do so would be to add one or more MMR research questions to the list of existing quantitative and qualitative research questions. For example, here are two research questions that could be added to the list at the beginning of a study to insure that the researcher would take an MMR perspective and produce MMR results rather than multi-methods results:

1. What did we learn from the classroom observations and interviews that informed the development of the open-ended and numerical questionnaire items?
2. To what degree do the data from the qualitative classroom observations help in understanding why the quantitative results turned out as they did?
3. In what ways do the various data sources contradict each other?

Let me provide you with a concrete example. Pierce (2012) performed an evaluation study for a new Second Language Studies (SLS) undergraduate BA program at our university. Based on data from 35 students and 13 faculty members, she analyzed the results for four instruments: focus groups, interviews, Internet-based surveys, and a Delphi technique. (According to Turnoff and Linstone, 2002: "Delphi may be characterized as a method for structuring a group communication process so that the process is effective in allowing a group of individuals, as a whole, to deal with a complex problem" – a process which usually happens in a series of stages; for an excellent example, see Pierce, 2012: 52–53; 62–63; Appendix 3). The findings indicated that the students generally felt a need to acquire teaching experience during their studies and that the value of the program would be increased if it had a teaching internship or practicum. However, she also found that different stakeholders held quite divergent views of what constituted the professional identities of these students.

Interestingly, Pierce openly considered the value added by the MMR approach that she used in a section headed "Strength of the Study" which started as follows:

> A mixed methods research (MMR) design was employed in the process of the evaluation. MMR can be defined as the use of qualitative and quantitative research approaches, including methods, analysis, etc. for the purpose of greater depth of understanding and corroboration of findings. (Johnson, Onwuegbuzie, and Turner, 2007, p. 124) Though the use of different data collection instruments arose in order to address ambiguity and questions at different stages of the project, the added benefit of employing mixed methods allowed for triangulation of findings across data and a deeper understanding of what the findings meant. (Pierce, 2012: 80)

She also provided a concrete example of how she put together a more comprehensive picture of the students' teaching experiences by combining her survey findings with the Delphi technique and the focus groups. Pierce also noted how the process of synthesizing the quantitative surveys and qualitative focus group data helped her to understand the students' needs and provided an example of how the department could best meet those needs:

> For example, providing information to students in order for them to gain teaching experience through self-directed teaching was the highest ranked option for departmental support on the surveys. However, this finding was not corroborated in focus groups and self-directed teaching was found to be selected due to concerns about student choice and department resources rather than an actual preference for the option. Moreover, focus group findings suggested that students needed, and the department should provide, a higher degree of support. Had findings been restricted to those in the surveys and not further explored in focus groups, an incomplete and less accurate picture of students' needs would have driven program development. (Pierce, 2012: 80–81)

While Pierce did not explicitly use terminology like "convergence," "divergence," "elaboration," "clarification," "exemplification," and "interaction," some of these concepts were clearly operating in her analyses.

Conclusion

I hope that the explanation above convinces you that MMR does not have to be complicated. Using either the nine legitimation strategies that Onwuegbuzie and Johnson (2006) described and I defined above – i.e., sample, inside-outside, weakness minimization, sequential, conversion, paradigmatic mixing, commensurability, multiple validities, or political legitimations – or the six practical techniques that Brown (2014) suggested – convergence, divergence, elaboration, clarification, exemplification, and interaction – in the future should help you create a quantitative-dominant, qualitative-dominant, or pure MMR study, wherein 1 + 1 (+ 1) = 3, that is, wherein quantitative plus qualitative (plus MMR strategies or techniques) equals three. In other words, the MMR whole should be greater than the sum of the quantitative and qualitative parts.

To help keep this whole process relatively simple, it may help to note: a) that MMR researchers do *not* have to apply all 15 (9 + 6) of the strategies and techniques described above for the study to be sound MMR; b) that these strategies and techniques might best be seen as a list of options from which the researcher should choose strategies and techniques to use in planning, carrying out, and reporting the MMR with the goal of enhancing and defending its quality; c) that the choice of options should obviously be governed to some extent by whatever constraints are found in the research situation; d) that the choice of options should be made to maximize the legitimation and quality of the MMR; e) that an adequate number of strategies and techniques should be selected to be able to convince readers that the study was well designed, carried out, and reported; f) that no study is perfect, but that more support for the quality of an MMR study will usually be more convincing than little support; and g) that MMR investigators should certainly build arguments for the convergence of various types of data, but also should investigate divergence, elaboration, clarification, exemplification, and interaction arguments.

Discussion Questions

1. What is MMR? How is it different from multi-methods research (aside from the lip curl)?

2. How is MMR different from pure qualitative research? From pure quantitative research?

3. How do quantitative-dominant MMR, qualitative-dominant MMR, and pure MMR differ?

4. What would be the benefits of using some of the legitimation concepts described above to enhance and defend an MMR study?

5. Which of the following legitimation strategies for enhancing and defending an MMR study do you think are most important generally and for your own research in particular: sample, inside-outside, weakness minimization, sequential, conversion, paradigmatic mixing, commensurability, multiple validities, or political legitimations? How would you discuss whatever legitimation strategies you selected in defending the value of an MMR?

6. Which of the following practical techniques for enhancing and defending an MMR study do you think are most important generally and for your own research in particular: convergence, divergence, elaboration, clarification, exemplification, and interaction? How would you explain and discuss these concepts in defending the value of an MMR?

7. How would any three of the practical techniques listed in number six enhance the meta-inferences that result from an MMR study such that the MMR whole would be greater than the sum of the quantitative and qualitative parts?

8. Write three research questions that would help guide your MMR with regard to: a) convergence, b) divergence, and c) exemplification.

References

Alyousef, H. S., & Picard, M. Y. (2011). Cooperative or collaborative literacy practices: Mapping metadiscourse in business students' wiki group project. *Australian Journal of Educational Technology*, 27(3), 463–480.

Brown, J. D. (2001). *Using surveys in language programs*. Cambridge: Cambridge University Press.

Brown, J. D. (2004). Research methods for applied linguistics: Scope, characteristics, and standards. In A. Davies & C. Elder (Eds.), *The handbook of applied linguistics* (pp. 476–500). Oxford: Blackwell.

Brown, J. D. (2014). *Mixed Method Research for TESOL*. Edinburgh, UK: University of Edinburgh Press.

Chang, L. Y.-H. (2007). The influences of group processes on learners' autonomous beliefs and behaviors. *System*, 35, 322–337.

Johnson, R. B., Onwuegbuzie, A. J., & Turner, L. A. (2007). Toward a definition of mixed methods research. *Journal of Mixed Methods Research*, 1(2), 112–133.

Kletzien, J. A. (2011). On the merits of mixing methods: A language program evaluation. *Second Language Studies*, 30(1), 49–94. Retrieved from http://www.hawaii.edu/sls/sls/?page_id=135

Miyazoe, T., & Anderson, T. (2011). Anonymity in blended learning: Who would you like to be? *Educational Technology & Society*, 14(2), 175–187.

Onwuegbuzie, A. J., & Johnson, R. B. (2006). The validity issue in mixed research. *Research in the Schools*, 13(1), 48–63.

Phuong, L. L. T. (2011). Adopting CALL to promote listening skills for EFL learners in Vietnamese universities. In *Proceedings of the International Conference "ICT for Language Learning"* (4th ed.). Retrieved from http://www.pixel-online.net/ICT4LL2011/common/download/Paper_pdf/IBL26-175-FP-Phuong-ICT4LL2011.pdf

Pierce, S. (2012). Utilization-focused evaluation for program development: Investigating the need for teaching experience within the Bachelor of Arts Program in Second Language Studies. *Second Language Studies*, 30(2), 43–107. Retrieved June 3, 2013 from http://www.hawaii.edu/sls/sls/?page_id=135

Turnoff, M., & Linstone, H. (2002). *The Delphi Method: Techniques and applications* [online version]. Retrieved from http://is.njit.edu/pubs/delphibook/

SECTION 2C

CHOOSING A RESEARCH TYPE

In section 2C, Choosing a Research Type, the chapters cover the issues involved in choosing a specific research type within the more global quantitative, qualitative, or mixed-methods paradigms. There are ten chapters in this section that will help you think more specifically about some of the many research types in our field:

Chapter 11 covers critical research, which is informed by the main tenets of critical theory and critical applied linguistics and includes at least a critical agenda – for example, challenging and changing current practices – and a critical research question. A number of research methodologies can be used in critical research including action research, critical discourse analysis, critical ethnography, and ideology critique. The chapter discusses each of these and provides a demonstration of how critical research can be applied.

Chapter 12 deals with action research (AR) which it defines as "… a research approach that is grounded in practical action (the action component) while at the same time focused on generating, informing and building theory (the research component)." The author examines the development of AR, criticisms and constraints that AR has faced, how AR is conceptualized, and its different forms. The chapter also explains the main features of AR and the processes that make AR flexible, adaptable, and dynamic. The chapter ends with an exploration of links between complexity theory and AR.

Chapter 13 explores teacher research, which it defines as "… systematic inquiry conducted by teachers, individually or collaboratively, which aims to enhance teachers' understandings of some aspect of their work, and is made public in some way … ." The chapter goes on to explain that the literature on the topic includes manuals to help teachers do such research, edited collections of teacher research, and studies of the teacher research process. After explaining attitudinal and practical barriers teacher researchers face, the author suggests actions that school leaders can take to promote teacher research and create a productive teacher research environment.

Chapter 14 examines case study research, which is generally a holistic and in-depth approach to characterizing an individual entity within its context; such an entity can be a single language learner, a classroom, an institution, or even a country. After defining case study research considerably more precisely than we have, the authors trace developments in case study research since the 1970s and stress the increasing importance of narratives as data. The chapter also explains the crucial elements and steps involved in case study research, explores single- versus multiple-case studies, and describes sampling strategies that are often used.

Chapter 15 deals with corpus research, which the authors define as "…a method of using computers to investigate patterns of language use within a large, principled collection of authentic texts, or a corpus … ." The chapter describes a number of freely available online corpora and explains developments in corpus-based research on vocabulary, grammar, and register, as well as the usefulness of creating learner corpora. The chapter ends with a detailed discussion of four classroom uses of corpora as well as suggestions for how teachers can do corpus research, with examples of the sorts of research questions that can be addressed.

Chapter 16 describes conversation analysis (CA) as that subset of discourse analysis research that focuses on interactions in spoken conversation. The chapter describes the transcription process and covers developments over the years in CA. The author also discusses three ways that CA has impacted language teaching and learning: by using naturalistic data, by viewing language as co-constructed, and by maintaining an agnostic attitude toward the language user's identity. The chapter ends with concrete suggestions for applying CA concepts in language classrooms.

Chapter 17 covers discourse analysis (DA), which, briefly, is the examination of patterns of language across texts while considering many social and cultural issues. After providing a much fuller definition, the chapter describes developments in DA including DA's relationship to pragmatics, structure of texts, genre analysis, critical DA, multimodal DA, identity, conversation analysis, classroom DA, and corpus-assisted DA. The author continues by discussing the implications of DA for language teaching and learning, and for cross-cultural communication.

Chapter 18 explains quantitative replication research, which is research that repeats a previous study using the same procedures with the possibility of confirming or not confirming the results of that previous study. The author discusses the scarcity of replication research and the consequences of that scarcity, then goes on to describe three types of replication studies: exact, approximate, and conceptual. After discussing the background of replication research and what can/should be replicated, the author explores some of the obstacles to replication research in the social sciences.

Chapter 19 covers ethnographic research which the author defines as "studying human activity and trying to understand the unwritten cultural rules which participants work by." After further describing the characteristics of ethnographic research, the chapter provides several example studies and covers the nature of ethnographic data of various sorts. The author continues by describing the general steps involved in ethnographic research, and ends the chapter by discussing recent developments in ethnography in online contexts and critical ethnography.

Chapter 20 covers narrative inquiry, which – according to the authors – is the systematic gathering, analysis, and representation of the stories that people tell. The chapter discusses the definition of narrative inquiry in more detail as well as the background of this type of research and its characteristics in the English language learner literature. The authors then zero in on one form of narrative inquiry known as autoethnography, which they describe in terms of its special uses and characteristics. The chapter then describes the stages and steps involved in doing narrative inquiry research as well as challenges that may arise.

Editors' Preview Questions

1. Which of the following research types are you familiar with: critical research, action research, teacher research, case study research, corpus research, conversation analysis, discourse analysis, quantitative replication research, ethnography, and narrative inquiry?

2. What is the primary characteristic that makes each of the research types listed above distinct?

3. What characteristics do all of the research types listed above have in common?

4. Which research type(s) are you most interested in? How might your choice help you to understand language learning and teaching, and to solve problems in your classrooms and professional life?

CHAPTER 11

Critical Research in TESOL and Language Education

Salah Troudi

INTRODUCTION AND BACKGROUND

In his book *Critical applied linguistics: A critical introduction*, Pennycook (2001) introduced what was then considered a new area or field of study in language education and TESOL. Pennycook's book can be considered as the *official* ushering in of a new era in the study of a number of domains such as discourse analysis, classroom methodologies, and literacy. These language-related areas have been framed within a critical approach to education and informed by mainly a theoretical framework of critical theory. Prior to Pennycook's publication of 2001, there were of course empirical studies and theoretical papers in the areas of TESOL and language education that reflected critical agendas of change, improvement, and questioning of taken-for-granted definitions and practices. For example, a special issue of *TESOL Quarterly* (1999, Volume 33) was dedicated to critical approaches to TESOL covering an array of topics such as race and gender by Ibrahim, classroom discourse analysis by Kumaravadivelu, and non-native English speaking professionals in TESOL by Brutt-Griffler and Samimy. In fact, the last decade has seen a clear surge in TESOL publications of a critical nature. However, critical research in TESOL and language education is still in its infancy and is considered as a newcomer in comparison to more established traditions such as positivistic, also referred to as scientific, and interpretivist approaches to research. What is still missing in research manuals in applied linguistics is a clear place for critical research as an approach with its theoretical perspectives, agendas, methodologies, methods, and criteria of evaluation. This chapter is an attempt at filling this gap and at introducing this approach to research to English language teachers, and novice and early-career researchers.

One possible explanation of the late arrival of critical approaches to the domains of language education and TESOL in particular is the relatively strong hegemony mainstream and apolitical approaches to English language teaching in the last few decades of ELT in general. With the wide spread of English and discourses of globalisation, development, proficiency, accountability and standardisation, the main focus of TESOL research was on improving learners' language proficiency by looking for efficient classroom methodologies, reliable testing measures, effective teacher education programmes, and interesting and motivating syllabuses and materials. In a recent and valuable publication on how to understand and critique research in applied linguistics, Perry (2011: 76) classifies research designs by using three continua: exploratory–confirmatory, quantitative–qualitative and basic–applied. The continuum exploratory–confirmatory is a reflection of research agendas that can be traced to two major research approaches/paradigms: the interpretive/constructivist and the scientific positivistic. What is missing in Perry's classification of research is the critical approach. One plausible reason for this gap is that because many critical researchers often use the same qualitative research instruments, open-ended interviews, observations, an association and, as a result, a mixing up is made between interpretive and critical research. An important point to clarify in this context is that similarity at the level of methods should not imply that critical research is synonymous with interpretive approaches, which are also known as qualitative. Critical research has a different agenda from the constructivist interpretive approach. For example, while an interpretivist researcher in TESOL aims at understanding a particular teaching or learning process from the perspectives of the teachers or learners, a critical researcher will be aiming at challenging and changing certain practices having identified a problem in the first place. There are also some major distinctions at the level of research methodologies or designs as will be addressed below.

Given that critical research is contextual and responsive, the reader should not expect a formulaic style or design with a rigid and a linear step-by-step process. However, like other main approaches, critical research needs to be systematic, theoretically justifiable, and credible.

Research on this Topic

Critical research in language education, TESOL, and applied linguistics in general has been appropriately associated with the wider philosophical framework of critical theory. The works of the Frankfurt School, with scholars such as Habermas, Horkenheimer, Adorno, and Marcuse, were influential in the twentieth century in setting up the main agenda of critical theory and its research, which was to help establish an equitable society. This is done through a research approach that is emancipatory, seeking action and change in order to alleviate pain in society and redress forms of alienation, discrimination, injustice, exploitation, and marginalisation. This research agenda is based on a general view of society and social realities as shaped by the hegemony of powerful economic and political structures, social and educational institutions, and discursive practices. Critical theorists such as Foucault, Freire, Bourdieu, Giroux, McLaren, and Shor among others, who in fact represent a multitude of critical theories and a general dissensus among them on the nature of criticality, seem to share a "conception of society as stratified and marked by inequality, with differential structural access to material and symbolic resources, opportunity, mobility and education" (Talmy, 2010: 128). Critical theorists have distanced themselves from a Marxian historical conceptualisation of society as an economic struggle between social classes and its deterministic revolutionary alternatives. Instead, they go beyond the economic analysis to incorporate "cultural and ideological analyses in [their] understanding of why the contradictions of late capitalism, including the everyday oppressions and accompanying widespread sense of alienation, are still sustainable" (Collins, 2007: 67).

Critical theory has been influential in the general area of education and more recently in language studies and teaching English as a foreign language (TEFL) and as second language (TESL).

PRACTICAL APPLICATIONS

The general procedures and principles of doing critical research from designing one's research questions to writing the final report and disseminating it publically through publications and presentations do not differ radically from interpretive or even positivistic quantitative research. See Richards, Ross, and Seedhouse's (2012) accessible introduction to different phases involved in conducting a research study in language teaching. They do not address critical research or its methodologies, but their work is useful to critical researchers at the level of methods of data collection.

STARTING WITH A CRITICAL AGENDA

To do critical research in language education the researcher needs to be guided by a critical agenda. This, for example, can be done by seeking to challenge a taken-for-granted educational practice or discourse, questioning a policy, raising awareness about the quality of teacher education or lack of professional development opportunities in some contexts, problematizing some testing practices or highlighting the effects and consequences of a language of instruction policy on the quality of educational opportunities for students and the quality of their learning experiences. Developing a critical agenda for a study in the field of language education reflects one's commitment to issues of equity, access, quality, learners' and teachers' views, and relevance of content and methodology to the lives, interests, and learning styles of the learners among many other critical issues. Perhaps an important step in developing a critical research agenda is the awareness that education in general and English teaching in particular are not apolitical. It is beyond the scope of this chapter to delve into the political and bureaucratic dimensions of education and the financial corporatization of TESOL under the hegemony of the globalisation movement. Critical researchers like Kumaravadivelu (2006:1) offer a critique of the "dangerous liaison" between globalization and TESOL. His work can serve as background to TEFL and TESL teachers who are interested in a critical stance on TESOL structures and practices.

DEVELOPING A CRITICAL RESEARCH QUESTION

Once a particular problem has been identified and a critical agenda and objectives have been formulated, a researcher needs to develop one or more research questions. This is the foundation upon which every research project should be based. The following critical areas suggested by Troudi (2006: 288) can be turned into research questions:

- English-only policy in the TESL classroom;
- the status of the EFL/ESL teacher as a professional;
- pedagogical hegemony: the tyranny of communicative language teaching;
- the spread of English and its effects on native languages;
- students' choice of language of instruction;
- students' voice in assessment;
- students' choice of content of their learning;
- job insecurity and low pay for teachers;
- job satisfaction and disenchantment.

Research projects and questions are contextually bound and researchers will have to consider socio-political and cultural factors in designing their studies. There are also issues of feasibility and constraints and these will vary according to the context of each study. The following are research questions with a critical agenda:

1. What are the impacts of an English-only policy on the learning experiences of EFL learners in a particular context?
2. What is the effect of an English medium of instruction policy in content areas on the quality of the educational experiences of first year university students in X country?
3. How does a particular testing approach affect EFL learners' attitudes to English?
4. What recruitment, promotion, and leadership opportunities do bilingual and multilingual teachers of English have in a particular professional context?
5. What world view is represented in EFL textbooks?

In the case of the fourth question the term "non-native speaker" is not used because of the embedded issues of power and marginalisation the term connotes. Instead, the terms "bilingual" and "multilingual" are meant to empower teachers and represent their strength.

DECIDING ON A METHODOLOGY

With clear research questions researchers are in a position to develop a methodology for their study. Methodological decisions are about the overall strategy and design that will guide research in the whole process of the study. This is different from the research methods or instruments which are techniques of data collection and can be either quantitative or qualitative, such as surveys, interviews, diaries, and observation among others. A number of methodologies have been associated with critical approaches to research such as action research, critical discourse analysis, critical ethnography, and ideology critique. These methodologies have in common a stress on action, change, and empowerment.

ACTION RESEARCH

Perhaps of all the above methodologies action research (see Chapter 12) is the one mostly linked to critical research and that's because of a clear emphasis on action. There is an abundance of theoretical and practical literature on action research. For example, in the fields of TESL and TEFL, Burns (1999, 2010) and Wallace (1998) offer a version of action research that is strongly aligned with the movement of teacher research and professional development. This is likely to be the approach of action research most familiar to ELT teachers and the one mostly reported in mainstream TEFL/TESL literature. The focus here is on improving classroom practice resulting in an action research that is pedagogically centred and that "reflects a mainstream conceptualisation of what constitutes teacher knowledge" (Troudi, 2008: 438).

Carr and Kemmis (1986) and Kemmis and McTaggert (1988) offer a solid introduction to critical action research as critical praxis which resolves around the central element of change and improvement of the social conditions of people's lives. It is this emancipatory version of action research that is appropriate to serve critical agendas and not a version that is imposed on teachers as part of a professional development plan or a teacher evaluation scheme.

On the practical side of conducting action research there are a number of models and steps suggested in research manuals and literature. Most models revolve around a cycle of four main elements. For example, in his emancipatory action research design Zuber-Sklerrit (1996: 3) suggests the following four phases:

1. strategic planning
2. action – i.e., implementing the plan
3. observation, evaluation, and self-evaluation
4. critical and self-critical reflection on the results of points 1–3 and making decisions for the next cycle of action research

This model bears very strong resemblance to the cyclical model suggested by Kemmis and McTaggart (1988) and, based on this model, other designs emerged that included additional steps such as reporting, writing, and presenting which come towards the end of the project (Burns, 1999).

ACTION RESEARCH DEMONSTRATION

In the case of the research question "What is the effect of an English medium of instruction policy in content areas on the quality of the educational experiences of first year university students in an X country?", a researcher or team of collaborating researchers can explore the effect of EMI policy by developing an intervention plan with experimental and interventionist elements. Researchers can select a group of students at an equivalent language level and teach them content through English for a given period of time and in the students' mother tongue for a second period. This is possible in many monolingual settings where all students share the same native language. At the end of the two intervention stages students can be asked about their experiences about learning via English and their mother tongue.

See Troudi (2007) for a collaborative and empowering action research project that sought to challenge some attitudes and stereotypes regarding multiple repeaters and their abilities in English at a university in the United Arab Emirates. This was done through a set of qualitative methods, individual and group interviews, classroom observation, and open-ended questionnaires, that allowed participating students to suggest pedagogical alternatives which were used by the researcher to design implementation. As a result of the project 70% of the students passed their final exam and, more importantly, the image of the multiple repeaters as passive and uninterested students was challenged at university level. See also Mack's (2012) action research project on classroom participation.

CRITICAL DISCOURSE ANALYSIS

Critical discourses analysis, like its mainstream counterpart discourse analysis, is an area of study, but can also be considered as a major methodology that can help the critical researcher investigate and answer questions about the use of discourse in language education. With a critical discourse analysis framework the researcher transcends the view of the study of discourse, in all its forms: written, oral, formal, and informal, as consisting of linguistic and sociocultural elements to explore socio-political dimensions. This is considered necessary to uncover and redress issues of ideology, power, and inequality which are produced and reproduced via discourse (Fairclough, 1995).

In the field of TESOL and drawing on the works of critical theorists and in particular post colonialists such as Said and postmodernists like Foucault, Kumaravadivelu (1999) established a conceptual framework for critical classroom discourse analysis. Classroom discourse, he argues, needs to be studied within a macro socio-political and socio-cultural context and beyond the classical and established suprasentential level. This is because classroom discourse is not neutral or only the result of pedagogical events. It is seen as "socially constructed, politically motivated and historically determined ... and the L2 classroom manifests, at surface and deep levels, many forms of resistance, articulated or unarticulated" (p. 472). Research about classroom discourse therefore should not be "confined to the acquisitional aspects of input and interaction, to the instructional imperatives of form-and function-focused language learning activities, or to the conversational routines of turn-taking and turn giving sequences" (Ibid).

CRITICAL DISCOURSE ANALYSIS DEMONSTRATION

In the case of this research question 'What world view is represented in EFL textbooks?' a researcher can adopt a critical discourse analysis framework to look at the main ideologies, world views, and cultural representations that are dominant in a set of materials in use. Researchers can look at how social groups are portrayed and the roles assigned to them. The focus can also be on how society at large is portrayed. Many textbooks reflect a sanitized, safe, and idealized version of social reality with no social problems such as crime, corruption, economic exploitation, racism, or modern slavery. These discursive practices in EFL textbooks are not neutral or apolitical and reflect reproductive agendas. Critical discourse analysis tools can therefore help researchers uncover such agendas and redress issues of misrepresentation, absent discourses, and marginalized social groups in EFL materials.

Novice researchers can consult some studies that have looked at racial and ethnic stereotypes and how EFL textbooks and materials perpetuate and present racialized representations of roles and images of certain groups (Kubota and Lin, 2009). Other useful studies, using critical classroom discourse analysis, have considered issues of gender and how female characters were poorly represented in terms of visibility and gender stereotyping (Sunderland, 2000).

Lin (1999) critically analyses discourse patterns in four English classrooms situated in different socioeconomic backgrounds in Singapore and demonstrates how classroom discourse patterns and practices can contribute to the reproduction of social inequalities or help transform students' worlds. Classroom interaction was technically transcribed using conversation analysis techniques but meanings and implications were investigated within a critical discourse analysis framework drawing on notions such as cultural capital, habitus, and symbolic violence (Bourdieu, 1991).

CRITICAL ETHNOGRAPHY

Having identified a critical topic a researcher might consider critical ethnography as a methodological choice. According to Thomas (1993) critical ethnography differs from conventional ethnography in the nature of its agenda. They do share fundamental characteristics such as the prolonged investigation of micro and macro contexts and a central role for qualitative methods and data. However, Thomas (1993: 4) argues that critical ethnographers "celebrate their normative and political position as a means of invoking social consciousness and societal change." Kumaravadivelu (1999: 476) summarizes the task of critical ethnographers, explaining that they are "actively engaged in dealing with powerful systems of discourse. They seek to deconstruct dominant discourses as well as counterdiscourses by posing questions at the boundaries of ideology, power, knowledge, class, race and gender." To do so they have at their disposal the same array of research methods used by mainstream conventional ethnographers such as interviews, observations, field notes, photography, and diaries among others. The main difference between the two versions is that the critical one insists on challenging systems and practices in order to change them rather than just understanding and reporting practices.

CRITICAL ETHNOGRAPHY DEMONSTRATION

The research question "How does a particular testing approach affect EFL learners' attitudes to English?" can be answered through a critical ethnography project. This is of course in case a researcher or a group of researchers have identified a critical topic in the area of language testing, which is often wrought with controversies and differing views about the most effective way to measure learners' language competencies. A starting point in such a project can be a stage of data collection on all aspects of testing in a particular educational context, and then a focus on how learners experience testing and its effects on their daily lives in the classroom, at school, and beyond. This will involve direct classroom observation, informal chats with learners about their test preparations and concerns, attending test preparation sessions, and interviewing students about the effects of testing systems on their learning experiences and futures. The overall purpose of the ethnography will be to expose the inadequacy of a test-driven educational culture and to replace it with a progressive and more humanistic approach.

Goldstein (2004) used critical ethnographic data and turned it into a critical ethnographic play in her teacher education class to help teachers respond to issues of language choice, racism, and discrimination in multilingual and multicultural schools. In this case data and findings from a critical ethnography have been designed to develop transformatory pedagogical units thus establishing a direct link between research and practical change. Canagarajah's critical ethnography (1993) study of a Sri Lankan classroom shows how Tamil students manage to resist discourses of cultural alienation and ideological domination represented in a U.S. textbook through a choice to learn grammar in a product-oriented approach.

IDEOLOGY CRITIQUE

As one of the established methodologies associated with critical theory, ideology critique has contributed to studies of cultural systems, politics, and other areas in social sciences. It is relatively less known in education and even more so in TESL/TEFL studies. However, given the power of ideologies, described by Burbules (1992: 7) as representing "a version of the world that helps people make sense of their circumstances" and a belief of critical theorists that ideologies emanate from powerful groups in society that want to maintain their privileges while excluding others, ideology critique can certainly contribute to investigate issues of power and ideologies in language education.

IDEOLOGY CRITIQUE DEMONSTRATION

Ideology critique can be used to challenge some taken-for-granted ideologies and practices in such areas as TESOL teachers' recruitment, promotion, and job security. In certain parts of the world, some TESL teachers whose first language is not English find it difficult to secure employment because of their first language. Such discriminatory practices have been legitimized by discourses of efficiency, competencies, and common good for the students. As a result, many competent bilingual and multilingual teachers could not compete for jobs and continue to be excluded. An alternative to this situation can be offered via a systematic ideology critique. Adopting Habermas' model (1972), a researcher needs to do the following:

1. Describe and interpret current situation, policy, attitudes, and practices.
2. Investigate the reasons and purposes behind recruitment and promotion policies and how they have become legitimate practices. This should include an investigation of how bilingual and multilingual teachers view themselves as professionals and how they might be perpetuating distorted practices and discourses that contribute to their own marginalisation.
3. Develop an agenda to challenge and change the situation and empower the teachers.
4. Evaluate the situation in practice and see if any change has taken place.

A combination of documents analysis, interviewing, and observation methods can be used in such a project.

Offering a fully developed account of how to do critical research in language education and TESOL is a project beyond the scope of this chapter. Readers are, therefore, encouraged to consult the educational research literature for approaches to data analysis and reporting of findings. Canagarajah (1996) offers a critical view on how to report critical research and urges scholars in TESOL to seek alternate forms that fit the purposes of critical research instead of following systematic formulas prescribed by academic genres.

CONCLUSION

Critical research has its fair share of challenges and criticisms, and questions have been raised about some of its theoretical assumptions about truth, social realities, and especially whether it can lead to real change. This is referred to as catalytic validity. In fact, Starfield (2004) asks whether research can be emancipatory within a climate of globalisation, marketization and corporatizing. However, I argue that critical researchers in language education should not be discouraged if they see little change happening as a result of their investigations. It is important to acknowledge that changes to attitudes, practices, and policies are often very slow and necessitate vital stages of problematization and raising awareness.

If we want to be educators and intellectual teachers (Giroux, 1988) rather than consumers and perpetuators of hegemonic structures and dominant discourses then our research ought not to be stripped of its critical agenda (Kincheloe, 2003: 109).

Discussion Questions

1. What language teaching areas can be explored through a critical research project?
2. Select one area and state what the main problem is in your teaching context.
3. Is it possible to develop a critical agenda to conduct a study about your chosen area?
4. Develop some research questions.
5. Which critical methodology is best suited for your research questions?
6. What research methods will you select for your study?
7. Are there any ethical issues to consider before and after data collection?
8. What strategy will you use to analyze your data and disseminate your findings?
9. How will you check that your research had an impact on practice, attitudes, or policy?

References

Bourdieu, P. (1991). *Language and symbolic power*. (G. Raymond & M. Anderson, Trans.). Cambridge, MA: Harvard University Press.

Brutt-Griffler, J., & Samimy, K. (1999). Revisiting the colonial in the postcolonial: Critical praxis for non-native English-speaking teachers in a TESOL program. *TESOL Quarterly*, 33(3), 413–431.

Burbules, N. C. (1992). Forms of ideology-critique: A pedagogical perspective. *International Journal of Qualitative Studies in Education*, 5(1), 7–17.

Burns, A. (1999). *Collaborative action research for English language teachers*. Cambridge: Cambridge University Press.

Burns, A. (2010). *Doing action research for English language teachers. A guide for practitioners*. New York: Routledge.

Canagarajah, S. (1993). Critical ethnography of a Sri Lankan classroom: Ambiguities in student opposition to reproduction through ESOL. *TESOL Quarterly*, 27(4), 601–626.

Canagarajah, S. (1996). From critical research practice to critical research reporting. *TESOL Quarterly*, 30(2), 321–330.

Carr, W., & Kemmis, S. (1986). *Becoming critical: Education, knowledge, and action research*. London: Routledge Falmer.

Collins, M. (2007). Critical approaches to research in practice. In J. Swann & J. Pratt (Eds.), *Educational research in practice* (pp. 67–83). London: Continuum.

Fairclough, N. (1995). *Critical discourse analysis: The critical study of language*. London: Longman.

Giroux, H. A. (1988). *Teachers as intellectuals: Toward a critical pedagogy of learning*. Boston: Bergin & Garvey.

Goldstein, T. (2004). Performed ethnography for critical language teacher education. In B. Norton & K. Toohey (Eds.), *Critical pedagogies and language learning* (pp. 311–326). Cambridge: Cambridge University Press.

Habermas, J. (1972). *Knowledge and human interest* (Trans.). London: Heinemann.

Ibrahim, A. E. K. (1999). Becoming black: Rap and hip-hop, race, gender, identity and the politics of ESL learning. *TESOL Quarterly*, 33(3), 349–369.

Kemmis, S., & McTaggart, R. (Eds.), (1988). *The action research planner* (3rd ed.). Geelong: Deakin University Press.

Kincheloe, J. L. (2003). *Teachers as researchers: Qualitative inquiry as a path to empowerment*. London: Routledge.

Kumaravadivelu, B. (1999). Critical classroom discourse analysis. *TESOL Quarterly*, 33(3), 453–484.

Kumaravadivelu, B. (2006). Dangerous liaison: Globalization, empire and TESOL. In J. Edge (Ed.), *(Re)Locating TESOL in an age of Empire* (pp. 1–32). London: Palgrave/Macmillan.

Kubota, R., & Lin, A. (2009). (Eds.). *Race, culture, and identities in second language education: Exploring critically engaged practice*. London: Routledge.

Mack, L. (2012). Does every student have a voice? Critical action research on equitable classroom participation practices. *Language Teaching Research*, 16(3), 417–434.

Lin, A. M. Y. (1999). Doing English-lessons in the reproduction or the transformation social worlds? *TESOL Quarterly*, 33(3), 393–412.

Pennycook, A. (2001). *Critical applied linguistics: A critical introduction*. London: LEA.

Pennycook, A. (2008). Critical applied linguistics and language education. In S. May & N. H. Horberger (Eds.), *Encyclopaedia of language and education: Volume 1: Language policy and political issues in education* (pp. 169–191). Boston: Springer.

Perry, F. L. Jr. (2011). *Research in applied linguistics: Becoming a discerning consumer*. London: Routledge.

Richards. K., Ross, S., & Seedhouse, P. (2012). *Research methods in applied language studies*. London: Routledge.

Sunderland, J. (2000). Issues of language and gender in second and foreign language education. *Language Teaching*, 33(4), 203–23.

Starfield, S. (2004). "Why does this feel empowering?": Thesis writing, concordancing, and the corporatizing university. In B. Norton & K. Toohey (Eds.), *Critical pedagogies and language learning* (pp. 138–157). Cambridge: Cambridge University Press.

Sunderland, J. (2004). Classroom interaction, gender, and foreign language learning. In B. Norton & K. Toohey (Eds.), *Critical pedagogies and language learning* (pp. 222–241). Cambridge: Cambridge University Press.

Talmy, S. (2010). Critical research in applied linguistics. In B. Paltridge & A. Phakiti (Eds.), *Continuum companion to research methods in applied linguistics* (pp. 127–141). London: Continuum.

Thomas, J. (1993). *Doing critical ethnography*. Qualitative Research Methods Series. Vol. 26. London: SAGE.

Troudi, S. (2006). Empowering ourselves through action research. In P. Davidson, M. Al Hamly, J. Aydelott, C. Coombe, & S. Troudi (Eds.). *Proceedings of the 11th TESOL Arabia Conference: Teaching, Learning, Leading* (pp. 277–290). Dubai: TESOL Arabia.

Troudi. S. (2007). Negotiating with multiple repeaters. In C. Coombe & L. Barlow (Eds.), *Language teacher research in the Middle East* (pp. 161–172). Alexandria, VA: TESOL.

Troudi, S. (2008). Reflection on action research. In A. Jendli, C. Coombe, & S. Troudi (Eds.), *Proceedings of the 13th TESOL Arabia Conference: Best Practice in English Language Teaching* (pp. 433–445). Dubai: TESOL Arabia.

Wallace, M. J. (1998). *Action research for language teachers*. Cambridge: Cambridge University Press.

Zuber-Skerrit, O. (Ed.). (1996). *New directions in action research*. London: Falmer.

CHAPTER 12

Action Research

Anne Burns

INTRODUCTION

Action research (AR) is a research approach that is grounded in practical action (the action component) while at the same time focused on generating, informing, and building theory (the research component). These two components work in combination, each mutually informing and supporting the other. It is a constructivist approach to research that involves processes of collaboration, dialogue, and action among the participants in the surrounding social system – typically the language classroom in the field of English language teaching (ELT). Reason and Bradbury (2001: 2) stress that "action research is about working towards practical outcomes and also about creating new forms of understanding, since action research without understanding is blind, just as theory without action is meaningless." They go on to emphasize other essential elements of AR:

> Since action research starts with everyday experience and is concerned with the development of living knowledge, in many ways the process of inquiry is as important as the specific outcomes. Good action research emerges over time in an evolutionary and developmental process, as individuals develop skills of enquiry and as communities of enquiry develop within communities of practice. (Reason and Bradbury, 2001: 2)

In this chapter, I first highlight some of the developments contributing to the growth and prominence of action research and then provide a brief commentary on some key issues related to the implementation of AR. This discussion is followed by a short review of recent AR studies and the chapter ends with discussion of the practical implementation of AR.

BACKGROUND

Philosophically and materially, AR stands in contrast to positivist, experimental approaches, which seek objective, logical, value-free, and generalizable knowledge. Positivist approaches, despite their dominance over a long period in educational and other fields, have been criticized, however, for not being readily applicable to the practical challenges of the professional communities they claim to serve. Action research sets out to generate knowledge that is localized, based on practical enquiry, and leads to informed change. It offers a route into systematic enquiry that provides options that are usually more meaningful to practitioners than other forms of investigation.

AR has become recognized, since its inception in the 1940s by Kurt Lewin, as an alternative empirical approach that seeks to identify and investigate the immediate concerns and interests of the participants. In the field of ELT it emerged mainly from the late 1980s and has grown in influence, because of its potential for increasing practitioner engagement in research, offering a means of school-based professional development, and generating contextualized and situated theories of teaching and learning.

A major influence on AR was the shift towards learner-centered concepts of curriculum development, which gave a more prominent role to the teacher as a central agent in the decision-making processes of the classroom. It also paralleled growing interest in classroom-based research to illuminate how learning and teaching operated in language classrooms. Another reason AR has gained ground is that it has been part of a more general movement in teacher education and professional development towards "teacher learning," influenced by theoretical advances and research in teacher cognition, reflective teaching, the knowledge-base of teaching, and the socio-cultural turn in language teacher education (Johnson, 2009). AR also aligns with the general shift in the applied linguistics field from the early 1980s towards interest in exploratory, qualitative, and ethnographic research approaches. In the sections below, I highlight three key issues that are debated in recent discussions of AR in ELT.

CRITICISMS AND CONSTRAINTS

In the field of applied linguistics, AR is by no means a well-accepted or established research methodology (Jarvis, 2002a, 2002b). It has been criticized – particularly by those who adopt a positivist stance – for a lack of rigour and subjectivity; methodological limitations, including a lack of established research methods and data procedures; problems of reliability and validity; lack of generalizability/replicability; and unclear ethical implications and processes (for example, see Dörnyei, 2007; Ellis, 2010). Doubts also center on the limited research training and therefore the capacity of teachers to undertake research and the relevance to the field of knowledge generated by teacher research. Commentators have also questioned whether any teachers actually do AR, and if so, why so little research has been published by teachers. Various studies of teacher engagement in (action) research (for example, Borg, 2010) have also highlighted impediments experienced by teachers themselves, such as institutional barriers, lack of knowledge of AR, limited time and materials, restricted research training, and little reason/motivation, recognition, or reward for doing research.

CONCEPTUALISATIONS OF ACTION RESEARCH

AR is not easily defined. It is frequently referred to as a type of qualitative research. However, advocates of AR would argue that it is motivated by a different worldview from both quantitative and qualitative paradigms and is a kind of "third way." A central concept is "praxis," that is, reflection combined with action in an ongoing process that leads to understanding and transforming social practices. Because of their participatory role, action researchers are subjectively involved in their research in ways that do not apply in other paradigms. Researchers seek freedom from bias, rather than objectivity, by using procedures such as cross-checking sources (triangulation), self-reflexivity, and member checks (referring their findings back to participants for feedback). AR should be viewed as an approach to research rather than a specific methodology, one that uses a family of methods and processes depending on the amount of controlled experimentation or open-ended exploration that is required. Although early examples of AR in ELT tended to be predominantly qualitative in design, recent studies also exemplify the usefulness of quantitative or mixed methods approaches – for example, Matsuzawa, 2012.

FORMS OF ACTION RESEARCH

Although AR has become more widely accepted in ELT, the majority of published studies have tended towards technical-practical (or problem-solving) forms of research involving practical solutions to local classroom issues. Crookes (1993) drew attention to the lack of studies adopting critical-emancipatory (or problematization) perspectives guiding the work of more critical strands of AR. These movements follow a line of research that is deliberately political and seeks to transform existing educational policies and practices in radical ways. AR studies that link issues of power, identity, inclusivity, and equality and that incorporate a diverse range of stakeholders beyond teachers and learners are still limited, although there is some evidence that this line of research is beginning to develop.

RESEARCH ON THIS TOPIC

Since the early 1990s – when there were hardly any accounts of AR studies to be found in the ELT literature – there is now a much more robust body of publications from which AR practitioners can draw for the purpose of conducting their own investigations, whether doing small-scale classroom studies, undertaking projects as part of teacher qualifications, or completing doctoral programs. Publication of many of these accounts has been facilitated by international professional associations, such as TESOL, through its series for teachers, such as *Case Studies in TESOL Practice* and *Language Teacher Research*. Its *TESOL Journal*, published online, also encourages publications by practitioner researchers, as do journals such as *Language Teaching Research* and *Language Learning and Technology*. These publications increasingly offer examples of research from locations not typically represented in the literature, thus encouraging teacher research in a wide range of contexts and expanding knowledge about conditions for learning and teaching internationally. Regional or local journals directed towards professional practice may also encourage AR publications, a notable example being the journal *Profile*, published since 2000 by the National University of Colombia. Published teacher researcher accounts have also come from various structured initiatives, such as action research integrated into undergraduate courses (see Burns, 2010, for a description of examples of these), or nationally funded professional development (e.g., the joint Cambridge English Language Assessment – English Australia Program projects published in *Research Notes* since 2011).

I have reviewed the development of this literature in various previous publications (e.g., Burns, 2011), so confine myself here to an overview of the types of studies completed and published in journals from 2011 to give a flavour of the kind of topics that are now of interest. Journal articles continue to form an important source. Recent examples show that while there is still an emphasis on applications for practice – for example, the use of ICT, skills development, affective dimensions of learning, developing learner autonomy, materials development – interest is growing in areas such as: the social roles of teacher researchers – for example, personal and professional identities; the nature of the AR experience for teachers – for example, self-development, impact on practice, personal theory development; discursive practices – for example, collaborative, dialogic interaction, nature and potential of teacher narrative, genres of reporting; teacher cognition in AR – for example, conceptual change, reflective thinking; the positioning of teacher action research – for example, within national educational reform movements, conceptualisations of effective professional development; the role of teacher educators/facilitators – for example, nature of support, scaffolding of teacher learning processes, roles and relationships vis-à-vis practitioners; and the interactions of AR with other research philosophies – teacher research as a hermeneutical (interpretative) and ontological (concerned with the nature of being and becoming) process, AR and complexity theory. This diverse range of publication topics provides growing evidence of greater sophistication and expanded possibilities for research adopting an AR orientation.

Practical Applications

Various models of AR have been put forward since Lewin first proposed a cycle of planning, action and fact-finding to motivate social change. The main features of these models present AR as:

- *cyclical*: developments in understanding and changes in practice occur over time through a reiterative and spiralling process;
- *open-ended*: start and end points for the research are not fixed but depend on the time and resources available;
- *systematic*: observation and reflection provide evidence for further action;
- *exploratory*: the outcomes of the research are not open to prediction.

While models of AR are useful, it needs to be kept in mind that AR is flexible, dynamic, and adaptable to the circumstances of the research. Essentially, it adopts a series of interrelated processes which look something like the following:

- explore teaching or learning as they currently occur;
- identify an area of interest or concern (a puzzle, dilemma, or issue);
- discuss with colleagues/other participants if possible how the issue might be addressed and involve them in the research;
- put a plan of action in place and observe how it plays out in the setting of the study;
- collect data to observe what is happening as the action takes place (for example, student questionnaires, observation reports, journal entries);
- reflect on what insights or findings are emerging from the observations;
- plan further strategic actions based on the data to address the issue;
- re-enter the cycle to deepen understanding, enhance practices, and identify further directions.

To shape the starting point, action researchers may develop questions or statements for their investigations, although more traditional forms of research questions are likely to be found in studies for formal qualifications. Classroom practitioners doing small-scale investigations are liable to ask questions such as "What would happen if I did X (for example, allowed students to choose their own reading material) in my classroom?" or to work from personal observations such as "I'm frustrated by my tendency to do X (for example, control what students choose to read) in class." Typically – whatever the motivation for the study – the direction of the research and the kinds of questions that emerge shift considerably from where they started, as researchers deepen their understanding of their practices.

As suggested earlier, action researchers have available a wide variety of data collection methods from those used in both qualitative studies (observation, field notes, diaries/journals, questionnaires, personal narratives/interviews, recordings using a range of technologies, or visuals of various kinds), and quantitative designs (control/experimental groups, pre-post testing, surveys, think-aloud protocols). The choice of methods will depend on the focus of the investigation and the amount of time, research skills, and theoretical knowledge available to the researcher, as well as the nature and purpose of the research.

Data analysis, as in other research, involves a gradual focusing or crunching of the data to refine reflections and to identify key themes or practices. Because of the cyclical and reflective nature of AR, formative analysis occurs throughout the whole process and informs practical action; however, most forms of AR reach a summative point where the whole of the data need to be analysed. Depending on the methods used for collecting data, a researcher might develop codes to illustrate key messages from interview data, provide diary extracts to illustrate important teaching insights, or extracts from classroom transcripts to identify particular interaction patterns between teacher and students. Where a researcher has used more quantitative methods, descriptive statistics, such as calculating means or standard deviations, followed by standard reliability procedures, may be used.

Data analysis in action research is a contentious area and has been criticized for its lack of rigour and even its absence from some accounts. For these reasons, some commentators question whether AR can be counted as research. However, AR should be judged more by its relevance to catalytic validity, that is, the extent to which it contributes to improving and changing educational practices, democratizing research, and leading to new practitioner learning, than its adherence to standard scientific measures. AR and the analyses it involves are more to do with practitioners adopting an attitude of enquiry and questioning, and taking a problematic position on taken-for-granted local practices for the benefit of themselves and their students. It relies less on whether causal changes can be demonstrated than on providing rich descriptions of the experiences of the participants (Burns, 2011).

Conclusion

Second language acquisition research is currently being influenced by insights from dynamic systems and complexity theories. These theories reject the idea that phenomena like language learning and teaching can be easily explained through simplified and reductive causal explanations. Similarly, they critique the principle that variables in the social situation of the research can be readily controlled. Complexity theory aims to understand and explain systems such as the classroom that are complex and dynamic, where actions, decisions, and behaviors must be open-ended, unpredictable, and even chaotic. AR aligns with this movement in that it recognizes:

- *change*: the notion of change is central. AR is concerned with documenting and explaining change as it occurs for the various classroom participants and stakeholders;
- *social situatedness*: classrooms are part of a wider system of schools, organizations, policies and theories that have an impact on the way the classroom operates;
- *social contextualisation*: learning and teaching inevitably take account of the nature of the classroom within a particular physical, social, cognitive, and cultural setting;
- *variability*: classroom behavior is dynamic and can only be understood by investigating the classroom as it is operates in its day-to-day reality;
- *flexibility*: outcomes cannot be predicted in advance as research processes seek emerging understanding and practices.

A key challenge for the ELT field is to deepen understanding of the conditions that impact on language teaching across the world. Teacher action research can potentially assist in positioning the knowledge base for teaching alongside other forms of research in the SLA/ELT field.

Discussion Questions

1. To what extent are there opportunities for practitioners in your context to engage in AR?
2. What conditions are needed to support teachers to become engaged in AR?
3. What kinds of topics or questions would lend themselves to action research in your context? Think of topics that could be researched: a) within your individual classroom; b) across your school or teaching center.
4. What potential ethical issues could arise where the researcher is also the classroom teacher?
5. Have you had any experience of addressing such issues?

References

Borg, S. (2010). Language teacher research engagement. *Language Teaching*, 43(4), 391–429.

Burns, A. (2010). Teacher engagement in research: Published resources for teacher researchers. *Language Teaching*, 43(4), 527–536.

Burns, A. (2011). Action research in the field of second language teaching and learning. In E. Hinkel (Ed.), *Handbook of research in second language teaching and learning*. Vol II (pp. 237–253). New York: Routledge.

Crookes, G. (1993). Action research for second language teachers: Going beyond teacher research. *Applied Linguistics*, 14(2), 130–144.

Dörnyei, Z. (2007). *Research methods in applied linguistics*. Oxford: Oxford University Press.

Ellis, R. (2010). Second language acquisition, teacher education and language pedagogy. *Language Teaching*, 43(2), 182–201.

Jarvis, S. (2002a). Research in TESOL Part I. *TESOL Research Interest Section Newsletter*, 8(2), 1–2.

Jarvis, S. (2002b). Research in TESOL Part II. *TESOL Research Interest Section Newsletter*, 9(1), 1–2.

Johnson, K. E. (2009). Trends in second language teacher education. In A. Burns & J. C. Richards (Eds.), *The Cambridge guide to second language teacher education* (pp. 20–29). New York: Cambridge.

Matsuzawa, T. (2012). Action research: Using narrow listening to improve business comprehension for business teleconferencing. *The Asian ESP Journal*, 8(2), 103–124.

Reason, P., & Bradbury, H. (2001). *The Sage handbook of action research: Participative inquiry and practice* (1st ed.). London: Sage.

CHAPTER 13

Teacher Research

Simon Borg

INTRODUCTION

Teacher research is systematic inquiry conducted by teachers, individually or collaboratively, in their own professional contexts, which aims to enhance teachers' understandings of some aspect of their own work, and is made public in some way – i.e., it is not a wholly private activity. Methodologically, teacher research is inclusive and allows for a range of both qualitative and quantitative strategies for collecting and analyzing data. Teacher research is not synonymous with action research (see Chapter 12), nor with reflective practice. It is a broader term which covers various approaches to research conducted by teachers in their own contexts. Action research is but one of these approaches and is defined by a cyclical research design and a concern for introducing and evaluating practical change; whilst reflective practice may occur privately and does not require the levels of systematicity, transparency, and public scrutiny that teacher research – in common with all types of research – must be subject to.

BACKGROUND

Teacher research can be traced back to the emergence of action research in the USA in the 1940s, through the teacher research movement in the UK in the 1970s, and the growth of reflective practice in 1980s, again in the USA. Common to these movements was a drive to democratize education and make it a more participatory process; from this perspective it was desirable to view teachers as autonomous investigators of their own work. In language education, interest in teacher research dates back to the 1980s, a time when greater emphasis started to be placed on the importance of research grounded in the realities of the classroom. In time, it was also recognized that teachers themselves were ideally placed to undertake such research. Today, teacher research is recognized as having the potential to be a powerful transformative force in the professional development of language teachers and numerous benefits to teachers, learners and schools of teacher research have been identified in the literature (see, for example, Sharp, 2007). However, despite these benefits – claimed or proven – in practice, the global prevalence of teacher research in language education remains low. In the next section I will outline some of the key issues related to teacher research that have been highlighted in the literature.

Research on this Topic

The literature associated with teacher research in language education is vast. One strand of work consists of practical manuals which give teachers advice on how to conduct research in their own working contexts. A second strand consists of publications that have been generated as a result of teacher research (for a recent review of collections of language teacher research, see Burns, 2010b). A third, and more recent, strand of work examines what research means to language teachers and what factors hinder or support their efforts to be research engaged. I will comment on these different strands of literature in turn.

In terms of practical research manuals for teachers, several exist. Generally, though, it is often difficult to discern much in them that is distinctively about teacher research rather than about educational research more generally. This emphasizes the point that in terms of methodological procedures – for example, the way that data are collected and analyzed – teacher research is not in fact distinctive. In other words, teacher research is not defined by its methodological procedures but by the identity of the researcher (one or more teachers); the site of the research (teachers' context); and the purposes of the research (primarily understanding one's context). One other observation I would make about research methods manuals for teachers is that they often imply that doing research is mainly a matter of technical competence and gloss over the attitudinal and practical problems that are often a significant barrier to productive teacher research engagement. Teachers do of course need the technical competence to conduct satisfactory studies, but this is only part of the equation, and many teachers' reluctance or inability to be research engaged does not stem from a lack of methodological knowledge.

Moving on to the second strand of work noted above, a growing body of published accounts of teacher research in language education has emerged in recent years. These typically take the form of edited collections – for example, TESOL's *Language teacher research in ...* series, with volumes from different continents. The volume of published teacher research is not insignificant – in the sense that it would take some time for anyone to read through every individual paper published. However, relative to the scale of language education as a global enterprise, teacher research remains a minority activity. There are clear reasons for this, as I discuss below. Two further critiques (see Borg, 2010) of much published teacher research are that a) the teachers are very often university-based (rather than in schools) and b) the research done has been completed as part of an academic degree. There is nothing fundamentally objectionable about either of these phenomena; their prevalence, though, does support my general view that teacher research remains a rather exclusive activity. The fact that teacher research often occurs in the context of formal programs of study also highlights two features which do make a significant positive difference to the extent to which teacher research is productive. The first is the availability of a mentor; in formal contexts this is typically the supervisor, but in other more general contexts it is equally important for teachers to have access to a more experienced and expert (in research terms) mentor who can provide appropriate guidance. The second is structure: the need to complete a task within a specific time-scale during formal study does focus the mind; in contrast, teacher research – which is open-ended – runs a greater risk of never being finished. I return to these and other considerations for improving the productivity of teacher research later.

The third strand of literature relevant to teacher research introduced above is characterized by a concern for understanding, from the perspectives of language teachers, what research is and what role it plays in their professional lives. My own research in recent years has focused on these issues (for example, Borg, 2013) and has provided insight into some of the key conceptual, attitudinal, and practical barriers which exist in relation to teacher research. Conceptually, one enduring problem is the multiple ways in which 'research' is interpreted by language teaching professionals – teachers, managers, and teacher educators – around the world. These interpretations exist on a continuum, with highly formal academic notions of scientific – for example, large-scale, experimental – research at one end, and very loose, informal, often pedagogical – for example designing instructional materials – views of what constitutes research at the other. Neither of these extremes is satisfactory as a definition of teacher research, allowing it to function as a productive strategy for the professional development of language teachers. In contrast, the definition proposed at the start of this chapter – while acknowledging the need for systematicity and transparency in teacher research – also emphasizes the teacher-driven and pedagogical-professional orientation of such inquiry.

Attitudinal barriers also hinder productive engagement in research by teachers. These often stem from inappropriate conceptions of what research is – for example, a teacher who believes that research must be large-scale and statistical will not feel it is an activity they can engage in. In my research, teachers and managers have also referred to colleagues they knew who were interested in research, but incompetent classroom practitioners: the argument in this case is that being research engaged is not related to one's quality as a teacher. The converse argument – that many good teachers are not interested in research – has also been presented to me on several occasions. I do not dispute either of these arguments. The response to the first is that teacher research is but one of many professional development options available to teachers and it would be wrong to suggest that all teachers should be doing teacher research. Regarding the second argument, the assumption that professional development is not required because there are no obvious problems to be addressed is professionally limiting: teacher research has the potential to support professional growth even in excellent teachers. Overall, attitudinal barriers stemming from misconceptions about what teacher research is and of its role in teachers' lives are among the most powerful obstacles to making teacher research a more widespread and productive feature of language teaching.

Practical barriers to teacher research, of course cannot be ignored. In particular, a lack of time is the most commonly cited reason teachers give when asked why they do not engage in and with research more often. Lack of access to mentoring and to resources – for example relevant literature – are also commonly reported obstacles. It is clear that if, as a field, we are serious about transforming the rhetoric that surrounds teacher research into practice, attention must be given to creating conducive conditions, and for this a significant part of the responsibility resides with decision-makers such as ministry officials, head teachers, and school directors. Yet teachers often sense a tension between what their institutions are encouraging them to do vis-à-vis research and the actual support the institution provides. Clearly, understanding the practical conditions that support teacher research and considering ways of creating these need to be central considerations in any attempt to enable teachers to be research engaged.

I have discussed three strands of literature which are relevant to our focus here on teacher research in language education. An analysis of this work indicates that the profile of teacher research in language education continues to grow and much practical advice for teacher researchers exists. However, it is also the case that a concern for technical matters – for example, collecting and analyzing data – tends to obscure powerful conceptual, attitudinal, and practical constraints which limit the extent to which teacher research can function as a productive professional development strategy for language teachers, and much more research into these issues is required.

Practical Applications

I will comment here on the implementation of teacher research from three perspectives – that of the teacher researcher, the school leader, and the facilitator of teacher research. In each case my focus will be on practical strategies for making teacher research work.

From the teacher's perspective, the starting point for teacher research needs to be their desire to understand some aspect of their work; this need may be expressed as a question, a problem, or a puzzle (see Allwright and Hanks, 2009, for a discussion of puzzles in an approach to teacher research called exploratory practice). It is important, though, to avoid an exclusively deficit-oriented approach to teacher research – in other words, teacher research is not simply a strategy for resolving problems. In fact, a narrow focus on finding immediate solutions to pedagogical problems oversimplifies the purposes of teacher research and limits its potential to support the longer-term development of teachers. Once teachers have identified a focus for their inquiries, decisions must be made about the evidence required to provide insight into the issues under study. This is the stage of data collection and numerous options are available here to teachers – for example, anecdotal field notes, drawings and photos of classroom events, audio or video recordings of classroom events, samples of student work, feedback from students on reaction slips or evaluation forms, assessment data, curricular documents and individual, group, and class discussions with students. In order to make teacher research sustainable it is desirable for teachers to integrate it as closely as possible into their routine classroom practices, and data can very often be generated without substantial modifications to what teachers normally do. However, while integration of this kind is desirable, it is inevitable that teacher research, in common with any form of professional development that teachers engage in, will make some additional demands on teachers' time. It is therefore important that the scope of teacher research – for example, the kinds of questions that are being addressed, the volume of data that is being collected, and the timetable that teachers set for their work – is kept realistic. Sustainability can also be enhanced when teacher research is collaborative among teachers and possibly with support from an external collaborator or mentor.

The evidence that teachers collect will need to be processed in some way – it is through data analysis that evidence becomes transformed into results. Analysis in teacher research very often takes place alongside data collection rather than after it. Teacher research will not normally call for high levels of expertise in processing data (for example complex statistical analyses); teachers, though, will need some familiarity with basic procedures for working with numerical data (for example, frequency distributions and other descriptive statistics) or for making sense of non-numerical data (e.g., visuals, interviews). Support with such matters is provided in manuals of the type discussed above, both within language education and in education more broadly (for example, Campbell, McNamara, and Gilroy, 2004). When the evidence has been analyzed, teachers examine their results in order to understand what conclusions can be extracted from them and what pedagogical decisions the results suggest might be of value to learners. The results may also suggest issues that can be examined through a further cycle of teacher research, although it would be unrealistic to expect teachers to be doing teacher research in an ongoing manner; it will be more feasible as a periodic activity that takes place at times during the school year when conditions are most conducive. Finally, we must not forget that because research is not a private activity teachers should share their findings in some *public* way; various more and less formal options for doing so exist (orally and/or in writing) and Burns (2010a) provides an excellent discussion of these.

School leaders also have a significant influence on the extent to which teachers work in an environment that is conducive to teacher research (Sharp, Eames, Sanders, and Tomlinson, 2006). The following are examples of the kinds of actions (based on Borg, 2013) that school leaders can take to promote such an environment:

- actively promote teacher research and give it a high profile within the school;
- ensure that teachers and managers in the school have a shared understanding of the value of teacher research;
- support the development of networks of teacher researchers within the school;
- find out which teachers are interested in doing teacher research and what support they need;
- help teachers identify research that is relevant to the school's work;
- create opportunities for teachers to share their research findings with other teachers;
- support teachers in gaining access to relevant resources;
- provide training for teachers which support teacher research;
- reward teachers' commitment to research;
- show an interest in and acknowledgement of the research teachers do;
- use the results of teacher research to inform policy and practice in the school.

By creating a conducive working environment school leaders can have a significant impact on the extent that teacher research takes place and contributes to the development of teachers, learners, and the school generally.

Finally, teacher research is often supported by a facilitator; this may be a more senior or experienced member of staff within a school, an external collaborator from a local college or university, or an external consultant brought in (perhaps even from overseas) by an organization or Ministry. Desirable characteristics for the facilitator are that they are active researchers themselves, understand what teacher research is, are sensitive to teachers' contexts, and are skilled in supporting and motivating teacher research. Facilitators often lead teacher research within the framework of a project or a course and with such a context in mind, here are some practical measures that facilitators can take to make teacher research a more productive experience for teachers:

1. Provide space for teachers to explore their beliefs about research and to clarify their understandings of what teacher research is. It is important to do this at an early stage.
2. Make quality a core concern from the outset – the findings of teacher research cannot provide a reliable basis for pedagogical or institutional decision-making if the research has not been done carefully.
3. Make teachers' own investigations the focus of the initiative; theoretical input and discussion should support practical inquiry rather than becoming an end in itself.
4. Facilitate as far as possible teachers' access to resources, such as electronic journals and books on how to do research.
5. Encourage teachers to investigate issues that are of professional relevance to them and to their schools, and which have potential benefits for their learners.
6. Create some degree of choice for teachers in deciding what to focus their projects on and how to carry out their research.
7. Support teachers in creating a structure for their teacher research projects – for example, by helping them create a timetable with intermediate milestones.
8. Work towards a final concrete output – for example, a short written report and/or presentations at a staff meeting or similar event.

9. Advise sponsors so that the time made available to teachers to do teacher research is realistic. Projects should develop thoughtfully rather than being rushed.
10. Ideally, workshops for teachers taking part on a teacher research course should alternate with phases of practical activity during which teachers complete parts of their research. This is preferable to completing all the input before teachers have started their projects.
11. Create mechanisms (online and/or face to face) through which teachers can receive regular feedback on their work from the facilitator and from one another.
12. Keep sponsors updated on teachers' progress and on any support they need.

Conclusion

Teacher research has undeniable potential for supporting teacher professional development and enhancing the quality of the educational experience learners receive. It does, however, make demands on teachers which they can only cope with when working conditions conducive to teacher research exist. Research conducted in recent years has provided much valuable insight into the factors which hinder efforts to promote teacher research, and while a lack of time remains a central constraint for teachers, it is also clear that there are additional and in some cases more powerful conceptual, attitudinal, contextual, physical, and technical barriers which need to be addressed if we are to promote teacher research more effectively in our field. It is also clear – as I noted earlier – that teacher research is but one of many professional development options available to teachers; the argument, then, should never be that teachers *should* be doing teacher research but that, where appropriate, it can promote powerful teacher learning. In other cases, where the conditions are patently unfavorable, teacher research will be neither desirable nor appropriate, and other forms of professional development will be more germane.

The facilitation of teacher research is one particular issue where our understandings remain undeveloped. I have listed here some practical suggestions, based on my own experience around the world, which individuals who facilitate teacher research can benefit from. However, we need more empirical insight into these matters – for example, via case studies from diverse contexts which focus on the work of the facilitator and through which we can develop a knowledge base that is grounded in and can subsequently inform the many substantive, instructional, and organizational decisions that facilitators must make when they are setting up and delivering workshops, courses, and projects to support teacher research. In education, there is a literature on how to teach research methods courses more generally and there has been some similar work in language education (for example, Diab, 2006); insights into what facilitators do when they *teach* teacher research, however, remain limited.

Discussion Questions

1. Think of a language education context you are familiar with and assess how conducive you feel it is to teacher research. What elements in the context are supportive of teacher research? Which elements hinder teacher research?

2. Have you conducted any teacher research yourself? If you have, what were the main challenges you faced in doing it? What benefits did you or anyone else (including your learners) experience as a result of the work?

3. This chapter argues that teacher research is not a private activity and that the findings therefore need to be made public in some way. If you design a study, collect and analyze

data systematically, but keep the results wholly private, do you think that this should or should not be called research?

4. This chapter also distinguishes between teacher research, action research and reflective practice. What do you feel the distinctions between these activities are? Do they have anything in common?

5. Have you ever facilitated teacher research by supporting others in doing it? If so, describe your experience and comment on effective and less effective aspects of your work as a facilitator.

6. Some teachers feel that their job is to teach, not to do research. What arguments might you use to encourage teachers to question this belief?

7. In teacher research, do you think that it is necessary for teachers to find out about what has already been written relevant to their topic? Or can teacher research be conducted without any reference to the existing literature?

8. Should the quality of teacher research be assessed against the same criteria that are applied to research generally? Or should criteria unique to teacher research be used?

References

Allwright, D., & Hanks, J. (2009). *The developing language learner: An introduction to exploratory practice*. Basingstoke, UK: Palgrave Macmillan.

Borg, S. (2010). Language teacher research engagement. *Language Teaching*, 43(4), 391–429.

Borg, S. (2013). *Teacher research in language teaching: A critical analysis*. Cambridge: Cambridge University Press.

Burns, A. (2010a). *Doing action research in English language teaching. A guide for practitioners*. New York: Routledge.

Burns, A. (2010b). Teacher engagement in research: Published resources for teacher researchers. *Language Teaching*, 43(4), 527–536.

Campbell, A., McNamara, O., & Gilroy, P. (2004). *Practitioner research and professional development in education*. London: Paul Chapman.

Diab, R. L. (2006). Teaching practice and student learning in the introductory research methods class. *TESL-EJ*, 10(2), no page numbers.

Sharp, C. (2007). *Making research make a difference. Teacher research: A small-scale study to look at impact*. Chelmsford: Flare.

Sharp, C., Eames, A., Sanders, D., & Tomlinson, K. (2006). *Leading a research-engaged school*. Nottingham: National College for School Leadership.

CHAPTER 14

Case-study Research

Patricia A. Duff and Tim Anderson

Introduction

A *case study* generally constitutes a qualitative, interpretive approach to understanding the experiences, features, behaviors, and processes of a bounded (a specific or defined) unit. The essence and value of a case study resides in its – typically – holistic and in-depth characterization of individual entities within a particular context, which permits researchers and readers to gain grounded new understandings of certain issues. Generally, the 'cases' in our field are language learners, teachers, speakers, or writers, but the case can be representative of other entities, such as a family, a program, a school, or even a country, where particular language practices are salient and the complexities, interactions, and dynamics of the system can be examined within the fullness of the case.

Case-study research has been used productively in second language teaching and learning research for many decades, as well as in other areas of applied linguistics, the social sciences, and other fields. One of the most compelling aspects of case-study research is that researchers can describe and account for the many factors and contingencies (for example, social, cultural, political, geographical, temporal, inter- and intra-personal) affecting a single entity. When that entity is a person, moreover, it is possible to gain a nuanced first-hand perspective of the participant's experiences and what they mean for him or her, in addition to the researchers' and others' perspectives on a person's attributes, behaviors, or performance. The concrete presentation of the case within this kind of ecology of factors, interactions, and interpretations can provide a vivid illustration or exemplar of more abstract principles.

For an example of how this process might work, let us consider Anna, a hypothetical case. Anna is an international graduate student from Asia attending an English-medium university in North America. Although quite proficient in oral English and academically very strong, Anna struggles with writing. Yet to perform well in her current courses and continue with graduate studies, she must become a more confident and capable writer in English according to the norms and expectations in her field. She has therefore enrolled in an "English for Academic Purposes" (EAP) writing course. As a researcher, you wish to find out more about Anna's educational background and her experiences, growth, challenges, interactions, and resourcefulness as a writer. You decide to examine Anna's progress through her EAP course, and monitor her performance in her content courses over two semesters. From the many possible aspects of Anna's writing to be explored, you decide to focus on her socialization into written academic discourse – that is, the forms of assistance provided by past and present instructors, tutors, peers, and other resources (for example, textbooks, sample essays, word-processing supports) that mediate her literacy practices; how she engages with those human and other resources within this socio-educational context; and the writing that results. You note that recent reviews of the L2 writing literature reveal that this is a promising avenue of research of relevance to scholars in applied linguistics and academic writing as well as for EAP instructors, L2 writers, and university programs. Anna is therefore a case of EAP writing, socialization, and development, and the evolving identity of an academic writer in a particular university context.

Background

Since the 1970s, when the fields of second language acquisition (SLA) and L2 education first blossomed, case-study research has played a critical role in theory development, research, and even teaching methods (see Duff, 2008, 2012a, 2012b, 2014, for more detailed overviews). Early studies offered analyses of individual learners' first-language (L1), bilingual, or L2 development, typically with English as a target language. What emerged were vivid and detailed descriptions of emerging linguistic systems affected by a number of factors, such as the learners' L1 knowledge, the linguistic properties of the L2, creative hypothesis-testing, generalization, the restructuring of learners' knowledge based on new experience (and other cognitive/psychological processes), and the socio-educational and sociolinguistic context in which learning or language use took place. In contrast with other research approaches, however, the field also came to know the case-study participants as unique people – children, adolescents, or adults involved in L2 teaching, learning, and use in particular linguistic, cultural, and social settings (even if those settings were not at the time fully described by the researchers). The case-study participants, the phenomena being examined, and their social contexts are in many ways inseparable, as current theorizing in SLA informed by dynamic systems, sociocultural theory, and ecological perspectives demonstrates.

Many seminal case studies came out of first-generation and subsequent case-study research. In the interim, the research questions addressed and populations sampled have expanded considerably to include a wider range of social, affective, personal, cultural, linguistic, and political factors in multilingual and transnational contexts. These include (foreign) language immersion, study abroad, refugee settlement, and language revitalization within indigenous communities, among many other contexts (see Duff, 2008, 2012a, 2012b, 2014). Research participants now range from very young children to the elderly, engaging with language(s) in particular ways, in their primary home communities or in others. Also featured increasingly are people in intercultural situations (including educational contexts) negotiating the complexities of the globalized knowledge economy where certain languages/literacies, ideologies, cultures, knowledge(s), and practices are privileged over others. Learners' linguistic and other (for example, textual) identities, dispositions, behaviors, and production have been examined in case studies in relation to their current or prospective communities of practice and in terms of their learning trajectories (past, present, and future). Indeed, an examination of people's experiences, development, and participation in particular communities over a longer term is much more feasible in case study than in studies with larger numbers of participants.

The narratives of case-study participants, such as teachers, learners, and speakers or writers describing their experiences, are becoming more common sources of data than in the past, although interactional data and other forms of observational and documentary evidence (for example, artifacts) are also included in many analyses (see Table 14.1). In the hypothetical study of Anna, for instance, researchers would normally want to elicit an oral or written narrative of her history and ongoing experiences as a writer. In much contemporary case-study research in applied linguistics, multiple case studies rather than single cases are the new norm, providing several instances of the phenomenon in question and thereby addressing – to some extent – issues of typicality and variation between and among cases that are often not possible to address in a single case. Recruiting several of Anna's classmates to participate in the study would likely reveal intriguing differences across them as well as similarities.

Research on this Topic

The remainder of this article describes how to conduct case-study research. The discussion and examples that follow pertain to case studies involving L2 writers, such as Anna, a common context for case-study research given the educational stakes associated with being a proficient, strategic, and effective writer, especially in English (Casanave, 2002). For a more comprehensive introduction to case-study research in education in terms of underlying principles and practical methods for undertaking studies, and examples, consult Merriam (1998), Stake (2006), and Yin (2014). Dyson and Genishi (2005) discuss case-study research methods in the area of L1 language/literacy, especially with young learners in classrooms. For sample studies and guidelines for L2 case studies across a broad range of themes, populations, and languages, see Duff (2008, 2012a, 2012b, 2014).

The first two steps in conducting case-study research are a) finding a suitable, timely, and interesting issue to investigate that is informed by current theoretical and empirical research, and b) identifying a potential site (context) or individual(s) in which to explore the target issues. (Sometimes the latter step occurs first, such as when a researcher encounters a student with unusual challenges, behaviors, circumstances, or abilities and the researcher seeks to investigate the situation and broader issues as a result; alternatively, one can start with an issue in mind and then recruit participants – or seek cases – accordingly.) A number of other aspects of a case study must then be explored, related to the sampling and selection of participants (cases), the unit(s) of analysis, methods and types of data collection, data analysis and interpretation, and the writing up of the report (for example, as a thesis, a dissertation, a journal article or chapter, or a technical report). Table 14.1 presents some of these key considerations and components in case-study research to be discussed in the following section.

Practical Applications

Qualitative case-study research in applied linguistics has robust and diverse possibilities. In seeking explanations for specific – often exciting and illuminating – phenomena, case studies typically employ a variety of data collection methods and options, as shown in Table 14.1, and unfold over a span of time involving either individuals or groups constituting the bounded systems or cases sampled. One consideration when conducting case-study research is the benefits and limitations of a single versus multiple case study and which

Crucial elements in case-study research

Preparing/defining research parameters:
- research questions
- theoretical rationale and relevant existing research
- contextualization and description of individuals/sites
- reflexivity about the researcher's own positionality and role with respect to the case, site, or issue
- research ethics, protections of case(s), issues of reciprocity with participants
- methodology – choice of research design and case (population/sites) and units of analysis

Recruitment and sampling strategy:
- one or more focal cases? rationale? others to include from case context, such as instructors, tutors, or other writers?
- sampling: e.g., random, convenience, purposeful?
- selection for relative representativeness (typicality/atypicality – and how that is ascertained) or maximal variation (e.g., contrasts, extreme cases)? explanation
- duration of study: shorter-term or longitudinal, and reasoning for choice and for interpretations (especially when drawing developmental inferences)

Data collection:
- direct observations (if relevant): in what manner, by whom, how often, with what duration, and recorded by what means?
- captured by introspection, through think-aloud protocols, measurement, through narrative retrospection, through drafts and final products of the writing itself (with or without oral/written feedback on writing that might have been obtained)?
- data elicited through interviews, solicited narratives (e.g., journals, logs), email correspondence, stimulated recall, or other sources?
- other document analysis, such as course outlines, writing models, policies, test results, PPT slides from presentations, etc.

Data analysis:
- using computer-assisted qualitative data analysis tools or more manual coding (if relevant)?
- thematic coding or linguistic/textual coding?
- within-case analysis and cross-case analysis?
- measurement and/or data reduction strategies?
- discussion of "trustworthiness" or "dependability" of analysis
- possible role of research participants in providing feedback (member checks) on transcription or data analysis
- triangulation (if relevant) of data from multiple sources and perspectives

Written report:
- presented case by case (or with clusters of cases), theme by theme, or in sequence in response to individual research questions?
- use of vignettes?
- selection of data (e.g., excerpts) to be included, and explanation of selection strategy and means of interpreting and representing findings
- relationship between findings and existing research literature
- discussion of limitations or constraints on generalizability or transferability (analytical/theoretical or statistical/inferential)
- implications for education and for future research and theory
- issues of researcher/writer "voice" and genre in written report and ways of capturing research participants' voices

Table 14.1   Crucial Elements in Case-study Research

type would best suit the phenomenon being investigated. For example, a case study conducted on the socialization of L2 writers into academic discourse practices at the tertiary level could focus on a single writer (a single case study, such as Anna); several writers (a multiple case study, such as Anna and three of her classmates); or even a writing support group or cohort (which might constitute its own case with several focal participants or cases embedded within it; or, alternatively, Anna's EAP course could be the case, with Anna and several classmates as cases nested within this larger unit). The unit of analysis, in turn, might be the production of the final term paper for the course and the various social, cognitive, linguistic/literate, and educational factors affecting its production.

The benefits of a single case-study design include the ability to deeply explore phenomena by concentrating on only one research participant (Anna), a single L2 writer in this case, and one bounded phenomenon such as the socialization of the participant into L2 writing practices in a particular field. A single case study of an individual L2 writer can reveal factors impacting the participant's academic discourse socialization at both a given period of time and longitudinally (over an extended length of time). One could examine, for example, the influence of the student's supervisor, advisor, or others on writing development, and how feedback practices can shape written discourse and one's sense of legitimacy as a writer. In this way, the co-construction of academic (discursive) expertise and identity could be investigated. Not all single case studies are longitudinal, though, and there are several potential challenges with longitudinal studies aimed at capturing change over time: these include the possibility that the lone participant will be unable to remain in the study for logistical reasons (for example, due to heavy workload), or might prove less interesting than expected in terms of writing processes and reflections on them, or might withdraw from the study for other reasons. Unlike a multiple case-study design involving several participants, having one person withdraw from a single case study effectively terminates the research process until another suitable participant can be recruited.

Multiple case studies, on the other hand, investigate several related cases of a similar phenomenon and involve two or more people or groups – where the group is considered a unit or case of something. Such a case study might be ethnographic in nature, exploring social and cultural processes, patterns, and meanings, or it might not fundamentally deal with such sociocultural issues. In L2 writing research, for example, a multiple case study might investigate various international tertiary – for example, college or university – students' production of academic discourse and could involve interviews and narrative inquiry, as well as other methods such as observations in class or when participants meet with supervisors, professors, or tutors to discuss writing. The benefits of a multiple case-study approach in this scenario include its potential for uncovering various factors which contribute to the socialization of L2 writers, yielding different exemplars and possibly contradictory experiences, perceptions, and outcomes with respect to those writers. Multiple cases allow for a multiplicity of voices (perspectives) to be heard and enable the researcher to subsequently draw on multiple data sources during analysis and writing (see sample studies in Duff, 2008, Chapters 3–4). For example, Casanave's (2002) study of five MA students in an applied linguistics program in the U.S. investigated the "writing games" that both L1 and L2 graduate students learned to take part in during their academic programs, and the importance of acquiring not only appropriate linguistic conventions and academic genres but also political and social strategies to survive and thrive as graduate students. Casanave's study offers valuable insights into many aspects of these L1 and L2 writers' lives as budding (English) academics and teachers, the barriers they encountered on their journeys, the struggles and successes they faced, and the games (strategic enterprises) they engaged in to succeed. Although multiple case studies can provide abundant information to describe and explain certain phenomena, one potential challenge in comparison to single case studies is the increased time, resources, and skill required to collect, manage, analyze, interpret and then represent multiple data sources in one study or report. On a more positive note, the richness, similarities, and differences among cases make it a particularly fruitful approach to case-study research because it also reveals potential disparities and possible explanations for them. These can be discussed in within-case and cross-case analyses.

Another essential consideration (see Table 14.1) is the sampling strategy to be used. One approach might be to seek typicality or representativeness (meaning the features of the cases are fairly common in the set or population from which they are drawn) or homogeneity in case selection – i.e., selecting cases that are very similar to one another in terms of, for example, age, ethnicity, proficiency, gender, or other features deemed most relevant. Alternatively, sampling might involve contrasting very different and even extreme cases: these could be very atypical cases or outliers, or cases demonstrating maximum variation, such as being opposites – for example, extremely skilled and effective writers vs. extremely unskilled ones. Some might argue that all cases are, by definition, unique, particular, singular, and therefore non-representative of others. However, there may be ways of demonstrating relative degrees of typicality within a particular context or group – for example, through the use of surveys (Duff, 2008). Finally, after conducting the case study – taking into account the features in the table related to research ethics, methods for undertaking the study and analyzing data, and reporting decisions – the researcher must decide how best to present the cases, contexts, and themes arising from the analysis in such a way as to make the report engaging, original, and theoretically (and educationally) relevant.

Conclusion

Case study remains a very powerful methodology for language researchers and for theory development in applied linguistics and language education. What it may lack in generalizability, it makes up for in its detailed portrayal of issues, settings, individuals, and interactions. Just as biographies help readers understand the lives of individuals in all their complexity and are not intended for generalization to the wider population, the case study researcher and reader come to know the focal participant(s) well and gain empathy for them and an understanding of their linguistic experiences and circumstances within their unique – but possibly common – learning ecologies. New understandings of what it means to be a contemporary language learner, teacher, or user in a particular area result.

Discussion Questions

1. What kinds of case studies in second language acquisition or education or other fields have you read before? Which have appealed most to you, and why? (You can find many examples in Duff, 2008, Chapter 3 or in Duff, 2014.) What strategies did the researchers/authors use that you found especially helpful and engaging?

2. If you were to conduct a case study in your teaching/learning context, what might your focus be? Why? What other research has been conducted on that recently? Who would your research participants be? Would you choose a single case study or a multiple case study and what would your sampling strategy be?

3. What characteristics and issues of the case would you focus on? Would there be sufficient characteristics and issues to be investigated? Could you get access to enough data sources? Would the study design be short-term or longitudinal?

4. What types of data collection techniques might be best suited for the study? Do these techniques enable you to answer the *how* and *why* of the phenomena?

5. How might you write up the study to make it interesting to readers?

References

Casanave, C. (2002). *Writing games: Multicultural case studies of academic literacy practices in higher education.* Mahwah, NJ: Lawrence Erlbaum.

Duff, P. (2008). *Case study research in applied linguistics.* New York, NY: Lawrence Erlbaum/Taylor & Francis.

Duff, P. (2012a). How to carry out case study research. In A. Mackey & S. M. Gass (Eds.), *Research methods in second language acquisition: A practical guide* (pp. 95–116). Malden, MA: Wiley-Blackwell.

Duff, P. (2012b). Case study research. In C. Chapelle (Ed.), *The encyclopedia of applied linguistics.* Malden, MA: Wiley-Blackwell.

Duff, P. (2014). Case study research on language learning and use. *Annual Review of Applied Linguistics,* 34, 233–255.

Dyson, A. H., & Genishi, C. (2005). *On the case: Approaches to language and literacy research.* New York: Teachers College Press and the National Conference on Research in Language and Literacy.

Merriam, S. (1998). *Qualitative research and case study applications in education* (2nd ed.). San Francisco: Jossey-Bass.

Stake, R. E. (2006). *Multiple case study analysis.* New York: Guilford.

Yin, R. K. (2014). *Case study research: Design and methods* (5th ed.). Los Angeles, CA: Sage.

CHAPTER 15

Corpus Research

Jesse Egbert, Shelley Staples and Douglas Biber

INTRODUCTION AND BACKGROUND

Corpus linguistics is a method of using computers to investigate patterns of language use within a large, principled collection of authentic texts, or a corpus (plural: corpora; see Biber, Conrad, and Reppen, 1998). Findings from corpus research inform our understanding of how words and grammatical features are actually used. These patterns of language use are usually not addressed in traditional language textbooks, so the findings from corpus research can play an important role in language teaching, complementing traditional treatments.

There are many corpora that are freely available for language teaching and research. The 100 million-word British National Corpus was designed to be a representative sample of British English in the 1990s. It can be accessed for free via a number of web-based interfaces. The largest available corpus of American English is the Corpus of Contemporary American English (COCA). COCA is a powerful and user-friendly corpus that is widely used by language teachers and learners. Two additional examples are the Michigan Corpus of Upper-level Student Papers (MICUSP) and the Michigan Corpus of Academic Spoken English (MICASE). These two freely available corpora are especially useful for English for Academic Purposes (EAP) applications.

According to Reppen (2010), there are four main ways in which corpora can be used in the classroom: a) using published materials that are informed by corpus research; b) creating your own materials based on corpus research; c) having students use existing corpora to do their own investigations of language (data-driven learning or DDL); and d) creating your own corpus to meet your learners' needs. These four uses of corpora represent four levels of involvement that teachers can have with corpora, beginning with simply using existing materials based on authentic language use and ending with actually performing corpus research. As most language teachers are likely to be more interested in effective curriculum and teaching methods than in empirical research, this chapter will focus mostly on uses a) and b). However, we will also discuss c) and d) in the section titled "Corpora in the Classroom."

In this chapter, we will begin by giving an overview of the use of corpora – large and principled collections of authentic language – in different areas of language research, including vocabulary, grammar, register variation, and learner language. We will then discuss findings and advances in corpus linguistics in terms of their practical applications for language teaching and materials development. We will conclude with a brief summary of key issues and future directions in corpus research. In each of the sections we will focus on corpus research of English, but it should be noted that corpus methods are used to study many languages of the world.

CORPUS-BASED RESEARCH

VOCABULARY

There has been a long tradition of relying on corpora for the development of dictionaries. In addition to improving the comprehensiveness of dictionary entries, corpus-based lexicography is employed to order word senses based on their relative frequency. The use of large corpora has also facilitated the development of word frequency dictionaries and collocation dictionaries, which describe commonly co-occurring word patterns (see McEnery and Hardie, 2012). These dictionaries are particularly useful for learners. Learner dictionaries rely heavily on corpus data in order to base dictionary entries on the relative frequencies of words and word senses, and to introduce key collocational patterns. The Collins Birmingham University International Language Database (COBUILD) is widely recognized as the first large-scale effort to develop a monolingual learner dictionary (a learner dictionary written entirely in the target language) based on the Bank of English corpus. Since the publication of the *Collins COBUILD English Language Dictionary* in 1987, many corpus-informed learner dictionaries have been published, including the *Longman Dictionary of Contemporary English* and the *Cambridge Advanced Learner's Dictionary*.

For decades, corpus research on vocabulary use has been largely concerned with creating lists of commonly used words. These word lists have been compiled for general English, as well as for more specific domains and varieties. Such lists can be used by teachers to determine essential vocabulary, particularly for EAP and English for Specific Purposes (ESP). A particularly influential example is Coxhead's (2000) *Academic Word List*, which contains 570 words selected based on their raw frequencies in a corpus of 3.5 million words of written academic English, balanced across four major disciplines and 28 subject areas. A newer academic word list, the *Academic Vocabulary List,* has recently been developed by Davies and Gardner. The complete *Academic Vocabulary List,* along with several useful tools that allow users to input their own texts to learn about vocabulary use, can be found at: http://www.wordandphrase.info/academic/.

Phraseology studies can be seen as an extension of lexical research to multi-word units, often called "formulaic expressions," or strings of words that commonly co-occur – for example, "on the other hand." Corpus research has revealed that such expressions are an important part of native and native-like speech and writing. Within academic writing in English, studies have shown that the use of formulaic sequences by learners, especially lower-level learners, differs from that of native English speaking writers (for example, Staples, Egbert, Biber, and McClair, 2013). English language teachers can draw on a number of corpus-based studies that have helped to identify multi-word units frequently used by native speakers in natural conversation as well as academic speech and writing (see, for example, Biber, Johansson, Leech, Conrad, and Finegan, 1999: Chapter 15; Simpson-Vlach and Ellis, 2010).

GRAMMAR

Corpus linguists have performed extensive research on the grammar of English, as well as many other languages. However, Biber and Reppen (2002) found that ESL/EFL materials often present English grammar in a way that does not represent patterns of authentic language use. For example, many grammar textbooks introduce progressive aspect before simple aspect, but Biber and Reppen (2002) used corpus data to show that the simple aspect is much more common in both conversation and writing.

The development and use of corpus-based pedagogical grammars is a more recent trend, but one that is quickly gaining popularity. The most comprehensive corpus-based grammar textbook to date is the *Longman Student Grammar of Spoken and Written English* (Biber, Conrad, and Leech, 2002) and the accompanying Workbook (Conrad, Biber, and Leech, 2002). These are the first corpus-based pedagogical textbooks on English grammar which include both authentic examples and information regarding the use of grammatical features in spoken and written registers of American and British English. For example, one pattern often overlooked by traditional ESL grammars is the use of a noun to modify another noun (for example "behavior modification" or "compression process"). Biber, Johansson, Leech, Conrad, and Finegan (1999: 588–596) show that these noun-noun sequences are especially important in academic prose and newspaper writing. For example, "nouns account for almost 40% of all pre-modifiers in news, and c. 30% of all pre-modifiers in academic prose" (p. 589).

In addition to looking at lexical or grammatical patterns separately, corpus linguistics has also revealed that certain grammatical patterns favor particular lexical choices. For example, Biber et al. (1999: 477–480) find that certain verbs – for example, "based on," "positioned," "analyzed" – prefer the passive voice so strongly that they rarely occur in active voice. Findings such as these suggest that the traditional method of teaching vocabulary and grammar separately may limit learners' knowledge of both domains.

Teachers and students can perform their own corpus searches of lexical and grammatical features using freely available online corpora. One example of a user-friendly and powerful online corpus is COCA (www.americancorpus.org), which was created by Mark Davies. For example, a teacher can generate a list of the most frequent progressive aspect verbs by simply logging into COCA (free of charge), and entering the progressive aspect tag, which can be selected from the "POS list" dropdown menu, into the search field. This would yield a list of verbs that are frequently used in the progressive – for example, "going," "being," "doing," "trying," "looking," etc.

REGISTER

A register is a variety of language associated with a particular set of situational characteristics. A register may be defined generally – for example, academic writing – or more specifically – for example, introductory university textbooks. Regardless of the level of specificity, research on register variation has demonstrated that the use of language within a given context is functionally motivated by the situational characteristics of that context. One approach to the study of register variation is to use corpus linguistic methods to describe variation in the use of individual linguistic features. For example, as Biber et al. (1999: 486–490) show, both modals – for example, "can," "should" – and semi-modals – for example, "ought to," "be going to" – occur much more frequently in conversation than writing.

In addition to research that has looked at individual features, register differences can also be studied by analyzing the relationships among many language features. Multi-Dimensional (MD) analysis is one method that incorporates the frequencies of many linguistic features in order to produce comprehensive descriptions of registers (see Biber and Conrad, 2009: Chapter 8).

Register variation can be easily investigated by teachers and students using online tools such as COCA, and other related corpora from Mark Davies. As mentioned above, two other free corpora that can be used to look at that language of university registers are MICASE and MICUSP.

LEARNER CORPORA

Recently, interest in gathering corpora of learner language – writing and speaking by individuals who are in the process of learning a second or foreign language – has increased. One of the initial projects in this area was the International Corpus of Learner English (ICLE), a collection of argumentative essays written by EFL learners in 16 L1s (for example, Swedish, Chinese; Granger, Dagneaux, Meunier, and Paquot, 2002; 2009). The ICLE has been used to explore the use of interlanguage and innovation by learners of different language backgrounds (see, for example, Waibel, 2005; Paquot, 2013; Rimmer, 2011). Paquot (2013) explored the use of three-word recurrent sequences using a lexical verb in the French component of ICLE as compared with nine other ICLE sub-corpora, showing transfer effects of L1 French on the use of formulaic language. A spoken learner corpus, the Louvain International Database of Spoken English Interlanguage (LINDSEI), is now available as well (Gilquin, De Cock, and Granger, 2010). Most learner corpora research has focused on differences between L2 English writers/speakers and L1 English writers/speakers. Two comparable corpora have been developed for use with ICLE and LINDSEI, the Louvain Corpus of Native English Essays (LOCNESS) and the Louvain Corpus of Native English Conversation (LOCNEC), respectively. Using these corpora, researchers have investigated learners' use (or over- or underuse) in areas that have previously been identified as problematic, including use of coherence devices such as discourse markers, temporal adverbs or signaling nouns, as well as formulaic language (see, for example, Agerström, 2000; Aijmer, 2011; Paquot, 2013; Römer, Roberson, O'Donnell, and Ellis, 2011). Aijmer (2011), for example, investigated the use of "well" by learners and native speakers by comparing data from the Swedish component of LINDSEI with the speech of native English speakers in LOCNEC, finding that Swedish learners overall overuse "well" when compared with native English speakers. Importantly, though, many individual differences were noted. A useful bibliography of such studies can be found at http://www.uclouvain.be/en-cecl-lcbiblio.html. Learner corpora can be developed by teachers to determine common issues their own learners are having. However, coding for errors has proven to be challenging, and only a small number of corpora, such as the Cambridge Learners' Corpus (CLC), have attempted to comprehensively code the corpus for errors. Such corpora have a great deal of potential usefulness for teachers, however. For example, errors found in the CLC were used to inform the grammar series *Grammar and Beyond*, allowing the authors to empirically identify common errors made by learners.

Although all the corpora discussed above are focused on English language learners, a smaller number of corpora exist for learners of other languages, such as French (for example, French Interlanguage Database – FRIDA) and Spanish (for example, Northern Arizona University Spanish Learner Corpus). Asención Delaney and Collentine (2011) conducted a MD analysis of L2 Spanish showing that learners of Spanish are sensitive to register differences (here, narrative and expository writing), and that third-year learners showed greater development in expository writing as compared with second-year learners.

Practical Applications

Corpora in the Classroom

At the beginning of this chapter, we introduced four main ways that corpora can be used in the classroom: a) using corpus-informed materials; b) creating corpus-informed materials;

c) data-driven learning; and d) creating corpora to meet the needs of learners. This section contains details and examples of each of those four uses. While not the norm in materials development, the number of ESL and EAP textbooks that are informed by corpus findings is increasing. These books take two primary approaches (Reppen, 2010: 5–17). One is to integrate findings from corpora into a more traditional format. A recent example is the 2012 Cambridge University Press ESL grammar series *Grammar and Beyond*. This series uses research from the Cambridge International Corpus and other previous studies to present important grammatical patterns based on frequency of use and register differences. The sequencing of the forms was also based on information from the corpus (for example, present progressive is not presented until after the simple present and simple past, reflecting the frequency of these forms). In addition, the CLC is used to present common errors on particular forms covered. Other examples include a number of ESL textbooks based on the *Academic Word List* (for example, *Focus on Vocabulary*). A second approach looks quite different from traditional approaches and focuses on approaching language from a corpus-based perspective. *Real Grammar* (Conrad and Biber, 2009), for example, provides a brief summary on traditional treatments of grammatical forms, but primarily covers areas not found in textbooks. Unit 3 of the textbook focuses on "discovery verbs and existence verbs" (for example "show" vs. "consist") and how verb tense and aspect varies by the semantic category of verbs.

A second way in which corpora can be used in the classroom is for teachers to develop their own materials based on corpus research. For example, teachers might use one of the available corpus-based word lists to develop materials for use in their classroom as a supplement to a more traditional vocabulary textbook. This can be especially helpful when students are learning English for a specific purpose (for example, academic writing).

Another area which has seen increasing interest recently is data-driven learning or DDL. In this teaching method, students are guided by teachers to search corpora for particular forms – for example, vocabulary items or grammatical patterns – in context. Alternatively, students may be given output from a corpus search by teachers. Benefits to this type of instruction include learners' ability to see the frequency and constraints of forms and to develop a greater depth of understanding about forms – for example, collocations for vocabulary items – and increased noticing. For example, to work on verb + preposition patterns, teachers can ask students to search the word "consist" in COCA to see what prepositions commonly follow that verb – for example, "consist of."

Finally, teachers can create their own corpora for pedagogical purposes. For instance, by creating a corpus of students' readings, this can allow the teacher to determine frequent vocabulary that they might want to pre-teach if it is not already known by students. A pedagogical reading corpus also provides language at an appropriate level for learners, since texts from preexisting corpora may be too advanced for learners.

DOING CORPUS RESEARCH

In previous sections, we have introduced several online tools that are available to teachers for corpus investigations. In this section, we briefly introduce methods and tools that are available to teachers and students for performing research on their own corpora. These tools can be useful for many purposes, such as analyzing patterns of language use in a corpus composed of student essays or generating word frequency lists of course readings and materials. After introducing how to build a corpus and how to use a concordancer to perform simple searches, we will introduce how to calculate appropriate frequency counts and what statistics are useful for corpus research.

A concordancer is a software program that allows users to search for words and patterns in a corpus of plain text files (.txt). Concordancers typically display search results in concordance lines – lines of text that contain the search term at the center along with surrounding context on the left and right. One example of a free, easy-to-use concordancer is AntConc, created by Laurence Anthony (http://www.antlab.sci.waseda.ac.jp/software.html).

Concordancers can also generate frequency counts for words and linguistic patterns. However, corpus users must be aware that frequency counts for words and features can be misleading if they are not properly normalized (or normed). Norming is a simple calculation that standardizes frequency counts by transforming them into a rate of occurrence per a set number of words using the formula: (frequency of feature / number of words in (sub-)corpus) multiplied by the basis for norming (for example, 1,000 words). In this way, the number of occurrences of a particular word or pattern can be accurately compared in two corpora of different sizes.

Some research questions can be answered by simply looking at the overall normed rate of occurrence for a word or pattern across an entire (sub-)corpus. However, while this approach produces a measure of how frequent a feature is overall, it gives no indication of how the use of that feature varies across texts in the (sub-)corpus. This simple frequency approach also makes it impossible to apply many statistical procedures that require measures of central tendency (e.g., mean) and variance (e.g., standard deviation). By calculating individual counts for each text in a corpus, researchers are able to statistically compare the means of two or more groups (e.g., using t-test or ANOVAs) or measure the strength of relationships between variables (e.g., using correlation).

Conclusion

Three areas of development in corpus linguistics could be especially helpful for language teaching: development of more principled learner corpora, development of spoken corpora, and additional research on the effectiveness of using corpora for language teaching (either through DDL or materials development).

One issue with available learner corpora (see the learner corpora section above) is that they generally do not clearly identify proficiency levels and also do not tend to have balanced numbers from different proficiency groups, so it is difficult to examine linguistic correlates of learner development. In addition, there are few longitudinal learner corpora, so the development of individual learners is even more difficult to map. New learner corpora can be developed with a more principled design – for example, with the use of stratified sampling to capture sufficient spoken or written data from given proficiency levels and the inclusion of standardized proficiency information as demographic variables. In addition, samples from existing corpora could be evaluated using standardized rating criteria rather than relying on self-reported proficiency.

Spoken corpora are by nature more difficult to compile than written corpora. One important area that is often neglected is phonetic and phonological information – for example, intonation, stress, segmental features. One recent exception to this is the *Hong Kong Corpus of Spoken English* (Cheng, Greaves, and Warren, 2008), which provides prosodic information – for example, stress, intonation, pitch – in the transcript. This allows teachers and researchers to see patterns of prosodic use across registers and, to some extent, language groups (Cantonese native speakers as well as English native speakers are included in the corpus). Much more work in this area is needed, however, before conclusions can be made and applications developed for the classroom. Another example for languages other than English is the C-ORAL ROM group of corpora (Cresti and Moneglia, 2005), which provide some prosodic information for Italian, French, Spanish, and Portuguese. Another issue with most spoken corpora, including in the examples above, is that it is difficult to gain access to the audio or video recordings for privacy and other reasons.

A final area for further development is in research investigating the use of corpus-based methods and materials in the classroom. There are currently too few studies on the use of corpora in the classroom to provide definitive conclusions on its effectiveness for language development. In addition, few studies have examined the impact of corpus-based materials on language learning. Since materials development has the potential to have a much more widespread effect than corpus-based methods, it is an important area for future research. Studies of this nature might include looking at the effect of corpus-based materials on student learning and motivation at different levels of learner proficiency.

Discussion Questions

1. Do any of the textbooks or course materials you currently use rely on corpus research? If so, what differences do you see between those textbooks/materials and traditional textbooks/materials? If not, in what ways could corpus-informed materials or information supplement your current textbook/materials?

2. What are the most important registers for your population of language learners (for example, academic writing, business communication)?

3. What advantages could your learners gain by using authentic texts or findings from corpus-based research?

4. How might learner corpora help teachers identify common issues for learners?

5. What factors need to be considered before applying the results from learner corpora to a different group of learners (for example, proficiency level, L1 background)?

6. In what ways could you use student writing (or speech) to develop your own small-scale corpus to investigate your learners' needs? What areas of language use would you focus on?

7. How could you use a concordancer to find patterns of interest in an existing corpus or one you have developed from classroom data?

8. What statistical measures would you use to evaluate the patterns you find in the corpus you investigate?

References

Asención Delaney, Y. & Collentine, J. (2011). A multidimensional analysis of written L2 Spanish. *Applied Linguistics*, 32, 299–322.

Agerström, J. (2000). Hedges in argumentative writing: A comparison of native and non-native speakers of English. In T. Virtanen & J. Agerström (Eds.), *Three studies of learner discourse. Evidence from the International Corpus of Learner English* (Vol. 10, pp. 5–42). Rapporter Från Växjö Universitet.

Aijmer, K. (2011). Well I'm not sure I think ... The use of *well* by non-native speakers. *International Journal of Corpus Linguistics*, 16(2), 231–254.

Biber, D., & Conrad, S. (2009). *Register, genre and style*. Cambridge: Cambridge University Press.

Biber, D., Conrad, S., & Leech, G. (2002). *Longman student grammar of spoken and written English*. London: Pearson Education.

Biber, D., Conrad, S., & Reppen, R. (1998). *Corpus linguistics: Investigating language structure and use*. Cambridge: Cambridge University Press.

Biber, D., Johansson, S., Leech, G., Conrad, S., & Finegan, E. (1999). *Longman grammar of spoken and written English*. London: Pearson Education.

Biber, D., & Reppen, R. (2002). What does frequency have to do with grammar teaching? *Studies in Second Language Acquisition*, 24(2), 199–208.

Cheng, W., Greaves, C., & Warren, M. (2008). *A corpus-driven study of discourse intonation*. Amsterdam: John Benjamins.

Conrad, S., & Biber, D. (2009). *Real grammar: A corpus-based approach to English*. White Plains, NY: Longman.

Conrad, S., Biber, D., & Leech, G. (2002). *Longman student grammar of spoken and written English workbook*. London: Pearson Education.

Coxhead, A. (2000). A new academic word list. *TESOL Quarterly*, 34(2), 213–238.

Cresti, E., & Moneglia, M. (2005). *C-ORAL-ROM: Integrated reference corpora for spoken Romance languages*. Amsterdam: John Benjamins.

Gilquin, G., De Cock, S., & Granger, S. (2010). *Louvain international database of spoken English interlanguage*. Louvain-La-Neuve, Belgium: Presses Universitaires de Louvain.

Granger, S., Dagneaux, E., Meunier, F., & Paquot, M. (2002, 2009). *International corpus of learner English*. Louvain-La-Neuve, Belgium: Presses Universitaires de Louvain.

McEnery, T., & Hardie, A. (2012). *Corpus linguistics: Method, theory and practice*. Cambridge: Cambridge University Press.

Paquot, M. (2013). Lexical bundles and transfer effects. *International Journal of Corpus Linguistics*, 18(3), 391–417.

Reppen, R. (2010). *Using corpora in the language classroom*. Cambridge: Cambridge University Press.

Rimmer, W. (2011). Learning the game: Playing by the rules, playing with the rules. *English Today*, 27(1), 22–27.

Römer, U., Roberson, A., O'Donnell, M., & Ellis, N. (2011). Linking learner corpus and experimental data in studying second language learners' knowledge of verb-argument constructions. *ICAME Journal*, 38, 115–135.

Simpson-Vlach, R., & Ellis, N. (2010). An academic formulas list: New methods in phraseology research. *Applied Linguistics*, 31(4), 487–512.

Staples, S., Egbert, J., Biber, D., & McClair, A. (2013). Formulaic sequences and academic writing development: Lexical bundles in the TOEFL iBT writing section. *English for Academic Purposes*, 12(3), 214–225.

Waibel, B. (2005). Corpus-based approaches to learner interlanguage: Case studies based on the International Corpus of Learner English. *AAA, Arbeiten aus Anglistik und Amerikanistik*, 30(1–2), 143–176.

CHAPTER 16

Conversation Analysis

John Hellermann

INTRODUCTION

Conversation analysis (referred to hereafter as CA) is a specialized approach to doing discourse analysis that focuses on the analysis of spoken conversational interaction. CA is not designed to elicit a particular language structure or language-use pattern, rather, the researcher attempts to make recordings (video or audio) of natural, mundane conversation, either from face-to-face or telephone interaction. Once the data are collected, extremely detailed transcriptions are made using a standardized system of transcription conventions. Along with capturing the words spoken by participants in the interaction, the transcriber attempts to put into writing details such as (in the excerpt below) the precise placement of overlapping talk (indicated by the [ ), timed pauses (line 6), in breaths (.hh at the start of line 16), and intonational contours (the period in line 7 indicates falling intonation). Such transcripts are, perhaps, the most immediately recognizable trait of CA research.

```
[Jim/Judy what is it 2:04]
02  Max    you don't need to use it [in the
03  Judy                            [what's in
04         that contain[er.
05  Max                [United States
06             (.5)
07  Judy   what i:s that.
08  Jim    I dun[no (.) it doesn't look very attractive anyway.
09  Judy        [probably something greasy
10  Judy   yeah.
11             (.)
12  Judy   something grea:sy American [that we don't know about
13  Max                               [p r o bably tomato
14            looks like [tomato sauce
15  Judy               [or we
16         .hh why would (.) they give us tomato sauce,
```

127

The details in the transcripts are an important aspect for CA because – rather than using a prior theory to interpret the structure of an interaction – CA researchers attempt to describe the language use and show how the participants are hearing, interpreting, and reacting to one another's turns of talk. Instead of trying to interpret the language use of the participants, the researcher attempts to show evidence for any kind of analytic claim about the language use and organization in the perspectives that are displayed by the participants in the talk. For researchers trained in qualitative, ethnographic methods in which drawing on multiple data sources for interpretation is seen as a methodological strength, this aspect of CA can be seen as limiting. However, from the perspective of CA researchers – especially those trained in linguistics – mining everything available in an analysis of just the sequence of turns of talk without resorting to information from outside the conversation itself is, if not the final word on the analysis, at least the necessary first step. Using such a procedure, we hope the data speak for themselves and the potential for analyst bias is reduced.

Background

CA developed in the field of sociology in the micro-sociological work of Erving Goffman and Harold Garfinkel. These researchers were interested in attending to language behavior of everyday interaction as a sociological phenomenon. Goffman's inquiries were socio-psychological, focusing on roles that we play in society and the way we consciously and unconsciously present ourselves to one another. Garfinkel, on the other hand, turned researchers' attention to the practices or methods that people use to do common-sense things. These ideas influenced Harvey Sacks (1992) and colleagues – notably, Emanuel Schegloff and Gail Jefferson – to develop a rigorous method to provide more precise empirical evidence for how social organization is constructed by participants by using language in their interactions. These methods focused on the close analysis of language and took advantage of newly accessible recording technology. Using this new technology, Sacks thought that researchers could best uncover the organization of the language that makes up social interactions through repeated listening to a recorded conversation and then to transcribe, in great detail, both the sequence of turns of talk and the minute phonetic and interactional details that make up each turn of talk.

Along with the detailed transcripts, Sacks advocated engaging in 'unmotivated looking.' That is, the analyst is advised to start an analysis without research questions, instead, noting any remarkable instance in the recorded data that seems to warrant further attention. Through repeated listening and – after the 1970s with the advent of accessible video recording – viewing of the data, the analysis builds from these initial noticings. Soon after its development in sociology, linguists became interested in this rigorous method for the analysis of language use.

There are three key impacts that CA has made on research relevant to language teaching and learning. These are: a) the use of naturalistic data for analysis; b) the treatment of language as a co-constructed practice; and c) an agnostic stance toward the identity of users of a language.

Naturalistic Data

The analysis of language data that is not elicited for purposes of research (ordinary conversations, talk in classroom interaction, etc.) allows the language learning researcher to uncover the very raw material for language use and organization. The lack of control in the design of the data collection means that the researcher need not worry whether the language collected is skewed by the collection instrument (a test, a task, etc.). The researcher, therefore, has a great deal of confidence in claiming the data are reliable as samples of the language being studied. The lack of a controlled design and controlled data collection means that CA research is used for exploratory investigations of the organization of language use in a particular context. A strength of the method is the potential for the discovery of phenomenon not previously noted in research or theorized. One downside to the use of the method, of course, is that carrying out an analysis is much more time consuming as the constructs for analysis emerge from the data.

CO-CONSTRUCTION

The approach to language as a collaborative process of co-construction means that individual grammatical categories like sentence, morpheme, phoneme, etc. are not analyzed without the sequential context in which they were used. The method forces the analyst to focus on language organization outside the heads of individual speakers to see how it is done in a cooperative way. As the review below illustrates, for language teachers this means thinking about the teaching of language use in new ways.

AGNOSTIC STANCE TOWARD NON-NATIVE SPEAKER IDENTITY

Perhaps the greatest impact CA has for research on multilingual, second language speakers has been its theoretical and methodological insistence on maintaining an agnostic stance toward social categories and identities. When a second language acquisition (SLA) analysis starts from the assumption that native speakers' grammaticality or acceptability judgments are the basis of grammatical competence (Ionin, 2011), the use of the label non-native speaker (NNS) implies lack of competence and a focus for analysis becomes the degree to which the language of the NNS is in error or incomplete. Following CA methods, however, the researcher does not foreground the identities of participants as native speaker (NS) or NNS; instead, the analyst focuses on the competencies of participants to organize their tasks and interaction through talk. This opens up the possibility for seeing language in interaction in new ways. For the researcher, this means that old contexts and sources of data can be re-examined, looking for details of the talk-in-interaction that may have been overlooked if an analyst was focusing solely on errors or deficiencies of learners.

RESEARCH ON THIS TOPIC

Although developed by sociologists, this description of CA shows that it is, at its core, a method for language research. From the start, the method was clearly of interest to linguists as seen by the fact that two of the foundational studies in CA were published in the linguistics journal *Language*. Shortly after, functional linguists saw the advantage of using naturalistic rather than constructed data examples for analyses and some began using CA as a method for analysis.

After linguists became familiar with the method, attention turned toward the analysis of data from language learners. For this context, CA research has studied core CA concepts such as the language practices that participants use to co-construct social organization, for example, repair, assessments, and turn-taking in language learning classrooms. However, most of the CA research on language learners now focuses on SLA, research encouraged by the seminal paper of Firth and Wagner (1997).

In that paper, the authors encouraged SLA research to use naturalistic data and to focus on important details that occur in language use. They also alerted the field to the effect that the use of the identity labels NS and NNS has on research. Rather than starting a research study by assuming a deficiency in the participants (implied by the NNS label) and searching for errors in the interaction, Firth and Wagner advocated describing the competencies of the participants. They also advocated using data from second language speakers using the multiple languages outside of classrooms to show how identities such as NS and NNS are rarely relevant for participants who are using a second, third, or n^{th} language for their interaction.

Although Firth and Wagner's own research focused on second language speakers rather than learners, their paper showed how CA methods offer the field of SLA an increased ability to see learning processes. They showed that using CA methods, we can see the step by step or microgenetic[1] focus on language use by learners engaged in language learning activities. Even without an explicitly stated theory of learning, CA researchers have developed ways of discussing learning by using longitudinal data sets for CA research. As discussed earlier, CA tasks the researcher with backing up analytic claims with evidence from interpretations of data (talk and interaction). Thus, CA research that attempts to discuss learning does not rely on standardized assessment scores or speculation on inner cognitive states, but – by using longitudinal data – it can show the competencies of a learner in some area of language use (for example, the way a learner makes a request) at various points in time and describe the trajectory either as evidence of change in that competency or not. CA research on learning describes learners' variable competencies for language in use (see Kasper and Wagner, 2011, and Hall, Hellermann, and Pekarek Doehler, 2011, for reviews of CA research on language learning).

Practical Applications

CA research has investigated and reported on the ways that the sequential structure of talk-in-interaction is used to organize classroom discourse since the 1970s. A recent classroom discourse study especially relevant for language learning teachers is that by Seedhouse (2004). Although there is a long history of research on classroom discourse, Seedhouse notes how using CA methods can provide new insights into the use of language for teaching and learning. His research illustrates much of the interactional work that is "hidden" to practitioners who do not have the privilege of seeing transcripts or video of themselves as they teach. Some of this work includes how a teacher-designed task cannot go precisely as planned. The CA perspective Seedhouse brings to the analysis shows how the contingencies that are fundamental to talk-in-interaction, turn construction, and turn taking, mean that instructors should think of language learning tasks as inherently variable. Seedhouse also illustrates how teachers resist direct negative feedback to students and the interactional outcome of such resistance. Related to this, he discusses the CA context of repair with respect to how repair and correction work in the classroom.

While Seedhouse (and others) describe the mechanisms of talk-in-interaction in the classroom, other research has taken findings from basic CA research and provided ideas for its application to tasks for language teaching. The most comprehensive such application has been done by Wong and Waring (2010). Their book introduces language teachers to CA by giving a summary of the major research foci in CA and their findings and then suggesting ways in which these findings can be used in the classroom. The authors focus on four aspects of CA research that serve as a heuristic[2] for understanding language competence as interactional competence: turn construction and turn taking; sequencing; overall structuring; and repair. The book then leads practitioners through these concepts with discussion questions and activities. At the end of each chapter, the authors include suggestions for practitioners regarding how they can use CA methods in general for purposes of better understanding their own practice, their task design, and the content for their language instruction. Importantly, the authors do not suggest that teachers have students memorize certain typical scripts that learners might use outside the classroom. Rather – in the chapter on sequencing practices, for example – the authors provide pairs of turns taken from actual conversations for learners to analyze and to illustrate sequences. For the productive part of the task, the authors suggest having learners write typical first turns and ask their peers to provide possible second turns to those first turns or to provide cards with first turns or second turns on the cards and ask students to find their matching adjacency pair. In this way, awareness is raised about sequence organization: learners see and hear a number of possibilities for sequences of talk, and have a chance to be creative in producing their own language while at the same time following the sequential formatting uncovered by CA research.

A place where readers can find an example of the application of CA to teaching a particular language use format is Huth and Taleghani-Nikazm's report on the use of research findings from CA to develop instructional materials for teaching telephone openings (2006). In this paper, the researchers used CA research to make cross-linguistic comparisons of the way telephone openings are done in English and German. The comparison was made for the purpose of understanding how teachers of German might go about helping their students understand this sequence of speech acts and how it might be taught. The authors report on their methods for teaching this sequence which included having students analyze both German and US English data from CA research on telephone openings, and then practicing by making telephone calls in German to their instructor and to other German speakers – attending to the normative format for conversational telephone openings in German. The authors show evidence that such awareness raising and practice led to the learners producing more German-like formats for telephone openings.

Conclusion

Apart from the uses mentioned above, there is one future direction in the use of CA for research and practice by language teachers that I see as important, and that is in the area of learners as CA researchers. As the previous review of the literature showed, the direct teaching of conversational routines found in CA research is antithetical to the theoretical grounding of CA. Consequently – rather than rote memorization of scripts – learners are made aware of sequential practices uncovered by CA and work on using those mechanisms for organization during their own interactions. Such awareness-raising can be further enhanced when learners are asked to do their own recording, transcribing, and analysis of conversations in the language they are learning. Although this activity, of course, needs to be adapted for proficiency level, by having learners record and transcribe conversations, teachers are providing them with opportunities for agency and providing methods for discovery of the language they are learning, both of which are acknowledged to be effective pedagogically.

One research method in linguistics (corpus analysis) is now used regularly in language learning classrooms for student-initiated research, and CA methods offer the same potential for learners to gain a deeper understanding of spoken language use by recording interactions in the language they are studying; transcribing that interaction; and then analyzing issues such as the grammar and phonology of turn construction, the pragmatics of particular turns and sequences, and lexical choice for spoken language registers. As a next step, once a transcript is produced, the detailed transcript can be used for performances of excerpts of the recorded conversation using the transcript as a script. Such work is not only fun for students (provided it is adapted to not frustrate them), but also gives them a chance to experience a more truly "embodied" practice of language and culture. The affective aspect of performing their transcribed conversations allows students to step into a new identity, removing potential face threats, and – in the details of the turn construction and sequential structure of the recorded everyday conversation – to experience how the culture of the language unfolds. In the process, an often un-instructable "feel" for the language develops.

Discussion Questions

1. What seem to be the most unusual or surprising aspects of CA that you learned about in this chapter? What do you find yourself attracted to? What do you find yourself disagreeing with?

2. The Huth and Taleghani-Nikazm paper mentioned earlier illustrates one CA research study and application of findings (teaching telephone openings). What are other ways you can think of that you might want to use CA findings for learning content in your classroom?

3. Given how CA understands language as a co-constructed phenomenon, how might that influence the way you assess language learners?

4. CA is not a theory of language learning, but how might CA methods help you understand competence or learning in new ways?

5. What are reasons for or against using the label "non-native speaker" for someone learning a language?

References

Firth, A., & Wagner, J. (1997). On discourse, communication, and (some) fundamental concepts in SLA research. *Modern Language Journal*, 81, 285–300.

Hall, J. K., Hellermann, J., & Pekarek Doehler, S. (Eds.) (2011). *L2 interactional competence and development.* Bristol, UK: Multilingual Matters.

Huth, T., & Taleghani-Nikazm, C. (2006). How can insights from conversation analysis be applied to teaching L2 pragmatics? *Language Teaching Research*, 10(1), 53–79.

Ionin, T. (2011). Formal, theory-based methodologies. In S. Gass and A. Mackey (Eds.), *Research methods in second language acquisition: A practical guide* (pp. 30–52). Malden, MA: Blackwell.

Kasper, G., & Wagner, J. (2011). A conversation-analytic approach to second language acquisition. In D. Atkinson (Ed.), *Alternative approaches to second language acquisition* (pp. 117–142). New York: Routledge.

Sacks, H. (1992). *Lectures on conversation.* (G. Jefferson, Ed.). Oxford: Blackwell.

Seedhouse, P. (2004). *The interactional architecture of the language classroom: A conversation analysis perspective.* Malden, MA: Blackwell.

Wong, J., & Waring, H. Z. (2010). *Conversation analysis and second language pedagogy: A guide for ESL/EFL teachers.* New York: Routledge.

Notes

[1] Microgenetic design is a method of scientific examination in developmental psychology in which the same subjects (usually children) are studied repeatedly over a short period of time. Whilst longitudinal and cross-sectional designs provide broad outlines of the process of change, microgenetic designs provide an analysis of behavior as it is changing.

[2] The noun "a heuristic" describes a specific rule of thumb or mental short cut derived from experience. (The adjective "heuristic" is derived from the Greek *heuriskein*, meaning "to discover" and relates to the process of gaining knowledge or another desired result by a process of experimentation or guesswork, rather than by following rules or some established formula.)

CHAPTER 17

Discourse Analysis

Brian Paltridge

INTRODUCTION

Discourse analysis examines patterns of language across texts and considers the relationship between language and the social and cultural contexts in which it is used. Discourse analysis also considers the ways that the use of language presents different views of the world and different understandings. It examines how the use of language is influenced by relationships between participants as well as the effects the use of language has upon social identities and relations. It also considers how views of the world, and identities, are constructed through the use of discourse.

BACKGROUND

The term "discourse analysis" was first presented by Zellig Harris (1952) in a seminal paper of that title. Harris was interested in connected speech and writing and the use of language beyond the level of the sentence. He was also interested in the relationship between linguistic and non-linguistic behavior; that is, how people know, from the situation they are in, how to interpret what someone says, or writes. Both of these themes have become important in the area of discourse analysis. Halliday (2009), for example, has discussed linguistic aspects of discourse as well as how, in order to understand the meaning of what a person says or writes, we need to understand both the context of culture and context of situation in which the communication is taking place.

Hymes's (1972) notion of communicative competence is also important for discussions of spoken and written discourse. Communicative competence involves not only knowing a language, but also what to say to whom, and how to say it appropriately in a particular situation. That is, it includes not only knowing what is grammatically correct and what is not, but also when and where to use language appropriately and with whom. It includes knowledge of rules of speaking, as well as knowing how to use and respond to different speech acts; that is, how, for example, to apologize or make a request, as well as how to respond to an apology or a request, in a particular language and culture. All of this involves taking account of the social and cultural setting in which the speaking or writing occurs, speakers' and writers' relationships with each other, and the community's norms, values, and expectations for the kind of speech event, or genre[1].

Research on this Topic

The relationship between linguistic and non-linguistic behavior is of interest to people working in the area of pragmatics as well as in the area of discourse analysis. While pragmatics is often treated as a separate area of research from discourse analysis, a number of authors include it in their discussion of discourse as well, as I do here. Pragmatics examines what people mean by what they say, rather than what words in their most literal sense mean by themselves. Thus, if a person says, "It's cold in here," they are probably doing something more than just stating a fact. They may also be making a request, or a suggestion, for someone to close the window. Pragmatics also considers the underlying assumptions of what a person says and what this means for the person with whom they are speaking. One of my students, Jun Ohashi (2008), was interested in the speech act of thanking in Japanese. Previous research had suggested that thanking in Japanese has mutual, reciprocal aspects to it and that these need to be taken into account when understanding what thanking means in Japanese. His research, however, showed that thanking in Japanese is much more complex than this. Thanking in Japanese also involves achieving a mutual debt-credit equilibrium as well as a denigrating of credit between speakers. For this reason, responding to thanking in Japanese is often more complex and more prolonged than it is in English.

Discourse analysts are also interested in the structure of texts in the sense of what people typically say first, and what they say next, and so on in a conversation or in a piece of writing. This is something that varies across cultures and is by no means the same across languages. When I was working in Melbourne, one of my students examined the promotional literature sent out by the Japanese department store Daimaru, which had a store there at the time. She looked at the flyers it sent to its Japanese and its English customers and found they were quite different in terms of how they organized information and the topics they addressed, even though both sets of texts had the same goal, advertising the upcoming spring sale. The Japanese texts all started with seasonal greetings such as "What lovely spring weather we are having. The flowers and trees in the park are coming to life and everything is looking so pretty." The English texts did not do this at all. When I asked one of my Japanese students the reason for this, he said it is too blunt to go straight to the point in Japanese letters. This is why, he said, letters in Japanese often start with what seem to people from some cultures as irrelevant topics, such as the weather, when the goal of the letter might be to sell something.

Genre analysis has examined the discourse structures and language features that are typical of texts such as academic essays, business reports, university lectures, and seminar presentations. More recently, genre analysts have used ethnographic data such as interviews, surveys, field notes, and observations, as well as an analysis of texts that surround the texts in order to get a view of the world in which the texts are written. I recently carried out a study with colleagues where we looked at the writing that visual and performing arts students submit for examination in their doctoral degrees (Paltridge, Starfield, Ravelli, and Tuckwell, 2012). We were interested not only in the language and discourse features of the students' texts, but also in the extent to which the texts that the students wrote were reflective of the doctoral dissertation genre in other, more conventional areas of study. We were particularly interested in finding out what the external influences were that lay behind the students' writing. In order to answer these questions, we collected a set of students' texts, carried out a survey, and conducted interviews with students and their advisors. We also looked at university handbooks and prospectuses, and read published research into visual arts PhD examination. We read in-house art school publications, attended roundtable discussions, and also went to doctoral students' exhibition openings. What we found was that students wrote texts that were, in some cases, very different from traditional doctoral dissertations, even though they still addressed the same criteria (such as originality and contribution to knowledge) that is required of all doctoral dissertations. Often, they took more traditional components of a doctoral dissertation (such as the literature review) and reconceived it in a way that better suited their project and the particular goal of their study. Through the ethnographic data, we were able to gain an understanding of why the students wrote the texts that they did which we would not have gained had we looked at the texts alone.

Critical discourse analysis is an approach which examines why language is used in particular ways and what the implications are of this use. One particular aim of critical discourse analysis is to reveal the (often hidden) values, positions, and perspectives that underlie texts that people write. Another student, Wei Wang (2007), drew on critical discourse analysis for a study in which he examined newspaper commentaries on the events of 9/11 in Chinese and Australian newspapers. His study examined the discourse structures of the Australian and Chinese commentaries and intertextual features of the texts. He also considered possible contextual factors, values, and points of view which might contribute to ways in which the commentaries were produced in the two different languages and cultures. To do this, he explored the role of the mass media in the two different cultures and considered implications of this for the texts he had examined. He found that Chinese writers often use explanatory rather than argumentative expositions in their commentaries. That is, they explained the situation to their readers rather than attempted to make a case. They also distanced themselves from outside sources and seldom indicated any endorsement of their sources. The Australian writers, on the other hand, predominantly used argumentative expositions to put forward their points of view. They also integrated outside sources into their texts in various ways to establish and provide support for the views that they expressed. My student argued that these textual and intertextual practices are closely related to contextual factors, and especially the role of the media in contemporary China and Australia. His study, then, by providing both a textual and contextual view of the texts he was examining, aimed to move beyond the text in order to explore reasons for the linguistic and rhetorical choices made by the writers of the texts.

Multimodal discourse analysis examines how texts combine the use of words with other modalities, such as pictures, film, video images, and sound. Helen Caple (2009) examined a newly emerging newspaper genre, image-nuclear news stories, from this point of view. Image-nuclear news stories are very short stories which comprise just a photograph and a heading, and/or a short caption. She showed how newspapers draw on the strength of visual images in these stories to capture and retain the interest of their readers. She also found an allusion to films (as well as television, songs, literary works, and sporting events, etc.) is common in these kinds of texts and often requires very specialized knowledge for the text-image relation to work. For example, in an image-nuclear story she examined about drought in China there was an image of dry, cracked earth which had central prominence in the photo with a row of people in the background carrying work tools. The heading that accompanied the image, "Dry hard with a vengeance," was a play on the 1995 American movie title *Die hard: With a vengeance.*

Discourse analysis has also examined the notion of identity, mostly taking a poststructural perspective, a view that rejects fixed and definitive ways of talking about things such as social categories, seeing identity as something that is both socially constructed and in a constant process of development and change as people interact with each other. Online communities are a particular place where social relations and identities are constructed through people's participation in the community's activities and their interactions with each other in the online setting. The environment in which they do this is very much a multimodal one, using not just words to express how they want to be seen, but also images, layout, design, a different view of grammar, and a different way of communicating with each other than they might use in their offline worlds (see Zappavigna 2012 for a discussion of discourse and social media; Myers 2010 for the discourse of blogs and wikis). A further way in which identity has been explored is through the use of narrative analysis; that is, the collection of stories in the form of journals, letters, autobiographies, memoirs, interviews, and orally told stories that enable us to gain insights into people's beliefs, experiences, and identities (see Baynham 2011 for further discussion of this).

There are also other approaches to discourse analysis that have not been discussed in this chapter, including conversation analysis (Wilkinson and Kitzinger 2011), classroom discourse analysis (Hammond 2011), and corpus-assisted discourse analysis (Gray and Biber 2011). These are further important approaches to discourse analysis which are making increasingly important contributions to our understanding of how people communicate with each other through the use of spoken and written discourse.

PRACTICAL APPLICATIONS

The research referred to in this chapter has important implications for language teaching and learning, as well as for cross-cultural communication more generally. For example, if a Japanese speaker does not know it is perfectly acceptable to say, "You're welcome" and nothing more in English after they have been thanked, they may likely say something like, "I'm sorry you had to go to so much trouble, and I am sorry to have bothered you, but thank you very much all the same" or, "Thank you for the kind thought but it really was just nothing" which, to many English speakers, might seem excessive. Many students from language backgrounds other than English may also not realize, for example, that it is perfectly acceptable to get straight to the point when they are writing an email, say, to their teacher or professor. In fact, if they do not do this, their reader may wonder what the reason for the email is and be frustrated as they cannot easily work out what it is about. Students may, thus, not realize that the way they do things in their first language and culture may be very different from how people do things in other languages and cultures and that they can very easily be misunderstood if they do not know this.

An experience I had a number of years back illustrates this. I was working in a language school in Sydney that was located in a high-rise tower building. There was a café on the ground floor of the building where students often went to buy their lunch. The café was very busy so orders had to be placed quickly, especially in the section which was making sandwiches to order. One day, the owner said to me "You know, your Japanese students are so rude. They never say please or thank you when they order their lunch." Now, I knew that my students were not rude, and I also knew from having been in Japan that it is quite common to place a fast-service order in Japan without saying please or thanks. At the next class, I talked about buying and selling in different cultures with my students, then set them the task of going to the café and observing native-speakers buying their lunch and to look for any particular linguistic routines they used for doing this. When the students came back they were surprised at how often people said "please" and "thanks" while they placed their orders, even though the interactions they observed had been very short. We role-played the situation in class and practiced ways of fitting "please" or "thanks" into ordering food as the people they observed had done. A few weeks later, the owner of the café said to me, "I don't know what's happened to your students, but they are so much nicer now!" My students had not changed at all. They had always been nice. They had just learned the particular way of doing something in the different language and culture, in this case in Sydney, Australia. The same interaction in other English-speaking cultures may, of course, be different. This is something that students need to learn, and anticipate, when they are using the same language in what might seem to be the same social situation but in another geographical location.

The study I described earlier on doctoral writing shows how it is important for writing teachers to avoid prescriptive models of what particular texts should look like in writing classrooms. Teachers need to be aware of specific ways of writing within particular settings, looking at previous students' texts as a guide to how they might present sample texts to their students. Often they will find there is much more variation than they expect in the texts and that there are often specific local, institutional reasons for this variation.

Critical discourse analysis also has very practical goals in that it can help people understand how they are being positioned by texts and the ways in which authors use language to do this. Multimodal discourse analysis, similarly, can show how the use of images and other modalities can contribute to a particular reading of a text which a person can choose to align themselves with, or resist. Identity research can help learners understand the role the use of language (or rather discourse) has in the construction of identities and how people read a particular identity from particular uses of language.

Conclusion

Discourse analysis, then, examines how, through the use of language, people achieve certain goals, perform certain acts, participate in events, and present themselves to others. It considers how people manage interactions with each other, and communicate within particular groups, as well as how they communicate with other groups, and with other cultures. Discourse analysis also focuses on the ideas and beliefs that people communicate as they use language.

Each of the areas discussed in this chapter will, no doubt, develop further in the future. This includes multimodal discourse analysis which is still – in some ways – in the process of development. The study of ways in which identity is expressed across different modes of communication and in different languages is also likely to develop further. Discourse analysis, then, is in many ways, a work in progress, but it is one that is able to tell us a lot about people's social worlds and how they communicate within them. This is especially important for language learners who are wanting to become part of these worlds, and to participate in them.

Discussion Questions

1. Think of a research question that could be answered by the use of discourse analysis. What data would you collect?

2. Which approach to discourse analysis outlined in this chapter would you use to examine your data?

3. What would you look for in the data?

4. How would you use this analysis in a classroom?

5. How, more broadly, could you use the results of discourse analysis in your teaching?

References

Baynham, M. (2011). Narrative analysis. In K. Hyland & B. Paltridge (Eds.), *The Bloomsbury companion to discourse analysis* (pp. 69–84). London: Bloomsbury.

Caple, H. (2009). Multisemiotic communication in an Australian broadsheet: A new news story genre. In C. Bazerman, A. Bonini, & D. Figueiredo (Eds.), *Genre in a changing world, perspectives on writing* (pp. 243–254). Fort Collins, CO: The WAC Clearinghouse and Parlor Press.

Gray, B., & Biber, D. (2011). Corpus approaches to discourse analysis. In K. Hyland & B. Paltridge (Eds.), *The Bloomsbury companion to discourse analysis* (pp. 138–152). London: Bloomsbury.

Halliday, M. A. K. (2009). Context of culture and of situation. In J. J. Webster (Ed.), *The essential Halliday* (pp. 55–84). London: Continuum.

Hammond, J. (2011). Classroom discourse analysis. In K. Hyland & B. Paltridge (Eds.), *The Bloomsbury companion to discourse analysis* (pp. 293–307). London: Bloomsbury.

Harris, Z. (1952). Discourse analysis, *Language*, 28, 1–30.

Hymes, D. (1972). On communicative competence. In J. B. Pride & J. Holmes (Eds.), *Sociolinguistics: Selected readings* (pp. 269–293). Harmondsworth: Penguin.

Myers, G. (2010). *The discourse of blogs and wikis*. London: Continuum.

Ohashi, J. (2008). Linguistic rituals for thanking in Japanese: Balancing obligations. *Journal of Pragmatics*, 40, 2150–2174.

Paltridge, B., Starfield, S., Ravelli, L., & Tuckwell, K. (2012). Change and stability: Examining the marcostructures of doctoral theses in the visual and performing arts. *Journal of English for Academic Purposes*, 11, 332–334.

Wang, W. (2007). *Genre across languages and cultures: Newspaper commentaries in China and Australia*. Saarbruecken, Germany: VDM Verlag Dr. Müller.

Wilkinson, S., & Kitzinger, C. (2011). Conversation analysis. In K. Hyland & B. Paltridge (Eds.), *The Bloomsbury companion to discourse analysis* (pp. 22–37). London: Bloomsbury.

Zappavigna, M. (2012). *Discourse of twitter and social media: How we use language to create affiliation on the web*. London: Continuum.

Note

[1] A genre is a particular way of using, presenting, and framing language according to audience and purpose: examples of genres could include a political speech, an interview, a church/mosque sermon.

CHAPTER 18

Replication Research in Quantitative Research

Graeme Porte

INTRODUCTION

A cornerstone of scientific research is the possibility of confirming (or otherwise) existing theory, hypotheses, or results by repeating previous procedures. The outcomes of such a repetition, or replication study, would ideally show us how far we can separate knowledge from the particular circumstances of time, place, procedure, or subjects which were part of the original experiment or study.

The so-called pure or hard sciences have long since embraced the need for replication of studies as part-and-parcel of scientific progress. However, in the social sciences – and in particular in applied linguistics research – such research is notably absent from the literature, rarely discussed outside learned journals, and equally rarely seen in published experimental or classroom research papers. One possible reason is the fact that many social scientists are more likely to use qualitative, non- or quasi-experimental research techniques that are difficult to repeat (see Practical Applications below); moreover, ever-changing social and historical research contexts can influence outcomes. Thus, an exact replication finding which did not repeat the original result is likely to generate even more doubt about the original in the social sciences than in the natural sciences.

However, there remains a strong argument that some kind of re-visiting of previous key studies' findings has to be undertaken by researchers to enable the self-correcting nature of science to be fulfilled. Yet the large majority of experimental studies undertaken and published remain follow-up or extension studies (see below) and, in these, work which follows a quantitative paradigm is often characterized by an over-reliance on statistical inference and the production of (often specious) statistically significant results – perhaps driven by perceived needs of journals which tend to publish mainly papers that report the rejection of null hypotheses[1]. Indeed, there is more than a suggestion that researchers sometimes use inappropriate analytic procedures in an attempt to increase their chances of publication by obtaining statistically significant results, increasing the likelihood that published findings are subject to Type 1 errors[2] (Nassaji, 2012). Against this background, I have argued (see Porte, 2012) that journal editors must assign space for the publication of replication studies and also encourage a broader acceptance of such research approaches by also publishing those that fail to replicate earlier results (see also Conclusion below).

One of the regrettable consequences of the scarcity of replication research in our field is precisely the fact that we might remain unaware of what such research contributes and how it is best defined. For many, the word "replication" means of necessity repeating something, in this case the previous experiment/study. However, an *exact* replication of a previous study is precisely the one least encountered and the least practical of the possibilities for replication research in our area. Study B can never be an exact replication of study A; the second study might be more or less similar but can never be the same in all respects of subjects, method, procedure, or context. Indeed, if they were the same, essentially we would not have two different experiments and that is precisely the aim of replication research! What we do need is confirmation (or otherwise) of a previous outcome. By introducing subtle changes in variables in the original study we increase the confirmatory power of each subsequent replication. These changes are incorporated in two further definitions of replication research.

In an approximate (sometimes referred to as partial) replication, we begin to alter the variables as described above in an attempt to see how reliable and/or generalizable the original findings were. We might, for example, choose a different age set of students, or gender and see how far the original results compare. Similarly, we might want to introduce subtle changes in the measuring instruments used in the previous analysis (and perhaps indicated by the previous author as in need of refinement) while keeping the other main variables constant and describe the outcomes.

Conceptual (also known as constructive) replications test previous hypotheses or results against a different experimental design. This kind of replication is often used when the original study presented outcomes which might have been affected by the methodology used and so we need a replication which uses a different methodology to test those outcomes. Indeed, since there really is no such thing as a precise measurement or treatment and because any study's validity can be increased if we find the same result using different measures or treatments, there are large numbers of key studies that might benefit from a conceptual approach to replication. Similarly, different ways of collecting data might be envisaged, such as observation instead of self-report, or qualitative methods used alongside the quantitative ones relied on in the original study. A successful conceptual replication provides stronger support for the original findings precisely because evidence shows outcomes were not just artifacts of the original methodology. It figures that the more manipulations of the effect of a particular construct that we have, the more (or less!) confident we can be that this effect is (or is not) actually present.

Doubtless, it has already become evident that there are likely to be large numbers of studies that might benefit from either or both approaches to replication. This is not to say, of course, that a single replication is likely to provide the answers we need – and in the pure sciences the norm would be that a series of replications focus on a key study and conclusions are drawn from them. Thus, for example, by systematically varying the conditions or procedures across a series of replications, it is made easier for researchers to determine the precise nature of a previous study's results and the extent to which they also hold for different populations and situations.

A distinction needs to be made between what I referred to above as "follow-up" or "extension" studies and the subject of this particular chapter. In follow-up studies, the methodology might be similar to a previous study but the objective is to present novel data – perhaps from a new context with different subjects and perhaps a different treatment. The focus is firmly on the latest results and what these bring to current knowledge. However, the end result does not mean we can – or wish to – compare the present outcomes with ones previously obtained in a similar study. In general, the more variables one introduces into the new study, the more distant that study becomes from what was done originally – and therefore, less comparable. With replication studies we seek always to compare one study with another, the replication with the original. To this end we would read continuous signposts throughout the text indicating in what way the author sees similarities and differences with the original study. Therefore, it is fair to say that in a replication study the focus is firmly on what the replicated study has to say about the original study.

Background

I have already indicated above that independent replication is considered one of the building blocks of scientific methodology. This rigorous approach to research is based on the assumption that we need to further validate and more clearly define theory in an attempt to get at the truth. It follows that any outcomes based on or triggered by such theory need to be treated with initial skepticism. By further validating and defining what we observe we can begin to have more (or less) confidence that the scientific method we employ is leading to reliable outcomes. When we observe a history of such outcomes, we can begin to have similar confidence in applying those findings elsewhere – for example, in the language teaching classroom. In this way, for example, "pure" scientists have succeeded in building a solid foundation for progress in medicine since they continually establish which findings are predictable and reproducible, and which are not. This aim of replicability or reproducability is sound if one accepts that all science attempts to reveal the set of rules by which the world operates. If a result cannot be replicated, we need to re-think our approach – effectively "go back to the drawing board." It would be wrong, however, to conclude that science makes no progress at all because our research consists only of constant repetition! Rather, we are presented with a research process which "… is one of flux, wherein future studies are often suggested as a result of a present finding. Implicit is the acceptance that the advancement of knowledge is not a straightforward endeavor but rather one which is most likely to proceed piecemeal as more and more information is acquired about a particular effect or relationship" (Porte, 2012: 12).

Furthermore, not every study needs, nor requires, nor merits replication. But many do need to be re-visited in this way (see Practical Applications below) and will reward further investigation. Indeed, in some fields, it is normal procedure for a researcher to have to replicate his or her own results before publication to ensure results were not an artifact of the original research design.

Research on this Topic

In a much-cited paper, Campbell and Stanley (1963: 3) already warned that research in the social sciences needed to be equally susceptible to further investigation: "…We must increase our time perspective, and recognize that continuous, multiple experimentation is more typical of science than once-and-for-all definitive experiments. The experiments we do today … will need replication and cross-validation at other times and under other conditions before they can become an established part of science, before they can be theoretically interpreted with confidence."

Muma (1993) went so far as to suggest that a study was incomplete until some kind of replication had been applied to its findings. Schneider (2004), in lamenting the scarcity of replication research in the social sciences, also observed the difficulties which confront those who choose to replicate others' work and try to publish it.

Within the field of applied linguistics and language teaching, there have been sporadic reminders of the need for replication and numerous calls which, in essence, re-iterate the need for "observations that can be repeated and verified by others" (American Psychological Association (APA), 2010:44). This, in turn, has been accompanied by an increasing, if somewhat belated, acknowledgement that there exist large numbers of studies which not only merit re-visiting, but urgently need replication (for example, Santos, 1989; Ortega, 2008; Mackey, 2012). Santos (1989), for example, discovered that of the 100 quantitative studies she selected in *TESOL Quarterly* and *Language Learning*, there had not been a single replication. Valdman (1993) was one of the earliest, explicit calls for such research from an applied linguistics journal yet the end result has been only four such studies to date. Polio and Gass (1997) showed there had been only two commentaries prior to 1997 on the topic of replication within applied linguistics. The lack of such work has led to criticism that researchers are prioritizing specious one-off research enquiry rather than seeking more valid, proven lines of investigation (Polio and Gass, 1997).

In the most recent initiative to promote more replication research, *Language Teaching* – a Cambridge University Press journal dedicated to critical reviews of research – published a question-and-answer commentary on replication research in which some of the journal's panel addressed a number of issues on how and why to undertake replication research (*Language Teaching* Review Panel, 2008). The same journal has recently initiated a further drive for more submissions by inviting researchers to nominate studies they feel are ripe for replication and suggesting how those interested might go about doing so.

Practical Applications

There are a number of sources of possible replication research studies but – as with much of the other research we undertake – one guiding factor will be the extent to which the research question or study itself continues to be relevant to the field. Thus, the question(s) should be perceived to be insufficiently answered in the previous literature and thereby suggest the appropriateness of further or additional investigation. The added impetus provided here is that a more recent or oft-cited study is more likely to be perceived as salient enough to warrant the interest of readers.

A further source of ideas can be within the original author's own observations about the perceived limitations to their research, a section often found towards the end of an experimental research paper. Our own critical reading can, and should, alert us to possible unanswered questions or doubts about the study presented us. Typically, an inner voice is set up during our reading of a piece of research and we find ourselves identifying possible weaknesses in the methodology or the explanations of results provided or wondering whether a potentially significant variable has been adequately controlled for or whether a different variable entirely might have brought about a different effect (Porte, 2010). There is a particular need always for approximate and conceptual replications to be carried out when the research we are reading is part of an area of research or a topic which has not been carried out in multiple settings or when a re-definition of a particular construct might be hypothesized to affect the results.

Classic studies that are considered key for the basis of theoretical claims are also good candidates for replication. Likewise, when the results reported are not those expected through the application of a particular theory or seem to contradict that theory, a conceptual replication might help us re-visit that theory and refine it.

My focus in this chapter has been on what can and needs to be replicated in terms of replication of quantitative research. Nevertheless, and despite numerous calls for more replication research in the social sciences, the fact remains that research with humans presents a number of obstacles to replication research, not least of which is the fact that the *material* with which we work is – by its nature – susceptible to continuous change. Many have therefore dismissed replication of qualitative research as being impossible in most research contexts (for example, Casanave, 2012). However, research outcomes cannot remain unaddressed: they should be – at the very least – re-visited with a view to establishing both their internal and external validity (Porte and Richards, 2012). Porte and Richards suggest that some of the traditional objections to replication of qualitative research can now be countered and argue that "… changes in features of the physical, social, and interpersonal context over time make replication problematic, but if detailed delineation of specific contexts is possible … this could be seen as an opportunity for replication rather than a barrier to it" (p. 288). They also argue that technological advances in data-storage mean that much more data is potentially available to qualitative researchers, with which they might better compare outcomes.

Conclusion

One of the problems for social scientists undertaking replication is precisely the fact that they are perceived to be working with old data and that the outcomes of the research has insufficient novelty value to be widely acceptable in terms of publication value. A further, and more insidious, problem has arisen as a result of the constant need for recognition and research funding: the perception that statistically significant and positive results are those which are most publishable. This perhaps not-totally-false view of journal needs makes it more palatable to many researchers to cherry-pick results and contribute to the bias towards researching only the kind of work that will most probably yield that kind of outcome.

It is refreshing to see a few learned journals in our field actively encouraging replication study submissions, for this is key to promoting more interest in the methodology. And this is as it should be since large areas of applied linguistics present findings from classroom-based, experimental studies which appear to have passed unchallenged into received wisdom and often then materialized in teaching methodology or onto textbook pages without having been addressed or challenged through sufficient replication.

Discussion Questions

1. What is the difference between a "follow-up study" and a "replication study"?
2. What variables might you consider useful to address when starting work on an approximate replication study?
3. How might you set up a conceptual replication study of an original study which obtained data on the decrease in students' written errors after a three-week special teaching course on the subject?
4. Why is replicating previous studies an important element in knowledge building?
5. What studies have you read that you think might benefit from being replicated?
6. How might one encourage more replication studies from novice researchers?

References

American Psychological Association. (2010). *Publication manual of the American Psychological Association* (6th ed.). Washington, DC: American Psychological Association.

Campbell, D. T., & Stanley, J. C. (1963). *Experimental and quasi-experimental designs for research*. Chicago: Rand McNally.

Casanave, C. (2012). Heading in the wrong direction. A response to Porte and Richards. *Journal of Second Language Writing*, 21(4), 296–297.

Language Teaching Review Panel (2008). Replication studies in language learning and teaching: Questions and answers. *Language Teaching*, 41, 1–14.

Mackey, A. (2012). Why (or why not), when and how to replicate research. In G. Porte (Ed.), *Replication research in applied linguistics* (pp. 21–46). Cambridge: Cambridge University Press.

Muma, J. R. (1993). The need for replication. *Journal of Speech and Hearing Research*, 36, 927–930.

Nassaji, H. (2012). Statistical significance tests and result generalizability: Issues, misconceptions, and a case for replication. In G. Porte (Ed.), *Replication research in applied linguistics* (pp. 92–115). Cambridge: Cambridge University Press.

Ortega, L. (2008). Foreword. In S. Wa-Mbaleka. *A meta-analysis investigating the effects of reading on second language vocabulary learning* (pp. iii–v). Saarbrücken, Germany: VDM Verlag.

Polio, C., & Gass, S. (1997). Replication and reporting: A commentary. *Studies in Second Language Acquisition*, 19, 499–508.

Porte, G. (2010). *Appraising research in second language learning: A practical approach to critical analysis of quantitative research* (2nd ed.). Amsterdam/Philadelphia: John Benjamins.

Porte, G. (2012). *Replication research in applied linguistics*. Cambridge: Cambridge University Press.

Porte, G., & Richards, K. (2012). Replication in second language writing research. *Journal of Second Language Writing*, 21(4), 284–293.

Santos, T. (1989). Replication in applied linguistics research. *TESOL Quarterly*, 23, 699–702.

Schneider, B. (2004). Building a scientific community: The need for replication. *Teachers College Record*, 106, 1471–1483.

Valdman, A. (1993). Replication study (editorial introduction). *Studies in Second Language Acquisition*, 15, 505.

Notes

[1] In statistics, the null hypothesis represents a theory that has been put forward (either because it is believed to be true or because it is to be used as a basis for argument) but has not been proved. In other words, the null hypothesis is the theory being tested. The alternative hypothesis is the theory to be accepted if and when the null hypothesis is rejected.

[2] In a hypothesis text, a Type 1 error occurs if the null hypothesis is rejected when it is in fact true. A Type 2 error occurs when the hypothesis is not rejected when it is in fact false. A Type 2 error is frequently due to sample sizes being too small.

CHAPTER 19

Ethnography

David M. Palfreyman

INTRODUCTION

Ethnographic research involves studying human activity and trying to understand the unwritten cultural rules which participants work by. The ethnographic perspective was articulated by Western anthropologists researching exotic communities, who tried to gain an insider perspective on the societies that they studied. Later the ethnographic perspective was applied to understand the cultural aspects of a wide range of groups and subcultures in Western and other societies, including working class youth, political elites, and school classrooms. Ethnography can lead us to valuable insights into the everyday workings of language and education.

BACKGROUND

Ethnographic studies usually work mainly with qualitative data, drawing on observation – for example, of behavior, language, or use of space – interviews with participants, photographs, documents, realia, or any other relevant source. However, ethnography is more than a set of techniques: it is a perspective on human activity, which seeks to unearth and piece together participants' own perspectives and values.

An ethnographic study aims for an emic[1] (insider) perspective: a view of what is going on in terms of the participants' own understandings. This contrasts with an etic[1] perspective: the possibly objective, but sometimes naïve or misguided, view of an outsider. The researcher is often a "participant observer," researching a familiar context or taking time to join and interact with a group as they go about their business. Ethnographers aim for "thick description" (Geertz, 1973): a description which captures not only observable features/events but also the significance which these have for actual participants in the social situation. Geertz refers to the example of a wink, which may be described in very precise objective terms as a specific movement of an eyelid (thin description), but which in context may have various significances – joking, signaling a conspiracy, being suggestive, etc. – for the person who winks and those who see and interpret it. In the case of language teaching, an activity may be interpreted quite differently by students than by their teacher – for example, as an opportunity to show off rather than as a learning activity – and an observer watching a class for the first time is even more likely to miss 'in-jokes' and other aspects of a particular class's culture. Ethnography necessarily involves referring to and understanding the context, which is often a community of some kind, large or small – for example, university education in China, or a group of three students working on an assignment. An ethnographic study thus tries to gain an in-depth understanding of the system of perceptions which the participants themselves are using to organize what they do and say; this may take a long time, as the researcher gradually comes to understand and articulate what is going on 'under the surface' of what he or she sees or hears.

Ethnography – like historical analysis or medical diagnosis, for example – tends to begin with data, and uses initial data to generate tentative hypotheses which are then confirmed or adapted in the light of further data. There is thus an emphasis on seeing things afresh: like a teacher newly arrived in an unfamiliar school or an unfamiliar country, the ethnographic researcher tries to work out the local rules of engagement, taking nothing for granted. Beginning research with rigidly preconceived aims may lead the researcher to overlook or misinterpret data or concepts which are of significance to participants, so ethnographic researchers try to begin their data gathering with an open mind about what is significant. They explore a culture in a principled way, gradually focusing in on points which challenge or confirm their understanding of 'what is going on' from the point of view of the participants. Consequently, rather than beginning with very specific research questions or universal hypotheses, they tend to begin with a more tentative foreshadowed problem – which is typically adapted or even discarded as the researcher develops a thick description as described above. This process of coming to understand a context/culture is itself part of the data, and ethnographic studies may be presented partly in narrative form.

A key strength of the ethnographic perspective is that it deals with everyday, possibly familiar situations, but takes nothing for granted. A researcher taking an ethnographic approach will not begin to observe an event such as a lesson (even her/his own lesson) with the assumption that they know what sort of lesson "should" take place, or that a student who is apparently inactive is "doing nothing": rather, they will wait and observe, looking out for unexpected occurrences (or non-occurrences) which reveal assumptions made by the teacher and the students. These rich points can then be explored through further observation or other methods such as interview. The ethnographic approach is particularly suitable for investigating complex, new, and/or developing situations such as the use of new technology or methodologies, or situations of contact between different cultures.

Ethnography is often refreshingly down to earth, making a close study of specific, everyday interactions and situations (a micro perspective); on the other hand, these often make sense only within a broader context such as participants' home life, their history, or the values of their society (a macro perspective). Ethnographic analysis develops by understanding the participants' perspectives, rather than assuming a priori that they will behave according to the researcher's preconceived ideas about their society. Ethnographic perspective therefore lends itself to critical investigation of the social forces which shape daily life.

Since an ethnographic study is usually based around a particular case or set of cases, and is inherently linked to understanding a specific context, objective truth and general applicability in a positivist sense are often not applicable criteria for evaluating such research. However, it may be evaluated according to somewhat different criteria. One criterion is authenticity for insiders: member checking – or showing, explaining, or discussing the researcher's conclusions with the informants – can help to support this. Since the ethnographic analysis aims to explain how participants see social situations, the final analysis should be recognizable to the participants themselves (although not all participants in a situation will be aware of the perspectives of everyone around them). Another criterion is comprehensibility or coherence for an outside audience – explaining insider knowledge such that outsiders can appreciate why participants behave and communicate the way they do. An ethnographic analysis may also be transferable in the sense of helping to understand similar situations elsewhere. Another criterion is reflexivity: the extent to which the researcher shows awareness of his/her own bias or influence in interpreting – and participating in – the context studied. Since ethnographic analysis is always to some extent subjective, reflexivity is crucial in enabling readers to evaluate the conclusions of a study.

Research on this Topic

An ethnography is, strictly speaking, a fairly in-depth, immersive, long-term study of a community and their subjective world. An ethnographic perspective may be applied to understanding various aspects of various educational or learning contexts; for example, Willis (1977) studied how working class youth respond to schooling and become channeled out of education and into manual jobs. This involved extensive study of how these young people, and those around them, talked and thought about education, work, and other topics both in and outside school, in order to understand how work became more important in their lives than education was. Sterponi (2007), on the other hand, conducted intensive study of children's reading behavior, comparing their preferred informal reading behaviors – which included sharing and discussing texts with their friends – with the ways of reading promoted by their school – primarily silent, solitary reading. Sterponi analyzed pupils' speech, movements, bodily position, and gaze – using video and audio recording of their reading lessons – as well as verbal data from their teacher and posters and other texts produced by the school; she arrived at an understanding of what "reading" meant to the teacher and the pupils in her particular context, and how these participants negotiated between these formal and informal reading practices in lessons.

Other studies focus on other aspects of education, such as assessment: how does the teacher view and approach an assessment event, for example? How is the "same" event interpreted and participated in by various kinds of student, or by other direct or indirect participants such as school authorities or parents? What social influences shape these perceptions, and what social consequences (short or long term) result from these ways of understanding the experience of education for the students or others involved? The concept of a social performance is often invoked in ethnographic analysis: how do different individuals enact the role of being a student or a testee, of becoming a teacher, of participating in professional development or being expected to against one's will? How are roles – for example, "bright student" or "unmotivated student" – assigned and constructed by teachers as well as students? Note that in an ethnographic study often a role is not something decided beforehand, but emerges as data is gathered and the researcher begins to understand the categories which participants use in thinking and talking about their experience.

As well as focusing on a set of participants who seem to form some sort of community, ethnographic studies often look at related contexts to identify common participants, roles, or themes among them. For example, a researcher might observe students interacting with the teacher in class and in the corridor, or interview teachers about their use of technology with their students and in other areas of their life. Especially in the modern world, a community may consist of people who do not know each other – for example, students and librarians in a university library – or who are in different locations – for example in an online community. Nevertheless, these people will share some norms, and perhaps negotiate and enforce new ones, forming a hybrid culture; and an ethnographic approach would seek to understand the shared (or conflicted) perceptions and responses which appear in such situations. An ethnographic study may also focus on an object – for example, a textbook, a curriculum, or an iPad – and examine how it is perceived or adapted and the significance it has for the network of people who promote, distribute, resist, use, or abuse it.

Language is a key element of the culture of a group, and is involved in various ways in the processes discussed above. Much ethnographic data – for example, from interviews, or from notes on lessons or other events – consists of language, although this is typically tied in with other kinds of data such as people's actions or expressions or their use of objects. In the case of language education, language is also the content of what people are engaged in, and it is closely tied to culture. The ethnography of communication – for example Carbaugh, 2005 – studies how different communities organize talk, silence, writing, and non-verbal communication – for example, in terms of who speaks to whom, in what way, with what precedence and using which forms; this area of research also considers how individuals make use of these norms to their own ends. In recent decades, beginning with the Communicative Language Teaching movement, learning a language has come to be seen as intimately tied with learning the cultural norms of the community using that language. "Cultural (or 'intercultural') competence" (Byram, 1997) has become an element in many language courses, aiming to help learners use language forms appropriately and to become aware of non-linguistic aspects of culture as well. Thus, understanding a culture has come to be seen not just as something that researchers do, but an important goal for language teachers and learners too.

As mentioned earlier, ethnographic studies can use a great variety of data. Interviews are a common and effective way of gathering data; however, people's responses in interviews should not be taken simply at face value. People are often unaware of or unable to articulate certain norms, even those which they unconsciously take account of; they may also be unwilling to express certain ideas – for example, because of the way they perceive their relationship to the interviewer (Blommaert and Jie, 2010). For this reason it is important to maintain reflexivity – awareness of the researcher's and others' social biases and purposes – in analyzing interview data, and to triangulate between different types of data from different individuals or from different situations. Visual and audio data can include photographs or recordings, providing more direct evidence of places, artifacts, and physical behaviors. Again, however, this data should not be taken at face value: the researcher should understand and allow for preconceptions and biases influencing the selection of what to record and from which point of view. In fact, this "problem" has been developed into a principled way of gathering data: researchers may ask informants to take photographs, make video recordings, or draw pictures of key places or activities, and use these as prompts for discussions or interviews. In the case of less articulate informants, such as children, this can be a very effective way of building up valuable data. Documents (official or unofficial) such as emails, students' writing, or teaching materials can also give insight into a cultural setting. Documents or other evidence which have been adapted or reinterpreted by different participants may be particularly revealing; for example, Canagarajah's (1993) research in Sri Lanka analyzed how students' doodles and other inscriptions in the margins of their American textbook revealed cultural tensions and appropriation in the Sri Lankan context.

Practical Applications

It is sometimes a matter of controversy whether a given study can be described as ethnographic – *TESOL Quarterly* (2013) provides helpful guidelines for authors submitting ethnographic work, with a proviso regarding critical ethnographies (see below). Richards (2003) comments on mismatches between the approaches which researchers claim to take and those which they actually use; for example, terms like "ethnography" and "thick description" may be used to describe research which works within pre-set categories, lacks sufficient analysis of different participant perspectives, or lacks reflexive awareness of the researcher's own bias. On the other hand, Brice Heath and Street (2008) point out that a researcher may validly adopt an ethnographic perspective without doing a full ethnography; or they may make use of ethnographic tools, such as in-depth interviews or participant observation, within studies which are primarily oriented to another approach, such as action research. When reading a study which claims to be ethnographic, it is important to consider whether the researcher has consistently taken an ethnographic approach – including an emic perspective and a reflexive approach to his/her own roles in the social situation – and whether the data-gathering methods used are appropriate to the aims of the study. Inconsistency which is not acknowledged or explained can make the conclusions of the study suspect.

Ethnography is very close to everyday life and work, and compared with some other research methods it can be carried out with relatively few resources: the main requirements are time, an open mind, patience, and an ability to observe, listen, and reflect. It is also less intrusive than some other methodologies, and so can be carried out on an ongoing basis in the course of other activities such as teaching, observing peers, or just strolling around a place, or sitting in meetings or lessons. Ethnography is a way of researching contexts rather than language per se, but it can be used to understand the role that language plays in particular contexts or activities. It can be a practical and insightful approach for researching cultural aspects of language, of activities, of materials, or of approaches to education.

An ethnographic study can be very small scale. For example, a teacher might study one activity: how teacher and learners approach it; how they react to it; how they talk about it afterwards; how they try to repeat/avoid it in future. The study may start from an interesting event or observation – for example, you may notice that certain students avoid participating in activities, or that a colleague says something about students or the curriculum which catches you by surprise. An ethnographic approach would then involve exploring the reasons which, for example, prompt students to avoid activities, and the strategies they use to do so; how they perceive the activities; how they perceive their own role in the classroom and perhaps beyond it. It would refrain from assuming that it is "normal" to take part in an activity or that the aim of the activity which is in the teacher's mind is clear to the students: the aim is to discover what is going on from the point of view of the different participants. An ethnographic perspective would ask: what would a visiting Martian, or a visiting parent, see in this situation? What seems to count as "participation" for those involved, and what other things do people do which are discounted as "non-participation"? The aim is to take a fresh look, putting aside as far as possible your own assumptions, and to gain a tentative idea about the assumptions of those you are observing: the social dynamic which produces this set of events.

You can start ethnographic research by observing broadly around a topic of interest, rather than focusing too narrowly on a specific question (Holliday, 2007), for example, "how students enter the room and settle down (or not) at the start of the lesson," "how students use their mobile phone in lessons," or "how a teacher responds to students' contributions." Since context is so important in interpreting ethnographic data, it is often helpful to start by describing or sketching the environment, the participants, and their physical positions; then notes about behavior and events can be linked to this. Distinguish between detailed objective observations – for example, "Student X looks out of the window" – and subjective interpretation; mark the latter in your notes by putting it in brackets or in a different column of your notes, and try to phrase it tentatively – for example, "Student X looks bored? or thinking about what to write?" The latter kind of hypotheses can be checked later, by asking the student how they felt at different points in the lesson, by noticing what they do *after* looking out of the window – for example, yawning or returning to writing – or by looking at what they wrote: that is, by triangulation of data. Always keep a notebook nearby, to note observations or thoughts at any time. Remember that "there is always an observer's effect" (Blommaert and Jie, 2010: 27), and this effect itself is often a useful piece of the picture: how do the students behave when they are focused on a teacher or a stranger observing them? How does this compare with what you observe from a distance or when they seem to have forgotten your presence? What does this show about how they perceive teachers and how they interpret their own activity?

Open-minded observation is crucial at the early stages, but reviewing research notes regularly (preferably every day), noting ideas and connections, repeated patterns, or impressions can guide you in further observation or questioning. There may be a feeling at first that "nothing is happening," because everything looks so familiar. But wait and watch, and you may realize that something other than what you expected is happening. Make a list of repeated or puzzling details that you notice; think about why people would respond in this way in this situation, and what connections there might be between these different points. Make a note of your hypotheses about what is going on between the people you are observing, from their perspective. The aim is not only to describe the detail of what you observe in a particular context, but to develop hypotheses and ideas to explain what is going on under the surface; not only to develop hypothetical ideas, but to constantly compare these with existing or new evidence, from observation, interviews, or other sources. Some people find that using different colors to highlight points on hard copy notes helps them to keep track of themes which emerge in their data; others may type up their notes and other data on a computer, so that they can search through it for key words and easily insert their own comments and questions, or add links between different parts of the data, or even use specialist software such as NVivo, Atlas.ti, or Transana to help them analyze the data.

You may have a chance to interview – or just chat with – some of the participants in your chosen context. In an ethnographic interview, ideally the interviewee will do most of the talking, and will have the freedom to explore topics as s/he chooses; the interviewer's role is to listen and notice points and topics for further exploration later in the interview or in future observations or interviews. Since the aim is to elicit the interviewee's perceived reality, open questions are typically used, and the interview is often organized around prompts rather than a list of questions. These prompts might include materials or photos, or even a real place – for example, interviewing a teacher in her classroom so that she can look around and refer to parts of the room or materials. The interviewer might begin with a "grand tour" prompt (Richards, 2003: 70) related to the activity/context involved – for example, "Could you talk me through the lesson," or "Tell me about a typical day at school" – rather than focusing on specific themes/ideas. Narrative prompts like these allow the interviewee to present his/her own view of the topic within a natural framework. The interviewer should maintain an encouraging manner – for example, showing attention and interest – but allow the interviewee to talk as much as possible, when necessary prompting for further details by picking up on terms used by the interviewee – for example, "You said the first activity was boring; what made it boring for you?" Later in the interview, or in a section of the interview, the researcher may start to ask in depth about some specific points, but if the interview begins like this, there is the risk of the interviewee talking only about what the interviewer expects to hear.

It is important to remember that "an interview is a conversation" (Blommaert and Jie, 2010: 44). Indeed, the researcher may gather helpful data through casual conversations with colleagues or students about lessons or materials, which are not perceived as "interviews"; but even if the conversation is a specially-arranged interview, it is important to try to establish a comfortable atmosphere. For example, when interviewing a student, he or she may be asked to bring a friend to the interview, to provide security and perhaps also to respond and prompt further discussion between the two informants. The researcher should be aware of what kind of conversation it is; for example, the interviewee may be suspicious of the researcher, or trying to impress him/her: the researcher should look out for signs of different agendas in the interview, and interpret what is said in relation to these.

Ethnographic research raises certain ethical issues, largely because it aims to capture naturalistic data. For example, gaining signed, informed consent from every person observed or interacted with may be too intrusive and render the research impractical. In addition, publicizing the kind of informal comments or practices which form part of ethnographic data may have negative repercussions on the informants – for example, if an institution or a teacher becomes aware of covert behavior by students. In general, ethnographic researchers try to keep their sources anonymous in any reports of their research, and to make their role as a researcher known in a way which is appropriate to the local context.

Ethnographic research, even on a small scale, is a gradual learning process. As a teacher you may know a great deal about education, but becoming an ethnographic researcher means taking a fresh look around and asking questions about phenomena which may seem obvious at first. Because of its special qualities, the ethnographic approach can also be adapted for use by students, for them to learn about language and culture in context. Roberts et al. (2001) provide excellent examples of how students can be prepared to notice and analyze social patterns and perceptions when they are studying abroad in a new society. Even without traveling, learners of a language may benefit by observing native or non-native speakers of the second language in real contexts (either in local situations or in recorded media such as TV programs), noting how language is used in coordination with movement, gaze, silence, and other resources, for example, to enact politeness, closeness, or different interpretations of events. As well as improving their understanding of language and culture, discovering unwritten rules of language and culture and understanding the perspectives of others can help learners to improve their observation and critical thinking skills and to apply these to everyday situations.

Conclusion

Ethnography remains a widespread methodology for research in language education research as well as in many other disciplines. Ethnography is now applied to online contexts as well as face-to-face ones – for example, Androutsopoulos (2008). Its focus on the specifics of context also always reminds the researcher of how place and physical features such as gesture are still important reference points in the digital world. New forms of data continue to emerge, such as participant-filmed videos. New kinds of focus, such as the introduction of a particular technology or new forms of language, are also developing, as are new ways of presenting research, such as hyperlinked collections of multimedia, multimodal data which aim to give the reader insight into the process of the research.

Ethnography, like other approaches, has in recent years taken a critical turn. Critical ethnography sharpens ethnography's focus on underlying social patterns to investigate how power can shape social and linguistic opportunities for different people, for example, in English for specific purposes in South Africa (Johns and Makalela, 2011). By identifying and highlighting how social inequalities are enacted and perpetuated in everyday or professional activities, critical ethnography may also help to challenge power structures and propose alternative social-cultural orders, often leveraging the participatory nature of ethnography via collaborative work with informants (for example, Bhattacharya, 2008).

Discussion Questions

1 Think about a time when you entered a new context (for example, a new country, a new institution, a new role, or even a new profession). What did you notice in your first days there? What did you have to get used to? How did you come (rapidly or gradually) to put aside certain expectations and become an *insider*?

2 Think about your own experience as a language learner: how did you develop an understanding of the cultural aspects of the language you were learning? Do you remember any key episodes when you noticed or learned something about the *foreign* culture, and it became less foreign to you?

3 Think of a topic which interests you in your present working context. It could be an aspect of learning, teaching, assessment, or social activity. Is there something that puzzles you or intrigues you about this context? If you wanted to conduct some ethnographic investigation of this topic, what kinds of situation would you want to observe? Who would you want to talk with? What kind of issues might you face in understanding this area of activity?

References

Androutsopoulos, J. (2008). Potentials and limitations of discourse-centred online ethnography. *Language@Internet*, 5(8). Retrieved from http://www.languageatinternet.org/articles/2008/1610

Bhattacharya, H. (2008). New critical collaborative ethnography. In S. Nagy Hesse-Biber & P. Leavy (Eds.), *Handbook of emergent methods* (pp. 303–322). New York: Guildford Press.

Blommaert, J., & Jie, D. (2010). *Ethnographic fieldwork: A beginner's guide.* Clevedon: Multilingual Matters.

Brice Heath, S., & Street, B. V. (2008). *On ethnography: Approaches to language and literacy research.* New York: NCRLL/Teacher's College Press.

Byram, M. (1997). *Teaching and assessing intercultural communicative competence.* Clevedon: Multilingual Matters.

Canagarajah, A. S. (1993). American textbooks and Tamil students: Discerning ideological tensions in the ESL classroom. *Language, culture and curriculum*, 6(2), 143–156.

Carbaugh, D. A. (2005). *Cultures in conversation.* Mahwah, NJ: Lawrence Erlbaum Associates.

Geertz, C. (1973). Thick description: Toward an interpretive theory of culture. In *The interpretation of cultures: Selected essays* (pp. 3–30). New York: Basic Books.

Holliday, A. (2007). *Doing and writing qualitative research* (2nd ed.). Thousand Oaks, CA: Sage.

Johns, A. M., & Makalela, L. (2011). Needs analysis, critical ethnography and context: Perspectives from the client and the consultant. In D. Belcher, A. M. Johns, & B. Paltridge (Eds.), *New directions in English for specific purposes research.* Ann Arbor, MI: University of Michigan Press.

Richards, K. (2003). *Qualitative inquiry in TESOL.* Basingstoke, UK: Palgrave Macmillan.

Roberts, C., Byram, M., Barro, A., Jordan, S., & Street, B. (2001). *Language learners as ethnographers.* Clevedon: Multilingual Matters.

Sterponi, L. (2007). Clandestine interactional reading: Intertextuality and double-voicing under the desk. *Linguistics and Education*, 18(1), 1–23.

TESOL Quarterly (2013). *Qualitative research: (Critical) ethnography guidelines.* Accessed from http://www.tesol.org/read-and-publish/journals/tesol-quarterly/tesol-quarterly-research-guidelines/qualitative-research-(critical)-ethnography-guidelines

Willis, P. E. (1977). *Learning to labor: How working class kids get working class jobs.* New York: Columbia University Press.

Note

[1] Emic and etic are terms used in the social and behavioral sciences to describe different approaches to the subject. The emic, insider, or inductive approach takes the perspective of the research participants as a starting point; the etic, outsider, or deductive approach uses theories and perspectives from outside of the setting being studied.

CHAPTER 20

Narrative Inquiry

Lauren Stephenson and Barbara Harold

INTRODUCTION

Whilst there are a range of theoretical assumptions and approaches associated with narrative inquiry, there is, according to Stanley and Temple (2008: 276) "little shared sense of core concerns, of approach, and even of what narrative is seen as." This chapter aims to provide some coherence and practical guidance when engaging in narrative inquiry in language education. The chapter begins by providing an overview of narrative inquiry and its characteristics. A specific type of narrative inquiry, autoethnography – i.e., a form of narrative research that is conducted and represented from the point of view of the self with the objective of surfacing how culture shapes and is shaped by the personal and perceived as socially constructed knowledge and experiences (Canagarajah, 2012) – is explained and advocated by the authors for use in the field of English language learning (ELL) in this chapter. The steps of narrative inquiry are presented and considerations and challenges are discussed.

BACKGROUND

Narrative inquiry is a means by which we systematically gather, analyze, and represent people's stories as told by them. According to Clandinin and Connelly (2000) narrative inquiry captures personal and human dimensions of experience over time, and takes account of the relationship between individual experience and cultural context. Narrative researchers collect data about people's lives and construct a narrative about their experiences and meanings they contribute to those experiences. Narrativists believe that humans live out stories, are told stories, and are story-telling beings. Stories have always been an important means of communicating lived experiences and creative renderings (Richardson, 1999; Stephenson, 2012).

Narrative research has drawn attention since the 1980s, but only really gathered momentum since the early 1990s (Reissman, 1993). Over the past two decades, narrative research has been conducted in several different fields including sociology, anthropology, history, health education, criminology, family science, women's studies, sociolinguistics, and education. The field of education, with its increasing focus on critical reflection, teacher professional knowledge, and teacher voices, has significantly impacted the developing trends within narrative inquiry. It is only in the last ten years that there has been interest in narrative inquiry in English language learning (ELL). Whilst narrative research methods continue to develop along with the different forms it may take, there are some common themes that run through narrative research in each field and ELL in particular.

Research on this Topic

Narratives of experience are an effective means to structure beliefs and practices of English language learners and educators into meaningful units and to make sense of the behavior of others. For qualitative researchers, through storytelling, individuals engage in narrative theorizing which may result in further discovery and shaping of their professional identities, resulting in new or different stories. These views resonate with recent ELL literature. Hearing the voices and stories of individuals in the context of their own lives has enabled deeper insights about the social and cultural contexts found within the field of ELL, English language teacher education, ELL professional learning, and leadership in ELL.

Drawing on Connelly and Clandinin's (2006) work, researchers using narrative inquiry in ELL describe the lives of individuals, collect and tell stories about people's lives, and write narratives about those experiences and the meanings of those experiences for the individual. Just as these stories capture the experiences of individuals, they also empower the individual participants by allowing the individuals themselves a more legitimate and authentic voice. Narrative inquiry is a form of narrative experience that allows the complexities, challenges, and ambiguities of our individual and collective life experiences to be linked to experiential inquiry.

Characteristics of Narrative Inquiry in English Language Learning

A goal of narrative inquiry in ELL is to explore the way in which people understand who they are and how they come to know and learn English; how to teach English and English literature; how to teach other people how to teach English; professional learning; and leadership perspectives and practices in ELL. Narrative inquiry is best used as a methodological approach when there is first an interest and appreciation of people's storied lives and the chronological or temporal nature of events of experiences. Second, there is an interest in process and change over time. Third, there is an interest in the social dimension, the self, representations of the self, the concept of reflexivity, and an awareness that the researcher is also the narrator.

The 1960s and 1970s saw a reflexive turn in qualitative research. According to Altheide and Johnson (1998: 285) reflexivity means that "the scientific observer is part and parcel of the setting, context or culture he or she is trying to understand and represent." Researchers are expected to describe the interactions that have occurred in the field, their methodologies and the context and participants studied. Reflexivity is where researchers and their methods are interwoven with the social world they study to address criticisms by some of bias and preconceived notions affecting the final research text (Gubrium and Holstein, 1997). "Reflexivity provides a way of dealing with the issues arising from the knowledge that much of what the researcher sees is a result of her own presence" (Holliday, 2001: 154).

For Hammersley and Atkinson (1983), reflexivity requires explicit recognition of the fact that the social researcher in the research act itself is part of the same social world under investigation. Reflexivity acknowledges that the research act and its product are part of the same world. Therefore, reflexivity occurs through interaction with the researcher, the research process, and its product.

As a result of this reflexive turn, increasing numbers of ethnographers began to self-reflect and self-criticise, and as a result appreciate reflexivity's impact on the validity of qualitative research. This focus on the complexities of qualitative research has led to much debate about the nature of different forms of narrative research in ELL. Furthermore, issues related to representation, reporting, interpretation, and voice have become critical factors in defining the narrative methods a researcher adopts. The issue of whose point of view is taken to report the research findings is significant when researchers describe and analyze situations represented as narrative texts. These narrative texts are interpreted by readers who derive their own meanings of the text. Thus, the writing of the narrative becomes equally as important as what happens in the research setting.

AUTOETHNOGRAPHY: ONE FORM OF NARRATIVE INQUIRY

There are many forms of narrative research including: autobiographies; life writing; personal narratives; life histories; oral histories; narrative interviews; narratives of self; and autoethnographies (see below). Creswell (2008) suggests that these numerous types of narrative research can be categorized based upon several characteristics: who authors the account; the scope of the narrative; who provides the story; the theoretical/conceptual framework; and whether the elements are included in one narrative. In this section, we focus on autoethnography, which is one of the forms of narrative inquiry that the authors have used when conducting research in English language learning and teaching (Chang, 2008; Harold and Stephenson, 2010; Stephenson, 2008, 2010, 2012). Autoethnography is a form of self-narrative that places the self within a social context and explores the interface between culture and self (Chang, 2008; Ellis, 2009). It is composed from within a simultaneously personal and social space, a blending of autobiography and ethnography (Ellis, Adams, and Bochner, 2011). Significant interest in autoethnography as both a method and a text emerged as a constant theme in the qualitative research methods literature from 1995. During this period, a number of seminal ideas emerged in the literature and these are discussed below. Where narrative researchers collect data about people's lives and construct a narrative about their experiences and meanings they contribute to those experiences, autoethnographic researchers collect data about their own lives and construct narratives about their own experiences.

When doing an autoethnography, the researcher retrospectively, selectively, and analytically writes about remembered moments that have significantly impacted the trajectory of his/her life. These moments are "epiphanies that stem from, or are made possible by, being part of a culture and/or by possessing a particular cultural identity" (Ellis, Adams, and Bochner, 2011: paragraph 9). Advocates of autoethnographic methods argue that to understand others one should understand the self. It varies from traditional ethnographic methods because the writer is no longer an objective outsider in the texts. The autoethnographer draws on a research base and a set of theoretical and methodological tools to analyze and compare their experiences with the ways others may experience similar epiphanies.

A valuable use of autoethnography is to allow others' experiences to inspire critical self-reflection. Given that autoethnographic methods promote analysis of the self through lived experiences in context, as a result it is possible to learn about the general from the particular. It can help readers understand the way concrete details of a specific life convey a general way of life. Thus, this methodology is an appropriate way to understand how individuals learn English or learn to teach English in a variety of contexts and cultures.

> Autoethnography (re)positions the researcher as a project of inquiry who depicts a site of interest in terms of personal awareness and experience; it utilizes the self consciousness ... to reveal subjectively and imaginatively a particular social setting in the expressions of locally grounded impressions. (Crawford, 1996: 166)

The approach is relatively underutilized in ELL research but has a number of characteristics that make it appropriate for inquiry in this field. These include:

- the use of systemic sociological introspection and emotional recall;
- the inclusion of the researcher's emotional, physical, and spiritual self;
- the production of evocative stories that create the effect of reality;
- the celebration of concrete experience and intimate detail;
- the examination of how human experience is endowed with meaning;
- an encouragement of compassion and empathy;
- a focus on helping us know how to live and cope;
- the repositioning of the readers as co-participants in dialogue;
- the seeking of a fusion between social science and literature;
- the connection of the practices of social science with the living of life;
- the representation of lived experience using a variety of genres.

Unlike traditional ethnographic methods, the experiences of the ethnographer are written into the text in an autobiographical style. Autoethnographic researchers believe in sharing things that are private and unique to the self, based on personal experiences (Ellis, Adams, and Bochner, 2011). Given that one of the functions of post-structural research is to challenge single-minded values and authoritarianism, autoethnography seeks changes to academic discourses. Therefore, autoethnographic approaches encourage alternative forms of writing, which include short stories, novels, personal essays, poetry, conversations, photographic essays, journals, and memoirs.

Narratives about the contexts in which ethnography is produced are about our workplaces, disciplines, friends, family, and self and include our own personalities, histories, and relationships in ELL, as much as our ELL research. The self sees life from a different point of view at different points in life (Geertz, 1995), and the act of writing leads to self-reflection, action, and more reflection that may change the self and possibly the life (Ellis, Adams, and Bochner, 2011). Canagarajah's (2012) *Teacher Development in a Global Profession* is a good example of an actual autoethnography in the field of English language education. It represents the ways in which he "negotiated the differing teaching practices and professional cultures ... in an effort to develop a strategic professional identity" (p. 258).

The next section looks more broadly at the stages and steps of doing narrative inquiry in general.

Practical Applications

Narrative Inquiry: Stages and Steps

According to Connelly and Clandinin (2006), the stages of narrative inquiry involve the field, texts on field experience, and the research text which incorporates the field and the texts and represents those issues of social significance that justify the research.

Using narrative as a methodological tool, research can be conducted in several ways. Typically, though, the researcher either collects a) stories as data and seeks to understand underlying themes from the stories, or b) descriptions of events through interviews, journal entries, documents, artifacts, and observations, and it is important that there is evidence of triangulation of data sources. The researcher then synthesizes the data into narratives or stories where the outcome is a co-constructed narrative between researcher and participants. In narrative analysis, the researcher and participants co-construct meaning throughout the research process rather than as a separate activity carried out after data collection. As such, the process of data gathering and analysis becomes a single harmonious and organic process. The narrative research process is, therefore, highly personal as it requires a very close relationship between the researcher and the participant which needs to be mutually constructed and allows each voice to be equally heard. In contrast to traditional research, narrative research is typically more accessible due to the ability of the researcher to tell stories of specific events using engaging writing techniques of fiction, such as exaggeration, dramatic recall, and unusual phrasings to meet literary criteria of coherence, verisimilitude, and interest. The steps in the narrative research process could look something like this:

1. Identify purpose of the research study and a phenomenon to explore.
2. Decide on the particular narrative approach as the nature of the stages and steps will vary accordingly.
3. Identify an individual (self or other) or individuals who can help you learn about the phenomenon.
4. Develop initial narrative research questions.
5. Consider the researcher's role in relation to the participants and the context.
6. Develop data collection methods, paying particular attention to interviewing.
7. Collaborate with the research participant(s) to construct/co-construct the narrative and to validate the accuracy of the story.
8. Write the narrative account.

CONSIDERATIONS AND CHALLENGES IN NARRATIVE INQUIRY

Although narrative inquiry has become more widely used, it is also seen as controversial within the research community and has been criticized in relation to issues of subjectivity, reliability, validity, and generalizability. However, essentially qualitative research prefers different terms to those used in quantitative research such as trustworthiness, credibility, verisimilitude, and authenticity. These issues along with ethical considerations are now addressed.

The issue of subjectivity has been raised in the educational research literature (Coffey, 1999). Narrative inquiry has been challenged for its lack of rigor in the collection, construction, and analysis of data. This lack of rigor is linked to the problem of bias introduced by the subjectivity of the researcher and others involved in the study (Coffey, 1999). These biases may not be readily apparent to the researcher. Opportunities exist for excluding data contradictory to the researcher's views, thus important data may be overlooked merely because they are so familiar. This can be addressed through reflexivity, critical reflective practice, and by fact checking and discussion of perceptions with critical friends.

It has been said that autoethnographic texts are "self-indulgent writings published under the guise of social research and ethnography" (Coffey, 1999: 155), and that they are written from within events, they are subjective, hence questionable in terms of reflecting reality. However, one must question whether any researcher is completely objective. Instead, autoethnographies have subjective and positioned researchers who shape and are shaped by their experiences. For example, in ELL a teacher will be influenced by a variety of interconnected past and present lived experiences including their own language learning, their own teacher preparation, theories and philosophies of teaching and learning, students taught, colleagues encountered and so on. As researchers, our understanding of others can only proceed from within our own experience. Within the ELL context, these lived experiences will impact the interaction between researcher, participants, and the context.

As a particular narrative technique, autoethnography seeks to reveal one's experience to oneself rather than to generalize, although good autoethnography may speak beyond itself. Autoethnography cannot be free of connection to a world beyond the self because culture impacts every individual. The subjective and positioned autoethnographic researchers who shape and are shaped by their experiences add considerable depth to their research.

We believe that there is no single truth but rather, perceptions and images that convey lived experiences in the past and present, and that anticipate the future. These perceptions are open to different interpretations, just as research data is gathered in a more traditional way. It is therefore important for the researcher to acknowledge their own biases, presuppositions, and interpretations and analyse with those biases in mind. In order to address the charge of narcissism, it is necessary to include strategies suggested throughout the literature for achieving credibility (Sparkes, 2002) and authenticity (Ellis, Adams, and Bochner, 2011). In the wider field and in ELL contexts these include explaining data collection procedures, documenting fieldwork analyses, reporting negative instances, distinguishing between primary and secondary evidence, distinguishing between description and interpretation, tracking what was actually done during different stages, and devising methods to check the quality of the data such as conducting reliability checks or cross checks with critical friends. As such, the values that shape the research are identified so that readers can draw their own conclusions. Qualitative researchers acknowledge their influences on those that they study and the importance of the role of knowledge generated through participant observation. For Ellis, Adams, and Bochner (2011), the concept of reliability in its orthodox sense does not apply in narrative inquiry.

Similarly, Freeman (2006) warns us against looking for a validity that encourages us to think that data can be confirmed by the speaker, where voice is considered representative and meaning as something that can be right or wrong. However, language is not transparent and one single standard of truth does not exist. Thus, narrative research should be deemed valid because it seeks verisimilitude and it is authentic, lifelike, and possible (Polkinghorne, 2007).

Within the process of writing up the field texts in ELL the interpretation depends on the researcher's inner dialogue and finding their own way of representation. Writers of personal narratives try to verbalize and clarify experience by attempting to be as explicit as possible.

The subjectivity inherent in the writing of field texts has been criticized for blurring the borders of fiction and non-fiction. It is the readers who provide validation by comparing their lives to the narratives and by feeling that the stories inform them about other people or lives. Generalizations can be built up if the researcher is able to draw on knowledge and impressions of other contexts and mediate between one context and others. We believe the readers of narrative research texts also play a critical role in relation to verisimilitude and generalizability. The reader of an autobiography must exercise critical judgment given that it is a self-revelatory method. Narrative inquiry texts allow readers to interpret and focus on reference populations determined by the readers. They may also extend readers' experiences by challenging or reaffirming their knowledge, skills, and practices as teachers, teacher educators, and learners in the field of English language teaching.

According to Hammersley (1991), ethical considerations historically have revolved around five issues: participation, deception, privacy, consequences for others and for research. Just as in any research method, these considerations must be addressed explicitly and transparently in narrative inquiry where honesty and high levels of ethical and critical engagement are essential.

A primary focus must be to protect the anonymity of those who share their experiences, perceptions, and stories with the researcher. Identities of certain individuals could perhaps be identified by the circumstances described and this constrains the level of explicitness in relation to ethical considerations. Narrative researchers must stay aware of how these protective devices can influence the integrity of their research as well as how their work is interpreted and understood. Most of the time, they also have to be able to continue to live in the world of relationships in which their research is embedded after the research is completed (Ellis, Adams, and Bochner, 2011).

Conclusion

The foregoing discussion has outlined some of the key characteristics, strengths, and limitations of narrative inquiry as a research method and, through discussion of one particular strand – autoethnography – has highlighted how it might contribute to the ELL context. Narrative inquiry and autoethnography have been in use for almost two decades and many of the initial criticisms of it as self-indulgent and lacking rigor have been challenged in the literature (see Crawford, 1996; Ellis, 2009; Sparkes, 2002). And yet in the field there are still those who are unwilling to accept its different styles of reporting data as legitimate scholarship. However, Tierney's (1998: 68) call for researchers to "seek new epistemological and methodological avenues [and to] chart new paths rather than constantly return to well-worn roads [that] will not take us where we want to go" is as relevant today as when he first made it. More recently, Nelson (2011) revives the call for the TESOL community to consider writing narratives to respond to changing needs of research and new forms of knowledge production in a postmodern world.

The challenge for researchers using a narrative approach in language research is to continue to find ways to clearly demonstrate its scholarliness, honesty, and relevance in the 21st century. Nelson (2011) reminds us that the digital age, with its widespread use of social networking and e-learning, has allowed unexpected forms of self-narrative, authorship, and digital storytelling to emerge, and suggests that experience-based narratives can offer new perspectives in language education research. Researchers in ELL need to step courageously into these new domains to democratize and strengthen the knowledge base in the field.

Discussion Questions

1. What are the key characteristics of narrative inquiry?
2. What is autoethnography and what are its key characteristics?
3. Identify and discuss the strengths and challenges of autoethnography as a means of research?
4. How can narrative inquiry benefit the field of ELL?
5. How are issues of reliability and validity dealt with in narrative inquiry?

References

Altheide, D. L., & Johnson, J. M. (1998). Criteria for assessing interpretive validity in qualitative research biographical method. In N. K. Denzin & Y. S. Lincoln (Eds.), *Collecting and interpreting qualitative materials*. Thousand Oaks: Sage.

Canagarajah, A. S. (2012). Teacher development in a global profession. *TESOL Quarterly*, 46(2), 258–279.

Chang, H. (2008). *Autoethnography as method*. Walnut Creek, CA: Left Coast Press.

Clandinin, D. J., & Connelly, F. M. (2000). *Narrative inquiry: Experience and story in qualitative research*. San Francisco: Jossey-Bass.

Coffey, A. (1999). *The ethnographic self*. London: Sage.

Connelly, F. M., & Clandinin, D. J. (2006). Narrative inquiry. In J. L. Green, G. Camilli, & P. B. Elmore (Eds.), *Complementary methods for research in education* (pp. 477–487). Mahwah, NJ: Lawrence Erlbaum Associates.

Crawford, L. (1996). Personal ethnography. *Communication Monographs*, 63(2), 158–168.

Creswell, J. W. (2008). *Educational research: Planning, conducting, and evaluating quantitative and qualitative research*. Boston: Pearson.

Ellis, C., Adams, T. E., & Bochner, A. (2011). Autoethnography: An overview. *Forum Qualitative Sozialforschung / Forum: Qualitative Social Research*, 12(1), Art. 10. Retrieved from http://nbn-resolving.de/urn:nbn:de:0114-fqs1101108

Ellis. C. (2009). *Revision: Autoethnographic reflections on life and work*. Walnut Creek, CA: Left Coast Press.

Freeman, M. (2006). Life 'on holiday'? In defense of big stories. *Narrative Inquiry*, 16(1), 131–138.

Geertz, C. (1995). *After the fact: Two countries, four decades, one anthropologist*. Cambridge, Mass: Harvard University Press.

Gubrium, J. F., & Holstein, J. A. (1997). *The new language of qualitative method*. New York: Oxford University Press.

Hammersley, M. (1991). *Reading ethnographic research: A critical guide*. London. Longman.

Hammersley, M., & Atkinson, P. (1983). *Ethnography: Principles in practice*. London: Tavistock.

Harold, B., & Stephenson, L. (2010). Researcher development in UAE classrooms: Becoming teacher-leaders. *Education, Business and Society: Contemporary Middle Eastern Issues*, 3(3), 231–242.

Holliday, A. (2001). *Doing and writing qualitative research*. London: Sage.

Nelson, C. (2011) Narratives of classroom life: Changing conceptions of knowledge. *TESOL Quarterly*, 45(3), 463–485.

Polkinghorne, D. E. (2007). Validity issues in narrative research. *Qualitative Inquiry*, 13(4), 471–486.

Reissman, C. K (1993). *Narrative analysis*. Thousand Oaks: Sage.

Richardson, L. (1999). Feathers in our cap. *Journal of Contemporary Ethnography*, 28(6), 660–668.

Sparkes, A. C. (2002). Autoethnography: Self-indulgence or something more? In A. P. Bochner & C. Ellis (Eds.), (2002). *Ethnographically speaking: Autoethnography, literature, and aesthetics*. New York: Rowman & Littlefield.

Stanley, L., & Temple, B. (2008). Narrative methodologies: Subjects, silences, rereadings and analyses. *Qualitative Research*, 8(3), 275–281.

Stephenson, L. (2012). Leadership perspectives and influences: A conversation with five leaders in TESOL. *Arab World English Journal*, 3(4), 19–35. Accessed from http://www.awej.org/awejfiles/_156_12_2.pdf.

Stephenson, L. (2010). Developing curriculum leadership in the UAE. *Education, Business and Society: Contemporary Middle Eastern Issues*, 3(2), 146–158.

Stephenson, L. (2008). Investigating teacher learning: An autoethnographic perspective. In L. Stephenson & P. Davidson (Eds.), *Teacher education and continuing professional development: Insights from the Arabian Gulf* (pp.128–148). Dubai: TESOL Arabia.

Tierney, W. (1998) Life history's history: Subjects foretold. *Qualitative Inquiry*, 4(1), 49–70.

SECTION 3

DOING THE RESEARCH

SECTION 3A

PRELIMINARY STEPS

In Section 3, the chapters are about actually doing research, and thus, they examine ideas that need to be considered while conducting research projects. It is organized into three sections on: A) Preliminary steps; B) Data gathering; and C) Reporting findings.

In section 3A, the chapters cover the preliminary steps that need to be taken. These five chapters cover the important issues of doing a literature review and creating a research niche, conducting research ethically, dealing with human subjects reviews, creating effective research questions, and setting up sampling procedures that will serve the research well.

Chapter 21 describes doing a literature review and creating your research niche. A literature review discusses the pertinent parts of papers and books that are related to the study involved. The chapter describes the purposes and organization of a sound literature review, as well as the importance of creating a niche for the study. The author also discusses four advantages of reviewing the literature and ends with a practical list of dos and don'ts to help in writing a good quality literature review.

Chapter 22 examines ethics in research, but in terms of a) the conduct of researchers working with human participants, and b) the moral ends of research as an activity. The chapter covers important issues including respect for persons, beneficence, justice, informed consent, anonymity, confidentiality, and risk/benefit ratio, and then discusses macroethical and microethical principles. The author also provides practical guidelines for doing ethical research with informed consent when power is unequal, in multilingual and multicultural settings, as well as in digital environments.

Chapter 23, which is about human subjects review, examines the legal, ethical, and institutional issues involved in respecting the rights of the individuals involved as participants in a research study. The chapter discusses macroethical and microethical considerations and three central principles that should govern the conduct of research. The author then considers the researcher's responsibility to informants, various sets of professional organization guidelines, and the roles that human subjects review boards play in the research process. The chapter ends with a discussion of ethics questions that are currently being debated in language research.

Chapter 24 is about creating effective research questions (RQs). The chapter begins by explaining what RQs are and what purposes they serve in a study. The authors then explain issues that novice researchers often face including knowing: where to put the RQs in the research report, what the ideal number of RQs is, whether RQs must be accompanied by hypotheses, and how to order RQs (especially when combining qualitative and quantitative RQs). The chapter then compares quantitative, qualitative, and mixed methods RQs in terms of the qualities of good research questions (with examples of well-written RQs of all three types).

Chapter 25 covers sampling and what it means. *Sampling* is the process of selecting a small group (a *sample*) from a large group (a *population*). The author necessarily introduces concepts like generalization, external validity, and representativeness before describing two main types of sampling: probability and nonprobability. The chapter stresses the importance in probability sampling of random selection in order to achieve generalizability of results, and the fact that nonprobability sampling limits generalizability. The author also describes the steps involved in various sorts of probability sampling, and ends with a discussion of sample size issues.

Editors' Preview Questions

1. What specific area of research are you interested in? What specific topic within that area of research particularly piques your interest? How would you go about finding books and articles on that topic? (see Chapter 21)

2. What does *ethics in research* mean? What do you need to do in a research study to insure that it is ethical with regard to how you treat any students, colleagues, or others who participate in the study? What does your human subjects committee consider ethical research behavior? How would you insure that your research practices are ethical? (see Chapter 22)

3. Does your institution require you to go through a human subjects review? If so, who do you need to contact? What steps do you need to follow? What forms do you need to fill out? And, where do you need to file those forms? (see Chapter 23)

4. What is the purpose of research questions? Are research questions similar in quantitative, qualitative, and mixed methods research? What research questions would you like to address in your research? (see Chapter 24)

5. What is sampling? How would you go about sampling in your research? How would you make sure your sampling is effective and adequately serves the purposes of your research? (see Chapter 25)

CHAPTER 21

Doing a Literature Review and Creating Your Research Niche

Ali Shehadeh

INTRODUCTION

A literature review is a description of the literature and studies that are relevant to our research study. It gives an overview of prior research and constitutes the foundation for our research. A review of the related literature is a fundamental part of any good research study because it contextualizes our research in the relevant body of knowledge; helps us define the scope of our research and creates a niche for it; enables us to develop an assumption; and justifies our research study as a whole. In this chapter, I will first illustrate the main purposes of doing a literature review and the ways of doing it. After that, I will consider ways in which we create a niche, or slot, for our research based on the literature review. In the next section, I will illustrate some advantages of doing a literature review and I will conclude the chapter by presenting a number of practical suggestions that can help us avoid the common pitfalls and produce a strong literature review.

BACKGROUND

As mentioned above, a literature review is a description of the relevant literature that relates to our research study. A review of the relevant literature, first of all, helps us narrow down the focus of our research area to a specific topic and enables us to decide on the direction of our research. For instance, it helps us to know if our research topic is a hot or current one, or not; that is, whether or not the topic of our research is being currently researched and whether it appeals to other researchers or the professional community (Hatch and Lazaraton, 1991: Chapter 1; Lussier, 2010: Chapter 9). Editors, researchers, and the professional community are only interested in current or hot topics. Second, it helps us identify a list of unanswered questions or ideas for further research. Most discussion on the need for further research sections in research studies suggests ways or ideas for further research and for moving forward the research and knowledge base in the field. For example, Mackey and

Gass (2005: 17) remark that, "The conclusion sections of many articles suggest questions for future research."

Similarly, a review of the literature helps us justify our research by providing a rationale for it and contextualizing it in the related literature, for instance, by identifying gaps in the literature and creating a niche, or slot, for our research (see Creating a Research Niche below). The investigator's task is to synthesize different views and research findings, judge and evaluate them, take a definitive stand, provide supporting evidence, and construct a coherent and logical argument or a theory for his or her research study. A review of the related literature, therefore, is not just a collection of other people's views, but a coherently constructed presentation of an idea or a series of ideas that relies on other sources for clarification and verification. For instance, you find 15 studies in the literature on the effects of motivation on second language learners. In reading these studies, you realize that there are two distinct theories about motivation in these articles with about half of the researchers advocating for each. In your literature review, you organize the discussion into two sections, one for each theory. You then discuss each theory in turn, explaining how the literature defines the theory and how it works, but you end your literature review with a section that posits the possibility that both theories may be operating at the same time and complementing each other. Other researchers' views must be acknowledged and used in such a manner that they support rather than overshadow the investigator's views and arguments.

A literature review can be divided into two main (conceptual) parts. Part one reviews and synthesizes the established literature in the field to show theory, trends, consensus, or lack thereof. This might be termed "background research." Background research surveys and describes the relevant and established literature in the form of theories, models, and frameworks that have been developed and examined by researchers over the last two to three decades. The researcher's task is to review, synthesize, and summarize this literature in which they highlight the importance of the field or the topic of the research and demonstrate researchers' continuing interest in it. Background research also describes any possible trends, consensuses, agreements, and disagreements among researchers in our chosen area.

Part two reviews research that was carried out on the topic of the research or related areas in the last five to ten years. This might be termed "prior research." A review of prior research – alternatively called "past research," "prior studies," or "previous studies" – focuses more closely on the specific studies that have investigated the chosen area of research or related areas in the last few years. It describes and illustrates in a more detailed manner the handful of studies that have investigated variables, issues, or aspects relating to our chosen area of research. The task of the investigator here is to explicitly show who did what (specific focus); how they did it (methodology used); and what they found (results obtained); as well as the significance or importance of previous findings. At the same time, this review enables the investigator to identify a gap or gaps in prior research with respect to the variables, issues, or aspects of their chosen area of investigation, prompting them to identify areas for possible investigation – i.e., what still needs to be done – so that their research study is justified, grounded in theory, and contextualized in the relevant literature.

It is important to mention that a literature review can be done in one section only, or two separate sections as mentioned above: one specifically devoted to the background research and one to the prior research. This depends on a host of factors including – but not limited to – the length and type of the article (for example, full-length research article, review article, brief report and summary, short article, response article, magazine article, newsletter article, etc.); the journal's requirements; as well as the scope and limitations of the topic of the research study itself. So, for instance, for magazines, newsletters, and some practical journals – where the literature review section is purposely limited for scope, length, target audience readership, amongst other considerations – it is quite possible to have the background research and the prior research summarized, synthesized, and presented in one section only. However, for full-length research articles, where more weight is given to the previous literature and the theoretical background, it is more appropriate to keep these two sections separate: one for the background research and one for the prior research.

Overall, doing a good literature review for a research study involves providing a critical overview of a substantial range of sources in which the relevant and up-to-date literature is properly summarized, synthesized, and evaluated. This is important in part because it helps the researcher narrow down the focus of the research, contextualize it, and decide on its exact direction – as illustrated above. A good review of the literature also enables the researcher to identify a gap or gaps in the literature and create a research niche, which is the focus of the following section.

CREATING A RESEARCH NICHE

One of the main objectives of doing a literature review is to create a niche – i.e., a place or slot – for our research in order to justify our study and provide a rationale for it. This is usually achieved by an analysis and evaluation of the existing research, and identifying the gaps therein, and demonstrating the need for further research.

So how do we do this? That is, how do we identify a gap in the literature and create our research niche? One way of doing this is by finding inconsistent, inconclusive findings or contradictions in prior research – for example, the benefits of teacher's feedback vs. peers' feedback for second language (L2) high school students' oral skills; the effects of explicit feedback vs. implicit feedback on L2 students' compositions. Another way is by identifying an aspect, issue, variable, or something that has not been controlled for and is in need of further research – for example, the effect of online planning on young learners' performance in task-based language teaching; the role of high school teachers' views and attitudes in a successful implementation of task-based language teaching in an EFL context in the Gulf region. A third way is by extending research beyond its existing territories or domains – for example, middle school students' perceptions of collaborative writing and collaborative editing in an EFL context in China. Further, you might find a controversy that may have been left unresolved – for example, the role of L2 learners' reprocessing and restructuring of their output in second language acquisition. Mackey and Gass (2005: 17) add that "research investigations need to be current, which of course entails that the questions have not already been answered in the literature, or have only partially been answered and therefore require further or additional investigation." The information obtained in all these cases may constitute a good basis for your study or a follow-up study, assuming – and verifying from existing research – that other researchers have not conducted such studies (Mackey and Gass, 2005: 16–19). Indeed, explaining the gap in the literature and how your study will fill it, plus a clear set of research questions, is often presented as a complete subsection at the end of the literature review entitled *Purpose*.

Creating and explaining your research niche is based first and foremost on the belief that *you* have something important or useful to say; or that you have an original angle or approach to something, for instance:

- a new or different sample of data
- a further confirmation of existing theory/perspective/research
- an extension (theoretical or pedagogical) to existing theory/perspective/research beyond its current territories and boundaries

- a challenge to existing theory/perspective/research
- an application of a certain theory, perspective, research, or mode
- a research agenda to propose (theoretical or pedagogical)
- a way of evaluating and moving the field forward

Second, it is based on the assumption that you have an ability to successfully convey this belief to the interested reader, editor, or reviewer; and third that you have an ability to translate this belief successfully into a written form following the appropriate publishing conventions and guidelines (Shehadeh and Burns, 2011).

All these considerations need to be borne in mind in order to create a niche for your research; otherwise, you will run into the "so-what response" to your research by failing to meet the "so-what question" requirements (Lussier, 2010: 50; Mackey and Gass, 2005: 17). You can see yourself that, if readers and reviewers respond to your explanation of the niche for your study with a "so-what" question, your paper will stand very little chance of being read, much less published.

Issues to consider when trying to answer the "so-what" question include the extent to which your research study meets key publication criteria: is it making an original contribution to the field, providing implications for practitioners, or contributing to the theoretical interest in the field? In other words, it is not enough to say that this or that has not been done (investigated, explored, examined, tested, etc.) before – i.e., simply to identify a gap in the literature. It is equally important to demonstrate the value of your research and justify its contribution to the field and the related literature. Lussier (2010: 183) suggests a few hands-on tips, in the form of "why," "what," and "who" questions, as a guide for answering. However, it may be useful to expand the questions to include all of the newspaper writer's WH-questions: what, when, where, why, how, and who.

- What is the gap that you perceive in the literature? What briefly is your topic? And what are your research questions?
- When did you understand that there was a gap in the literature?
- Where does your study fit into the literature?
- Why would anyone care? Why is your research necessary, even valuable? Answering these two questions responds directly to the "so-what" question.
- How does your study fill the gap in the literature?
- Who will care? Students? Teachers? Administrators? Other researchers?

Other Advantages of Reviewing the Literature

In addition to demonstrating that you have consulted and understood articles and books relevant to your study (thereby showing how your work relates to the general body of knowledge in the field), providing a logical argument for your research, and creating your research niche – as described in the previous two sections respectively – doing a good literature review has a number of other advantages for your research study.

First, a review of the previous literature helps you arrive at your research questions or hypotheses and justify them. Good research questions or hypotheses quite often arise from the previous literature and are grounded in it, when, for instance, we develop these questions and hypotheses through suggestions made by other researchers (Andrews, 2003; Lussier, 2010; Mackey and Gass, 2005; Sunderland, 2010). For example, Andrews (2003:

17–18) argues that research questions must be grounded in the relevant literature and that there must be a consistency between the literature reviewed and the rest of the study. Similarly, Mackey and Gass (2005) state that "Most reasoned research questions come from a reading of the literature and an understanding of the history of current issues." (For other ways of arriving at your research questions, see Andrews, 2003; Hatch and Lazaraton, 1991: Chapter 24.)

Second, reviewing the relevant literature helps you in identifying and choosing, or deciding on the most appropriate way to approach the design and research methodology of your study, including the selection of a target population, methods of data collection, data collection procedures and treatment, and analysis of data. Indeed, it is very difficult to think of a sound methodology or research design, defined as a framework around which we organize our data collection, away from the related literature and the relevant theoretical background. For instance, Rasinger (2010: 57) argues that "research design, theoretical background and actual method used are inseparably linked and form the overall framework for our study, hence it is crucial that these three parts work well together."

Third, reviewing the literature helps you discuss, contextualize, interpret, and judge the findings of your study in reference to the previous literature in the field – which you have already reviewed in your introduction, and which has motivated your study in some way. For instance, did your study provide full or partial confirmation or support for prior research? Why? Why not? In what way? Thus, having analyzed the previous literature, you are in an excellent position to examine your results for how they fit into the more general developments in the literature. Do your results support findings in previous studies? Refute them? Find something entirely different? Equally important, you can compare your study critically in terms of its design, power, and limitations to other studies in the literature.

In addition, the discussion part of your study enables you to see whether and to what degree you were able to fill the gap or gaps you identified in your literature review. Some of the questions you will ask here might include: Did you fill a gap in the literature? How significant or important were your findings? What contribution did your study make to the previous literature and to the general body of knowledge in the field? It is important to explicitly state in your discussion whether and in what way your work has successfully filled a gap or contributed to the literature. Indeed, the value of your study and the importance of its contribution can only make real sense by comparing and contrasting its findings to the previous literature, and by the extent to which your findings were able to successfully fill a gap or gaps in the literature.

Fourth, finally, another advantage for doing a literature review is that it enables you to make principled and specific recommendations and suggestions for further research based on the findings of your study in conjunction with prior research, especially when there are contradictory or inconclusive findings. Suggestions for future research may include:

- Aspects of your original research questions that you were unable to address in your study
- Questions that arose because of the limitations of your study
- Questions that you did not feel were adequately addressed in your study
- New questions that popped into your mind while you were collecting the data, analyzing the results, or writing up the research report.

All of which can and should be framed in terms of the previous literature.

Viewed from this perspective, the value of doing a good literature review extends beyond your current research study to providing directions and suggestions for further research.

Conclusion

In this chapter, I have illustrated the main goals, advantages and ways of doing a good literature review, and ways of creating a research niche. I explained that doing a good literature review and using the previous literature to contextualize our work and justify it, enables us to create our research niche, and shows how our work and findings relate to the general body of knowledge in the field. All of these factors lend authority to our work and give credibility to our research as a whole.

Finally, Lussier (2010: 185–186) makes a number of practical suggestions that researchers must bear in mind when doing a literature review. These include citing all up-to-date research, in particular empirical research, that has relevance to our study; synthesizing and summarizing past studies by way of comparing and contrasting their findings and showing areas of consistent and inconsistent findings; highlighting major themes and trends arising from the relevant literature and past studies; identifying gaps in the literature and past studies in order to both provide rationale for our research project and contextualize it in the related research; and specifying clearly what new knowledge or original contribution our research project will have for the related literature.

If followed properly, these suggestions will help you avoid many of the pitfalls that weaken a potentially good literature review. Such pitfalls include, first, your review of the literature should avoid turning into a historical narrative, for example, if it starts with the turn of the twentieth century and includes anything and everything that directly or indirectly relates to the field or the purpose of the study. Second, the review should be selective rather than comprehensive or exhaustive citing virtually all the relevant articles that relate to your study. Third, the review should be up-to-date and avoid having mostly sources, especially the key ones, being out-of-date. Fourth, the review should lead to your research questions or hypotheses. Fifth and finally, the relevant literature should be properly synthesized or summarized.

Discussion Questions

1. Examine a recent research article in one of the tier-one or tier-two journals in your field. How have the authors identified a gap in the literature and created a niche for their research? Look at an article you recently published in a tier-one or tier-two journal. How did your literature review lead to or motivate your research questions or hypotheses, and/or your methodology and research design?

2. Look at the editors' or reviewers' reports of a recent research article you had submitted to a reputable journal in your field, but was rejected. What were their concerns about the so-what question concerning originality of your study, its contribution to the literature, its underlying rationale, or its contextualization in the relevant, up-to-date literature?

3. Examine a recent research article in one of the tier-one or tier-two journals. How did the authors discuss, contextualize, and interpret their findings in reference to the previous literature in the field and/or make recommendations and suggestions for further research based on their findings?

4. Examine a recent research article published in a reputable journal in your field. To what degree does its literature review resonate with the points made and explained throughout this chapter?

References

Andrews, R. (2003). *Research questions*. London: Continuum.

Hatch, E., & Lazaraton, A. (1991). *The research manual: Design and statistics for applied linguistics*. New York: Newbury House.

Lussier, R. (2010). *Publish don't perish: 100 tips that improve your ability to get published*. Charlotte, NC: Information Age.

Mackey, A., & Gass, S. (2005). *Second language research: Methodology and design*. New York: Routledge.

Rasinger, S. (2010). Quantitative methods: Concepts, frameworks and issues. In L. Litosseliti (Ed.), *Research methods in linguistics* (pp. 49–67). London: Continuum.

Shehadeh, A., & Burns, A. (2011). Action research in TESOL. Pre-conference Certificate Course offered on 9 March, 2011, at the 17th TESOL Arabia International Annual Conference. 9–12 March, 2011, Dubai, UAE.

Sunderland, J. (2010). Research questions in linguistics. In L. Litosseliti (Ed.), *Research methods in linguistics* (pp. 9–28). London: Continuum.

CHAPTER 22

Ethics in Research

Magdalena Kubanyiova

INTRODUCTION

Ethics in research typically refers to at least two important areas: the ethical conduct of the researcher working with human subjects and the moral ends of the research activity itself. The first set of concerns has traditionally been embedded in Institutional Review Boards (or IRBs) – the role of which is discussed further in Chapter 23 – and also in professional codes of ethical practice, such as *TESOL Quarterly Research Guidelines*, which specify the kinds of behaviors that underlie the responsible conduct of research and safeguard human subjects. The second concern – the values and moral purposes of applied linguistics research or, in other words, the consideration of what research is for and what purposes it should serve – has been debated at research conferences and in published articles (for example, Ortega, 2012).

A version of formal ethical clearance is required in most research institutions and contexts. Even if this may not be the case for certain forms of practitioner research, experienced language teachers are – by virtue of their in-depth understanding of the researched context – likely to be sensitive to the ethical considerations inherent in their research. Even so, with the rapidly changing landscape of language teaching around the world, involving people from diverse linguistic, sociocultural, and socio-political backgrounds who are learning, teaching, and using languages in a variety of settings – both material and virtual – explicit reflection on both moral ends and moral conduct is important in sensitizing the researchers to the ethical questions and dilemmas that may arise in these new territories. The purpose of this chapter is to offer an overview of some of the key themes in the current debates and outline practical guidelines for addressing ethics in language research.

BACKGROUND

Most research projects – particularly if these are funded by external funding agencies – require ethical clearance, typically granted by institutional committees set up specifically for this purpose. The general ethical criteria which inform these procedures are typically derived from three core principles that serve as moral standards for research involving humans: respect for persons, which binds researchers to protect the well-being of the research participants and avoid harm and/or potential risks; beneficence, that is, ensuring that the research project yields benefits while minimizing harm; and justice, or in other words, a fair distribution of research benefits.

To address the first principle, researchers are usually required to produce evidence of "informed consent" or, in other words, demonstrate that the research participants who have agreed to take part in the research project have been sufficiently informed of the research purposes and their responsibilities and have a clear understanding of the voluntary nature of their participation. Consent forms that the participants are normally asked to sign (for examples, see Mackey and Gass, 2005) contain a brief description of the project and an explanation of what the participants are asked to do, how the data will be collected and used, and how the participants can exercise their right to withdraw from the project if they wish. Additional measures for safeguarding the principle of respect for persons include the protection of the participants' identity (anonymity) and privacy (confidentiality), and the consent forms should normally incorporate an explanation of how these will be observed.

The principles of beneficence and justice have received far less attention in institutional codes of practice: the usefulness to communities who participate in our research and who are supposed to benefit from it is typically assessed only in the sense of offsetting potential risks, which has also been referred to as the risk/benefit ratio. However, reflections on the implications of these ethical principles have been included in the current debates in applied linguistics research. For example, Gass (2010) has raised a practical issue related to the principle of justice in experimental research. As she argues, even though our treatment may be seen as generally beneficial to the participants in our research, experimental researchers who recruit experimental and control groups are still in a position of having to deny those benefits to the latter group for the sake of the experiment. Some practical solutions to this ethical dilemma have been offered, such as providing the treatment at a later stage of the project when this would no longer interfere with the results of the experiment.

Considering the principle of justice and beneficence more broadly, Ortega (2012) has argued that the requirement of fair distribution of research benefits may be violated if our research persistently targets – often out of convenience – only certain types of, typically privileged, populations while overlooking or excluding the needs, concerns and personal, educational, socioeconomic, and linguistic realities of others. This, as she maintains, has particularly been the case in the instructed SLA domain and she has called for adopting an ethical lens as criteria informing researchers' theoretical and methodological decisions in their pursuit of socially and educationally valuable knowledge.

Research on this Topic

The current debates about ethics in research reflect a growing recognition that although raising researchers' awareness of the moral purposes of their research activity is important and their adherence to the ethical principles and codes of conduct is often mandated, these macroethical principles (cf. Kubanyiova, 2008) in themselves do not offer a blueprint for ethical language research. On the contrary, numerous tensions and dilemmas have been documented in research – despite the researchers' routine compliance with the common ethical principles embedded in institutional reviews – as well as in projects in which researchers pursued a deliberate reflection on the moral purposes of their activity and strove to promote social justice, empower the researched communities, or adopt an advocacy stance (for example, Holton, 2009; Kolouritis, 2011 and the other articles in the same special issue).

For instance, it has been pointed out that there may be issues of relevance and limits in consent depending on the specific context, that the matter of privacy is not resolved after access has been negotiated, and that even the best intentions and practices could lead to indirect coercion. More specifically, the so-called "ethically important moments" have been shown to arise when different macroethical principles clash in the course of a specific research project (Kubanyiova, 2008). This includes situations – typically found in highly contextualized research such as case studies, ethnographies, or specific types of action research – when securing confidentiality and anonymity of the research participants (principle of respect for persons) may not be possible without compromising the responsibility to produce accurate knowledge (principle of beneficence). Another issue may arise in projects aimed at changing attitudes and/or practices, when the best intentions of the researchers to serve the research community by actively promoting change (principle of beneficence) in fact violate the participants' right for self-determination (principle of respect for persons), when this change – however worthwhile and socially desirable it may be perceived to be by the researchers – is neither valued nor desired by the research participants. This dilemma is further augmented in contexts which do not offer an easy definition of who is representative of the researched community, and when the issue of whose voices should be heard and whose agendas advocated is far less clear (cf. Holton, 2009).

It appears, therefore, that although the macroethical principles are necessary, functioning as important signposts in the researcher's practice, they do not hold all the answers for making ethical choices in the actual practice of conducting research. Drawing on the work outside of applied linguistics and using examples from her research with teachers of English as a foreign language, Kubanyiova (2008) has proposed a more situated approach to ethical decision-making in language research, adopting a microethical framework for ethical decision-making grounded in "ethics of care" and "virtue ethics."

The underlying premise of the "ethics of care" model is that research is primarily a relational activity demanding the researcher's sensitivity to, and emotional identification and solidarity with, the people under study. This approach extends the concerns embedded in the macroethical principles by emphasizing the need to move beyond labels, such as vulnerable persons, and responding to the needs of specific individuals in specific contexts and in specific stages of the research project. Virtue ethics theory, on the other hand, originates in Aristotelian ethics and highlights the importance of the researcher's ability to recognize microethical dilemmas as they arise in the concrete research practice. The emphasis is therefore not on following principles but rather on the development of the moral character of the researchers, their ability and willingness to discern situations with potential ethical ramifications as they arise in the research practice, and their ability to make decisions that are informed by both macroethics of principles and microethics of care.

To sum up, the currently debated situated view of ethical research practice has highlighted the need to integrate both macro- and micro-perspectives of ethical research practice into the ethical decision making process. The reflection on the general principles of respect for persons, beneficence, and justice must be complemented by an ongoing cultivation of the researcher's ability to discern and respond to ethically important moments and dilemmas as they arise in the specific course of research. Focusing on selected issues documented in the applied linguistics research, the next section illustrates the practical applications of ethical reasoning grounded in the situated view of ethical research practice.

PRACTICAL APPLICATIONS

INFORMED CONSENT IN CONTEXTS WITH UNEQUAL POWER DYNAMICS

The notion of informed consent implies that research participants agree to being involved in a research project on the basis that they fully understand the nature of the research and their role in it and that they can exercise their right to opt out at any stage with no penalty. This, however, could be problematic in contexts with unequal research relationships, particularly when the researcher is also the research participants' teacher, teacher trainer, or supervisor and thus acts as a gatekeeper. Even though the signatures for the consent form may be fairly easily obtained in such settings, further reflection is needed on whether they in fact always guarantee a fully informed and voluntary agreement to take part in research.

Grounding the discussion in the research context of ESL education in Canada, Kolouriotis (2011), for instance, has identified research with international students, newcomers, immigrants to Canada, and Aboriginal people as especially prone to ethical challenges of this type, citing the lack of language proficiency (see also the next section) or different cultural norms and expectations underlying roles and responsibilities of those in positions of lesser authority as potential barriers to fully informed consent. Language teachers or teacher educators conducting research on their own classrooms in a variety of settings are therefore particularly likely to face such ethical dilemmas, especially if the students or teacher trainees may feel, as a result of their own sociocultural background and educational history, that they cannot refuse a request to someone in a position of authority without negative consequences for their academic, professional, or personal future.

Developing trusting relationships has been seen as one way of minimising the ethical threat arising from unequal power dynamics. Yet, as has been illustrated in the past research, good rapport between the researcher and the researched does not necessarily erase the power differences and is therefore no guarantee of informed consent demanded by the macro-ethical principles. This is because – as illustrated in Kubanyiova (2008) – feelings of coercion may arise precisely because of the participants' desire to please the researcher, and their efforts not to jeopardize the relationship may lead to undue pressure to comply with requests for participation, despite the participants' feelings of unease about their role in the project, which may remain unarticulated and, therefore, less easily accessible to the researcher.

Both examples demonstrate that applying the situated approach to ethics in the actual practice of ethical decision-making implies a recognition that an initially signed consent form is but the beginning of the researcher's systematic and ongoing inquiry into his or her ethical research practice. Such inquiry starts with a thorough examination of the initial, as well as evolving, power dynamics inherent in the researcher-researched relationship. Central to the researcher's task is the development of heightened awareness of possible "ethically important moments" when a formal consent may, paradoxically, breach the principle of respect of persons. As has been illustrated above, this issue can arise if consent is primarily motivated by the fear of negative consequences rather than a willingness to contribute to research. The researcher's responsiveness to the participants' assumptions, agendas, and anxieties may include one or more of the following:

- creating a genuine space for an open dialogue which allows the research participants to voice their concerns;
- providing verbal re-assurances of the entirely voluntary nature of the research at crucial moments of the research project (especially once potential issues have been identified);

- negotiating and adjusting the elements of the research design to address the participants' anxieties;
- encouraging the participants to consider withdrawal from some or all parts of the project (especially if it has become clear that the participants' sense of obligation to the researcher is preventing them from initiating such desired course of action explicitly).

LANGUAGE RESEARCH IN MULTILINGUAL AND MULTICULTURAL SETTINGS

Much of applied linguistics research involves multilingual speakers in a range of linguistic and cultural settings and ethical challenges may arise from at least two situations: a) the research is conducted in the research participants' L2 which may be of limited proficiency and b) the research generates unfavorable portrayals of research participants as deficient users of L2.

The guidelines offered by Burns (1999: 73) in order to address the first issue provide the researchers with a useful toolkit of solutions to potential ethical challenges associated with the research participants' limited language proficiency. The suggestions include:

- explaining the research in language appropriate to the level of the students and encouraging the students to ask questions about it;
- providing written information and discussing it in class;
- arranging for bilingual information or explanations through aides or other more advanced students;
- explaining the research to family members with higher levels of L2 proficiency.

Just which of these guidelines would safeguard ethical conduct in the actual research practice, however, depends on the researchers' assessment of the impact of their research conduct on the participants' well-being in the specific context of the research project. For example, Koulouriotis (2011) reports on the experiences of two researchers, one of whom discovered that by conducting her research in the participants' L2, she was not handicapping the L2 learners who took part in her research, as the common ethical concern may have been. Rather, she realized that choosing to conduct her interviews in the learners' L2 enabled her to create a context for authentic communication which was highly valued by the participants. Although this practice required intensive negotiation and listening effort on the part of the researcher, the participants' feelings of pride and accomplishment gave this researcher a reassurance that important moral ends were being met thanks to this decision. In contrast, the other researcher in a different research setting opted for the use of the participants' native language as the medium of research interaction. This ethical decision was grounded in her awareness of the research participants' needs and abilities and her resulting conviction that it was only through their mother tongue that the participants could access a deeper level of their experiences, thoughts, and feelings.

The second issue related to the practical applications of ethical research practice in multilingual and multicultural settings concerns a conscious reflection on the linguistic and social representations of bilingual research participants, particularly those with the developing competence in a second, additional, or heritage language or those with complex multilingual profiles. A typical discourse adopted in the past research has been that of deficiency which has treated any non-standard language production as errors and evidence of failure. This is now slowly being redressed in current debates (cf. Ortega, 2012) which have called for language research which recognizes the rich linguistic resources that bilingual speakers purposefully draw on as they make meanings in their interactions in a range of social settings in the pursuit of diverse social, educational, and identity goals.

ETHICS IN RESEARCHING DIGITAL ENVIRONMENTS

The rapid development of digital technologies has opened up new research avenues and numerous possibilities for collecting insightful language data, be it on interaction, learner language, negotiation of social and virtual identities, literacy practices, or many others. More accessible ways of capturing language interaction through audio and video recordings, including the increasingly widespread Web 2.0 tools, offer virtually unlimited options for studying linguistic practices of diverse populations. The question that is far from resolved in the contemporary applied linguistics research, but which researchers will have to continue to explore, is the extent to which the ethical landscape of researchers' roles and responsibilities has been transformed by such unprecedented opportunities for accessing online language data.

For example, although the new technologies have enabled access to a wide range of authentic language practices, to what extent does the participants' consent also imply their agreement to be portrayed in an unfavorable light when such authentic interaction involves all kinds of coarse vernacular language, including swearing? Related to this is an understanding that social media participants draw on diverse, often multilingual, communicative repertoires and choose to present different aspects of their identities as they engage with diverse audiences. Ethical research must therefore seek to represent both the authentic online interactions and the lived experiences of those who participate in them (Lee, 2014).

Yet, even this practical guideline does not fully address the highly contested nature of some of the most common categories for ethical reflection in digital research contexts, including the notions of harm, vulnerability, privacy, and human subjects (for example, to what extent should the principle of respect for persons apply to avatars in Second Life?). Fully aware of the far from clear-cut nature of these categories, Markham and Buchanan (2012), members of the Association of Internet Researchers' Ethics Working Group, have produced a comprehensive set of ethical guidelines which language researchers can draw on as they reflect on their ethical responsibilities in these new research environments. In line with the situated approach to ethical decision-making advocated throughout this chapter, these guidelines task the researchers with the responsibility to make such context-sensitive decisions within a specific research project, to be responsive and adaptable to continually changing technologies, and to acknowledge the possibility of multiple judgments, ambiguity, and uncertainty as part of the process.

CONCLUSION

This chapter has shown that ethics in research involves both adhering to well-established ethical guidelines, principles, and values, and discerning ethically important moments in action. The first sensitizes the researchers to potential ethical concerns and worthwhile research purposes and develops their understanding of the nature of research ethics. The second cultivates their ability to apply ethical principles in the actual practice of the research activity in the particular setting with particular people. The examples in this overview have shown that what is ethical research practice in language research needs to be constantly negotiated and renegotiated in the context of the specific research project. This approach to ethical decision-making resonates with Hornberger's (2006) view that in order to advance our understandings, we must approach our research with humility and respect for both communities and individuals.

Discussion Questions

1. How relevant is a reflection on the social value of research in relation to your research context?

2. What purposes does your research aim to fulfill and how valued are these by the research community?

3. Describe an ethically important moment that has recently arisen in your own research. How did you respond to it and, applying the terms in this chapter, how would you describe your approach to your ethical decision making?

4. The Practical Applications section describes three contexts which invite researchers to reflect on a situated approach to ethical decision-making. Think of another example within these or other contexts where macro- and micro-ethical principles may clash and provide an account of what researchers may do to respond to this dilemma.

5. Suggest ways in which the virtue ethics approach can be used in practice to cultivate novice researchers' ethical awareness and self-reflexivity.

References

Burns, A. (1999). *Collaborative action research for English language teachers*. Cambridge: Cambridge University Press.

Gass, S. (2010). Experimental research. In B. Paltridge & A. Phakiti (Eds.), *Continuum companion to research methods in applied linguistics* (pp. 7–21). London: Continuum.

Holton, G. (2009). Relatively ethical: A comparison of linguistic research paradigms in Alaska and Indonesia. *Language Documentation and Conservation*, 3(2), 161–175.

Hornberger, N. H. (2006). Negotiating methodological rich points in applied linguistics research: An ethnographer's view. In M. Chalhoub-Deville, C. A. Chapelle & P. Duff (Eds.), *Inference and generalizability in applied linguistics: Multiple perspectives* (pp. 221–240). Amsterdam: John Benjamins.

Koulouriotis, J. (2011). Ethical considerations in conducting research with non-native speakers of English. *TESL Canada Journal*, 28 (Special Issue 5), 1–15.

Kubanyiova, M. (2008). Rethinking research ethics in contemporary applied linguistics: The tension between macroethical and microethical perspectives in situated research. *The Modern Language Journal*, 92(4), 503–518.

Lee, C. (2014). Language choice and self-presentation in social media: The case of university students in Hong Kong. In P. Seargeant & C. Tagg (Eds.), *The language of social media* (pp. 91–111). Basingstoke: Palgrave Macmillan.

Mackey, A., & Gass, S. (2005). *Second language research: Methodology and design*. Mahwah, NJ: Lawrence Erlbaum Associates.

Markham, A., & Buchanan, E. (2012). Ethical decision-making and internet research: Recommendations from the AoIR Ethics Working Committe. Retrieved from http://www.aoir.org/reports/ethics2.pdf

Ortega, L. (2012). Epistemological diversity and moral ends of research in instructed SLA. *Language Teaching Research*, 16(2), 206–226.

CHAPTER 23

Human Subjects Review

Dudley W. Reynolds

INTRODUCTION

Almost without exception, the data for language research come from human informants or study participants. This means that there are ethical considerations involved in how the individuals providing that data are treated during the planning, data collection, and reporting phases of the research. From the very inception of a project, we must think about which societal groups we will know more about as a result of the research and whether we are privileging one group over others simply because they are easier to access or more advantaged. If we are working with existing data like published news stories or internet blogs, what are our responsibilities to the original producers of the data who probably never thought their work would become the subject of a research study? If we are interacting with individuals in order to gain data, what should we tell them about the project and when should we tell them? Similarly, what are acceptable methods for inviting and/or encouraging people to participate in a study? What are our responsibilities to a participant if something goes wrong or is unexpectedly revealed while we are collecting data? Once we have collected the data, what precautions should we take in how we store it? Finally, when we write up a study, what information should we provide about the individuals providing the data and what should we in turn share with them about our conclusions?

Respect for the rights of individuals in a research study is not only an ethical but also a legal requirement. Most governments, academic institutions, and publication outlets require a formal review of the procedures for recruiting participants, collecting data, storing data, and reporting conclusions prior to the start of any study involving human subjects. These review requirements have emerged in part as a reaction to high profile instances of questionable research including studies conducted on prisoners in Nazi Germany and a US government-funded study on the effects of syphilis where the participants were not informed about drugs that could have significantly improved their quality of life. Because of this history, some researchers, especially in the social sciences, unfortunately see the review requirements as designed to handle extreme cases of medical research and therefore overly protective. In reality, however, careful attention to the questions asked by the review process can serve as a guide for improving the quality of any study. They also point back to the more basic ethical considerations that any researcher needs to take personal responsibility for.

Background

Kubanyiova (2008) – and in the preceding chapter – makes a useful distinction between macroethical and microethical considerations involved in the conduct of research. Macroethical principles spell out the basic guidelines for responsible research as determined by a community. They may be established by regulatory bodies, professional or disciplinary organizations, or local institutions. One of the most often cited statements of this type is a report commissioned by the U.S. government's Department of Health, Education, and Welfare in 1979, known as "The Belmont Report" (*National Commission for the Protection of Human Subjects of Biomedical and Behavioral Research,* 1979). It identifies three basic principles that should guide the conduct of research:

1. *Respect for persons* – individuals have the right to make decisions for themselves and deserve special safeguards if something such as age, cognitive impairment, or incarceration limits their ability to make decisions;
2. *Beneficence* – research should seek to maximize its benefits, while minimizing its harm, for individuals and society;
3. *Justice* – both the benefits and risks associated with research should be shared equally across society.

More specific to the field of language research, the British Association for Applied Linguistics has issued a set of "Recommendations on Good Practice in Applied Linguistics," in which it identifies a general responsibility to informants:

> Applied linguists should respect the rights, interests, sensitivities, and privacy of their informants. It is important to try to anticipate any harmful effects or disruptions to informants' lives and environment, and to avoid any stress, undue intrusion, and real or perceived exploitation. Researchers have a responsibility to be sensitive to cultural, religious, gender, age and other differences: when trying to assess the potential impact of their work, they may need to seek guidance from members of the informants' own communities. In certain types of contract research, respect for informants cannot be guaranteed, and in these cases, researchers should consider carefully whether they should continue with the project. (The British Association for Applied Linguistics, 2006:4)

Most guides to ethical conduct issued by local institutions mirror those of the government regulatory bodies that require the institution to have a review process in place. There are instances, however, where particular departments may issue disciplinary interpretations of those broader regulations. For example, the Ontario Institute for Studies in Education at the University of Toronto has issued a statement to help students and faculty differentiate between field-based inquiry as an exercise in professional development, and formal research projects, the latter of which should undergo regulatory review (University of Toronto Research and Innovation, n.d.).

Public statements such as the Belmont Report or departmental guidelines provide useful gauges for ensuring that our research complies with the general expectations of society and our disciplinary community. We must also be prepared, however, for the issues that arise throughout the planning, implementation, and reporting of a study for which there may not be clear community guidelines, what Kubanyiova refers to as "microethical" questions. Discussions in the language research literature illustrate some of these questions. Ortega, for example, challenges language researchers to realize that a choice as basic as, for example, what to study and how to study it should be ethically-driven; she boldly asserts that, "the value of research is to be judged by its social utility; value-free research is impossible; and epistemological diversity is a good thing" (Ortega, 2005: 427). Others (for example, Baude, 2007; Dorian, 2010; Innes, 2010) have pointed out the ethical problems that arise when working with archival texts and corpora, including how to determine – and respect – the audiences and purposes for which the original speakers of those texts intended their words to be used. Lee (2011) highlights tensions that can emerge during a confidential interview when sensitive information or the potential for harm to others is revealed. Li (2011) discusses the difficulties associated with representing the voices of research participants during qualitative data analyses. Such discussions underscore the need to consider continuously and consciously the implications of our research not only for scientific knowledge but also for the individuals who make it possible.

Research

There are a number of professional associations which provide useful discussions and guidelines for addressing both macroethical and microethical concerns with relevance to language researchers (see the reference section for full list and details).

Practical Applications

The U.S. Department of Health and Human Services' *International Compilation of Human Research Standards* currently lists over 1000 regulations in more than 100 countries. It is therefore impossible to provide a detailed description of the applicable review process for every study. In general, however, such regulations specify the entities responsible for conducting a review, the procedures for a review, and the issues that should be determined through review.

In many countries, the entities responsible for reviewing research are located primarily within academic institutions. They operate under names such as "Institutional Review Board" (IRB) or "Research Ethics Committee." They may be comprised of faculty, staff, and administrators from the institution; outside experts such as medical doctors; and members of the general public. In cases where there is not an established review board to which it would be appropriate to submit a study, it is possible to set up a board for a particular study or hire a private company to conduct a review.

Often review boards are allowed to follow different procedures for different types of study. For example, the US *Code of Federal Regulations*, Title 45, Part 46 specifies three levels of review. Studies which pose minimal risk to participants and which involve minimally invasive procedures as defined in the regulation may be reviewed relatively quickly and determined to be exempt from further review. Studies which cannot meet the standards for exemption may still be reviewed under an expedited process provided that revealing participants' identities or their responses would not put them at risk legally, physically, or socially. The expedited process is a limited review in that it typically does not require convening the full board. Studies which do not qualify for an exemption or an expedited review must have a *full* review conducted during a called meeting of the review board. The type of review required may also be based on the ability of the individuals to make an informed choice about participating. The US regulations, for example, typically require that studies involving minors, pregnant women, and prisoners receive either an expedited or full review.

Formal review processes typically address certain key issues. The first is whether a study: a) qualifies as research, and b) involves human participants. Review boards take different positions – for example, on whether student projects conducted for a class should be considered research or simply a learning activity. Questions may be asked therefore about whether there is a possibility to present findings from the study at a conference or in published form. Questions about human participants often focus on what it means to participate. For example, are examples of speech acts overheard on public transportation data from human participants? What about comments taken from blog postings that are identified only by avatars? It is not always obvious whether a study is research involving human subjects, and the best policy is to consult the review board. In some cases, review boards will provide a formal assurance that a study does not require review.

Another determination that review boards frequently make regards the preparation and obligation of the investigators to handle ethical questions related to human participants. The board will look for assurance that all investigators have received training in both the ethical dimensions and legal requirements for working with participants and their data. They will also make sure that the investigators can be held accountable for implementing the requirements. For example, if a study involves investigators from different institutions, the review board for the lead investigator will want to make sure that the boards for the other institutions have approved the study and will monitor compliance for work done by their personnel. If the project is being conducted by a student, they will want assurance from a faculty supervisor.

Next they will examine a description of the research question(s) and procedures. Review boards are typically not qualified to review a protocol in the way that a faculty supervisor or publication reviewer might, but they will want to make sure that answers to the questions being asked would be worth the time or disturbance involved to the participants. They will also want to make sure that the planned procedures are likely to produce answers to the questions in a way that minimizes any potential risks. They may comment, for example, on the use of statistics; or if a study targets a specific population, they may ask questions about groups who are being excluded. They may also require an exact or potential list of questions that will be asked during an interview. Finally, they will look for whether the investigator(s) have considered who the study benefits and how.

Perhaps the two most important issues that a review board considers are the degree to which the research subjects will be willing participants and the level of risk to which they will be exposed as a result. With regard to participation, the board will examine how participants are recruited; whether inducements to participate, such as money or extra points on a grade, might cloud their judgment; how the goals and procedures of the study are explained to them; whether there is a mechanism for checking that the participants understood what was explained to them; and whether the participants know what to do if they change their mind about participating. In order to make these determinations they will closely examine recruitment texts and any forms used to document "informed consent." If a study involves language learners, they should also want assurance that everything is explained in a language the participant commands.

With language research, the most common questions related to risk focus on whether the information conveyed in the data is somehow sensitive and could damage the well-being of the participants if their identity were accidentally revealed. For example, previous demographic research about migrant workers might suggest that a study that asks farm workers to talk about their life history in order to gather a language sample for error analysis could bring up or reveal the informant's legal status in the country. In this case, the review board might want to make sure that not only the informant's name but also any details that might reveal where the interview was conducted would be excluded from data transcripts. If the interviews are recorded, they will want to know who will have access to the recordings, how the recordings will be stored, and what will happen to the recordings once the transcripts have been created. The responsibility of the review board is not to prevent research with risks from taking place, but rather to make sure that the risks are minimized.

While the bulk of the formal requirements for review of human research deal with the process for securing initial approval to begin a study, it is important also to be aware of the compliance requirements and responsibilities that apply once a study begins. Typically, requirements are in place regarding the storage and preservation of informed consent documents and study data. If we make video recordings of classroom interactions for a conversation analysis study of power dynamics, it is important to know therefore if we can keep the recordings once the results have been published. What happens if we decide at some point that we want to do another study comparing the effectiveness of different encouragement routines? Other requirements address the need to report unexpected consequences, such as inadvertently destroying data or breeching the confidentiality of an informant. Finally, boards may specify a time period or conditions that require a study to be reviewed again. For example, if putting up posters around campus does not generate enough volunteers for a study, it may be necessary to seek approval before deciding to send a request for participants over a listserve.

Across the social sciences especially, there are complaints about the impact of formal requirements for review on researchers' willingness to conduct certain types of research (see Bowern, 2010). Most boards, however, manage their reviews as a dialogic process. The investigators submit an application for review; the board considers it and responds with queries and suggestions; the investigators revise and respond; and so forth. Rarely will a board simply dictate what must happen. It is important therefore to know the principles and considerations that guide a board's responses and to use the opportunity for dialog to improve our own understanding of the ethical dimensions of our research.

Conclusion

The focus and methods of language research are constantly changing and evolving. With each new question, method, and source for data, new ethical considerations also arise. At the time this is being written, the US Department of Health and Human Services is considering changes to the guidelines for calculating risk that may impact the way studies are reviewed. These shifting perspectives are not a sign of the inadequacy of our current understandings and processes as much as they are an indication that ethical judgments must be reflexive. They are not requirements to be satisfied but rather responsibilities to work by.

Within the language research community, examples of questions currently being debated include:

- When does a research consultant providing information on ways of saying and interpreting become a research subject? (see Bowern, 2010; Thomas, 2009)
- If participants say they would like to be acknowledged for their contributions to knowledge of their language or culture, should we identify them? (see Bowern, 2010)
- Are language samples taken from internet and social media sites data from human subjects? If so, should researchers be required to seek some form of consent? Are there procedures for minimizing risks to the producers of such data? (see McKee, 2008)
- Should research funding agencies put more emphasis on what the Belmont Report referred to as beneficence and justice? If they do, will that disadvantage language research that does not have clear classroom applications? (see Ortega, 2005; Spada, 2005)

Such questions are a sign of a healthy and responsible community.

Discussion Questions

1. Think about a research project you are considering or have recently conducted. How does the study meet expectations for the respect of persons, beneficence, and justice?

2. Consider a proposed study where a teacher in an intensive language program wants to investigate the transfer of reading strategies from L1 to L2. The teacher proposes to recruit students from his or her class, but only those of whose first language the teacher has a working knowledge. What questions might a review board ask about the choice of participants and the recruitment procedures?

3. How would you feel if you discovered that a friend had copied postings to your social media page and was using them for a study of politeness moves in online discourse? How would you feel if you discovered the friend had done this when you saw the postings in a journal article? What guidelines would you suggest for a study like this?

4. Imagine that you are at an institution where the review board requires you to destroy data within three years of the time a study is reported as completed. How would this requirement impact your research? Are there steps you could take to minimize the impact?

5. Imagine a study in which you will interview recent immigrants, many of whom are classified as political refugees. The interview responses will be transcribed. What risk-minimizing guidelines might you set up before starting to transcribe about data that either should not be transcribed or should somehow be altered?

References

Baude, O. (2007). Legal and ethical aspects of the conservation and distribution of oral corpora. *Revue francaise de linguistique appliquee*, 12(1), 85–97.

Bowern, C. (2010). Fieldwork and the IRB: A snapshot. *Language*, 86(4), 897–905.

Dorian, N. C. (2010). Documentation and responsibility. *Language & Communication*, 30(3), 179–185.

Exemption from Ethics Review | U of Toronto Research & Innovation. (n.d.). Retrieved January 18, 2013, from http://www.research.utoronto.ca/for-researchers-administrators/ethics/human/at-a-glance/initiation/exemption-from-ethics-review/

Innes, P. (2010). Ethical problems in archival research: Beyond accessibility. *Language & Communication*, 30(3), 198–203.

Kubanyiova, M. (2008). Rethinking research ethics in contemporary applied linguistics: The tension between macroethical and microethical perspectives in situated research. *The Modern Language Journal*, 92(4), 503–518.

Lee, E. (2011). Ethical issues in addressing inequity in/through ESL research. *TESL Canada Journal/Revue TESL du Canada*, 28 (special issue 5), 31–52.

Li, Y. (2011). Translating interviews, translating lives: Ethical considerations in cross-language narrative inquiry. *TESL Canada Journal/Revue TESL du Canada*, 28 (special issue 5), 16–30.

McKee, H. A. (2008). Ethical and legal issues for writing researchers in an age of media convergence. *Computers and Composition*, 25(1), 104–122. doi:10.1016/j.compcom.2007.09.007

National Commission for the Protection of Human Subjects of Biomedical and Behavioral Research. (1979). *The Belmont report: Ethical principles and guidelines for the protection of human subjects of research*. Department of Health, Education, and Welfare. Retrieved from http://www.hhs.gov/ohrp/humansubjects/guidance/belmont.html

Ortega, L. (2005). For what and for whom is our research? The ethical as transformative lens in instructed SLA. *The Modern Language Journal*, 89(3), 427–443.

Spada, N. (2005). Conditions and challenges in developing school-based SLA research programs. *The Modern Language Journal*, 89(3), 328–338.

The British Association for Applied Linguistics. (2006). *Recommendations on good practice in applied linguistics*. Retrieved from http://www.baal.org.uk/public_docs.html

Thomas, M. (2009). Review article: Ethical issues in the study of second language acquisition: Resources for researchers. *Second Language Research*, 25(4), 493–511.

List of professional associations which provide useful guidelines for language researchers

The TESOL International Association. *TESOL Research Agenda* (August 2004). http://www.tesol.org/advance-the-field/research

TESOL Quarterly Research Guidelines (n.d.). http://www.tesol.org/read-and-publish/journals/tesol-quarterly/tesol-quarterly-research-guidelines

The British Association for Applied Linguistics. *Recommendations on Good Practice in Applied Linguistics* (2006). http://www.baal.org.uk/public_docs.html

Linguistic Society of America. *Linguistic Society of America Ethics Statement* (May 2009). http://www.linguisticsociety.org/about/who-we-are/committees/ethics-committee

American Educational Research Association. *Code of Ethics* (February 2011). http://www.aera.net/AboutAERA/KeyPrograms/SocialJustice/ResearchEthics/tabid/10957/Default.aspx

Association of Internet Researchers. *Ethics Guide* (n.d.). http://aoir.org/documents/ethics-guide/

Conference on College Composition and Communication. *Position Statement on Ethical Conduct of Research in Composition Studies* (November 2003). http://www.ncte.org/cccc/resources/positions/ethicalconduct

The U.S. Department of Health and Human Services' *International Compilation of Human Research Standards*, http://www.hhs.gov/ohrp/international/intlcompilation/intlcompilation.html

CHAPTER 24

Creating Effective Research Questions

Deena Boraie and Atta Gebril

INTRODUCTION

After you have identified your research topic and research purpose, the next step is to narrow down your scope and develop specific research questions (RQs). RQs work like a roadmap that shows which path to follow to reach your destination and what resources you need to take with you. A roadmap can also help you plan for any expected challenges during the trip and hopefully make your journey easier by showing the shortest way to reach your destination. RQs – as Dörnyei (2007) argues – serve a similar function in any research project since they help operationalize your research purpose. When you have a research project, you usually start with a general, and sometimes vague, idea. In other situations, you might have a very optimistic plan, which is not realistic at all. This is why RQs help researchers find focus for their work by making the research idea more specific. Furthermore, they prevent a researcher from running the risk of developing a research project that needs huge resources. Such projects need a lot of time and a team of researchers, which are not necessarily available for many of the projects we work on in applied linguistics.

RQs fall into three different categories/research designs: quantitative, qualitative, and mixed. The types of RQs asked in a research project depend on the nature of the topic you are interested in. For example, in correlational research RQs usually look into the relationship among a number of variables. In other contexts studies focus on the effect of a specific variable on other variables. Probably these two examples are more common in quantitative research. Conversely, in qualitative research RQs focus on a description of a certain phenomenon. In mixed research studies you can use mixed RQs or a combination of both quantitative and qualitative RQs.

BACKGROUND

It is very important to get the questions right and this process takes time; but it is time well spent. You should not rush this stage of the research study and try to think carefully about your choices. Do not panic if you have spent a lot of time since it may take weeks or even months to come up with solid RQs. Novice researchers sometimes go through bewilderment and frustration during this stage as described by this first-time thesis writer:

> In my opinion, the most difficult thing when writing the research questions is choosing questions that have not been chosen by someone else in order to get useful results in the field of my study from which the reader could benefit from. Also, it is important to find the research gap first, then decide on my research questions, but the problem in my case for example, that it is the same gap in all researches that I have read, and they all end up their papers by writing that more research is needed to figure out this problem. So, how could I know that I have chosen the correct research questions that would really solve that issue? Another issue is the quality of the research questions, they should be clear to the reader, feasible and straight forward; the question should not carry more than one meaning. However, it seems challenging for me to decide whether they are supposed to be more general or narrowed down. (MA thesis writer at the American University in Cairo, Spring 2012)

A closer look at the quotation shows the dilemmas that novice researchers usually encounter when developing their RQs. Their main concern is to avoid writing poor questions that can lead to a waste of time and resources.

Developing good RQs is at the heart of a well-designed and successful research study and they are the basis of developing a sound conceptual framework. Effective RQs focus your ideas and ensure that your research is doable and manageable within the available timeframe. Because RQs represent the core of your research study, it is essential to explicitly link them to other study sections. For example, your introduction usually establishes the context of your study and also provides a rationale into why this project is needed by introducing a research gap: there must be a logical progression from this introductory part to your RQs, which is achieved by ensuring that these RQs come from a well-identified research gap in the literature. As Mackey and Gass state (2005: 17), you must avoid a situation where you "run into a 'so what' response" to your research proposal. You should also demonstrate that your RQs have not yet been addressed adequately in the literature and that answering your RQs would contribute to the current body of knowledge. In addition, your methodology should by default be developed for the purpose of answering your RQs. Different study procedures, including design of study instruments, data collection procedures, and your data analysis plan, are mainly utilized to answer your RQs. RQs determine where, when, how, and why you collect and analyze your data and the strategies you use to ensure the validity of the results of your study. Figure 24.1 describes the relationship between RQs and other study sections.

One of the key sources of RQs is the section of "suggestions for further research" which usually appear at the end of articles or papers. These suggestions are invaluable since they represent questions that still need to be answered based on the opinion of an experienced researcher.

There are a number of issues that novice researchers usually struggle with when working on RQs, the first of which has to do with the location of RQs in the manuscript. Since RQs should stem from an identified need or research gap, as indicated earlier, it is logical to include your RQs right after your introduction where you have established the rationale for your study. After stating your RQs, you need to move to your "methods" section where you should lay out a plan for answering these questions.

Another issue that frequently comes up is whether there is an ideal number of RQs required in a research study. There is no set number, but typically the number of RQs ranges from one to three on average. Having said this, there are studies that include a larger number of RQs when the researcher investigates many variables. However, you have to

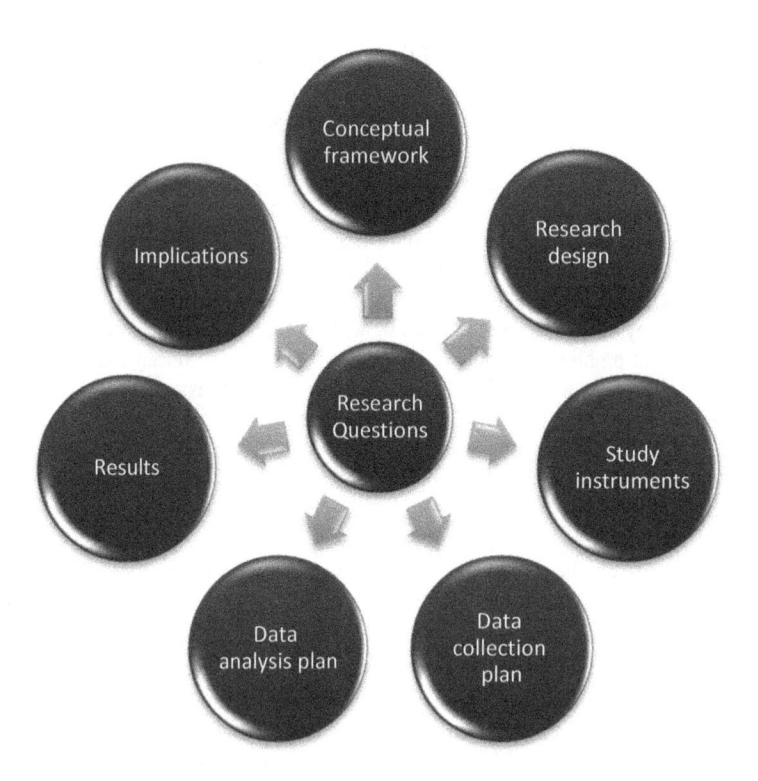

Figure 24.1 The Relationship Among Research Questions and Other Study Sections

be cognizant of your resources and also to be realistic when you decide on the number of questions you would like to investigate. Too many questions always come with a huge workload and might eventually result in the researcher being unable to finish the project. Therefore, always make sure that you have the right number of questions, keeping in mind the types of resources and skills you have.

Thirdly, a common question that researchers ask is whether they must produce a hypothesis for each quantitative RQ in their study. A research hypothesis is a prediction about the results of the study. Specifically, hypotheses are statements about the expected relationship among the variables that are under study (Johnson and Christensen, 2012). To answer this, we should examine the source of any research hypothesis. Research hypotheses are generated based on the findings of previous research which are discussed and presented in the literature review. A hypothesis may also emerge from your own previous experience or observation of the phenomenon under study. For example, you may have observed during your teaching of adult EFL learners that your students with a higher intellectual or occupational profile perform better than those with lower profiles. Based on this experience, you might formulate a hypothesis that students with higher intellectual and occupational profiles will achieve significantly higher scores at the end of a language program compared to students with lower profiles. Therefore, the answer to the question is that it depends. If you have support from the literature or from your own observations of events, then you could produce a hypothesis. Creswell (2009: 133) advises researchers to write only quantitative RQs, and not both RQs and hypotheses, to avoid redundancy. He notes that, "unless the hypotheses build on the research questions" there is no need to include hypotheses. Researchers also have to be very careful that they are not biased and plan to support their hypotheses regardless of the actual outcomes of the study (Johnson and Christensen, 2012).

Fourthly, when writing RQs for mixed methods research studies using a combination of quantitative and qualitative questions, you should pay attention to the order of your RQs. For example, if you are planning to use a two-phase approach and you have a quantitative phase followed by a qualitative phase in your study, then you should present the RQs in this order. If you only have one phase in your study, you may consider ordering the questions according to the importance of variables or the order used in presenting the variables in your introduction. In other cases, the questions are interdependent and for this reason you have to make sure that they are ordered logically since they build on each other.

Fifth, typically, in a mixed methods study researchers write separate qualitative and quantitative RQs in their studies. Creswell (2009) encourages researchers to separate mixed RQs instead or to include at least one mixed RQ in addition to the separate qualitative and quantitative questions.

Research on this Topic

This section describes the guidelines provided in the literature for how to write effective RQs in qualitative, quantitative, and mixed methods designs. A brief discussion of related terminology is also presented.

Quantitative, Qualitative, and Mixed Methods RQs

In quantitative research, RQs usually investigate whether there are differences or relationships between two variables or more. For this reason, quantitative RQs are written in an interrogative format and seek to either examine relationships between the independent and dependent variables or to identify differences between groups on an independent variable (Perry, 2005). A related concept associated with RQs in quantitative studies, as discussed earlier, is research hypotheses. Hypotheses can be written in the form of a null or a directional or non-directional hypothesis. A null hypothesis, which represents the traditional approach, is a statement that predicts no relationship between the variables or no significant difference among the groups. An example of a null hypothesis is that there is no difference in scores between students with high test anxiety compared to students with low text anxiety. The directional hypothesis is a statement that predicts the relationship that exists among the variables being examined. For example, the researcher can formulate a hypothesis that students with high test anxiety will score lower compared to students with low test anxiety. The non-directional hypothesis is also a prediction that a difference exists but the researcher does not know the exact direction (either higher or lower) of the difference. The non-directional hypothesis will state there will be a difference in scores between students with high test anxiety compared to those with low test anxiety (Creswell, 2009).

A qualitative research question is usually written as an "interrogative sentence that asks a question about some process, issue or phenomenon that is to be explored" (Johnson and Christensen, 2012: 76). Qualitative RQs focus on how a specific phenomenon happens, and why it takes place in a specific way, and what aspects of this phenomenon are related to this pattern. This reflects the main purpose of doing qualitative research, which is to understand a personal experience, a human behavior, or a specific phenomenon. There is also flexibility in the way you develop qualitative RQs. Qualitative research is iterative and emergent and that is why new research questions can be added later. This does not mean that you can start a qualitative research project without any research questions. The researcher starts with a broad and central question that is worth investigating. From this central question, you can formulate several sub-questions which provide focus for the study without limiting the inquiry and allow exploring and developing new insights. Typically, qualitative RQs start with question words, such as "what," "why," and "how."

The mixed-methods RQ is a relatively new trend that is a hybrid or integrated question which includes both the quantitative and qualitative strands of the study (Creswell, 2008). Mixed-methods RQs are challenging because they combine two different approaches – being both specific and open-ended at the same time. The mixed-methods RQ integrates the quantitative and qualitative phases of the research project. An example of a mixed-methods RQ could be: "How do the themes that emerge from qualitative interviews with teachers and students explain why students with high test-anxiety perform poorly on tests compared to students with low test-anxiety?"

QUALITIES OF GOOD RESEARCH QUESTIONS

The basic qualities of good RQs are clarity, specificity, feasibility, significance, interest, and relevance. All types of RQs should meet these criteria. When writing your RQs, make sure that they meet the following criteria: (Brown, 2001; O'Leary, 2004; Boudah, 2011):

- RQs must be *clear*. RQs questions should be clear and free from ambiguity. You have to make sure that your RQs are understood similarly by different people. Otherwise, this will cause confusion for readers of your research report and sometimes for the researchers themselves.
- RQs must be *specific*. They should be clearly written and not vague. The key terms and concepts in the RQs must be clearly and operationally defined. If your RQs are not clear then most likely your research proposal will not be accepted because it indicates you are not ready to begin your study.
- RQs must be *realistic*. You should write practical and feasible questions. You should not pose RQs that you cannot answer within the set timeframe for conducting the study. You must also make sure that you have the technical expertise and access to the resources needed to obtain answers to the RQs.
- RQs must be *significant*. RQs must contribute to the existing literature and they must be based on an identified need. If the field does not gain anything from the answer to the RQ, then you should reword it or change the topic. RQs should not pose questions that seek opinions. You must provide a satisfactory justification for your RQs.
- RQs must be *interesting* to you. Conducting research requires a great deal of work and "a lot of intellectual, physical and emotional energy" (Nunan and Bailey, 2009: 31). If you are not sufficiently motivated and enthusiastic, then chances are you will not complete the study.
- RQs must be *relevant*. RQs should be relevant in your instructional context and consequently should have useful implications. Language teachers always need to find answers for problems in their classes and that is why attempting to do so makes the research project worthwhile and beneficial.

PRACTICAL APPLICATIONS

This section provides and discusses examples of well- and poorly-written quantitative, qualitative, and mixed RQs. When evaluating the quality of RQs the criteria mentioned above must be considered.

A WELL-WRITTEN QUANTITATIVE RQ

"What is the difference between using face-to-face classroom collaborative writing activities and using Wikis collaboratively on students' individual writing in terms of fluency, accuracy, and complexity?"

This is a good quantitative RQ because it is specific and the variables are clearly indicated. The independent variable is the type of collaboration used in the teaching/learning of writing, whether face-to-face activities or using Wikis, and the dependent variable is the quality of the students' writing clearly defined in terms of three separate measures. The RQ would be most likely realistic and interesting for teachers who teach writing and use online teaching resources. The significance of this study would be that it contributes to effective classroom practice and provides information to teachers about the effectiveness of using specific types of collaborative activities on students' individual writing.

A POORLY-WRITTEN QUANTITATIVE RQ

"What are the differences between native and non-native writers?"
This question is problematic in terms of its scope and feasibility. As for scope, this is a very general investigation which does not specify what writing features the researcher is interested in. Is she interested in discourse features such as fluency, lexical richness, syntactic complexity, or grammatical accuracy? Is she interested in stylistic issues? Or is she interested in organizational patterns and cohesive ties used by the two groups? In terms of feasibility, this is a project that is not realistic; it needs a team of researchers and a huge amount of resources as well as time.

A WELL-WRITTEN QUALITATIVE RQ

"How do Egyptian teachers represent English speakers and their respective cultures in the classroom? Specifically:

a. Which nationalities and ethnicities are featured referencing Kachru's circles of World Englishes?
b. How do teaching materials (i.e. flashcards, texts, recordings, pictures, etc.) selected by Egyptian teachers reflect English speakers and their respective cultures?
c. Are these representations depicted positively, neutrally, or negatively?"

The RQ is clear in terms of the concepts being explored. The central RQ focuses on the phenomenon of English being viewed as a *lingua franca* in a globalized world and investigating the reality of how it is actually represented in the classroom in a context where English is a foreign language. The overall RQ also allows for an emerging design where additional factors may be identified that may have bearing on this phenomenon being studied. The initial subquestions also add some focus and can be used to guide data collection during the interviews, observations, or document reviews. The RQ is realistic, significant, and interesting for teachers teaching in the specific context since little research exists in this area at the time of writing this chapter. Insights would be gained into how teachers represent the L1 community, how they select materials, and how these materials represent the English speaking community.

A POORLY-WRITTEN QUALITATIVE RQ

"Should L1 be used in EFL classrooms?"
This is a broad question and not really researchable as it is written. This issue dates back to the direct method, which advocated that monolingual teaching was the only way to obtain best bilingual results and the use of L1 in the classroom was prohibited. A better research question investigating this phenomenon would be:

- What role should L1 play in EFL classrooms?

Some specific subquestions could be:

- What are the attitudes and beliefs of teachers and students towards the use of L1 in EFL classrooms?
- When do students and teachers code-switch in the L2 classroom?

A WELL-WRITTEN MIXED-METHODS RQ

"How can students' perceptions towards collaborative writing activities explain the differences, if any, between using face-to-face classroom collaborative writing activities and using Wikis collaboratively on students' individual writing in terms of fluency, accuracy, and complexity?"

This mixed-methods RQ integrates a good quantitative RQ as well as an open-ended qualitative RQ. The researcher intends to use qualitative data obtained from students using interviews or open-ended questionnaires to explain the quantitative results in more depth.

CONCLUSION

Writing RQs is not an easy task, especially for novice researchers who have just started navigating the research process. Good RQs are usually the product of a well-identified research gap. Once you have identified this gap, you should strive to develop RQs that are specific, realistic, and that contribute to the current literature. Also make sure that you have the necessary skills and resources needed to answer these questions. In addition, keep your eye on the other sections of your study while developing your RQs. As indicated earlier, your RQs should be linked to the other study parts starting from your literature review, to the methods, data analysis, and, of course, results sections. Another important piece of advice is to match your RQs with the research design employed in your project. It is very important to have RQs that are compatible with the issues of interest and the design used to answer these questions. Finally, always remember the analogy of roadmaps and RQs, since keeping this association in mind will help you reach your final destination. Have a safe journey!

Discussion Questions

1. Write down a research topic you are interested in on a sheet of paper. Take some time to think about potential issues you can investigate that are related to this topic. Then, write down a general question based on these issues – do not write a very specific question at this point.

2. After you have read all the literature available on your topic, it is time to make the general question you have written in the previous activity more specific. Think of subquestions that you can develop based on this general question. Write at least three specific questions.

3 Are the research questions that you have developed in the previous activity of good quality? In order to answer this question, have a look at the *Qualities of Good Research Questions* section in this chapter.

4. Which research design should you use to answer these research questions? Quantitative? Qualitative? Mixed methods? Why?

5. In this chapter, the researchers compared research questions to roadmaps. What do you think about this analogy?

References

Boudah, D. J. (2011). *Conducting educational research: Guide to completing a major project.* Thousand Oaks, CA: Sage.

Brown, J. D. (2001). *Using surveys in language programs.* Cambridge: Cambridge University Press.

Creswell, J. W. (2009). *Research design: Qualitative, quantitative, and mixed methods approaches* (3rd ed.). Thousand Oaks: CA: Sage.

Dörnyei, Z. (2007). *Research methods in applied linguistics.* Oxford: Oxford University Press.

Johnson, B., & Christensen, L. (2012). *Educational research: Quantitative, qualitative and mixed approaches* (4th ed.). Thousand Oaks, CA: Sage.

Mackey, A., & Gass, S. (2005). *Second language research: Methodology and design.* Mahwah, NJ: Lawrence Erlbaum Associates.

Nunan, D., & Bailey, K. (2009). *Exploring second language classroom research: A Comprehensive guide.* Boston, MA: Heinle.

O'Leary, Z. (2004). *Essential guide to doing research* [Electronic version]. Thousand Oaks, CA: Sage.

Perry, F. L. (2011). *Research in applied linguistics: Becoming a discerning consumer* (2nd ed.). New York: Routledge.

CHAPTER 25

Sampling and What it Means

John McE. Davis

INTRODUCTION

When investigating any unit of analysis – be it a single case study or many thousands of individuals – the researcher has likely isolated members (or a member) from a larger group and thus engaged in the process of sampling. That is, a smaller group (a sample) has been selected from a larger group (a population) in order to learn something about the larger group (Vogt, 2007). Social science researchers use samples to apply their findings to individuals (or non-human units) beyond their study. That is to say, researchers often want to generalize their findings – they want to claim that the way members behave in a study is how similar members out in the world would behave as well. Researchers are able to do this because of the special properties samples retain: they can capture quite accurately the characteristics or trends of the population from which they are drawn. However, the degree to which a researcher can generalize results will depend on the sample size and, more importantly, the sampling method.

BACKGROUND

Generalization – the extent to which findings can be applied to a defined population – depends on sample representativeness, or how well a sample captures particular characteristics of a population: "the degree to which the sample represents a population is determined by the degree to which the relevant attributes in the target population are found in the sample" (Perry, 2011: 60). If a researcher intends to generalize findings, she/he must demonstrate that the sample is representative of the group to which findings are being applied. The sampling method a researcher chooses – as well as the sample size – will have important consequences for the degree to which the sample represents the larger group.

There are two main categories of sampling in social science research: a) probability sampling; and b) nonprobability sampling. The difference between the two has to do with whether all the members of a population are known and whether each has a chance to be selected in the sample. Probability sampling refers to the random selection of units (e.g., students, teachers, schools) from a population list. In probability sampling, since all the units of the population are listed, each member has a known chance of selection. Crucially, random selection gives the sample important properties. When every member of the population has an opportunity to be included in the sample, bias is reduced. Bias refers to differences between the sample and the population on a characteristic of interest, the consequence being that the sample no longer resembles the population. Random selection reduces bias since units are selected on the basis of chance and not on other factors, such as the unconscious desires of the researcher, or the availability and/or accessibility of particular subgroups. For example, if a researcher wanted to investigate the views of educators throughout a school district, and interviewed colleagues at her/his school only, the sample would likely fail to collect the spectrum of views in the district. Results would be biased toward the overrepresented views of the responding group. Drawing a probability sample, rather, in which each teacher in the district is identified and listed, would provide all members an equal chance of selection and would more likely capture the range of views extant in that population.

The other category of sampling method is nonprobability sampling. Nonprobability sampling methods offer a number of research advantages (see below), yet their ability to capture trends in a population – that is, their representativeness – is regarded as limited. Nonprobability sampling refers to sampling techniques in which selection proceeds without a full listing of population members/units and without randomized selection. Rather, nonprobability sampling involves selecting members on the basis of availability, accessibility, or convenience. Since there is no random selection from a population list, and since some population members are unidentified/unlisted, sampling may miss the full range of variation in a phenomena of interest. Therefore, there is general agreement in the applied linguistics research methods literature that nonprobability sampling techniques limit generalization, primarily because of the unknown representation of the population by the non-randomly selected sample.

In applied linguistic research, probability samples are rare and nonprobability samples the norm. Nevertheless, prescriptions are clear for researchers who want to generalize findings: a probability sample is required. Steps can be taken to improve – and arguments made for – the representativeness of a nonprobability sample (see below). Yet, if a nonprobability sampling procedure is used, current methodological advice calls for researchers to be explicit about the nonprobability sampling method, to concede the likelihood of bias, and to be clear that the results are relevant for members within the study only.

Research on this Topic

The above summarizes current disciplinary advice on research sampling and implications for external validity given a particular sampling method. The thinking on sampling in language education research (in the quantitative methodological paradigm) has been in line with methodological traditions in social science research, these traditions taking the position that external validity and generalization are contingent on sample representativeness, which is in turn contingent on random selection.

This view has been historically consistent in applied linguistics methods advice. Hatch and Lazaraton (1991:42) stake out the position early: a "way to attempt to obtain a representative sample is via random selection." The axiom has remained up to the present: "a large enough sample of randomly selected members is widely accepted by researchers to be approximately representative of the population from which it was taken" (Brown, 2012: 3. See also Brown, 2006; Dörnyei, 2007; Mackey and Gass, 2011; Perry, 2011). The need for random sampling is likewise echoed by experts in survey research in which sampling and generalization are methodologically central: "[u]sing appropriate probability sampling helps support the generalizability of the results of survey research" (Wagner, 2010: 25. See also Brown, 2001; Dörnyei and Taguchi, 2010).

The corollary to this position, of course, has been that nonprobability samples limit generalization. Again, Hatch and Lazaraton (1991: 42) make the point early on: "… if the group has been selected by "convenience sample" (they happened to be the group available), no … generalization is possible." As noted prior, generalization is inappropriate due to lacking representation of the population. That is to say, experts take the view that the representativeness of a nonprobability sample drawn from a partial listing of a population is biased: "purposeful samples will almost always produce biased samples" (Perry, 2011: 70). Thus, methods experts uniformly agree on the implications for external validity when using nonprobability samples – generalization is severely limited: "the extent of generalizability in [a nonprobability] type of sample is often negligible" (Dörnyei, 2007: 99).

Again, probability methods in applied linguistics research are atypical and nonprobability techniques common practice. This state of affairs is due largely to the practical difficulties associated with undertaking random sampling methods, but also partly because of the difficulty in defining the population types common to language research (Brown, 2012). The necessities of nonprobability methods notwithstanding, experts have observed that nonprobability methods do not prevent researchers from making unwarranted generalizations of findings (Brown, 2006; Perry, 2011; Wagner, 2010).

Practical Applications

Decisions about sampling method and sample size will depend mainly on the research goals of the study, but also on practical considerations such as time, available resources, and member accessibility. Different sampling methods have different strengths and weaknesses, and when planning a study, researchers will want to know what can and cannot be accomplished using a particular method.

Very few applied linguistics studies undertake probability sampling, but, if a researcher endeavored to do so, the following procedures would be involved. The first step is to clearly identify the population of interest and specify the relevant attributes of members within that population. It will stand to reason that using a sample to make claims about a population will necessarily require specifying and defining that population.

The second step is to create a list of every member/unit in a population such that each has an equal or non-zero[1] chance of selection (a known challenge in language research). At this stage, care should be taken to avoid what is known in survey research as "coverage error": the exclusion or overrepresentation of relevant units in the population list/sample frame. Excluding units from selection potentially skews results toward the response patterns or behaviors of included members, thereby reducing similarities between sample and population characteristics. Over-representing units gives them a greater chance of selection, and likewise skews results. For example, drawing a random sample from an inaccurate alumni email list could cause coverage error in two ways. First, if the list is not regularly updated or contains addresses with typographical errors, relevant individuals may be excluded from the sample frame. Second, if there are erroneous duplicates, then certain individuals may be oversampled and their views disproportionately represented in the study.

Once a population list is constructed, a number of random sampling techniques are possible depending on the needs and goals of the research project. The prototypical probability sample type is a simple random sample (SRS). A simple random sample involves selecting a subgroup by chance, typically using a random number table or a random number generator in a spreadsheet application. For example, a random sample can be drawn by entering a list of units into a spreadsheet and assigning a random number to each unit (using the =RAND() function in Excel). Next, the units are sorted – i.e., ranked – from smallest to largest, and the desired number of units in the sample – the first 100 units, say – is selected from the ranked list.

A variation on the SRS technique is systematic sampling. Systematic sampling involves selecting members from a list at set intervals (every n^{th} unit). Systematic sampling is useful when units are not easily "thrown into a hat" for selection – that is to say, assigning units random number codes or listing units in a spreadsheet is difficult or impossible. A common systematic sampling example is the selection of members from a phone book. If a phone book were to be used as a sampling frame, copying every name into a spreadsheet, or assigning every name a random number code would be impractical. Rather, a researcher could read through the phonebook selecting a different name at a set interval – for example, every tenth name. If, for instance, a researcher wanted to draw a sample of 1000 individuals from a phonebook, they could divide the total number of names in the phone book (for example $N = 50,000$) by the desired sample size (50,000 /1000 = 50) and then read through the names selecting every fiftieth name until 1000 names had been selected. However, a known disadvantage of systematic sampling is that the selection process can be biased by a periodic, consistent trait within the population.

If a researcher is interested in the characteristics of specific groups, stratified random sampling can be employed. Stratified random sampling involves identifying subgroups of interest – or strata – within a population and then randomly selecting units from within each of the groups/strata. For example, if a researcher was interested in studying the views of heritage versus non-heritage language learners at a university, two population lists would be created, one with heritage language learners, the other with non-heritage learners. Next, two separate samples would then be selected, randomly, from each list. Stratified sampling can be used to ensure that the sizes of groups in the study are similar to their proportions in the population; this method is known as proportional random stratified sampling. Nonproportional random stratified sampling involves forming sample groups that differ from their proportions in the population. Nonproportional random stratified sampling can be used when a researcher aims to compare subgroups and requires similar group sizes rather than in population proportions. Moreover, nonproportional sampling can be used to increase stratified samples when groups are small and assumptions cannot be met for certain statistical analyses (e.g., minimum sample sizes).

Another type of probability sampling is cluster sampling, an approach that addresses a known difficulty with random selection in applied linguistics research: creating the required list of population units. Cluster sampling is helpful when populations are large, widely dispersed over geographic regions, or otherwise inaccessible due to lacking resources or time. The procedure initially involves identifying sampling units that cluster or group the individual members of interest together. For example, teachers and students are typically grouped in classes, schools, clubs, departments, or universities. Such entities have the advantage of being fewer in number, identifiable, more easily accessible, and thereby easier to collect into a list. Once a list of these grouping units is created, the next step is to draw a random sample of cluster units. For example, if a researcher is interested in the views of college language majors at universities in a particular geographic area, instead of attempting to list every student at every university, the researcher would list all the language major programs instead – the cluster units that group students together – and then select a random sample of language programs from that list. At this stage, two options are possible. The first is to take a census and include all members within the cluster units in the study – that is, *all* students in the sample of language major programs are selected to participate in the study – i.e., one-stage cluster sampling. The second option is to sample once again, this time randomly selecting students from within each of the cluster units – referred to as multi-stage cluster sampling. Using the cluster sample method makes the task of random selection more manageable since, in the example above, less time and fewer resources would be required to construct the list of major programs at each university than would have been needed to generate a list of every language student at every university. (See Ajayi (2008) for an example of one-stage cluster sampling in language education research.)

Nonprobability sampling, again, refers to member selection without randomization. Despite issues with representativeness and generalization, nonprobability techniques serve a number of useful research purposes. Perhaps the chief advantage is practicality: nonprobability techniques may be the only sampling alternative when resources and/or time are in short supply. As Dörnyei (2007) notes, nonprobability techniques involve a trade-off in which representativeness is sacrificed to accommodate the means of the ordinary researcher. Moreover, nonprobability sampling techniques may be the only way of getting at populations that are difficult to access, and in such instances any results are better than none.

A common nonprobability method is convenience sampling (Perry, 2011), or the selection of respondents who are most readily available, such as students or teachers at a researcher's school. Other nonprobability sampling options include varieties of purposive sampling, or techniques that select members to achieve a particular research goal (Perry, 2011). The main types of purposive sampling include expert sampling – i.e., sampling a group of experts/pundits; heterogeneity/diversity sampling – i.e., purposeful inclusion of units capturing a range/variability of population characteristics; snowball sampling – i.e., members recruiting additional participants who would be difficult to identify otherwise; and typical case/modal instance sampling – i.e., sampling the most frequently occurring member or typical case in a population.

Purposive sampling methods can also be applied to stratified and cluster techniques (Brown, 2012). For example, proportional and nonproportional stratified samples can be drawn without randomization; these approaches are referred to as proportional quota or nonproportional quota sampling. As with the probability varieties of these techniques, the researcher selects desired proportions of members from relevant subgroups, though, again, without using random selection. Likewise with cluster sampling: cluster units and the units within clusters can be selected in a variety of purposive ways. These principled sampling approaches can be regarded as improving the representativeness of nonprobability samples (to a limited degree) in that relevant groups from the population – and/or their proportions – are present in the sample.

A study by Yihong, Yuan, Ying, and Yan (2007) provides an example of proportional quota sampling. The study investigated relationships between language learning motivation and self-identity among university students in China. First, the researchers identified the different university types in China (comprehensive, normal, foreign language, etc.), and then selected university types matching the proportions in the population of all Chinese universities. For example, "comprehensive" universities comprise 13.5% of all universities in China; thus 13.5% of universities in the study sample were the comprehensive type. Next, groups of students were selected from the stratified university sample matching the student population proportions for a given university type. For example,

21.5% of all Chinese undergraduates are enrolled at "comprehensive" universities, thus 21.5% of the sample was comprised of "comprehensive" university students. Using this principled method, 2278 undergraduates were selected from 30 universities, to "represent the population of more than five million university undergraduates in mainland China" (Yihong et al., 2007: 137).

Clearly, representation of the university population of Chinese EFL learners is achieved to some degree in this study given the careful proportional quota technique. However, without randomization at each stage of sampling, the claim of population representation – strictly-speaking – goes too far. Without random selection, it is impossible to know the degree to which the full range of characteristics in the population strata are reflected in the stratified sample as well. As Dörnyei (2007: 99) points out, "[n]o matter how principled a non-probability sample strives to be, the extent of generalizability in this type of sample is often negligible."

An important consideration of sample representativeness has to do with sample size, an issue discussed briefly here. Determining an appropriate sample size, however, is not a straightforward matter. As a general rule, the greater the proportion of the population, the more representative the sample (Brown, 2012; Dörnyei, 2007). Some recommend "magic" sampling fractions (commonly one to ten per cent of the population) though such parameters do not always apply. Clearly, a sample comprising one per cent of a population of 100 will lack representativeness. When sampling from smaller populations, then, researchers should err on the side of larger proportions; Dörnyei (2007) points out that when the above percentages are applied in survey research, 100 is regarded as a minimum. Moreover, note that while the "more-is-better" axiom generally applies to probability and non-probability samples, sample size alone cannot compensate for unrepresentative selection techniques. A large sample comprising a large proportion of a population can still be biased if it omits important population segments – a particular risk with nonprobability methods. By contrast, a relatively small random sample – drawn from carefully researched strata or clusters – can capture characteristics of very large populations with a high degree of accuracy. For example, a representative sample of roughly 1000 voters can capture voting trends in the entire U.S. population. The important point, then, is that both sample size and random selection help to maximize sample representativeness.

Additional advice on sample sizes relates to minimum n-sizes needed for reliable statistical procedures. For example, a normal distribution can be achieved with 30 units; 50 units enables correlational procedures; 100 allows for factor analysis and other multivariate procedures (see Brown, 2012; Dörnyei, 2007).

Finally, techniques used by survey/questionnaire researchers provide guidance on minimum sample sizes if certain population parameters are known. Sample sizes can be computed if a researcher specifies: a) a desired confidence level (e.g., 95%); b) an acceptable confidence interval or amount of sampling error (e.g., ±3%); c) the size of the population; and d) an estimate of population variability on a statistic of interest. Using such an approach, however, requires knowing population statistics in advance (often requiring a pilot study), as well as a certain amount of statistical and survey methods expertise (Dillman, 2007).

Conclusion

Probability samples are difficult to achieve (and rare) in applied linguistics research. Non-probability samples are thus standard practice. This state of affairs is unlikely to change, though it will be worth pointing out, in passing, that the external validity of studies purporting to investigate language learner/user populations would be greatly strengthened if researchers endeavored to use random samples. Since methodological practice is unlikely to change in this direction, a more realistic change might be to reduce the commonplace tendency of generalization on the basis of nonprobability samples. A final suggestion, then, is that researchers be mindful of the limitations of their sampling methods. Again, disciplinary advice calls for researchers to be explicit about the type of sampling method used, to concede potential bias if it is a nonprobability technique, and to limit generalizing claims accordingly.

Discussion Questions

1. Describe and justify a few example scenarios in which nonprobability sampling would be the preferred method to probability sampling.

2. How might the representativeness of a nonprobability sample be increased?

3. Even when using "principled" sampling strategies, why is generalization unwarranted for nonprobability samples?

4. A paper-based survey is administered to attendees at a national annual conference for college language educators (the survey is included in the conference packet). The study is investigating the types of language assessments used in college language programs. What type of sampling method has been used? What arguments might be made that the sample is representative of the population of college language educators? In what ways might the sample be biased? That is, what factors would cause the responses of conference attendees to differ from the population of college language educators?

References

Ajayi, L. (2008). ESL theory-practice dynamics: The difficulty of integrating sociocultural perspectives into pedagogical practices. *Foreign Language Annals*, 41(4), 639–659.

Brown, J. D. (2001). *Using surveys in language programs*. New York: Cambridge University Press.

Brown, J. D. (2006). Generalizability from second language research samples. *Shiken: JALT Testing & Evaluation SIG Newsletter*, 10(2), 21–24. Retrieved from http://jalt.org/test/bro_24.htm

Brown, J. D. (2012). Sampling: Quantitative methods. In C. Chapelle (Ed.), *The encyclopedia of applied linguistics* (pp. 1–6). Chichester, West Sussex, UK: Wiley-Blackwell. Retrieved from http://onlinelibrary.wiley.com/doi/10.1002/9781405198431.wbeal1033/pdf

Dillman, D. A. (2007). *Mail and internet surveys: The tailored design method* (2nd ed.). New York: John Wiley & Sons.

Dörnyei, Z. (2007). *Research methods in applied linguistics: Quantitative, qualitative, and mixed methodologies*. New York: Oxford University Press.

Dörnyei, Z., & Taguchi, T. (2010). *Questionnaires in second language research: Construction, administration, and processing* (2nd ed.). New York: Routledge.

Hatch, E., & Lazaraton, A. (1991). *The research manual: Design and statistics for applied linguistics*. New York: Newbury House.

Mackey, A., & Gass, S. (2011). *Second language research: Methodology and design*. Mahwah, NJ: Lawrence Erlbaum.

Perry, F. L. (2011). *Research in applied linguistics: Becoming a discerning consumer* (2nd ed.). Mahwah, NJ: Lawrence Erlbaum.

Vogt, P. W. (2007). *Quantitative research methods for professionals*. Boston, MA: Pearson.

Wagner, E. (2010). Survey research. In B. Paltridge & A. Phakiti (Eds.), *Continuum companion to research methods in applied linguistics* (pp. 22–38). New York: Continuum.

Yihong, G., Yuan, Z., Ying, C., & Yan, Z. (2007). Relationship between English learning motivation types and self-identity changes among Chinese students. *TESOL Quarterly*, 41(1), 133–155.

Note

[1] A *non-zero* chance of selection refers to the practice of *weighting* units in the sample frame such that their probability of selection is increased or decreased to improve sample representation.

SECTION 3B

DATA GATHERING

In Section 3B, Data Gathering, the chapters cover the data-gathering processes necessary for any research. The seven chapters cover the processes of conducting interviews, constructing questionnaires, conducting focus groups, using introspective methods, designing and using rubrics, conducting diary studies, and analyzing your data statistically.

Chapter 26 is on the topic of conducting interviews. According to the author, a research interview is "… an interactional event in which one party asks questions on topics relevant to the goal of the study and the other party answers these questions." The chapter covers a number of key concepts: survey interviews, structured interviews, qualitative interviews, semi-structured interviews, ethnographic interviews, life history interviews, sociolinguistic interviews, and oral proficiency interviews. After discussing theoretical perspectives, the author ends by discussing the role of interviews in research, as well as the analysis and representation of interview data.

Chapter 27 is about constructing questionnaires. Questionnaires are written instruments on which respondents read a series of questions or statements and respond by writing their answers or selecting from a list of possible answers. The chapter explains what the different types of questionnaires are, why questionnaire research is useful, and what qualities good questionnaires have. The authors also discuss the issues involved in designing and formatting questionnaires, as well as common concerns with response rates. They also make suggestions for writing, administering, and analyzing questionnaires, and end by discussing the ethical principles of questionnaire research.

Chapter 28 discusses conducting focus groups, which are defined as "organized discussions with homogenous groups led by a moderator, following a set plan, where participant interaction is leveraged for increased understanding." The author describes the characteristics, benefits, and limitations of focus groups before addressing some of the key issues involved in focus group research methodology. The chapter ends by discussing common practices in the use of focus groups as well as the value of combining focus groups with other research methods.

Chapter 29 covers the use of introspective methods, which involve the elicitation and collection of data directly from participants about the ways they "approach, organize, and understand information and learning." The authors explain the goals of introspective research, where it came from historically, and its guiding principles. The chapter also covers key concepts like verbal reporting, stimulated recall or retrospection, interviews, and diary studies. The authors end by discussing considerations that researchers should keep in mind when conducting introspective research and providing a classification scheme for eliciting introspective data.

Chapter 30 examines the use of rubrics. A rubric is a set of instructions for assessing performance in a language that lists possible scores and describes the expected features of performance for each outcome. The chapter describes three types of rubrics and provides examples. The author explains why rubrics are important, the advantages and disadvantages of the different types, the importance of matching rubrics to research uses, and approaches to building rubrics. The chapter ends by describing an example rubric research project and how the author dealt with various problems, as well as currently active areas of research on rubrics.

Chapter 31 covers diary studies, which typically involve analyzing diary or journal entries written by language teachers or learners or teachers. The chapter explores key concepts like introspection, think-aloud data, stimulated recall data, concurrent introspection, intermediate and delayed retrospection, as well as primary and secondary introspection. The author also discusses various ways that diary studies have been applied in theoretical and practical second language acquisition research, and provides practical advice for keeping and using a teaching journal.

Chapter 32 examines statistical data analysis. The chapter begins by defining research data as "a collection of facts, measurements, and observations used to describe or make inferences." The chapter also discusses concepts like hypothesis testing, identifying and measuring variables, preparing data for statistical analysis, screening data for statistical analysis, and deciding on statistical tests (including discussions of cross-tabulations and chi-square, phi and Cramer's V, correlations, t-tests, analysis of variance, and effect size procedures). The authors end with advice on what should be included in selecting and reporting on statistical procedures.

Editors' Preview Questions

1. Which of the following data-gathering techniques are you familiar with: interviews (see Chapter 26); questionnaires (see Chapter 27); focus groups (see Chapter 28); introspective methods (see Chapter 29); rubrics (see Chapter 30); diary studies (see Chapter 31); and statistical data gathering (see Chapter 31)?

2. What is the primary characteristic that makes each of the data-gathering techniques listed above distinct?

3. What characteristics do all of the data-gathering techniques listed above have in common?

4. Which data-gathering technique(s) are you most interested in? How might your choice(s) be able to help you to understand language learning and teaching, and to solve problems in your classrooms and professional life?

CHAPTER 26

Conducting Interviews

Gabriele Kasper

INTRODUCTION

Interviews are a standard activity for producing knowledge in language research across the methodological spectrum (Gubrium, Holstein, Marvasti, and McKinney, 2012). They serve a variety of purposes and are designed, conducted, analyzed, and represented in research reports accordingly. As an activity type, a research interview is an interactional event in which one party asks questions on topics relevant to the goal of the study and the other party answers these questions. The interview's defining question-answer structure – with or without a third-turn response by the questioner – builds on a fundamental interactional organization in which social members anywhere participate in the course of their daily lives.

BACKGROUND

What distinguishes the interview from question-answer adjacency pairs in ordinary conversation is that: a) the question and answer turns are pre-allocated to the interviewer and the respondent in a complementary fashion; and b) that the topical content comes from the purpose of the interview. These generic features categorize the interview as an institutional activity. The parties can be multiple interviewers and multiple respondents, but predominantly, interviews are conducted between two participants. Increasingly, focus groups and other forms of group interview are also used.

RESEARCH ON THIS TOPIC

STANDARDIZED SURVEY INTERVIEWS

A survey interview is a delivery mode of a survey (Brown, 2001) and – as such – its purpose is to enable generalizations to be made from the sample of interview participants concerning the characteristics of the population that the sample is meant to represent. In applied linguistics, survey interviews are used in a wide range of subfields: these include social-psychological studies of individual differences in language learning; program evaluation; language variation and change; and societal multilingualism. In order to ensure consistency and facilitate coding and quantification, interviews are based on a questionnaire or schedule that specifies the order and formulation of the scripted questions (structured interview). Standardized survey interviews also prescribe the allowable answer categories and how the interviewer delivers the questions, responds to the answers, addresses problems in question understanding, and records the responses. Large-scale surveys such as the European Commission surveys – for example, the 2012 survey on multilingualism in Europe – are conducted by many different interviewers who are not the designers of the instrument, making it all the more important that interviewers adhere to the interview protocol in order to obtain reliable data. However, as an extensive body of research shows, interaction can only be standardized to a certain extent. No amount of training and standardization can eliminate the fundamental unpredictability of interaction, and rigid adherence to the protocol can adversely affect the respondent's participation and answer quality. Therefore, students of interaction in standardized survey interviews recommend a measure of flexibility for question delivery, ordering, and reformulation (Houtkoop-Steenstra, 2000), arguing that the loss in formal consistency will be compensated by substantive gains in answer quality.

Qualitative Interviews

The term qualitative interview refers collectively to various types of interview conducted in qualitative research. Some of these are more or less distinct genres – such as ethnographic interviews and life history interviews – others are more diffusely called qualitative interviews without further specification of their particular characteristics. They converge on the goal to enable a profound understanding of the participants' opinions, beliefs, attitudes, experiences, and identities in a particular domain or domains as these are described by the participants. Since qualitative interviews aim for descriptions from the participants' perspective, they are typically conducted in a flexible format that allows the respondent to take extended turns and the interviewer to follow up responses contingently with further probing and explore unexpected directions in the participants' talk. In open-ended formats, the interview is initially guided by a few, broadly formulated questions that encourage the participant to produce topically rich and thoughtful descriptions and accounts. In semi-structured interviews, the interviewer references more targeted, pre-specified questions, which allow for easier comparability of question-answer sequences across participants. However, the question order, formulation, and interviewer's uptake of the responses are not prescribed: questions that have already been addressed or pre-empted can be omitted or re-contextualized and "re-entextualized"; and questions not included in the written set may be raised as the interview develops. Since the aim of open-ended and semi-structured interviews is not to "standardize away" the contingencies of normal interaction, there is less risk of increased difficulty in understanding; at the same time, the full availability of the repair apparatus enables participants to address problems of understanding as they arise. In longitudinal interview studies, the two formats of interview organization are commonly deployed sequentially, such that a study will begin with open-ended interviews and progressively move to more focused questions, targeting specific topics that emerged in prior interviews. In this way, the study can advance from initial exploration to inductively achieved hypothesis-formation and subsequent hypothesis testing. The outcomes of the last phase may complete the study or open up new topics, starting up a new investigative sequence. Qualitative interview studies typically explore complex problems that unfold in interrelated topic components generated during and across interviews. Therefore the exploration–hypothesis formation–hypothesis testing sequence often takes several cycles on multiple time scales.

Ethnographic interviews are a standard component of ethnographies and ethnographic studies. They complement participant observation, recordings of interactions in their indigenous settings, and collections of documents and artifacts and investigate the cultural lives of social groups and institutions from the members' perspectives. Although the purpose of collecting multiple types of data is to gain a multiperspective view on the groups' or institution's cultural practices, norms, and values, research reports of ethnographic studies in applied linguistics often privilege the interview data (Talmy, 2010). Life history interviews (also called autobiographic interview, narrative interviews, or memoirs) seek to offer insights into the human condition through the stories that individuals tell about their life experiences (Roulston, 2010). In applied linguistics, autobiographic interviews are the key data source for language biographies, that is, bilingual and multilingual speakers' narrative accounts of how they came to use, learn, change, or lose languages and language varieties throughout their lifetime or during a specific period. Analytical emphasis is placed on elucidating "subject realities" or "life realities" (Pavlenko, 2007), although both foci can be addressed through the same interview study.

SOCIOLINGUISTIC INTERVIEWS

Other differences aside, in the interview genres considered so far, the organization of the interview and the language(s) it is conducted in serve as a vehicle to elicit information about a particular phenomenon in the respondents' life-worlds. In sociolinguistic interviews, however, the topical content serves as a platform to elicit information about language and discourse. Whereas all other types of interview discussed originated in other disciplines within the social sciences, the sociolinguistic interview was designed specifically for the purposes of linguistic and applied linguistic research. William Labov (1972) developed the sociolinguistic interview as a measure to offset the Observer's Paradox[1] in participant observation. The interview enables the researcher to select respondents according to the desired social variables and to manipulate the interview interaction so that different speech styles can be elicited. Topics typically center around informants' life history, experiences, and views on various issues. Interview respondents are not aware of the investigative focus. One design feature recommended by Labov (1972) was to ask informants about life-threatening experiences, since affectively loaded topics successfully triggered casual speech. The "danger of death" question has not proven equally effective across research contexts, but affective engagement may still be conducive to vernacular speech. While the data are gathered through a semi-structured qualitative interview, the analysis focuses on selected phonological variables and their correlations with demographic variables and speech style. In addition to variationist sociolinguistics[2], sociolinguistic interviews have also been found useful for the study of discourse organization and management. Schiffrin (1987) conducted informal group interviews with couples and friends to investigate discourse markers in English. The interview interaction provided sequential environments for several discourse markers to be used repeatedly, such as "well" in dispreferred answers and request-compliance sequences, and "oh" in response to repair and explanations, and as acknowledgement.

A type of sociolinguistic interview designed for the purpose of spoken language assessment is the oral proficiency interview (OPI). Typically, though not exclusively, organized as a dyadic interview between the language tester as interviewer and the L2 speaking candidate as respondent, the OPI serves to elicit samples of target language speech from the candidate for the purpose of language assessment. OPIs are differentially pre-structured. The OPI developed by the American Council of Teachers of Foreign Languages (ACTFL), for instance, has a semi-structured format. Question topics are selected to probe the candidate's foreign language ability at one or more of four major levels of language proficiency, specified in the ACTFL Guidelines. The topics that have to be covered for each proficiency level are pre-determined, but the order in which the questions are asked and their linguistic form are left to the interviewer's discretion. The interviewer is also allowed to preface and reformulate questions to facilitate the candidate's understanding, and there are no prescriptions of how to repair understanding difficulties. A large literature has examined OPI interaction from a range of discourse-analytical perspectives, with the purpose of determining its relationship to ordinary conversation (the target domain) and to examine, among other things, interviewer practices, the relation of candidate's performance and scores, and changes in candidates' interactional competences between successive interviews. The speaking test of the International English Language Testing System (IELTS) is designed to assess how L2 speakers will perform in an English-medium study or work environment. While also organized in a dyadic format, the IELTS speaking test is conducted as a standardized structured interview. Interviewers are required to strictly adhere to the examiner frame – a script prescribing question topics, form, and order for each of the nine IELTS bands and proscribing reformulation and unsolicited comments. Seedhouse (2013) compares the interactional organization of the IELTS with that of L2 classrooms and academic content classes at universities in order to assess the extent to which L2 classrooms prepare students to participate in the IELTS test and to what extent IELTS represents the kinds of interaction typical of university courses. While question-answer sequences are prevalent in all three activity types, the rigid format of IELTS contrasts strongly with the varying organizations of L2 classrooms and university content classes, which allow these instructional activities to be flexibly adjusted to local needs and objectives.

THEORETICAL PERSPECTIVES

Interviews are pervasive in modern and late-modern society. Partly fuelled by media preoccupation with people's opinions and attitudes towards matters of public interest, partly by poststructuralist concerns with the role of identities in language learning and education, interviews have become the data production device of choice in much qualitative applied linguistics since the mid-1990s. However, this upsurge in use has not been accompanied by an effort to get a conceptual handle on the interview as a machine for producing knowledge. Consequently, interviews have been treated in a commonsensical fashion in the great majority of interview studies in applied linguistics, and for several decades, sociologists, anthropologists, and psychologists have been urging social scientists to locate the interview in its epistemological, sociocultural, and sociohistorical contexts, understand it as an activity type, and consider that interview responses are unavoidably shaped by the interviewer's questions and other conduct. In the last few years, applied linguists (Talmy, 2010; Talmy and Richards, 2011) and sociolinguists (De Fina and Perrino, 2011) have extended this much-needed discussion to their disciplines. Roulston (2010) distinguishes neo-positivist, romantic, constructionist, postmodern, transformative, and decolonizing approaches to the (qualitative) interview. Other authors contrast the interview as a resource with the interview as a topic for study (Seale, 1999), or the interview as research instrument with the interview as social practice (Talmy, 2010). In the resource/instrument perspective, the interview is treated as a transparent access device to facts about the respondent's external social world and revelations about their internal mental life. Behind this commonsense understanding lies a view of language as neutral conduit and a transmission model of communication; conceptualizations that few contemporary applied linguists would explicitly endorse. As Briggs (1984: 3) warned, the interview-as-instrument concept "smuggle(s) outmoded preconceptions out of the realm of conscious theory and into that of methodology." This is a concern for applied linguists because, as Talmy's review (2010) shows, the great majority of interview studies in (qualitative) applied linguistics implicitly adopt an instrument perspective, even if its inbuilt assumptions conflict with the study's conceptual framework.

As a social practice that requires examination as a research topic in its own right, the interview is treated as interaction in which the participants jointly produce descriptions and accounts at particular moments in their talk: interactional and representational practices – including selections from the participants' linguistic repertoires – are key analytical interests, since it is through them that the participants construct descriptions, stories, and stances. While the instrument view pays no heed to the interactional methods through which the interview is accomplished, the social practice view holds that these methods require careful analytic attention since it is only through them that the topical content of the interview becomes available in the first place.

PRACTICAL APPLICATIONS

TO INTERVIEW OR NOT TO INTERVIEW?

The conceptualization of the research interview has direct consequences for research practices. In other words, what the interview *is* for the researcher shapes what the researcher *does* with the interview. Roulston (2010) offers a comprehensive and very helpful discussion of how different theoretical perspectives on the interview are associated with particular methodological practices and strategies for quality assurance. Here I want to consider the first design decision that researchers have to make when they develop a research plan: is the interview an appropriate choice for the purpose of the study? Does it answer the research questions? Unless the researcher adopts the realist view that participants' reports about practices in their social worlds provide true descriptions of actual facts, interviews are not an adequate choice to learn about how people live their social lives. In order to find out how people go about their activities, including using, learning, teaching, and assessing language, researchers need to observe participants' conduct in natural settings. However, to answer questions about participants' opinions, beliefs, attitudes, feelings, knowledge, and experiences, interviews are an appropriate choice. Even so, when the study addresses psychological questions, they should not be the default option since people constantly make their psychological states known to each other through their conduct, about and to which they may make psychological claims and attributions. Although interviews are often treated as privileged contexts to generate stories from participants, it has to be considered that storytelling is a high-frequency activity in people's daily lives. Stories regularly provide the occasion for psychological displays and, conversely, such displays are regularly achieved through stories and their delivery modes. Whether they occur in daily interaction or in the research interview, stories and psychological matters are unavoidably occasioned and accomplished through interaction and recipient designed. Consequently, interviews are no delivery platform for unadulterated psychological states and true stories. In fact, the same story told at different times in a series of research interviews (Prior, 2011) or delivered in different languages (Koven, 2001) shows marked differences between versions. These considerations do not distract from the value of the research interview when the participants' discursive representations of their worlds are at issue. They are meant to encourage applied linguists to choose interviews judiciously, consider alternative options, and examine psychological matters and stories in relation to the discursive contexts in which they are produced.

ANALYSIS AND REPRESENTATION

The theory of interview adopted by the researcher will have critical implications for analysis. From an instrument perspective, interview responses are scrutinized for their thematic content, read off a scripted version of the responses. The research report includes summaries of interview responses and quotations with or without commentary. A sophisticated, rigorous style of thematic analysis is offered by grounded theory method (GT) (for example, Bryant and Charmaz, 2007). It involves four successive stages of analysis: initial inductive open coding; the collection of codes into concepts; and of concepts into broader categories; and finally the formulation of a theory that interlinks the categories. Through constant comparison, the various types of category and concept are compared with each other and new data. GT requires a persistent interplay between data collection and analysis. The later stages of data collection operate in a deductive mode that enables theoretical sampling. Although some interview studies in applied linguistics claim to have used GT, it is rarely apparent from the research report how GT's elaborate apparatus was used to generate theory.

Under the social practice view, the interview is analyzed as interaction. Rather than deleting the interviewer from the analysis, responses are analyzed as co-produced by the interviewer's questions and other interviewer conduct. Examining the interview as coordinated action-in-interaction requires that analysts pay close attention to the understandings that the participants display to each other through their responses. By examining the details of turn construction – including grammatical and lexical resources, prosody, the temporal structuring of turns, and (if the interview is video-recorded) nonvocal conduct – it can be shown how the participants accomplish actions, identities, epistemic and affective stances, and social relations. While these are necessarily local accomplishments, they show how the participants relate themselves to matters outside the interviews. Finally, the research report includes detailed analyses of representative excerpts from the data, transcribed with sufficient granularity to clearly display the phenomenon of interest. This representational policy enables readers to critically co-analyze the excerpts and in the given case disagree with the author.

CONCLUSION

As elsewhere in the social sciences, research interviews in applied linguistics are overused, under-theorized, and under-analyzed. In the past few years, applied linguists have taken important steps to catch up with the older social sciences in their effort to put research interviews in our field on a reflected, conceptually profound, and empirically rigorous footing. This new direction needs to be pursued further. There is an urgent need for more studies of various types of research interviews. In order to develop an empirically grounded theory of interview methodology, applied linguists are called on to turn their own critical apparatus on the research interview in order to achieve a sophisticated understanding of the interview as a knowledge-generating activity. Such studies will enable applied linguists to select interviews more judiciously; enhance their practices of conducting, analyzing, and representing research interviews; and produce insightful research that coherently transforms theory into methodology.

Discussion Questions

1. Make a list of specific research topics and research questions. Decide which of the questions can appropriately be answered through a research interview and which are better addressed through other types of data collection methods.

2. For the topics and questions that are good candidates for an interview study, which of the theories of interview proposed by Roulston (2010: Chapter 3) will you choose?

3. What methodological decisions will you make in order to transform your chosen theory of interview coherently into research methods?

4. Choose five interview studies published in an applied linguistic journal or edited volume. Describe the studies in light of Table 1 "Contrasting conceptualizations of the research interview" in Talmy (2010: 132). Discuss what evidence in the research report fits with the research instrument or social practice perspective.

References

Briggs, C. L. (1984). Learning how to ask: Native metacommunicative competence and incompetence of fieldworkers. *Language in Society*, 13, 1–28.

Brown, J. D. (2001). *Using surveys in language programs*. Cambridge: Cambridge University Press.

Bryant, A., & Charmaz, K. (2007). Grounded theory in historical perspective: An epistemological account. In A. Bryant & K. Charmaz (Eds.), *The SAGE handbook of grounded theory* (pp. 31–57). Los Angeles: Sage.

Council of Europe (2012). *Special Eurobarometer 386: Europeans and their languages*. Available at http://ec.europa.eu/

De Fina, A., & Perrino, S. (Eds.) (2011). *Narratives in interviews, interviews in narrative studies*. Special Issue, *Language in Society*, 40(1).

Gubrium, J. F., Holstein, J. A., Marvasti, A. B., & McKinney, K. D. (Eds.) (2012). *The SAGE handbook of interview research* (2nd ed.). Thousand Oaks, CA: Sage.

Houtkoop-Steenstra, H. (2000). *Interaction and the standardized survey interview*. Cambridge: Cambridge University Press.

Koven, M. (2001). Comparing bilinguals' quoted performances of self and others in telling of the same experience in two languages. *Language in Society*, 30(4), 513–558.

Labov, W. (1972). *Sociolinguistic patterns*. Philadelphia, PA: University of Pennsylvania Press.

Pavlenko, A. (2007). Autobiographic narratives as data in applied linguistics. *Applied Linguistics*, 28, 163–188.

Prior, M. T. (2011). Self-presentation in L2 interview talk: Narrative versions, accountability, and emotionality. *Applied Linguistics*, 32, 60–76.

Roulston, K. (2010). *Reflective interviewing*. London: Sage.

Schiffrin, D. (1987). *Discourse markers*. New York: Cambridge University Press.

Seale, C. E. (1999). *The quality of qualitative research*. London: Sage.

Seedhouse, P. (2013). Oral proficiency interviews as varieties of interaction. In S. Ross & G. Kasper (Eds.), *Assessing second language pragmatics* (pp. 199–219). Basingstoke, UK: Palgrave Macmillan.

Talmy, S. (2010). Qualitative interviews in applied linguistics: From research instrument to social practice. *Annual Review of Applied Linguistics*, 30, 128–148.

Talmy, S. & Richards, K. (Eds.) (2011). *Qualitative interviews in applied linguistics: Discursive perspectives*. Special Issue, *Applied Linguistics* 32, 1.

Notes

[1] When speakers are aware of being observed, they may talk differently from when they are not being observed. Yet in order to study how people normally talk, researchers need data from unobserved natural language use. Sociolinguist William Labov referred to this dilemma as the Observer's Paradox.

[2] According to variationist sociolinguistics, language is systematically variable. Variation is probabilistic rather than categorical and related to such factors as speaker characteristics, social orientations, speech situation, and linguistic environment. Language change emerges from the variable use of linguistic features.

CHAPTER 27

Constructing Questionnaires

Christine Coombe and Peter Davidson

INTRODUCTION

Questionnaires are amongst the most common research tools that ELT researchers use, mainly because they are useful, versatile, quick to implement, and the data they generate can be analyzed relatively quickly and easily. As teachers and researchers, we are continually bombarded with requests to complete questionnaires from our colleagues and students. In reality, however, good questionnaires that generate useful data are particularly difficult to write, so inexperienced developers often base their own instruments on ones in the public domain that have deficiencies. This chapter summarizes best practices with regard to questionnaire design, development, and administration.

BACKGROUND

Questionnaires are any written instruments that present respondents with a series of questions or statements to which they are to react either by writing out their answers or selecting them from among existing answers (Brown, 2001). They are often referred to by different names such as inventories, forms, tests, batteries, surveys, scales, profiles, and indexes (Aiken, 1997). The major objective in questionnaire research is to obtain accurate and relevant information or data about the topic under study. Another important objective in this type of research is to maximize the response rate (the proportion of respondents answering the questionnaire).

According to Dörnyei (2003), questionnaires in ELT research can yield three different types of data about the respondents, namely factual, behavioral, and attitudinal. Factual questions are those that attempt to find out information about who the respondents are. These types of questions yield what is known as demographic information. Behavioral questions are ones that ask respondents to report on what they are doing or have done in the past. Attitudinal questions find out what people think and investigate respondents' opinions, beliefs, interests, and values.

RESEARCH ON THIS TOPIC

WHY DO QUESTIONNAIRE RESEARCH?

Proponents of questionnaire or survey research point to a number of advantages associated with this type of quantitative research. First, surveys can be used to research virtually any aspect of teaching and learning and can be easily used in field settings such as classrooms (Nunan, 1992). Questionnaires are also easier and less expensive than other forms of data collection (Seliger and Shohamy, 1989; Brown, 2001). According to Dörnyei (2003), conducting research with questionnaires provides us with unprecedented efficiency in terms of researcher time, effort, and financial resources. As noted by Mackey and Gass (2005), questionnaires are more practical and economical than interviews, and they can easily elicit comparable data from a number of respondents.

Other reported benefits of questionnaires are that they are relatively easy to analyze and they reduce bias because of the uniform question presentation. Additionally, the researcher's own opinions do not influence the respondent and there are no verbal or visual clues to influence the respondent. Finally, questionnaires are familiar to most people as nearly everyone has had some experience completing them so they do not make respondents apprehensive.

Despite the numerous advantages associated with survey research, there are some noted disadvantages that must be taken into consideration. One major disadvantage of questionnaire research is the inability on the part of the researcher to probe responses. Because questionnaires are structured instruments that consist of, for the most part, selected response items, they do not allow respondents to qualify their responses which often results in superficial data (Walonick, 1997–2004; Mackey and Gass, 2005). Another disadvantage that has major implications for research conducted in foreign language and second language contexts is respondent literacy. It is often assumed that respondents can read and write well and this is often not the case (Mackey and Gass, 2005).

A number of biases in research have implications for questionnaire research and could be considered as disadvantages of this type of data collection. Prestige bias, or the fact that people do not always provide true answers about themselves, happens because respondents often want to please the researcher by providing the "right" response, and they usually have a fairly good idea of what the desirable or acceptable response is. Acquiescence bias or the tendency that some people have to agree with sentences they are unsure of or are ambivalent about is another bias that is prevalent in questionnaire research. Fatigue effects often kick in if questionnaires are too long or monotonous.

QUALITIES OF GOOD QUESTIONNAIRES

According to Walonick (1997–2004), questionnaires should have the following qualities:

- *Questionnaires should evoke the truth.* To achieve this, questionnaires must be non-threatening. If a questionnaire has controversial or sensitive items, it is important to clearly state your policy on confidentiality. If respondents are concerned about the consequences of answering a particular question, their responses might not be truthful.
- *Questionnaires should ask for an answer on only one dimension.* Good questions ask for only one piece of information. A question that asks for a response on more than one dimension will not provide the researcher with the information they are

seeking. Avoid the use of double-barreled questions that ask about two facets, but only allow for one response, for example "Do you agree or disagree? Grammar and vocabulary are important for advanced learners."
- *Questionnaires should accommodate all possible answers.* When conducting research using surveys, it is important to provide the respondent with all the possible responses. Asking a question that does not accommodate all possible responses can confuse and frustrate the respondent.
- *Questionnaires should have mutually exclusive options.* A good question should have only one correct or appropriate choice for the respondent to make and it will leave no ambiguity in the mind of the respondent.
- *Questionnaires should produce a variability of responses.* Good survey items produce a variability of responses.

PRACTICAL APPLICATIONS
DESIGNING AND FORMATTING A QUESTIONNAIRE

Most problems associated with questionnaires can be traced back to the design phase (Walonick, 1997–2004). The design and formatting of a questionnaire is important on many levels. For one, a well-formatted survey makes it easier for the respondent to read and complete, which will in turn improve response rates (Bradburn, Sudman, and Wansink, 2004). In addition, it can reduce measurement error, as respondents will be more likely to follow the flow of the survey, and be less likely to misread or overlook questions (Dillman, 2000).

Dörnyei (2003) recommends designing a questionnaire with the following parts: title, instructions, items, additional information, and a final thank you. The purpose of the title is to provide respondents with an initial orientation to the topic under study and to activate background knowledge or schema. Interestingly enough, questionnaires with titles are generally perceived as more credible than those without, thereby increasing their face validity. Another important part of the questionnaire design is the instructions (Walonick, 1997–2004). According to Dörnyei (2003), there should be two types of instructions: general and specific. The former is intended to provide a general greeting at the beginning of the questionnaire and should include information like: what the study is about and why it is important, the organization and/or individual responsible for conducting the research, an emphasis that there are no right or wrong answers, a promise of confidentiality, and a thank you. The latter type of instructions are those that are specific to the question groupings. These instructions should explain and demonstrate how respondents should answer questions. The last two sections of a questionnaire are the additional information section and the final thank you. The additional information section can include the contact details of the researcher, how the questionnaire should be returned, a note promising a copy of the results, and an invitation for a follow-up interview if applicable.

GENERAL CONSIDERATIONS OF QUESTIONNAIRE DESIGN

Once you have decided on a format and an overall design of the questionnaire, it is necessary to make decisions on a number of other points. The first, and perhaps most important, is deciding what to ask. Generally in research we ask questions that provide us with information on what we are primarily interested in (our dependent variables) and information which might help explain the dependent variables (our independent variables). We must also be aware of confounding variables that distort the results of our research and have to be adjusted for.

LENGTH

Determining the length of the survey is also an important consideration. Dillman (2000) recommends that before making a determination of survey length that the researcher must consider the respondents' level of responsibility, commitment, and interest. The general temptation of a novice researcher is to cover too much ground by asking everything that might turn out to be interesting. Experts in the field agree that anything over four to six pages that requires more than 30 minutes to complete is too long (Brown, 2001). Stamina is another factor in survey response. If surveys are too long, respondents may begin to choose from only the first answer choices (Dillman, 2000). One way to ensure that fatigue does not negatively affect your study is to have respondents answer the most important questions in the survey (those that are directly related to the primary research questions) in the first half of the questionnaire.

QUESTION TYPES

Deciding on what types of questions to include in your questionnaire is another important decision the researcher will have to make. In general, researchers will choose from open or closed format questions. With the former, respondents formulate their own answers, whereas with the latter respondents are forced to choose between several given options. Some common open formats are:

- Open questions – e.g., How many languages have you studied?
- Clarification questions – e.g., If you rated the textbook you are using as **poor** or **very poor**, please briefly explain why.
- Sentence completion – e.g., One thing I liked about this workshop was …
- Short answer questions – e.g., What was it that you found most useful about this workshop?

Examples of closed format question types include:

- Choice of categories
  e.g., What is your marital status? Circle one: single, married, divorced, separated.
- Likert scale
  e.g., Language assessment is an interesting subject.
  Circle: SA   A   neutral   D   SD
  (SA = strongly agree, A = agree, D = disagree, SD = strongly disagree)
- Differential scales
  e.g., How would you rate this presentation?
  Very boring   1   2   3   4   5   6   7   8   9   10   Very interesting
- Checklist
  e.g., Circle the classroom activities that you are particularly interested in.
  Drill and practice
  Cloze
  Dictation
  Pair work
  Group work
  Silent reading

QUESTION ORDER AND GROUPINGS

The way in which a researcher orders questions on surveys is important as it establishes both the survey's logic and flow (Dillman, 2000; Bradburn, Sudman, and Wansink, 2004). It has been recommended that questionnaire designers pay special attention to the first question of a survey, as it is the key in engaging respondents to complete the remainder of the instrument (Fanning, 2005). Dillman (2000) recommends that the first question should:

- apply to all respondents;
- be easy to read, understand, and respond to (so closed response questions are better);
- be interesting;
- connect with the purpose of the survey.

Whatever type of questions you decide to use on your questionnaire, it is important to be consistent and to group question types together. When arranging questions on a questionnaire a number of strategies have been found to be useful. Some researchers go from the general to the more particular; others arrange questions from easy to more difficult. Still others move from factual questions to the more abstract ones. Some arrange questionnaires starting with closed format questions and move on to more open ended ones. It is recommended with questionnaires on sensitive or controversial topics to avoid starting with demographic or personal information questions. Research shows that respondents are less likely to respond truthfully to a sensitive item once they have already given identifying information about themselves (Dillman, 2000).

RESPONSE RATE

The response rate of a questionnaire is the single most important indicator of how much confidence you can place in the results (Walonick, 1997–2004). As a general rule, long questionnaires get fewer responses than shorter questionnaires. To maximize your response rate, it might be necessary to eliminate questions from your instrument. A good way to do this is to ask yourself the purpose of each and every question on the instrument and to try to relate each item directly back to the research question it is trying to answer.

SAMPLE SIZE

Sample size is another important consideration in questionnaire research. A common question posed by novice researchers is how large should a sample size be? According to the literature, there are no hard and fast rules on this. A general recommendation is 10% of the population under study. Hatch and Lazarton (1991) state that the basic requirement of a normal distribution equates to at least 30 respondents. For researchers who want to claim statistical significance, at least 50 respondents are needed, and for multivariate statistical procedures like factor analysis at least 100 respondents are necessary (Brown, 2001; for more on this topic see Chapter 25).

FEEDBACK AND PILOTING

According to Frary (2003: 1), it is a good idea to obtain feedback from a small but representative sample of potential respondents. Piloting the questionnaires can assist the researcher in "determining the relevance of the questions and the extent to which there may be problems in obtaining responses."

SUGGESTIONS FOR WRITING GOOD SURVEY ITEMS

Perhaps the most important thing when writing the actual survey items is to ask precise questions using simple and direct language. For the survey to be successful, the questions must be clearly understood by the respondent. Avoid the use of negatives if possible, and never use double negative in questions. In addition to being clear and concise, there should be a clear-cut need for every question on your survey. Questionnaire developers should take care when writing the first item on a survey. Experts recommend that this question should be general but pertain to the purpose of the survey (Fanning, 2005), otherwise there is the potential for losing the respondents' trust and focus (Dillman, 2000).

Questionnaire developers should be aware of the various biases inherent in survey research and take steps to avoid them. One way to do this is to ensure that respondents react to both positive and negatively worded survey items. This practice also helps prevent respondent response sets where respondents quickly give the same response (for example, "strongly agree") without actually reading the questions.

When response categories of a question represent a progression from a lower level of response to a higher one (i.e., "never, seldom, occasionally, frequently"), it is usually better to list them from the lower level to the higher level in left-to-right order (Frary, 1996). Another recommendation as put forth by Frary (1996) is to consider combining response categories. Combining "seldom" with "never" might be acceptable if respondents would be unlikely to mark "never" and if "seldom" would connote an almost equivalent level of activity.

ADMINISTERING THE QUESTIONNAIRE

Questionnaires are most commonly administered either in a paper format or – more commonly these days – electronically through online questionnaire development programs like Survey Monkey and Survey Select. Whichever way the researcher chooses to administer the questionnaire, there are a number of issues to consider. First, a cover letter/email should be included. This is necessary to help sell the questionnaire and to create rapport with potential respondents. One way to increase respondent motivation to answer the questionnaire, and therefore increase your response rate, is to provide an incentive for a properly-completed questionnaire. If the information gained from your instrument is of interest to the respondent, one good incentive is to offer to provide a summary report of your results once your study has been completed. A final consideration is to try to make completion and return of the survey convenient. If you are administering a paper questionnaire, providing respondents with a self-addressed stamped envelope will make return of the questionnaire more convenient.

ANALYZING THE QUESTIONNAIRE

According to Walonick (1997–2004), the researcher should start formulating a plan for the statistical analysis of a questionnaire during the design phase. Strategies for knowing how each question on the questionnaire will be analyzed and how missing data will be handled are crucial to the success of the research. If the researcher cannot specify how each question will be analyzed, it should not be included in the questionnaire.

CONCLUSION: ETHICAL PRINCIPLES OF QUESTIONNAIRE RESEARCH

Ethics has become a cornerstone for conducting effective and meaningful research. To ensure that questionnaire research meets the standards for ethics, Oppenheim (1992) recommends that researchers should adhere to five ethical principles (for more on this topic, see Chapters 22 and 23):

- No harm should come to the respondents as a result of their participation in the research;
- The respondents' right to privacy should always be respected;
- Respondents should be provided with sufficient information to complete the questionnaire;
- In the case of conducting research with children, permission from their caretakers should be obtained first;
- The researcher should not promise a higher degree of privacy and confidentiality than he/she can deliver.

In addition, for questionnaires to be successful research tools, they must be carefully designed to yield valid and reliable information. Attention must be paid to ensure that individual questions are relevant, appropriate, intelligible, precise, and unbiased. By carefully drafting and evaluating the need for every question used in the instrument, you will collect more meaningful data that can be more easily interpreted and analyzed.

Discussion Questions

1. When is it better to use questionnaires rather than interviews?
2. What can you do to encourage people to take time out to complete your questionnaire?
3. What considerations should you make when administering your questionnaire?
4. What steps can you take to ensure that your questionnaire meets ethical requirements?
5. What impact will technology have on question design, administration, interpretation and use?

References

Aiken, L. (1997). *Questionnaires and inventories: Surveying opinions and assessing personality.* New York: John Wiley.

Bradburn, N., Sudman, S., & Wansink, B. (2004). *Asking questions: The definitive guide to questionnaire design.* San Francisco: Jossey-Bass.

Brown, J. D. (2001). *Using surveys in language programs.* Cambridge: Cambridge University Press.

Dillman, D. (2000). *Constructing the questionnaire: Mail and internet surveys.* New York: John Wiley & Sons.

Dörnyei, Z. (2003). *Questionnaires in second language research: Construction, administration and processing.* Mahwah, NJ: Lawrence Erlbaum.

Fanning, E. (2005). Formatting a paper-based survey questionnaire: Best practices. *Practical Assessment Research and Evaluation*, 10(12). Retrieved April 23, 2012 from http://pareonline.net/getvn.asp?v=10&n=12

Frary, R. (1996). Hints for designing questionnaires. *Practical Assessment, Research & Evaluation*, 5(3). Retrieved July 15, 2011 from http://pareonline.net/getvn.asp?v=5&n=3

Frary, R. (2003). *A brief guide to questionnaire development.* Retrieved from http://www.peecworks.org/PEEC/FV4-0001B459/S01795CAB-01795F65

Hatch, E., & Lazarton, A. (1991). *The research manual.* New York: Newbury House.

Mackey, A., & Gass, S. M. (2005). *Second language research: Methodology and design.* Mahwah, NJ: Lawrence Erlbaum Associates.

Nunan, D. (1992). *Research methods in language learning.* Cambridge: Cambridge University Press.

Oppenheim, A. N. (1992). *Questionnaire design, interviewing and attitude measurement.* London: Pinter.

Seliger, H. W., & Shohamy, E. (1989). *Second language research methods.* Oxford: Oxford University Press.

Walonick, D. (1997–2004). *Survival statistics.* Bloomington, MN: StatPac.

CHAPTER 28

Conducting Focus Groups

Sena C. Pierce

INTRODUCTION

Focus group research is one of the premier methods to collect, analyze, and report qualitative data in order to "get inside the heads" of a target population. The idea and use of focus groups has grown exponentially since its appearance over 50 years ago, and extensive use in many areas has somewhat clouded the definition of what exactly a focus group entails. This chapter aims to define the contemporary focus group method, discuss benefits, challenges, and key issues with use of the method, provide a brief review of foundational literature, and discuss practical application and considerations for its use in language research.

BACKGROUND

DEFINITIONS

Focus groups may be referred to interchangeably as a tool, technique, or method and, although these terms involve different levels of organization, focus groups are discussed here as a research method in order to bring to mind a higher level of organization with a history of use, accepted standards of practice, and rigor.

A general perception of focus groups may be of a group of people sitting at a big table sharing their opinions to someone standing at the front, clipboard in hand. The reality is far more intricate. At a minimum, most scholars define focus groups as a group discussion focused on a particular topic (Krueger, 1994; Krueger and Casey, 2009; Morgan, 1996; Stewart, Shamdasani, and Rook, 2007). Krueger and Casey (2009: 2) offered a more descriptive definition of the method: "A focus group study is a carefully planned series of discussions designed to obtain perceptions on a defined area of interest in a permissive, nonthreatening environment [where] each group is conducted with 5 to 10 people led by a skilled interviewer."

While Krueger and Casey's (2009) definition of focus groups is comprehensive, one missing element is participant interaction or, as Belzile and Öberg (2012: 460) referred to it, "the hallmark of the focus group method." Drawing closely from Krueger and Casey (2009), with the addition of interaction, focus groups are defined here as organized discussions with homogenous groups led by a moderator, following a set plan, where participant interaction is leveraged for increased understanding.

FOCUS GROUP CHARACTERISTICS

In a reflection on focus group research, the described godfather of the method, Robert Merton (Merton, Fiske, and Kendall, 1990: 565), discussed it as "a set of procedures ... that may help us gain an enlarged sociological and psychological understanding in whatsoever sphere of human experience." The expansive breadth of Merton's blanket definition serves to highlight the range of its use across widely diverse disciplines, including language research, with the most predominant users of the method being market researchers and public health specialists (Stewart, Shamdasani, and Rook, 2007; Morgan, 1996). In spite of the wide application of focus groups, there are key characteristics that distinguish it from other qualitative methods and group processes including:

- The goal of the group is to collect data for research purposes, rather than decision-making, therapy, etc.;
- The groups are small with approximately five to 12 individuals;
- Group members share similar characteristics – for example, age, experience, language background, profession, etc.;
- The method includes multiple groups or a series of focus groups;
- The groups are facilitated by a skilled moderator;
- The moderator follows a pre-established protocol – i.e., questions or prompts;
- The groups produce qualitative data – for example, audio, video, transcripts, notes, etc.

Common practices related to focus group characteristics are discussed further in practical applications.

Focus groups stand out as an important method for qualitative and mixed methods research for the ability to explore complex ideas, motivation, and behavior by accessing individual perspectives while leveraging conflict and consensus that emerges naturally during participant interaction. Like all research methods, there are distinct benefits and challenges to conducting focus groups, as well as key issues concerning their use. (Unless otherwise noted, focus group benefits, limitations, and key issues were drawn from Krueger (1994), Krueger and Casey (2009), and Stewart, Shamdasani, and Rook (2007).)

BENEFITS

FOCUS GROUPS ARE ECONOMICAL

A primary benefit of focus groups is the ability of researchers to generate a large amount of in-depth data quickly, and at a relatively affordable cost compared to other methods, i.e., individual interviews. Along with this, the use of focus groups can significantly increase the sample size of a qualitative study (Krueger, 1994).

FOCUS GROUP FINDINGS ARE TRUSTED

The results of a focus group are often easily understandable to stakeholders and the public and are believable (Krueger, 1994). Some have argued that this perception may give too much credibility to focus group results without the requisite scrutiny (Krueger, 1994; Stewart, Shamdasani, and Rook, 2007).

FOCUS GROUP DISCUSSIONS CAN BE CONTROLLED

As a discussion progresses, skilled moderators have the ability to probe, clarify, and pursue unexpected avenues of talk. Moreover, the role is flexible and allows for a range of more or less control of the group's discussion, depending on the study's design.

FOCUS GROUPS CAN ACCESS DIVERSE POPULATIONS

Unlike other forms of data collection, such as surveys or questionnaires, focus groups can be conducted with young children or other illiterate populations. The format also gives voice to research participants and has been used as a source of empowerment in participatory research, particularly for members of marginalized groups (Krueger and Casey, 2009; Morgan, 1996). This may be a particular benefit for language research conducted within culturally and linguistically diverse communities that may not be represented in the dominant culture or language group.

LIMITATIONS
INTERACTION IS MESSY

Though a distinct benefit, participant interaction is also a potential limitation. Interaction between group members, and the moderator and group members, may influence the flow of conversation, agreement or disagreement within the group, or group member contributions. For example, an outspoken participant may dominate the discussion or drive the group off-task. A moderator may also unintentionally provide cues that influence participant responses. A skilled moderator can help offset these challenges by controlling the flow of conversation and his or her own contributions.

FOCUS GROUP FINDINGS ARE NOT GENERALIZABLE

When conducting focus groups there is an underlying assumption that those who participate are representing the opinions of a larger population. However, like other methods such as interviews and surveys, individuals who elect or are directly asked to participate in focus groups may not represent the opinions of the target population. The dynamics of individual groups may also vary considerably ranging from quiet and fairly non-participatory to loud and energetic. Conducting multiple focus groups and analyzing data across groups both widens the sample pool and helps to balance the variability between groups.

ANALYSIS OF FOCUS GROUP DATA IS COMPLEX

Though not necessarily a limitation, focus groups introduce participant interaction as an additional layer to the data that must be contended with, to some extent, during analysis. There is not one set way to incorporate participant interaction into data analysis, though at a minimum, comments need to be interpreted within the context of the group's interaction.

RESEARCH ON THIS TOPIC
KEY ISSUES

The defining characteristic of conducting focus groups – participant interaction – has emerged recently as a key issue in the use and analysis of focus group data (Belize and Öberg 2012; Morgan, 2010). The primary issue of concern is the ambiguity of the role, and level of importance, that participant interaction plays in focus group research, and the need for more clarity about how researchers decide to use, analyze, and report it (Belzile and Öberg, 2012; Morgan, 2010).

In addition to researchers' use and analysis of participant interaction, the reporting of focus group methodology (or lack of reporting) in the research literature is also a key issue. There is great flexibility in how focus groups are conducted, which is both a strength and a challenge. On the one hand researchers are able to conduct focus groups in the best way possible to meet the goals of a study. On the other, there are no existing standards to direct key decisions in the use or review of focus groups as a method. Recognizing this situation in a comprehensive review of focus group research, Morgan (1996) called for more explicit reporting of design, implementation, and analysis decisions in order to drive the development of standards. Fifteen years later, the call for more transparency and detail in focus group reporting, particularly in data analysis and interpretation, remains a key issue (Belzile and Öberg, 2012; Morgan, 2010).

Focus groups developed out of Robert Merton's work conducting group interviews about morale during and after WWII (Merton, Fiske, and Kendall, 1990). Following in Merton's footsteps, focus groups were adopted by market researchers in the 1950s, becoming and remaining a prominent tool to collect and understand consumer opinions. It wasn't until the 1980s that focus groups reemerged within academic research by way of social scientists (Krueger and Casey, 2009). Krueger (1994) discussed the reemergence as a pendulum swing away from a focus on quantitative data that didn't quite answer questions about the human side – the how and why of observed phenomena.

FOCUS GROUP AS A RESEARCH METHOD

There is limited literature on the use of focus groups in language research or as a research method in its own right. One exception includes Li and Barnard's (2009) study of differences in participant contributions during individual interviews versus focus groups with English language teachers in New Zealand. Not surprisingly, Li and Barnard found qualitative and quantitative differences in teacher comments between the two methods and argued that both should be used in order to triangulate findings.

Much of the literature available in the broader field of social sciences has tended to report best practices – the *what* and *how* of conducting focus groups – over empirical investigation of the method (Belzile and Öberg, 2012; Li and Barnard, 2010; Morgan, 1996). In a comprehensive review of focus group use within social science, Morgan (1996) concluded that the absence of standards for use were likely due to its novelty in academic research. In absence of accepted standards, the broad consensus among scholars is that all decisions made in the planning, implementation, analysis, and reporting of focus groups must support the overall goal of the study (Belzile and Öberg, 2012; Krueger, 1994; Krueger and Casey, 2009; Morgan, 1996; Morgan, 2010; Stewart, Shamdasani, and Rook, 2007). Morgan (1996) identified key decision points in the design of focus groups and argued for a standard checklist of information that should be consistently reported. The checklist included: a) participant recruitment; b) the number and size of groups and participant characteristics; c) sampling and segmentation strategy, i.e., the organization of groups by participant characteristics; d) the level of standardization across groups; and e) question summaries and information about moderation – for example, structure and qualifications of the moderator(s).

PRACTICAL APPLICATIONS

Focus groups can be useful at all stages of a research cycle, particularly for exploratory research, but also as a tool for interpretation of findings, or as a confirmatory process to check hypotheses (Stewart, Shamdasani, and Rook, 2007). In addition to traditional research, focus groups can be used: to inform needs assessment and program development; to explore decision-making processes; to test new programs or ideas; to inform program improvement; to generate questionnaires; or as a check against additional data such as survey responses or individual interviews. Krueger and Casey (2009) provided an outline of four distinct areas of use including market research, academic research, public/nonprofit sector, and participatory research. In the field of language research, focus groups are and can be used as a stand-alone method or in combination with other methods and are generally used for two primary purposes: academic research – for example, theory building – and public/nonprofit sector research – for example, language education. Possible uses include exploring grammaticality judgments from speech community members, or soliciting needs of a language program from prospective students.

FOCUS GROUP PRACTICE

Due to the versatility of use and flexibility in the application of focus groups, knowing the right decisions to make in design and review of the method can be daunting, particularly in absence of standards as a guide. Although there is a lack of empirical work investigating the use of focus groups within language research, there is a broad literature describing common practices using the method in social science research and the public/nonprofit sector. The focus group characteristics here were drawn from Krueger (1994), Krueger and Casey (2009), Morgan (1996), and Stewart, Shamdasani, and Rook (2007). Drawing from this literature, the present section provides a brief overview of common practices and the use of focus groups in combination with other methods.

COMMON PRACTICE

There are a number of accepted practices that appear throughout the literature to guide decisions in the design, sampling, moderation, analysis, and reporting of focus groups. These include:

- Groups are generally as homogenous as possible with selected characteristics related to the research question or topic. It is assumed that discussion is better among group members with similar characteristics. Also, homogenous membership allows comparison across groups.
- Conducting multiple groups with similar characteristics and analyzing data across groups is preferred in order to balance out variability across groups. The number of groups depends on various factors including time and resources, however, Morgan (1996) suggested that the inclusion of four to six groups is ideal.
- The size of the groups range from five to 12 participants with fewer participants preferred for more complex or sensitive topics. Some have argued for no more than ten participants in studies other than market research at which point the groups are more difficult to control and there are fewer opportunities for participants to contribute (Krueger, 1994; Krueger and Casey, 2009).
- More standardization in implementation across groups, i.e., identical interview protocols and uniform facilitation, allows for easier comparison across groups though it may reduce opportunities for exploration of emergent ideas. A mixed approach to standardization follows a flexible protocol and facilitation in earlier groups from which a standardized protocol and procedures are developed for use in later groups (Morgan, 1996).
- The moderator may provide more or less control of the discussion in line with the level of standardization in the study's design. Generally more control prioritizes the

interest of the researcher and less control prioritizes the interests of the participants (Morgan, 1996).
- Most data analysis is conducted using transcripts of focus groups prepared from video or audio recordings of the groups. Researchers interested in the content of focus group discussion often conduct thematic analysis (most common), while researchers predominately interested in interaction conduct conversation or discourse analysis.

In place of common practices for reporting focus group findings, Morgan (2010) suggested three options for reporting participant comments including: a) providing sample quotes representative of the findings; b) restating key points made in discussion; or c) reporting an intact section of the interaction.

COMBINING FOCUS GROUPS WITH OTHER METHODS

Whether for linguistic research, classroom, or program needs, focus groups can be designed as a stand-alone method or in combination with other research methods, often viewed as strengthening the research design (Krueger, 1994; Morgan, 1996). The most common methods used in tandem with focus groups are individual interviews and surveys (Morgan, 1996). For example, focus groups can be used to further explore findings from individual interviews, or vice versa. Focus groups can also be used to develop suitable language for survey items. Less common but also used, focus groups can be employed to further explore survey findings. The use of focus groups in combination with other methods is generally part of an iterative design process where the findings serve as input for follow up data collection or as a means to confirm and/or further explore findings from interviews, surveys, or other methods. In a mixed methods design, focus groups may be used in similar combinations but with the explicit intent of triangulating findings across diverse approaches.

Conclusion

Focus groups are a method of collecting in-depth, qualitative data through group discussions which has been in use since the 1950's, only emerging in social science and language research in the last 25 years. They are an effective and efficient way to collect information about complex topics and are especially useful in exploratory studies. Qualitative and mixed methods researchers are also drawn to focus groups for the incredible flexibility in their use and the unique contribution of participant interaction as a component of the data. However, the flexibility in design and a lack of set standards for how to use and analyze participant interaction are key challenges when implementing focus group research. In order to address these challenges, there is a need for more empirical studies exploring focus groups as a method, as well as increased transparency and consistency in reporting decisions in design and implementation. This need is becoming increasingly urgent as the use of focus groups continues to expand and innovations from other disciplines, such as conducting focus groups online or by phone, are adopted in language research.

Discussion Questions

1. In light of the versatility in how focus groups can be used in language research, is it possible to develop a one-size-fits-all set of standards to guide their use and review?

2. In what ways can researchers effectively blend the analysis of data from individual comments and participant interaction?

3. When analyzing both content and participant interaction, does a researcher need to prioritize one over the other?

4. In what ways may the use of alternative formats such as online focus groups impact common practices in sampling and focus group moderation?

References

Belzile, J. A., & Öberg, G. (2012). Where to begin? Grappling with how to use participant interaction in focus group design. *Qualitative Research*, 12(4), 459–472.

Krueger. R. A. (1994). *Focus groups: A practical guide for applied research* (2nd ed.). Thousand Oaks, CA: Sage.

Krueger, R. A., & Casey, M. A. (2009). *Focus groups: A practical guide for applied research* (4th ed.). Thousand Oaks, CA: Sage.

Li, J., & Barnard, R. (2009). Differences of opinion: Methodological considerations regarding addressivity in individual interviews and focus groups. *New Zealand Studies in Applied Linguistics*, 15(2), 15–29. Retrieved June 8, 2013 from http://www.alanz.ac.nz/journal/

Merton, R. K., Fiske, M., & Kendall, P. L. (1990). *The focused interview: A manual of problems and procedures* (2nd ed.). New York: Free Press.

Morgan, D. L. (1996). Focus groups. *Annual Review of Sociology*, 22, 129–152.

Morgan, D. L. (2010). Reconsidering the role of interaction in analyzing and reporting focus groups. *Qualitative Health Research*, 20(5), 718–722.

Stewart, D. W., Shamdasani, P. N., & Rook, D. W. (2007). *Focus groups: Theory and practice* (2nd ed.): Vol. 20. Applied social research methods series. Thousand Oaks, CA: Sage.

CHAPTER 29

Using Introspective Methods

Sheryl V. Taylor and Donna Sobel

INTRODUCTION

Within the realm of language research, researchers investigate important questions about language learners' behaviors and knowledge. Researchers ask what learners are doing as they learn language and how they process language. Introspective research – the goal of which is to examine the underlying linguistic knowledge learners have gained of the second language and the source of that knowledge – is positioned within the tradition of qualitative research. Following the qualitative research tradition, introspective research relies on data elicitation methodologies such as interviews, diaries, "think aloud," and verbal reporting.

The primary aim of introspective research methods includes data elicited directly from participants about the way they approach, organize, and understand information and learning (Brown and Rodgers, 2002; Gass and Mackey, 2011). Introspective methodologies are a common source of data elicitation in language research, both second language research and foreign language research. These data elicitation methods seek to reveal the cognitive processes employed by participants that cannot be made evident through direct observation.

Given that most processes involved in learning language are not observable, the goal of introspective research is to examine the underlying linguistic knowledge learners have about the second language and the source of that knowledge. A major source of production data in introspective research includes utterances produced by language learners. The researcher presents a language task and participants are asked to report on the mental processes they use while completing the task. Data elicitation methods include spontaneous utterances or prompted utterances produced in spoken or written forms. Over the years, researchers have argued that spontaneous utterances provide an incomplete picture of the learner and prompted utterances are necessary to gain a comprehensive view of the learners' understanding and knowledge (Corder, 1973; Gass and Mackey, 2000; 2011). In this chapter, we present the key issues surrounding introspective research including an overview of its use in language research, examples of practical applications in the field of language education, and considerations for the future direction of introspective research methods.

Background

Introspective research methods have a long history in research traditions, in particular in language research (Gass and Mackey, 2000). Originally used in the fields of philosophy and psychology, and later in cognitive psychology, education, and linguistics, introspection is viewed as a way to access consciousness. Inherent in introspective research is the assumption that an individual can access and reflect on internal processes. As a result, introspective research methods have generated considerable debate. Questions address how effectively one can verbalize mental thoughts while concurrently completing a task and how accurate these self-reports may be. As purported by Dennett (1987), humans are sense-making beings who create reasonable explanations for mental activity without necessarily understanding fully what is happening. In other words, if pushed to self-report, will individuals develop a probable explanation whether they can justify it or not?

Introspective methods lost popularity when behaviorism gained favor in the first half of the twentieth century. Instead of looking inward, behaviorist methods promoted observing, measuring, then interpreting human behavior. With the influence of behaviorism, research became focused on observable behaviors. Language researchers collected speech samples to be analyzed according to linguistic generalizations and patterns of language use. Reports from the learner about cognitive processes were not accessed. During the reign of behaviorism, studies implementing introspective methodologies were nearly abandoned.

Advocates of introspection argue that introspective methods provide legitimate sources of scientific evidence that are otherwise unavailable. Combined with learners' spoken or written language production, the learners' reasoning provides information about what individuals are knowing, understanding, and doing as they produce language. Using introspective data avoids the risk that the researcher will rely solely on production data and infer the reasoning behind the learner's utterances.

Research on this Topic

The goal of introspective research in the field of language research is to examine the knowledge of an individual's second language and to determine the source of that knowledge by eliciting productive data in the form of either spoken utterances or written utterances (Gass and Mackey, 2000; 2011). Researchers using introspective methods in language research are focused on understanding how learners' knowledge of the language emerges. Given that many aspects of language learning are not explicitly observable, prompting language learners to introspect about their internal processing sheds clarity on the language learning process.

Introspection has been integral to research since early times. Commonly cited early practitioners of introspection as a mode of exploring reasoning include Aristotle, Augustine, and Plato (Lyons, 1986). Long-term fundamental questions about introspective methodology involve the use of certain types of introspection and whether one type is more effective than another in producing accurate results. When asked to introspect about one's mental function from events in the past, how reliable is the recall? What role does memory play in this case? Are learners' acceptability judgments reliable data? Is introspection sabotaged as a result of humans' tendency to generate explanations even when the explanation may not be warranted? Such questions contributed to arguments that introspective methods were untrustworthy.

Behaviorism became a generally accepted view of human learning during the first half of the twentieth century. This was consistent in the field of language learning where stimulus-and-response approaches dominated outlooks on language learning and classroom language instruction. In other words, children hear language, imitate the sounds they hear used by adults, are rewarded, and then repeat the sounds. Eventually children learn to make the sounds in a sequence that carries meaning. Behaviorism upheld the view of environment acting on the individual. Introspective methods, meanwhile, underwent scrutiny which resulted in them losing favor as a trustworthy reporting method for scientific purposes during the first half of the twentieth century (Brown and Rodgers, 2002).

By the second half of the twentieth century, the view of human learning had shifted. With the rise in attacks on behaviorism including Chomsky's counter argument in the field of language and linguistics, behaviorism lost favor to cognitive science. Studies in psychology contributed to researchers' understanding of how children acquire language. In the fields of language and linguistics, researchers asked if children learn language much like they learn other things. With the surge in popularity of cognitive psychology, a new interest in introspection emerged. Language researchers looked to introspection as a means to access learners' language utterances and verbal reporting.

The interest in internal processing resulted in introspective methods gaining popularity in the field of education. Given that humans are social beings and use language to communicate, researchers in education began to study teachers' verbal reporting with respect to their thought processes before, during, and after instruction. Introspective methods focused on teachers' verbal reports about judgment and policy, problem solving, and decision-making. Arguments, led by Ericsson and Simon (1993), that psychological studies should consider mental processes contributed to the revival of introspective methodologies and to the design of principles for guiding introspective studies based on information-processing theory. These guiding principles include:

- Minimize the time transpired between mental operations and verbal reporting;
- Understand that verbalization increases the cognitive demands on an individual's mental processing and attend to this in order to insure quality results are achieved;
- Avoid any expectations for social and conversational conventions during verbal reporting of mental processes;
- Attend to the information in introspective reports that is contained beyond the actual words shared;
- Avoid prompting verbal reports of automatic processes; and,
- Structure the introspective research model with verbal reporting to allow for predictions about how mental operations will be organized by the individual.

(Brown and Rodgers, 2002: 55)

Verbal reporting, one type of introspective data elicitation methodology, gives voice to silent thinking and prompts individuals to vocalize about their internal processes as they perform a task or solve a problem. Researchers rely on verbal reporting to gain information about how individuals address tasks, problems, and judgments. Verbal reports provide researchers with the opportunity to observe how individuals may vary in the ways they approach the same task. Ericsson and Simon (1993) were instrumental in articulating three types of verbal reporting:

- *Talk alouds* (also called self-report). The report is shared in reference to a participant's general approach to something. For example, having the participant talk aloud while she spells a word or describe how she approaches learning a new skill.

- *Think alouds* (also called self-observation). The participant shares the verbal report concurrently while completing a task or within a short period after observing an event. For example, the participant reports on a specific task just performed.
- *Retrospective study* (also called self-revelation). The participant's report is ongoing and includes description, explanation, and interpretation of thought processes; it occurs subsequent to the participant completing a task. When prompts are provided, this reporting type is also called a prompted interview or a stimulated recall.

(Brown and Rodgers, 2002; Gass and Mackey, 2002; 2011)

Stimulated recall or retrospection has been used extensively in language research to gain information about what learners are doing as they produce language. In fact, there is significant cross over for the stimulated recall methodology to different domains of language research. Data collected using stimulated recall have been used in research on interaction, sociolinguistics, and pragmatics. In language research, using introspective methodologies helps researchers avoid an over-reliance on inferring the reasoning behind learners' speech or writing by primarily examining production data.

Also used in the field of education, retrospection or stimulated recall has been employed to evaluate teaching effectiveness. Using short video clips extracted from longer teaching episodes, researchers pose specific questions to classroom teachers. Teachers' verbal reports provide description and interpretations of their thought processes relevant to instruction and learning. However – as is the case with all data elicitation methodologies – there are advantages and disadvantages to verbal reporting. Disadvantages question the level and extent to which the report data are valid and reliable. Another concern addresses the accuracy of the reporting – for example, self-reports and self-observational data. In the case of verbal reporting, the advantages outweigh the disadvantages provided that verbal reports are recorded, both audio and video, thereby facilitating the data analysis. Verbal reporting offers researchers access to internal processes that would otherwise not be available. Given minimal passage of time and the presence of a tangible reminder of the task, verbal reports support the participant's vivid recall. Ericsson and Simon (1993) have demonstrated that participants' actual behavior corresponds with the results obtained using verbal reports. Their work has shown verbal reports to be reliable measures. All said, limitations do exist with the use of verbal reports. Despite a quick turn-around from task completion to verbal reporting, reports do sometimes lack accuracy. This absence of accuracy is attributed to individual participants and to the type of memory structure used in the recall procedure.

Another type of introspective methodology is interviews (also see Chapter 26), one of the most common methods for eliciting narratives. Interviews, frequently used in sociolinguistic research, are conducted one-on-one between the interviewer and individual participant. Interviews typically consist of open-ended questions that encourage the individual participant to comfortably respond. Depending on the purpose, interviews can be structured around a stimulus, part of a questionnaire, or in response to a video prompt. The result is often unscripted, conversational data. The researcher records the interview and later transcribes the interview data for purposes of analysis. In general, interviews are used with the intention of collecting three types of data:

- *Factual*, such as information about the learner's age, gender, background, language learning history;
- *Behavioral*, for example, the learner's lifestyle, approaches to learning language including strategies employed;
- *Attitudinal*, such as beliefs and opinions, interests and values. Attitudinal questions sometimes address learners' attitudes toward the language they are studying.

(Gass and Mackey, 2011)

Interviews present both advantages and disadvantages. An advantage is that the researcher has the control over the type of information solicited. Interviews can result in a breadth of information with learners prompted to describe detailed information about themselves. While experienced interviewers bring an understanding of how to put interviewees at ease, an inexperienced interviewer can be at a disadvantage. When the researcher is the interviewer, there is a risk she may influence how the interviewee responds. Other disadvantages of interviews involve the risk of participants filtering their responses. In other words, interviewees sometimes report what they think the researcher wants to hear.

Diary studies in language research are another approach to eliciting introspective data. When participating in a language acquisition diary study, learners record their perceptions about language learning. The purpose is for diary writers to describe the language learning process, make notes about their attitudes, and record their approach to language learning. In some cases, the researcher will provide structure for the diary, but in many cases the writer is unconstrained by predetermined topics. Diary writers are asked not to edit their thoughts while writing and to establish a writing routine that fits their daily schedule. Diary writers are encouraged to avoid writing about *everything* and instead to select writing topics of interest. In addition to providing information about learners' internal processes, diaries have proven to be useful in highlighting insights into language learners' attitudes toward language learning and language learning contexts.

Features identified as advantages of diary studies can also be represented as disadvantages. Advantages include the unstructured approach and absence of predetermined topics. Writing without a need for editing can be an advantage allowing for the writer's freedom of expression resulting in a sizeable quantity of introspective data. On the other hand, limited structure about topics may detour diary writers who need guidance. While editing is discouraged for diary writers at the onset, a disadvantage includes the need for the diary writer to remove all personal indicators in the diary prior to any public review of the diary contents and before data analysis begins. Lastly, keeping a diary during an extended period of time requires commitment on the part of the diary writer.

PRACTICAL APPLICATIONS

The goal of introspective research methods is to study language learners' internal processes in combination with the variables that influence the process. For those who are reading and/or conducting introspective research it is important to note that there are a variety of types and uses of introspective research. The methodologies addressed in this chapter cross over to different domains of language research including psycholinguistics, strategies-based research, linguistics-based research, interaction-based research, sociolinguistics, survey-questionnaire research, and classroom-based research. Introspective methodologies have been used within each of these domains with the intent purpose of investigating the way individuals approach, organize, and understand information, learning, and teaching. Whether reading or conducting introspective research, researchers must keep in mind a pivotal consideration to insure that the introspective task is appropriate for the linguistic and cognitive capabilities of the learner. This is especially important when working with second language learners in the new language. Hence, research reports need to include sufficient information about the background and abilities of the learner participants and a detailed description of the task. Researchers may want to conduct preliminary observations of the learners prior to selecting an appropriate introspective task to be used in their research.

A seminal work by Faerch and Kasper (1987) presents a classification scheme for the elicitation of introspective data that can be helpful to readers. This framework addresses the category of the study, an explanation about the verbal report, and a description of the participants. Expanding on the classification scheme, the following questions may be useful for readers of introspective research:

- What are the research questions? Are these useful and relevant to your interests?
- Is the task appropriate for the learner-participants' linguistic and cognitive capabilities?
- Is the task/procedure explicit yet straightforward? Are the instructions clear and concise?
- Which introspective data elicitation methodology is most appropriate for the research question and selected task?
- Did the researcher record the data elicitation in audio and video formats?
- Is the data coding system clearly stated? Is the data analysis consistent with the research question and coding?

Novice researchers conducting introspective research may choose to observe learners engaged in language learning tasks before selecting a research focus and research questions. Once research questions have been narrowed, the researcher's next step involves making decisions about data elicitation methods and acknowledging the integral connection between research findings and data collection measures. After reflecting on the aforementioned consideration questions, researchers may want to consider using a "critical friend" for the purpose of conducting interviews. Use of a critical friend removes the risk of researcher interference. Lastly, novice researchers will need to insure they have the necessary equipment for unobtrusive audio and video recording, and careful plans for the compiling, coding, and analyzing of data.

In addition to the resources in the reference list of this chapter, exemplary studies provide helpful illustrations of introspective data elicitation methods. One study that exemplifies retrospective stimulated recall by Silverberg and Samuel (2004) studied the effect of age on language acquisition and bilingual learners' organization of vocabulary by presenting participants with a vocabulary task. Schumann and Schumann's (1977) seminal work using diary study in which the researchers themselves were the diary writers focused on individual affective variables and the role they played in language learning across more than one context. The authors' classroom-based research used stimulated recall to tap classroom language teachers' verbal reporting of their instructional practices used to support students in culturally responsive classrooms (Taylor and Sobel, 2011).

Conclusion

While introspective research has generated considerable controversy and debate over the years, introspective data elicitation methodologies are presently recognized as valuable sources of data for studying participants' internal processes. Resting on the assumption that individuals can access and reflect on what takes place with their internal processing, advocates from a variety of fields contend that introspective research methods allow researchers to observe how mental operations are organized by individuals. Introspection as a mode of exploring learners' reasoning provides a method for revealing cognitive processes that is not evident through direct observation.

Discussion Questions

1. What features of language learners' internal processes are of particular interest to you?

2. After reviewing the research grounding introspective data elicitation methodologies, determine whether you are an advocate or skeptic of introspective research. What arguments articulate your stance?

3. Consider how you might begin to use introspective research methodologies to address a question about learners' or teachers' internal processes, decision-making, or problem solving.

4. What are two to three research questions that interest you?

References

Brown, J. D., & Rodgers, T. S. (2002). *Doing second language research*. Oxford: Oxford University Press.

Corder, S. P. (1973). The elicitation of interlanguage. In J. Svartvik (Ed.), *Errata: Papers in error analysis* (pp. 36–48). Lund: Gleerup.

Dennet, D. (1987). *The intentional stance*. Cambridge, MA: MIT Press.

Ericsson, K. A., & Simon, H. A. (1993). *Protocol analysis*. Cambridge, MA: Bradford/MIT Press.

Faerch, C., & Kasper, G. (1987). From product to process – Introspective methods in second language research. In C. Faerch & G. Kasper (Eds.), *Introspection in second language research* (pp. 5–23). Clevedon, UK: Multilingual Matters.

Gass, S. M., & Mackey, A. (2011). *Data elicitation for second and foreign language research*. New York: Routledge.

Gass, S. M., & Mackey, A. (2000). *Stimulated recall methodology in second language research*. New York: Routledge.

Lyons, W. (1986). *The disappearance of introspection*. Cambridge, MA: MIT Press.

Schumann, J., & Schumann, F. (1977). Diary of a language learner: An introspective study of second language learning. In H. Brown, C. Yorio, & R. Crymes (Eds.), *On TESOL 77* (pp. 241–249). Washington, DC: TESOL.

Silverberg, S., & Samuel, A. G. (2004). The effect of age of second language acquisition on the representation and processing of second language words. *Journal of Memory and Language*, 51, 381–398.

Taylor, S., & Sobel, D. (2011). *Culturally-responsive pedagogy: Teaching like our students' lives matter*. Bingley, UK: Emerald Publishing Group.

CHAPTER 30

Designing and Using Rubrics

Larry Davis

INTRODUCTION

In language education research we often want to judge the ability of learners to use spoken or written language to communicate. Rubrics are an important tool for evaluating such language performance in that they help produce judgments that are systematic, consistent, and relevant to the language abilities of interest within the research project.

For the purposes of this chapter, a rubric will be defined as a set of instructions used for evaluating language performance that does the following:

1. Lists the possible scores that may be awarded – for example, 1, 2, 3, 4; or "fair," "good," "excellent";
2. Describes the features of performance expected for each outcome; these features are termed descriptors.

This type of instrument is also referred to as a rating scale, and people who use rubrics to make scoring decisions are commonly called raters (Fulcher, 2003; Weigle, 2002).

TYPES OF RUBRICS

The task of judging language performance can be approached in a variety of different ways and this variety is reflected in different types of rubrics. Holistic rubrics specify how a single overall score is to be awarded and embody an approach where language performance is viewed as a complex whole. While a holistic rubric may specify a variety of different language features for each score level, raters are expected to integrate these features into a single judgment (Table 30.1). Primary trait rubrics define scores based on the presence or absence of certain features (Figure 30.1).

Score	Description
3	Introduction thoroughly describes the issue and indicates the writer's position. Argument is clearly organized and supported with several well-developed points. Few errors in grammar, vocabulary, and punctuation; these have no effect on sentence-level understandings.
2	Introduction superficially describes the issue, but the writer's position is generally clear. Argument is mostly clear with several brief supporting points. Some problems with grammar, vocabulary, and punctuation are present, but these generally do not cause confusion.
1	Little or no description of the issue is given, or the writer's position is unclear or not mentioned. Argument is difficult to follow; supporting points are missing or irrelevant. Problems with grammar, vocabulary, and punctuation make some sentences difficult to understand.

Table 30.1   A Hypothetical Holistic Rubric for an Argumentative Essay

In contrast, analytic rubrics divide language performance into different components, with each component awarded a separate score, and embody a view of language as consisting of different and separable parts (Table 30.2).

Primary trait rubrics do not attempt to fully describe the characteristics of performance at each level, but rather take the approach of focusing on only those specific language phenomena that are most important for the successful completion of the task.

Is the issue clearly described?

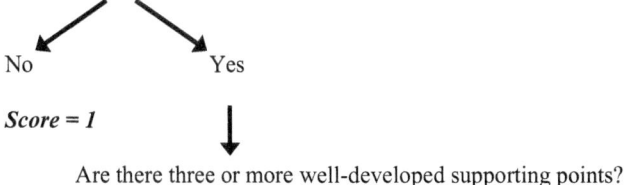

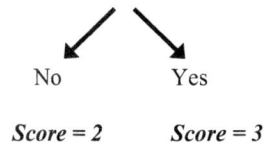

No → *Score = 1*
Yes ↓

Are there three or more well-developed supporting points?

No → *Score = 2*
Yes → *Score = 3*

Figure 30.1   A Hypothetical Primary Trait Rubric for an Argumentative Essay

Category	Score		
	1	2	3
Introduction	Little or no description of the issue is given; the writer's position is unclear or not mentioned.	Introduction superficially describes the issue; the writer's position is generally clear.	Introduction thoroughly describes the issue and clearly indicates the writer's position.
Organization and Support	Argument is difficult to follow with one or two poorly developed or irrelevant supporting points.	Argument is mostly clear with several brief supporting points.	Argument is clearly organized and supported with several well-developed points.
Mechanics	Problems with grammar, vocabulary, and punctuation make some sentences difficult to understand.	Some problems with grammar, vocabulary, and punctuation, but these generally do not cause confusion.	Few errors in grammar, vocabulary, and punctuation; these have no effect on sentence-level understandings.

Table 30.2 A Hypothetical Analytic Rubric for an Argumentative Essay

BACKGROUND

WHY ARE RUBRICS IMPORTANT?

Where research involves performance assessment, rubrics serve two very important functions:

1. They are statements of what counts for scoring; and
2. They promote consistency in the criteria used to award scores.

Rubrics play an important role in determining what scores mean; by matching specific language features to a score they describe the type of performance that a given score represents and, more broadly, the type of language ability (or construct) that the assessment measures. In addition, rubrics provide instructions for how to evaluate performance, which helps to ensure that performances are scored the same way every time, and that different raters produce comparable scores. Scoring consistency, whether it be across test takers, across time, or across different raters, is necessary for scores to be usable in research – or any other domain.

ADVANTAGES AND DISADVANTAGES OF DIFFERENT TYPES OF RUBRICS
HOLISTIC RUBRICS

Holistic rubrics have the advantage of allowing raters to evaluate the full complexity of performance, with the resulting scores hopefully reflecting this complexity. From a practical standpoint, holistic rubrics are relatively quick to use because only a single scoring decision is required; this may be especially helpful when scoring decisions must be made quickly and/or in real-time such as when scoring a live interview. On the other hand, holistic rubrics are based on the assumption that different aspects of language ability develop at the same rate (Weigle, 2004). If a test taker with mixed abilities displays aspects of both higher-level and lower-level performance, it can be difficult to assign a score. In addition, test takers with differing strengths may also receive the same score for different reasons, making it difficult to know what sort of performance a particular score actually represents. For example, one person who receives a certain mark in a speaking test might speak haltingly, but make few grammatical mistakes, while another person who receives the same score speaks fluently, but with many grammatical errors.

ANALYTIC RUBRICS

Analytic rubrics provide separate scores for various aspects of performance, and in this sense provide more detailed information regarding the test taker's abilities. They may also be easier for raters to use in situations where test takers differ in their strengths and weaknesses. The main disadvantages of analytic rubrics are: a) additional time may be needed for scoring because several different decisions must be made for each response; and b) decision-making can be cognitively challenging when several different categories must be monitored at the same time. This cognitive load may be reduced by reviewing the performance several times and scoring a different area each time, but this takes longer. Another potential problem is that raters may find it difficult to independently judge the different domains of performance and as a result award the same score across all categories (known as the "halo effect"). This is equivalent to scoring the performance holistically, and the benefits of analytic scoring are lost.

PRIMARY TRAIT RUBRICS

An advantage of primary trait rubrics is that it may be easier to make a binary yes/no decision regarding a specific feature than it is to judge how much of a complex language phenomenon is present. Primary trait rubrics are also transparent in that specific rules for decision making are made clear. The major disadvantage is that they are usually limited to a particular task and so a separate rubric must be constructed for each type of task used. For example, the specific features that make for a good oral presentation may have little relevance to success in ordering a meal in a restaurant, and so separate rubrics would need to be constructed for each task. Primary trait rubrics also require a thorough understanding of the characteristics that make for successful performance, which requires considerable experience and/or analysis of the language produced by people completing the task. Finally, only a limited set of very specific features are included in some versions of primary trait rubrics – for example, Figure 30.1 – which may represent a severe simplification of the original performance. For scoring efficiency and consistency, however, it might be argued that such an approach is desirable because it focuses the decision process on only those features that matter most for scoring.

APPROPRIATENESS FOR A GIVEN RESEARCH USE

For scores to be valid, the rubric must be appropriate for the research purpose for which it is used. In particular, it cannot be assumed that a rubric is acceptable simply because it was used in other research studies or in a well-known test. Rather, the appropriateness of the rubric for the research study must always be evaluated before the rubric is used; a few general factors to consider when evaluating (or designing) rubrics are given below. It should also be noted that the focus here is on the use of rubrics in research; for a discussion of how to evaluate rubrics for classroom assessment, see Brown (2012).

DOES THE RUBRIC COVER THE LANGUAGE ABILITIES OF INTEREST?

A rubric should include the language phenomena that make up the ability of interest, and exclude everything else. For example, if a researcher is interested in measuring general speaking proficiency, then the rubric needs to cover the full range of language features that are thought to be important for general oral proficiency. A rubric that focused just on grammatical accuracy would be inappropriate because it omits important aspects of speaking ability such as pronunciation, fluency, and the ability to interact with other speakers – which themselves are just a few of the many things that might contribute to successful oral communication.

DO THE RUBRIC DESCRIPTORS INCLUDE AN APPROPRIATE AMOUNT OF DETAIL?

Detailed descriptions of language performance at each score level provide more guidance for decision making, but come at the cost of potentially overwhelming raters with too much information. Conversely, overly brief or vague descriptors, or descriptors that differ only in the adjective used, such as few grammar errors, some grammar errors, many grammar errors, may result in varying interpretations by raters who have different definitions of few, some, and many. The scoring setup also matters: if decisions must be made quickly it will be more difficult to handle detailed descriptions, compared to situations where there is more time and/or opportunity to review the test taker's response.

DOES THE RANGE OF SCORES MATCH THE RANGE OF TEST TAKER ABILITY?

In many research situations we are interested in looking at differences either between groups, between treatments, or over time; it is difficult to detect such differences when everyone gets the same score. This result can happen when the range of a scale is too coarse to capture actual differences. For example, imagine a weight loss study where the weight lost by each person is measured in increments of 100kg; virtually all dieters would get a result of 0 even though some individuals might have lost a considerable amount. To avoid this type of situation, rubrics can be written so that there are some test takers at the bottom of the scale, some at the top of the scale, and most somewhere in the middle. This approach spreads out the test takers such that test takers with relatively subtle differences in ability are given different scores, which in turn gives the best chance of seeing differences between groups or treatments, if differences exist. (Note that if the purpose of assessment is to determine whether test takers have achieved a specific level of mastery, this approach may not apply.)

Research on this Topic

Approaches to Building Rubrics

One way to help ensure that a rubric is appropriate for the research purpose is to build your own. A variety of methods have been used to create rubrics, but these can be divided into two general approaches (Fulcher, 2003, 2012). The first approach relies on expert judgment to decide what should be measured and to describe the kind of performance expected at each score level. Brown (2012) gives a detailed description of the process used to develop this type of rubric; in brief, this involves: a) defining the goals for the assessment; b) choosing the type of rubric; c) selecting the categories of language performance to include; d) selecting the number of score levels; and finally e) writing descriptors for each category/score combination. These steps are guided by the knowledge and experience of the rubric creator, ideally augmented with input from colleagues or whatever other sources might be available. While constructing rubrics using the expert-driven approach can be relatively quick, such rubrics require experts; that is, people who are thoroughly familiar with the test task and test takers. Test takers may also behave in unanticipated ways, and raters may then find the rubric harder to use than expected. Accordingly, it is very important to try out expert-driven rubrics before use by scoring some sample performances and then evaluating how well the rubric matches actual test taker behavior.

The second approach starts with an analysis of what the learners do in carrying out the assessment task, which is then used as the basis for constructing the rubric. This approach to rubric construction is less common, perhaps because of the extra work involved. Fulcher (2012) describes three different methods that utilize this approach.

1. *Performance data based* – for example, Fulcher, 1996. Sample performances are analyzed for features that differ across different levels of performance, which are then used to construct the rubric.
2. *Empirically derived, binary-choice, boundary definition* – for example, Upshur and Turner, 1995. Experts are used to divide a random sample of written or recorded performances into stronger and weaker groups of equal size. The experts then choose the single most important feature that separates the two groups, which is then framed as a question such as "Does the paragraph contain a topic sentence?" The groups may then be further divided into subgroups using the same procedure.
3. *Performance decision trees* – for example, Fulcher, Davison, and Kemp, 2011. This is a combination of both one and two. Like method two, a random sample of performances is repeatedly divided into stronger and weaker groups (although not necessarily of equal size) and a single criterion is chosen that separates the groups. Like method one, detailed analysis of performance is used to determine the criterion.

These approaches all have the potential to produce rubrics that are very clearly tied to test taker performance, but that tend to be task specific.

PRACTICAL APPLICATIONS

An example of several issues described in this chapter can be found in Davis (2009), who investigated the question of whether test takers doing a paired speaking task received different speaking proficiency scores when working with a partner of stronger or weaker language ability. The speaking task came from the speaking section of a well-known test of English (the First Certificate in English Examination, or FCE); the rubric for the study was based on the rubric used to score the FCE, but was also informed by other rubrics published in the literature so that the rubric would be representative of typical rubrics used in similar tests of speaking. The final result was an analytic rubric where scores of from one to five were awarded in categories of grammar and vocabulary, pronunciation, fluency, and discourse management. An analytic rubric was chosen because: a) such rubrics were typical of common rubrics for paired speaking tasks; and b) it was possible that some aspects of speaking might be influenced by the partner (such as discourse management), while others were not (like pronunciation). Following data collection, the draft rubric was compared to test takers' responses and the descriptors were revised to: a) reflect the actual language produced by the test takers; and b) ensure that the rating scale was adjusted so that the weakest responses received a score of one, and the strongest received a score of five. Ultimately, it was found that partner proficiency had no consistent effect on scores.

As an example, this study illustrates a number of the issues mentioned earlier:

- The selection/development of rubric content covered the language features thought to be important for the study (typical formulations of general speaking proficiency);
- An analytic rubric was chosen because of the possibility of differential effects of partner on different aspects of language. In addition, raters scored recorded responses and could replay the responses as many times as needed, so making multiple scoring decisions for each test taker was felt to be doable;
- The rubric was adjusted to fit the specific characteristics of the actual test taker performances, in particular the range of speaking proficiency shown.

RECENT RESEARCH

Although the use of rubrics is "neither new nor novel" (Brown, 2012: 29), the scoring of language performance remains an area of active research and development. A few current issues are given here.

THE ACTUAL CRITERIA USED BY RATERS WHEN SCORING

Researchers continue to investigate how raters interpret rubrics when scoring, as this is important for establishing that the assessment measures the intended construct. The indigenous criteria used by individuals who have not received formal rater training are also of interest, since such criteria are useful for building rubrics and for understanding how people perceive complex language abilities such as interactive communication.

EXPERT-DRIVEN VS. DATA-DRIVEN RUBRIC CONSTRUCTION

The creation of rubrics through expert judgment is by far the most common approach; nonetheless, it has been argued that newer data-driven methods for constructing rubrics allow for a stronger link to be made between scores and what test takers can actually do (Fulcher et al., 2011). Practical issues have limited the use of data-driven approaches in many contexts, although rubrics created this way might be more feasible for research studies where analysis of language production may already be a part of the research effort.

THE RISE OF AUTOMATED SCORING

As natural language processing technologies have developed it has become possible to construct automated scoring systems to evaluate writing and speaking. Automated systems offer the advantages of speed and convenience, and are attractive because: a) it is very clear exactly what language features are used to make a scoring decision; and b) these features are judged the same way every time. Although automated systems reduce the need for human raters to make scoring decisions, the criteria used by the machine to generate scores still need to be identified, which entails many of the same design issues mentioned earlier in this chapter. Also, automated scoring systems are often trained to approximate human scores, and during this process a wide variety of measurements made by the automated system are compared to human judgments. The language features identified as useful for predicting human scores may in turn provide insight into what human raters are evaluating when scoring.

Conclusion

Rubrics are an important tool for encouraging clarity and consistency in the scoring of language performance, whether the context be classroom assessment, large-scale tests, or research studies. To be useful, however, a rubric must be appropriate for the research question(s) being asked; ensuring a proper match between rubric and research purpose requires careful consideration of the type of rubric to use, close examination of the content of the descriptors, and verification that the rubric actually fits the test takers and is practical for raters. Rubrics can be seen as a kind of measuring stick for language performance, and attention given to this measurement device will help to ensure that the resulting data are valid and useful for the research purpose.

Larry Davis works for Educational Testing Service. Any opinions expressed in this chapter are those of the author and not necessarily of Educational Testing Service.

Discussion Questions

1. A researcher is interested in evaluating the general English speaking proficiency of several hundred international college students. Some students come from countries where language instruction focuses on grammatical accuracy, while others come from educational contexts where a communicative approach is followed. What advantage(s) might an analytic rubric have for this study? Are there any reasons why the researcher might prefer to use a holistic rubric?

2. A researcher wants to know if the speaking ability of intermediate-level foreign language students improves after a four-week study-abroad program. The researcher plans to ask the students to complete a speaking task before and after the program, and will score the resulting performances on a three-point scale with levels of beginner, intermediate, and advanced. What will likely be the researcher's conclusion regarding the effectiveness of the study abroad program? What advice might you give the researcher regarding the design of the rubric?

3. Select several responses to a short writing (or speaking) task and split them into two equal groups of stronger and weaker performances. Then, note the most important feature that separates the two groups and turn this feature into a question that can be used to place each response into the correct group (see Figure 30.1 for examples). Next, for each group write several descriptors that describe typical performance in the group (see Tables 30.1 and 30.2 for examples). Which of the two methods of defining the groups was easier to write? If possible, ask someone else to divide the responses into two groups, first using the descriptors and then using the question. Do their groups match yours? Which method do they find easier to use?

References

Brown, J. D. (2012). Developing rubrics for language assessment. In J. D. Brown, (Ed.), *Developing, using, and analyzing rubrics in language assessment with case studies in Asian and Pacific languages* (pp. 13–31). Honolulu, HI: University of Hawai'i, National Foreign Language Resource Center.

Davis, L. (2009). The influence of interlocutor proficiency in a paired oral assessment. *Language Testing*, 26, 367–396.

Fulcher, G. (2003). *Testing second language speaking*. Harlow, UK: Longman.

Fulcher, G. (1996). Does thick description lead to smart tests? A data-based approach to rating scale construction. *Language Testing*, 13, 208–238.

Fulcher, G. (2012). Scoring performance tests. In G. Fulcher & F. Davidson (Eds.), *Routledge handbook of language testing* (pp. 378–392). New York, NY: Routledge.

Fulcher, G., Davidson, F., & Kemp, J. (2011). Effective rating scale development for speaking tests: Performance decision trees. *Language Testing*, 28, 5–29.

Upshur, J., & Turner, C. E. (1995). Constructing rating scales for second language tests. *English Language Teaching Journal*, 49, 3–12.

Weigle, S. C. (2004). *Assessing Writing*. Cambridge: Cambridge University Press.

CHAPTER 31

Conducting Diary Studies

Kathleen M. Bailey

INTRODUCTION

Diary studies constitute both a set of research procedures and a body of literature in second language learning and teaching. Diary studies consist of analyses of entries in diaries (journal entries made daily or at least very regularly) by language learners or teachers, which have been analyzed and are typically discussed in terms of a review of the literature. The primary data are usually written, though some researchers (e.g, Block, 1996) have analyzed spoken diary entries. Some studies have included other data in addition to the diary entries (for example, Ellis, 1989). The data may be analyzed through qualitative and/or quantitative means.

BACKGROUND

Diary studies make an important contribution to research on language teaching and learning because – to the extent that the diarists are willing to share their introspections – this body of literature allows us to see what may be unavailable to classroom observers: the learners' or teachers' actual feelings and reflections about their experiences of language learning and teaching. Thus diary studies are like first-person case studies: the diarists write about their own experiences and reactions to those experiences. In this regard, diary studies fit in the tradition of self-reported data and introspective research (see also Chapter 29).

As a research procedure, "introspection is the process of observing and reporting on one's own thoughts, feelings, motives, reasoning processes, and mental states, often with a view to determining the ways in which these processes and states shape behavior" (Nunan and Bailey, 2009: 285). Introspection has been widely used in psychology research and some forms of introspective data collection have been incorporated in applied linguistics research as well – most notably think-aloud procedures and stimulated recall. Gathering think-aloud data involves having research subjects talk about their ongoing mental processes while they are doing a task, such as revising a composition. In contrast, collecting stimulated recall data entails giving research subjects some kind of documentation to help them remember and retrospect about a past event. For instance, researchers can use video-recordings, audio-recordings, or observers' field notes about language lessons to get the teachers of those lessons to talk about what they were thinking and feeling while they were teaching. Thus the difference between think-aloud procedures and stimulated recall is the timing of the introspection relative to the event itself.

In fact, the question of timing is quite relevant to a discussion of diary studies. Building on work by Cohen and Hosenfeld (1981), Nunan and Bailey (2009) discuss the difference between concurrent introspection, immediate retrospection, and delayed retrospection. One difficulty in discussing these concepts is that the general term, introspection, covers all three of these concepts. To be more specific, however, Cohen and Hosenfeld (1981) designate concurrent introspection as occurring during the event about which the subject is introspecting. Think-aloud procedures are a clear example of concurrent introspection. It is the retrospective processes that are a bit fuzzier. Immediate retrospection is said to occur "right after the event, and delayed retrospection occurs hours or more following the event" (Nunan and Bailey, 2009: 285). So unless students and/or teachers are actually making journal entries during a class or while they are learning language in a naturalistic setting (outside of class), the diary entries would be data collected through immediate retrospection or delayed retrospection. It seems clear that diary entries made as close as possible to the event being discussed are more reliable than those made later, since particular details of memory can degrade over time.

In the late 1970s, when the first language learning diary studies were published, the data were typically analyzed by the diarists themselves, but later studies involved analyses by someone other than the original diarists. When the diarists themselves were also the analysts, the analysis was called a primary or direct or introspective analysis. In later decades, a researcher or teacher trainer would often have language learners and teacher trainees make diary entries which were subsequently analyzed by the research/trainer. This process was called a secondary or indirect or non-introspective analysis (Curtis and Bailey, 2009: 69). The advantage of the diarists themselves doing the analyses is that their introspection and memories of events can enrich the data. The advantage of people other than the diarists carrying out the analyses is that they may bring fresh viewpoints to the data and make connections that the diarists did not see.

One interesting problem of using teachers' or learners' diary entries as research data has to do with what ultimately gets recorded. If it is true that some teaching and learning go on outside of our awareness, then it is axiomatic that we can only report on those teaching and learning factors of which we are aware. It is also likely that some intentional or unintentional selection is involved in terms of what actually gets recorded in teachers' and learners' journals. Thus, diary entries most likely under-represent – and may skew our understanding of – the experiences of language teaching and learning, and the participants' reactions to it.

Research on this Topic

Diary studies have examined key issues in second language acquisition. For instance, research on learning styles and strategies has been influenced by accessing the thoughts and affective responses of the language learners themselves (see Carson and Longhini, 2002; Halbach, 2000). Other diary studies have investigated the construct of language learning anxiety (Hilleson, 1996). In addition, older language learners' needs and experiences have also been documented in diary studies (Schulz and Elliott, 2000).

Furthermore, teachers have kept journals which include investigations of both pre-service teachers' experiences (Numrich, 1996) and in-service teachers' work (Appel, 1995; Bailey, 2001; Verity, 2000). The roles and strengths of non-native speaking teachers, as well as some of the challenges they face, have also been addressed through diary studies (Lee and Lew, 2001; Matsuda and Matsuda, 2001). For an overview of diary studies of both language learning and language teaching through about 2008, please see the review by Curtis and Bailey (2009).

Practical Applications

There are practical applications of keeping a journal for both language learners and teachers. For students, trying to learn a new language can be frustrating, and making regular entries in a diary can help learners express (and perhaps deal with) their frustrations. Doing so can also help language students recognize both successful strategies and counter-productive behaviors. For instance, in rereading a journal that I had kept as a low-level student of French, I found that I had been rushing through the three in-class examinations and had actually skipped entire sections of each test – behavior I had not been aware of at the time (Bailey, 1983).

Doing diary studies of their own teaching can help language teachers address problematic issues and solve puzzles about their work, as well as make practical connections with theory. As an example, while I was teaching EFL to undergraduate university students in Hong Kong, I kept a teaching journal for two semesters. At first, making the diary entries served as a way for me to articulate problems in my lessons and to self-assess my efforts to deal with those problems as they arose (Bailey, 2001). Later, as I was analyzing the data, I was able to make several connections to the idea of pedagogical scaffolding from sociolcultural theory.

Keeping a teaching journal can be part of the data for an action research project. For example, if a teacher wanted to investigate her turn-distribution to make sure she wasn't overlooking any of the students, she could collect data by audio-recording or video-recording her lessons to document which students she called on, which ones bid for self-nominated turns, which ones responded to general solicits to the entire class, and so on. But in order to record what she was hoping to do and to document her successes and failures, her own introspective account would also provide useful data.

If you are a teacher, whether or not you want to publish your research, doing a diary study can be a valuable part of establishing a reflective practice approach to your own professional development. Recording what you do in your teaching, what you had hoped to do, how well a lesson turned out, and what worked as well as what went awry can all provide the basis for thoughtful reflection. Some teachers have used their teaching journals as the basis for group discussions about teaching. In Hong Kong, for instance, Brock, Yu, and Wong (1992) shared excerpts from their journals with one another on a weekly basis. As teacher trainees in California, Cole, McCarthy, Rogan, and Schleicher (1998) also benefited from sharing their group journal.

Some teacher educators have used the diaries kept by teacher trainees to learn about those trainees' needs and concerns. For instance, Numrich (1996) analyzed the teaching journals of 26 novice teachers who were enrolled in a TESOL practicum course. Her analysis of the trainees' diary entries about their practice-teaching experience allowed her to identify their concerns and frustrations. These frustrations, in decreasing order of frequency of mention (with the number of trainees citing each issue given in parentheses) were as follows: "managing class time (13), giving clear directions (10), responding to students' various needs (9), teaching grammar effectively (8), assessing students' learning (7)", and "focusing on the students rather than on themselves" (Numrich, 1996: 142).

Advice on how to go about keeping a language-learning or teaching journal is given in Nunan and Bailey (2009). They suggest that diarists do the following:

- Set aside time each day to write in your diary, as soon as possible after class;
- Write in a quiet, comfortable place and if you are word processing the journal entries, save them regularly;
- Carry a small notebook or personal digital assistant (PDA) in order to make brief notes as events occur;
- The time devoted to writing in the diary should be equal to the time spent in the language class; however, in an immersion context, you should consider focusing the diary entries on some part of the teaching/learning experience, so you don't get overwhelmed with the need to keep up with the generation of data;
- The diary should be kept in a safe, secure place so you can write candidly;
- When you are making journal entries, don't worry about style or grammar, especially if you are writing in your second language, as the journal entries can be edited later;
- When you write a comment in your journal, provide evidence for the statement and give concrete examples;
- Make notes at the end of each diary entry about thoughts or questions you may have, so you can address them later.

(For more detailed guidance, see Nunan and Bailey, 2009: 303–304.)

Conclusion

Some people find writing, either by hand or with a word processor, to be tedious and time-consuming. They may prefer to audio-record their journal entries. The difficulty with making audio entries is that if you wish to use those data in an actual analysis, you will probably have to transcribe those entries at some point – and transcription is much more onerous and time-consuming than writing is! However, in the future, speech recognition tools may make it easier to generate written journal entries by speaking, rather than writing, thereby short-cutting the need to transcribe.

Mixed methods studies (those that use both quantitative and qualitative data collection and analysis procedures) are now widely accepted and are becoming more common, and diary studies work well in mixed methods research on language learning and teaching as a means to tap into the perspectives of the teachers and learners themselves. For example, Ellis (1989) used this approach in a case study of Simon and Monique – two students who were enrolled in the same German course. Their similarities and differences were documented with several data collection measures, and their diary entries revealed that they had very different concerns about their success in their language course they were taking. Analyzing qualitative data has historically been a painstaking process of combing through the records looking for themes and patterns. With the advent of computer programs for analyzing qualitative data, such procedures will become easier and possibly more systematic. However, to be amenable to computer analyses, the diary entries must be word processed rather than audio-recorded or written by hand.

Another possibility for the future would be to establish one corpus of language learners' journal entries and another of teachers' journal entries. Corpora are digitized text files that can be searched for specific features, which can then be tallied and analyzed for surrounding linguistic features. Having such a corpus of language learners' and teachers' diary entries would allow researchers to compare learners' and teachers' concerns, strategies, and perceived successes across many different contexts.

Due to space limitations, it is not possible to discuss all the diary studies that have been conducted. Nor is there room here to cite the methodology articles about, or the critiques of, diary studies. If you'd like to learn more, please go to www.tirfonline.org/resources/references and scroll down to the topic of diary studies. There you will find a lengthy reference list that is regularly updated, and can be downloaded for free.

Discussion Questions

1. Would you ever want to keep a daily journal about your own language learning or teaching experience? Why or why not?

2. Some people find keeping a diary to be very demanding work, partly because writing can be difficult and time consuming. What would be some strategies you could develop to ensure that you would be able to make frequent and consistent diary entries while you study a language or teach a language course?

3. Sometimes introspecting honestly about oneself makes journal-keeping even more challenging. Some novice diarists make journal entries that are flat, factual reports, devoid of introspection or affective responses. Other diarists have written entries that are full of emotion – a veritable affective outpouring, with very few facts to help the reader understand the diarists' reactions. If you were to keep a journal, what steps could you take to help you achieve a balance between factual reporting, introspection, and interpretation?

4. Have you ever kept a journal of your experiences as a teacher and/or language learner? If so, what did you discover in the process? If not, talk to someone who has kept a diary and see what they learned by doing so.

References

Appel, J. (1995). *Diary of a language teacher*. Oxford, UK: Heinemann English.

Bailey, K. M. (2001). What my EFL students taught me. *The PAC Journal*, 1, 7–31.

Bailey, K. M. (1983). Competitiveness and anxiety in adult second language learning: Looking *at* and *through* the diary studies. In H. W. Seliger & M. H. Long (Eds.), *Classroom oriented research in second language acquisition* (pp. 67–102). Rowley, MA: Newbury House.

Block, D. (1996). A window on the classroom: Classroom events viewed from different angles. In K. M. Bailey, & David Nunan (Eds.), *Voices from the language classroom: Qualitative research on language education* (pp. 168–194). New York: Cambridge University Press.

Brock, M. N., Yu, B., & Wong, M. (1992). 'Journaling' together: Collaborative diary-keeping and teacher development. In J. Flowerdew, M. N. Brock, & S. Hsia (Eds.), *Perspectives on second language teacher development* (pp. 295–307). Hong Kong: City University of Hong Kong.

Carson, J. G., & Longhini, A. (2002). Focusing on learning styles and strategies: A diary study in an immersion setting. *Language Learning*, 52, 401–438.

Cohen, A. D., & Hosenfeld, C. (1981). Some uses of mentalistic data in second language research. *Language Learning*, 31(2), 285–313.

Cole, R., McCarthy, L. R., Rogan, P., & Schleicher, L. (1998). Interactive group journals: Learning as a dialogue among learners. *TESOL Quarterly*, 32, 556–568.

Curtis, A., & Bailey, K. M. (2009). Diary studies. *OnCUE Journal*, 3(1), 67–85.

Ellis, R. (1989). Classroom learning styles and their effect on second language acquisition: A study of two learners. *System*, 17, 249–262.

Halbach, A. (2000). Finding out about students' learning strategies by looking at their diaries: A case study. *System*, 28, 85–96.

Hilleson, M. (1996). "I want to talk to them but I don't want them to hear": An introspective study of second language anxiety in an English-medium school. In K. M. Bailey & D. Nunan (Eds.), *Voices from the language classroom: Qualitative research on language education* (pp. 248–275). New York: Cambridge University Press.

Lee, E., & Lew, L. (2001). Diary studies: The voices of nonnative English speakers in a master of arts program in teaching English to speakers of other languages. *CATESOL Journal*, 13, 135–149.

Matsuda, A., & Matsuda, P. (2001). Autonomy and collaboration in teacher education: Journal sharing among native and nonnative English-speaking teachers. *CATESOL Journal*, 13, 109–121.

Numrich, C. (1996). On becoming a language teacher: Insights from diary studies. *TESOL Quarterly*, 30, 131–151.

Nunan, D., & Bailey, K. M. (2009). *Exploring second language classroom research: A comprehensive guide*. Boston: Heinle, Cengage Learning.

Schulz, R. A., & Elliott, P. (2000). Learning Spanish as an older adult. *Hispania*, 83(1), 107–119.

Verity, D. P. (2000). Side affects: The strategic development of professional satisfaction. In J. P. Lantolf (Ed.), *Sociocultural theory in second language learning* (pp. 179–197). Oxford: Oxford University Press.

CHAPTER 32

Analyzing Your Data Statistically

Matthew A. Robby and Christina Gitsaki

INTRODUCTION

Research data are a collection of facts, measurements, and observations used to describe or make inferences. Data are basic units by which research results are collected, analyzed, interpreted, and communicated: they are the building blocks of knowledge developed and shared to enhance understanding and to promote advancement. It is therefore important to ensure the relevance, validity, reliability, and integrity of the data as well as to build checks and balances into the data collection process to identify data problems early. Inaccurate data reduce the ability to answer research questions and test hypotheses because they produce distorted and invalid findings (Isaac and Michael, 1997). Inaccurate data can also result in flawed decision-making and policy, as well as reduce the ability to replicate research and facilitate researchers performing future investigation.

BACKGROUND

Hypothesis testing is important in performing language research. A hypothesis is an informed statement which proposes a relationship or difference between an independent variable and a dependent variable. In research, it is helpful to always assume and test the null hypothesis that there will be no statistically significant relationship or difference between a causal variable and outcome variable. Approaching research from the standpoint of testing the null hypothesis with accurate statistics helps to include objectivity into processes. Statistics is the study of the collection, organization, analysis, interpretation, and presentation of data. Statistics can lend support for determining if a hypothesis is true or false, that is, if a result may have occurred by chance. An accepted standard in educational research is the probability or p value of less than .05, which determines if a result is statistically significant. That means that the probability is less than five in 100 that a result occurred by chance.

Research on this Topic

Identifying and Measuring Variables

Variables are approximations of the thing being measured. They can be characteristics, behaviors, and phenomena being researched. A key distinction is between independent and dependent variables. An independent variable may be described as a predictor, manipulated, or explanatory variable. It is often thought of as a causal variable as it can produce a degree of change or effect on a dependent variable, also known as a measured, response, or outcome variable. For example, we can evaluate the measurable effects of an independent variable or set of causal factors – for example, an EFL curriculum model, a set of teaching strategies, or a supplemental support program – on a dependent or outcome variable – for example, end of term assessment scores.

An important prerequisite for being able to perform effective language research is to understand how variables are different with varying attributes, how they should be organized, their level of measurement and scale, and especially how they will be used in research (Isaac and Michael, 1997). In terms of level of measurement, nominal data are qualitative and have no numeric significance or magnitude between attributes; examples include gender, ethnicity, and occupation. Ordinal data show general differences between attributes, characteristics, categories, or levels as one is greater than the other, but it is unclear how the categories differ in exact size. They are general approximations of magnitude. Examples include: a) small, medium, and large; b) an agreement survey scale: 4 = Strongly Agree, 3 = Agree, 2 = Disagree, 1 = Strongly Disagree. Interval and ratio data have ranking and magnitude between categories and they include precise and equal distances between categories. Interval data can be ordered and have equal intervals, but no true zero point; ratio data have the same characteristics but do have a true zero point. An example of interval data is reading comprehension scores, as distances between score levels are equal and most likely everyone who completed the exam would have scored above zero.

Preparing Data for Statistical Analysis

Research cannot occur unless data are first collected, organized, formatted, and prepared in spreadsheet form for statistical analysis. The focus here is on quantitative data – i.e. numerical data. Highly recommended is the use of the Statistical Package for the Social Sciences (SPSS) software for supporting language research with data processing and analysis. To facilitate applied research, action research, and/or formative evaluation of an educational program – i.e., curriculum model, set of instructional strategies, or use of technology – data must be collected from either electronic or hard copy records, and then merged to and formatted in a spreadsheet file. In the spreadsheet file, variables must be labeled, coded, and sometimes transformed into a different format and level of measurement for effective analysis.

Some variables may have limitations of use with certain statistics depending on whether they are in number or text format. Nominal data appearing as a string or text variable (e.g., gender, marital status, and high school) should be converted by assigning a number to each category of the variable. Doing so ensures that attributes of the variable can be counted, tabulated, and compared with other variables. There are various options, but one could code the above nominal variables as follows: a) gender: 1 = female and 2 = male; b) marital status: 1 = married and 0 = not married; and c) high school: 1 = public, 2 = private, or 3 = other.

Student age (e.g., ranging between 18 and 50) which is a continuous, numeric, and interval level variable, can be recoded according to natural breaks identified in the data as a result of reviewing information in frequency tables. In its original form, age is not easily reviewed in a table format with distinct categories because it is a continuous list of numbers. To facilitate table analysis with four groupings of age instead of dozens, age can be collapsed and recoded into 1 = *18 to 19*; 2 = *20 to 21*; 3 = *22 to 23*; and 4 = *24+*. Doing so allows for cross-tabulation comparisons of frequency and % differences among the four categories of age against, for example, an end of course assessment, either coded as 1 = passed and 0 = failed; or examined for differences with procedures which utilize the mean and standard deviations, such as Analysis of Variance (ANOVA).

PRACTICAL APPLICATIONS

SCREENING DATA FOR STATISTICAL ANALYSIS

Statistical analysis is critical in research. The following sections discuss frequently-used descriptive and inferential procedures for systematically analyzing collected data to answer primary questions and/or to test hypotheses. Descriptive statistics describe the basic features of the data – for example, frequencies, percentages, mean, median, mode, standard deviation, etc. Inferential statistics are techniques that allow us to use samples to make generalizations about the populations from which the samples were drawn. As part of the initial process of generating statistics to test hypotheses, it is important to produce descriptive data for a variety of reasons: a) to check for any mistakes with data entry or merging new variables to an existing data file; b) to verify the accuracy of the coding and re-coding of the data and the integrity of the data; c) to understand better the counts, percentages, and distribution of the data, which depends on the level of measurement; d) to ensure that statistical assumptions are not violated; and e) to thus be able to select appropriate statistical tests.

Producing and reviewing frequency tables of counts, percentages, valid percentages, and cumulative percentages of each variable can help to quickly identify any miscodes and to understand the proportion of cases with missing data. This preliminary data screening is critical to determine if there are any patterns of missing data. Sometimes the statistical software may interfere with the transfer and merging of data, so screening the data can provide opportunity to identify and correct problems and thus increase confidence in the integrity of the data.

If the variable is an assessment score, frequency tables can be supplemented with descriptive statistics to understand the mean, median, mode, and standard deviation of scores. Histograms help to visualize the distributions of scores relative to the normal curve. Any statistic which relies on the mean and standard deviation (for example, ANOVA and *t*-tests) must consider the distribution of scores. Some statistics are more robust against violations of the normal distribution assumptions. Preliminary screening can determine to what extent assumptions are violated. In fact, box plots, which are graphic representations of distributions, are helpful in identifying the central tendency of scores as defined by the median score (mid-point) and the measure of dispersion, as depicted by the inter-quartile range (scores between the 25th and 75th percentile of the distribution). Box plots also show scores which are outside that range, as well as the location of scores which are extreme outliers (Darren and Mallery, 2003).

DECIDING ON STATISTICAL TESTS

Clarifying what you plan to do in the research, the type of independent and dependent variables which are available, and understanding the level of measurement for the research variables are all critical for ensuring correct selection and use of statistical tests (see Figure 32.1 below). The type of statistical analysis should match the characteristics and level of your data. It is important to distinguish between non-parametric tests – i.e., those that examine the rank order of values and make no assumptions about the distribution of values – and parametric tests, which require the data being normally distributed (Darren and Mallery, 2003). Basic mistakes that could reduce statistical accuracy would be to use nominal or ordinal level data with inferential and advanced statistical analysis tools which rely on the mean and distribution; or using basic statistics with interval or ratio data as this is not correct and can limit the information derived.

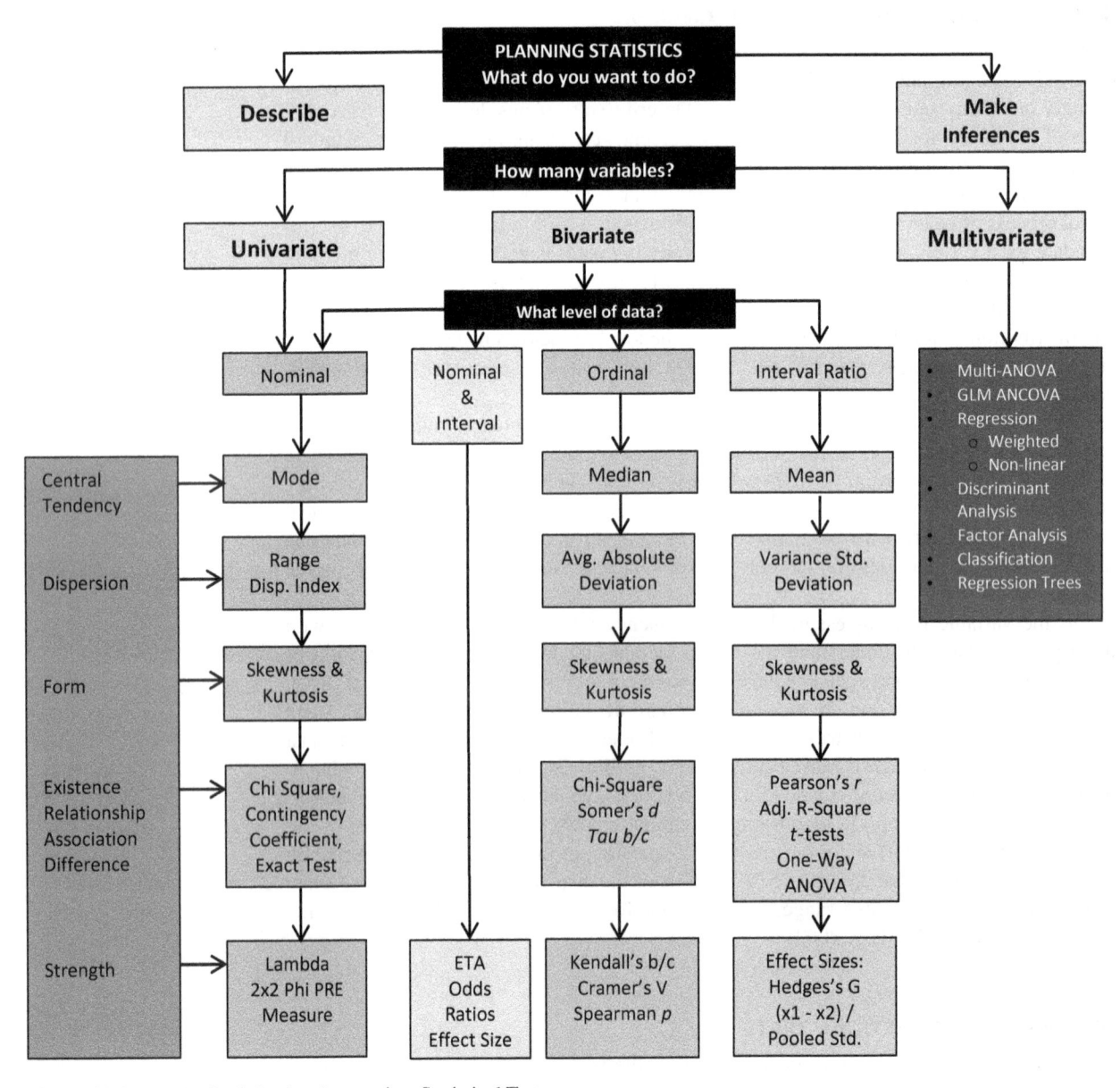

Figure 32.1 Model for Selecting Appropriate Statistical Tests

CROSS-TABULATIONS AND CHI-SQUARE

Typically an independent variable in columns is cross-tabulated through the dependent variable in rows. Frequencies and column percentages are often examined to understand how outcomes vary by categories of the independent variable. The chi-square statistic is used to test the null hypothesis and to thus determine if there is a statistically significant relationship between values in rows and columns usually in a 2x2 cross-tabulation table, but sometimes also in larger tables (Greenwood and Nikulin, 1996). Specifically, it examines the difference between the observed and expected frequencies, with larger differences resulting in a larger chi-square value (Belle, 2002). If the significance value is less than .05, then there is likely a statistically significant relationship or difference found in the table.

The chi-square procedure is appropriate for use with nominal and some ordinal level data. Practical table analysis of frequencies and column percentages can assist in understanding the relationships between variables; for example, whether passing the IELTS with an overall Band 5 (yes/no) varies by gender (females/males). Chi-square can help determine if any differences found are due to chance or actually represent true differences.

With the chi-square procedure, the reliability of the results may be questionable if sample sizes are not large enough. The procedure requires 80% of the cells meeting expected minimum frequency levels, so the total number of cases should be five times the number of table cells, and no one cell should have a frequency less than five (Belle, 2002). Often larger tables, like 2x4 (for example, gender by a four-point agreement scale), can be recoded and collapsed to meet frequency requirements for table cells. So the four categories of the agreement scale can be converted to two categories for comparison by gender. Numerous types of ordinal and interval variables can be recoded and better grouped into dichotomized categories for analysis. Here are two examples: 1) raw scores or scale scores in an assessment can be converted to 1 = passed and 0 = failed; and 2) a four-point Likert scale can be collapsed to 1 = Agree and 2 = Disagree. With small sample sizes, it is best to use Exact Tests, an alternative computation to chi-square that helps achieve greater accuracy when testing the null hypothesis in small samples.

PHI AND CRAMER'S V

While chi-square and the Exact Tests will indicate whether there is a statistically significant relationship, they will not tell you the strength of the relationship. Just because a statistically significant relationship is found does not mean that the null hypothesis should automatically be rejected. Practical table analysis should be used as well as the strength of the association to help determine if the alternative hypothesis should be accepted. Also, because a chi-square result can be influenced by sample size and the number of categories examined, the Phi coefficient should be used with a 2x2 table and the Cramer's V coefficient should be used with larger tables to determine the strength of any statistically significant relationship identified (Davenport and El-Sanhury, 1991). Phi and Cramer's V are measures of association which are standardized for interpretation between 0 and 1, with values closer to 1 indicating stronger associations. While interpretation may vary by academic discipline, a useful guide for interpretation of phi or Cramer's V in performing language research is as follows: a) .00 to .10 is negligible; b) .11 to .20 is slight; c) .21 to .30 is slight to moderate; d) .31 to .40 is moderate; e) .41 to .50 is moderate to strong; f) .51 to .70 is strong; and g) .80 to 1.00 is very strong.

CORRELATIONS

Bivariate Pearson correlations are used to determine if one interval or ratio level variable influences another; or if there is association between a number of independent variables and one or more outcome variables. A positive correlation suggests that as the value of one variable increases the value of another variable will also increase (Ravid, 2000).

Correlations are often examined in scatterplots to understand the pattern of the data relative to a regression line of perfect association. If a statistically significant relationship between two variables is found because the significance level is below .05, then the direction and strength of the relationship is interpreted between 0.0 and 1.0, with stronger correlations found as the value approaches 1.0. If too many of the cases (more than 80%) are in one category of a variable, then the variable may be considered non-normal and so the Pearson correlation could produce inaccurate results. A helpful alternative correlation to use when the distribution of data is non-normal is the Spearman rank order correlation.

T-TESTS

When, due to small sample sizes, there is doubt and potential bias that the results are accurate and the standard deviations represent the population examined, the independent sample *t*-test should be used to test the null hypothesis (Zimmerman, 1997). The *t*-test is a very useful tool for comparing the mean and distribution of scores between two different groups. The test assumes use of an interval level dependent variable, probability sampling, independent observations, and a normal distribution. The *t*-test is robust against violations of the normality assumptions with small sample sizes because it relies on the Central Limit Theorem (Durrett, 2004). A useful recommendation is for the total number of cases in a *t*-test to exceed 50 for meaningful analysis.

The statistical output often provided after running a *t*-test analysis shows the number of cases for each group, their means, standard deviation, standard error of the mean, mean difference between the groups, 95% confidence interval of the mean, and whether the equal variance assumption has been violated or not. If the significance level is less than .05 and the mean difference appears educationally meaningful, then it is likely that there is a true difference and there should be consideration for rejecting the null hypothesis.

In contrast with the independent sample *t*-test, which examines two different groups, the paired sample *t*-test can be used to examine pre/post score differences for the same group. This procedure assumes that there will be no baseline to follow-up difference in assessment scores for the same group. In addition to examining and revealing whether there is a statistically significant mean pre/post change for the same group (based on the two-tailed significance value, *t*-value, and mean difference), the correlation between test one and test two is also reported. The correlation helps to show if there was a statistically significant mean difference or change within the group, for example, whether students that scored high at baseline were also more likely to score high at follow-up.

ANALYSIS OF VARIANCE (ANOVA)

The inferential Analysis of Variance (ANOVA) procedure is used to test for any statistically significant mean differences between three or more groups. It tests the null hypothesis that the measures of dispersion around the mean are not different between the groups, and it is helpful because it does this simultaneously (Gelman, 2005). The test compares the variance within and between groups or samples. ANOVA requires an interval level dependent variable, which should be normally distributed and preliminarily screened for normality; it requires groups to be similar in their variances and determines this through the homogeneity of variances test; it assumes that the grouping categories examined are complete and relevant; and it assumes that random sampling has been used so that findings can be generalized to a larger population (Gelman, 2005).

The statistical significance value in table format based on the F-test (the higher the F value, the greater the difference) provides for direct interpretation. If the significance value is less than .05 there is a statistically significant difference in the means between certain groups, but perhaps not all the groups, so additional analysis should be performed. Thus, it is helpful when interpreting the ANOVA results to also examine the 95% Confidence

Interval (CI) of the mean between the groups. The true mean falls between the lower and upper bounds of the 95% CI. So where there is no overlap between the lower and upper bounds of the CI between the groups, it is more likely that there is a statistically significant difference and, if so, this may support the rejection of the null hypothesis. With ANOVA *post-hoc* comparisons can be made between the groups for detailed interpretation. There is an adjustment for more conservative results if the equal variance assumption has been violated; and there is a weighting option to increase accuracy of comparison if the sample sizes are too different between the groups.

ANALYSIS OF COVARIANCE (ANCOVA)

The Analysis of Covariance (ANCOVA) procedure is like ANOVA but it has the added feature of being able to control for covariates that are confounding intervention effects, thereby helping to isolate the effects of a program. The procedure provides a covariance design or 'noise reduction' design, for example, by implementing statistical control techniques of pre-test variability between groups – for example, experimental and control groups – and provides more accurate adjusted post-test estimates for comparison (Maxwell and Howard, 1981; Oaks, 2001). ANCOVA can reduce bias by adjusting for initial differences between groups before the treatment, and it can increase the precision of estimation and statistical power, thus being able to accurately detect an effect (Oaks, 2001).

EFFECT SIZE PROCEDURES

Statistically significant findings increase confidence that a true relationship or difference probably exists. Determining the magnitude, strength, practical significance, and whether the finding is educationally meaningful is a matter for further interpretation of information. Sometimes small improvements are educationally meaningful given the particular outcome being examined (Grissom and Kim, 2005). To help with interpreting whether statistically significant findings are truly meaningful, effect size measures should be calculated.

The Cohen's *d* effect size is a classic example of a useful procedure for examining the magnitude of the mean difference between two groups, usually an experimental and comparison group (Cohen, 1988). It is often calculated by deriving the pre-test to post-test change for each of the two groups, comparing the mean difference between them by dividing the result by the standard deviation of the control group. This helps to place findings in standard deviation units to help interpret the size of the effect of, for example, a language program, curriculum model, or intervention. The Hedges's *g* effect size is generally the same as Cohen's *d*, but has a correction factor for small sample sizes (Hedges, 1981).

Besides Phi, Cramer's V, Cohen's *d*, Hedges's *g*, and Pearson's *R*, there are numerous other types of effect size measures available for use in determining if a statistically significant finding is educationally meaningful. Here are a few examples: a) Eta squared, which examines a nominal variable by an interval in terms of the amount of variation accounted for in the outcome by the independent variable (Darren and Mallery, 2003); and b) odds ratios, sometimes used in 2x2 table analysis to measure association between two binary variables. For example, odds ratios can be used to compare the odds of passing the IELTS for a group of students who received classroom instruction versus a group that received the same instruction plus supplemental support and tutoring from a language learning center.

CONCLUSION

It is important to have an idea of what statistical techniques will be used before collecting data. Doing so is part of proper planning and is important for effective data collection to support the research, and also to ensure integrity of the research process. In selecting and reporting use of statistical procedures, one should include: a) describing the attributes of variables and their level of measurement – for example nominal, ordinal, interval, ratio; b) explaining why certain statistics are a good choice based on what they are intending to do, how measurement assumptions are met, and the filtering and control techniques applied; and c) why doing so is appropriate based on the research circumstances and for accurately describing phenomena or testing hypotheses. Also, research should not be limited to one statistical approach when more than one may make an important contribution to obtaining and verifying accurate findings (Isaac and Michael, 1997).

The advice provided in this chapter is based on the best use of certain statistics relative to a range of research circumstances, questions, variables, and strategies in an effort to reduce error and enhance accuracy. Adhering to the fundamental principles and correct use of descriptive and inferential statistics will improve the effectiveness of your research and help to build additional knowledge and understanding for professional practices and for promoting language acquisition. While not unusual, any deviations from the basic assumptions and purpose of certain statistics will likely require justification.

Discussion Questions

1. What would you need to do to prepare your data for performing language research?
2. What factors are important for consideration in selecting statistics for analyzing your data?
3. Why is screening your data important and what techniques would you use?
4. What techniques would you apply to control for threats to the validity of your statistical findings?
5. What procedure would you use to compare mean scores between three or more groups?
6. Why is it important to plan your research and what factors should be considered?

References

Belle, G. V. (2002). *Statistical rules of thumb.* Wiley series in probability and statistics. New York, NY: John Wiley.

Cohen, J. (1988). *Statistical power analysis for the behavioral sciences* (2nd ed.). Hillsdale, NJ: Erlbaum.

Darren, G., & Mallery, P. (2003). *SPSS for Windows step by step* (4th ed.). Boston, MA: Allyn & Bacon.

Davenport, E., & El-Sanhury, N. (1991). Phi/Phimax: Review and synthesis. *Educational and Psychological Measurement,* 51(4), 821–828.

Durrett, R. (2004). *Probability: Theory and examples* (4th ed.). Cambridge: Cambridge University Press.

Gelman, A. (2005). Analysis of variance? Why it is more important than ever. *The Annals of Statistics,* 33(1), 1–53.

Greenwood, P. E., & Nikulin, M. S. (1996). *A guide to chi-squared testing.* New York: Wiley.

Grissom, R. J., & Kim, J. J. (2005). *Effect sizes for research: A broad practical approach.* Mahwah, NJ: Erlbaum.

Hedges, L. V. (1981). Distribution theory for Glass's estimator of effect size and related estimators. *Journal of Educational Statistics,* 6(2), 107–128.

Isaac, S., & Michael, W. B. (1997). *Handbook in research and evaluation* (3rd ed.). San Diego, CA: Educational and Industrial Testing Services.

Maxwell, S., & Howard, G. (1981). Change scores – necessarily anathema? *Educational and Psychological Measurement*, 41(2), 747–756.

Oaks, M. J. (2001). Statistical power for nonequivalent pretest-posttest designs. *Evaluation Review*, 25(1), 3–29.

Ravid, R. (2000). *Practical statistics for educators*. Lanham, MD: University Press of America.

Zimmerman, D. W. (1997). A note on interpretation of the paired-samples t-test. *Journal of Educational and Behavioral Statistics*, 22(3), 349–360.

SECTION 3C

REPORTING FINDINGS

In Section 3C, Reporting Findings, the chapters cover the reporting of the findings that come out of a research project. The two chapters cover the important issues of presenting your research and publishing your research.

Chapter 33 explores the issues involved in presenting research beginning with the benefits of presenting research and the importance of visual support in presentations. The author also covers the costs and benefits of doing professional presentations, as well as the importance of tailoring the presentation to the audience in terms of aims, topic, terminology, abbreviations, speed, non-verbal behavior, audience interest, and so forth. The chapter ends by discussing the controversial issue of presentation as salesmanship and the importance of experienced presenters in our field writing about the issues involved in professional presentations.

Chapter 34 is about publishing research. The chapter begins with a discussion of why publishing is important. The author then addresses the steps involved more or less in the order in which they occur: choosing an appropriate journal (that is, the etic perspective on publishing, avoiding publication mills, the quality of the journal), submitting the manuscript, waiting for a response from the journal, dealing with the initial decision (that is, accept with revision, revise and resubmit, or reject), and what to do after acceptance (the contract, open-access issues, the production cycle, and celebration).

Editors' Preview Questions

1. Once a research project is finished, would you want to share it with your colleagues? With members of the field at large? How would you go about sharing/presenting the results of a study? To whom? Where? How? (see Chapter 33)

2. Once a research project is finished, would you also want to publish the results? Where would you like to publish your study? How would you go about doing that? What problems do you anticipate with publishing your study? How would you overcome those problems? Specifically, what would you do if the first journal you submit it to rejects it for publication? (see Chapter 34)

3. Personally, why would you want to present your results publically and publish them? How would you benefit from these professional activities?

CHAPTER 33

Presenting Your Research

Andy Curtis

INTRODUCTION

Research can, of course, be presented in many different ways, the two most common of which are through writing and through speaking. As the former is addressed elsewhere in this volume (see Chapter 34), the focus of this chapter will be on presenting your research orally, for example, at conferences, at department or faculty seminars, and to other professional groups within your community of practice.

In English, there are at least 20 meanings of the word "present," within three of the main parts of speech: noun, adjective, and verb. According to Harper (2012), the original meaning was the noun, which dates from 1200 AD and comes from Latin. At that time, the noun "present" was related to the notion of "the bringing of something into someone's presence," which developed into the Late Latin *inpraesent*, meaning "face to face," and from there, via Old French, meaning "a thing offered or a gift." All of the different meanings of the original noun form of present can apply to presentations. For example, effective presentations are those that are appreciated by the audience, which relates to the gift meaning, and are those that bring the research into the presence of the audience, by presenting the content in ways that connect with the audience. Without the audience appreciating the presentation, and without that audience-presenter connection, a presentation cannot be defined or described as effective.

By the following century, in the 1300s, "present" had developed into the verb used in the phrase "to give a presentation,"coming from the Latin *praesentare*, meaning "to place before, show, or exhibit," and again from there via Old French, meaning "to bring into the presence of; to introduce formally or ceremonially." The mid-fourteenth century adjectival meaning of "being there" is also relevant, as this relates to the point made above, about the importance of the presenter and the audience connecting is some way, on some level. Part of the Old French definition, related to formal introductions, also applies to modern-day presentations, which are usually formal, even if the style of the presentation is considered to be informal, as presentations are governed by set of rules and rituals, which relates to the notion of ceremonial.

Unfortunately, the ways in which rituals are carried out are often not made explicit to those new to the community (or academic tribe), and to those attempting to gain access to the tribe. However, if the rituals are carried out incorrectly, the presenter's entry into, or standing within, that community can be compromised. For example, if an audience is expecting a more formal, data-based presentation, and they receive an informal presentation, based on anecdotes and stories, then the assumptions and expectations of the audience and the presenter have been misaligned. This can have potentially serious consequences, for example, if the presentation is part of a hiring process.

Background

Being able to present your research is important, because the more widely known your research is, the more of an impact it can make, which can become a virtuous cycle, in which having your research more widely known supports the furthering of that research. One of the most common ways of spreading the word and communicating your findings with an audience is through publication, which can take many forms, such as scholarly and academic articles or book chapters, and/or more informal professional publications (see Chapter 34). However, published work can take years to see the light of day, and even then, the work may only be accessible to those who subscribe to that particular publication, or to those who have institutional access, for example, through a college or university library subscription. Therefore, the audience for work presented orally can be larger than the audience for published work, and there is the opportunity for face-to-face interaction with an audience, which is not usually possible with published work. Although articles submitted for publication are reviewed and written feedback is given, what that written system lacks is the immediacy of the feedback and the possibility of co-operative, collaborative, co-construction of ideas in real time, with an audience. This is an important chronological contrast between the years over which a written article might need to be revised and re-written, multiple times, for a top-tier journal, as a book chapter, etc.

According to its website, Vitae is a UK-based organization which is committed to helping doctoral level researchers in higher education and research organizations develop professionally and career-wise, as well as personally. Vitae, which is funded by a number of UK-government funded research agencies, argues that researchers need to develop the important abilities necessary for presenting research to an audience of peers in a range of contexts including at least in their own academic departments and in faculty seminars, as well as at international conferences. They also remind researchers that poster sessions are one legitimate form of presentation.

Vitae further points out the importance of tailoring the content to fit the audience in different presentations. For example, a seminar presentation to an interdisciplinary group with no specialized knowledge of the academic area involved should be very different from a presentation at a conference, where the audience is made up of specialists in the same academic area. Although the first point, about the importance of the presenter's awareness of their audience, might seem obvious, there are (far too) many presentations in which it is painfully clear that the presenter is so focused on their data, their slides and themselves, that they appear to be largely unaware of their audience, or at the very least, disconnected from their audience.

Another point made above, in the Vitae site, that may appear to be self-evident relates to presentations given to a non-specialist audience, who are unfamiliar with the models, methods, and materials in the presenter's field of expertise. Perhaps even more importantly, from the perspective of language educators, the language of the discipline may not be known or understood by a non-specialist audience. Therefore, developing an ability to present research, orally and in real-time to a live audience can be an essential skill, which sensitizes presenters to other people, many of whom may be outside of the presenter's areas of expertise. This awareness and sensitivity is essential, not only with face-to-face audiences, but it can also feed positively into the researcher-presenter's writing, with a heightened awareness of the potential or target readership for their writing informing the writing process. This relates to the notion of 'reflexivity' in research, five aspects of which were listed by Linda Finlay (2002: 209): "(i) introspection; (ii) intersubjective reflection; (iii) mutual collaboration; (iv) social critique; and (v) discursive deconstruction."

Research on this Topic

In the *Portable Mentor* (2003: 133–144), Cohen, Greco, and Martin devote an entire chapter to "Presenting Your Research," which is unusual for that kind of book, and a reflection of the importance those three writers attach to being able to present effectively. Also, although the book is subtitled "Expert guide to a successful career in psychology," the advice they give regarding presentations can apply to presenters from a multitude of disciplines.

For example, according to Cohen, Greco, and Martin: "When you consider submitting your research for a conference presentation, it is wise to weigh the costs and benefits of the endeavor" (p. 133). These will be different for each presenter, but is nonetheless important for all presenters to consider the costs and benefits, which will also help them to consider carefully the reasons why they are giving the presentation, and what purposes it is intended to serve. Cohen, Greco, and Martin go on to explain that: "The benefits include disseminating information to appreciative audiences, such as professors, students, clinicians, teachers, and other professionals interested in new ideas to assist them in their own work" (p. 133). However, for audiences to be appreciative they themselves must first feel appreciated by the presenter who shows his/her respect and concern for the audience, for example, by being well-prepared, clear, and concise. Presenters can show the audience that they are appreciated by being receptive to input and feedback from the audience, even if the feedback is critical – and in some cases, especially if it is critical.

In relation to the point made above, regarding the importance of feedback, Cohen, Greco, and Martin also note that: "As a personal gain, your audience may provide feedback on your research findings which may be invaluable to you in the development of your research program" (p. 134). In relation to the benefits of giving effective conference presentations, Cohen, Greco, and Martin give other reasons as well: "Presenting research at conferences also allows for the opportunity to meet potential future advisors, employers, collaborators, and/or colleagues. Conferences are ideal settings for networking and, in fact, many conferences have forums organized for this exact purpose (e.g., job openings listed on a bulletin board and networking luncheons)" (p. 135).

One of the recurring themes in the literature on presenting research is the use of visual support to increase the effectiveness of communicating the main points to the audience. For example, Polit and Beck (2003: 625) state that: "Most conference presentations can be greatly enhanced by including visual materials (e.g., slides, transparencies, PowerPoint materials). The visual aids should be kept very simple for biggest impact." Polit and Beck also note that: "Tables are difficult to read on slides or transparencies; they can, however, be distributed to members of the audience in hard copy form. Make sure a sufficient number of copies is available." Although transparencies are now used relatively rarely, the points about clarity of visual support still apply.

In the same way that Cohen, Greco, and Martin (2003) were writing for a psychology readership, although their advice regarding presentations can be just as useful for language research-presenters, Polit and Beck were writing for nurses, but again, their advice applies equally well to language researchers and presenters. Also noted above is the fact that much of the advice given by writers and researchers such as Cohen, Greco, and Martin (2003), and Polit and Beck (2003) may appear to be obvious. However, most people who have attended large numbers of presentations will know that the misuse of visual support can be extremely common, sometimes even with experienced presenters.

This negative experience of presentations, from an audience perspective, is succinctly summed-up on the OpenWetWare wiki website, which states that: "Effectively communicating your research starts with good data but does not end there. On the contrary, many good results are so badly presented that they do not reach the audience and do not stimulate the feedback that might improve your science." As the last part of the statement shows, the OpenWetWare website is aimed at scientists, but as noted above, advice on giving presentations from fields outside of language teaching and research can be just as useful as any advice given from within the field. The site goes on to point out that: "Good presentation of scientific results is not an easy or intuitive task. It requires the putting together of an interesting slide show, good oral presentation, and provoking feedback from the audience."

Practical Applications

Some of the practical applications of being able to present your research well – i.e., clearly, concisely, and engagingly, while showing respect and care for the audience – have already been explored in the section above. However, Cohen, Greco, and Martin (2003: 135) reiterate and expand on their earlier points about the practical considerations, in terms of a cost benefit analysis, of giving positive, professional presentations: "The costs include the time commitment of writing and constructing the presentation, the potential for rejection from the reviewers, the cost of attending the conference, the anxiety inherent in formal presentations, and the time and expenses of traveling to the meeting." In spite of these and other costs, Cohen, Greco, and Martin (2003: 153) tentatively conclude that: "Although we do believe that the benefits of presenting at conferences outweigh the costs, you should consider the specific pros and cons for you, your research, the specific meeting, and your particular situation before embarking on this experience." Also in relation to practical considerations, the OpenWetWare website referred to above gives the following advice to its readers: "You are most likely more specialized than the audience. Therefore, begin by stating your aim, introduce the topic, and explain terms and abbreviations," which relates to the point made above, about presenting to non-specialist audiences. The site also reminds presenters of the importance of time management and states that there can be "no good presentation without good data." The use of "good" here is not clarified, but it could be taken to mean, for example, clear, concise, and/or convincing, and "data" here could broadly refer to any details presented to the audience, whether qualitative, quantitative, or a combination of both, as well as more visual data or more written-word data.

From the audience perspective, the site notes that there is "no control of speed of input (unlike reading)" for the audience, which means the presenter must be aware of and responsive to audience feedback, especially non-verbal or paralinguistic signals, such as furrowed brows, which may indicate audience confusion, or the audience not being able to hear clearly, not being able to see clearly, etc. The importance of such signals has been recognized within the field of linguistics for nearly 50 years now. For example, David Abercrombie (1968: 55) pointed out that: "We speak with our vocal organs, but we converse with our entire bodies; conversation consists of much more than a simple interchange of spoken words." This reference to conversation can provide a useful guide for presenters who may be anxious or nervous about standing up in front a room full of their peers and/or their academic elders, and presenting their work. Such presenters can visualize themselves having a one-to-one conversation as a goal for their presenting style. In this approach, the audience is seen as a single entity, with the presenter engaged in a dyadic interaction. This can help avoid the natural flight or fight response, in which, when faced with large numbers of other animals, human beings are genetically hardwired to either run away, or to stand and fight. As neither reaction is usually acceptable in most modern-day encounters, visualizing the audience, no matter how large, as a single entity can help nervous or anxious presenters overcome their fear, which is also a natural reaction in stressful and high-stakes situations in which the outcome is unknown.

Abercrombie (1968: 55) went on to note that: "The term *paralanguage* is increasingly commonly used to refer to non-verbal communicating activities which accompany verbal behaviour in conversation," and he concluded that: "Anyone with a professional interest in spoken language is likely, sooner or later, to have to take an interest in paralanguage too." As writers are, almost by definition, somewhat logo-centric, and focused on the word, the sentence, the paragraph, and the page, this can tend to make non-word based communication – which in many languages and cultures is proportionally greater than word-based communication – challenging for writers. Also, as most researchers are, again almost by definition, writers, when researchers present their work, they can sometimes be relatively insensitive to the non-verbal messages being communicated to them by their audience, such as lack of interest or growing interest. In terms of audience interest – although the former is negative and latter positive – both kinds of signals must be immediately received and accurately decoded, which applies to any communicatively successful speech act. This is true whether the act is locutionary, illocutionary, or perlocutionary, with most presentations falling into the perlocutionary category, as they usually have a particular purpose, such as persuading or convincing. Austin (1962: 120) argued that speech acts occur at three levels: "… the locutionary act (and within it the phonetic, the phatic, and the rhetic acts) which has a *meaning*; the illocutionary act which has a certain force in saying something; and the perlocutionary act which is *the achieving of* certain *effects* by saying something". Or more clearly:

- A locutionary act is the actual utterance along with its surface meaning.
- An illocutionary act is the underlying, intended meaning, or "illocutionary force" (Austin, 1962: 100) of the utterance.
- A perlocutionary act is the actual effect of the utterance in getting the listener to do or recognize something.

No matter how well the presenter knows his/her material, without this sensitivity to the paralinguistic messages from the audience, the presentation is unlikely to be effective.

Conclusion

Currently, in the academic world, being able to present our work orally to an audience still tends to be the poor relation of being able to write well. This is shown by the fact that more time and energy is generally put into training new researchers how to write, compared with the relatively little effort that is put into training them how to present effectively. However, this publication-presentation imbalance is gradually being redressed, and this may be an example where a common business practice can be usefully adopted by the academic community, as successful businesses realize that, unless their sales people can pitch their product, the best product in the world will go ignored and unnoticed.

Although professional academics are often uncomfortable with the notion of business practices in the academic environment, the fact remains that any kind of presentation, on some level and to some extent, is selling, albeit the selling of intellectual ideas, academic concepts, scholarly perspectives, etc. Therefore, one possible future direction will be for educational institutions to learn to put the same emphasis on the importance of being able to present effectively as business organizations puts on such skills. This notion of educators as salespeople is a controversial one, but effective presenters need to be at least open to the possibility that "the market place of ideas" is not just a theoretical construct or an abstract metaphor, but a literal situation – for example, in the case of the buying and selling that occurs in academic conferences. In the future, it may then be that this academic resistance to learning from the business world will give way to a more pragmatic and realistic acceptance of the economic realities of education, in which effective researchers and presenters need to be effective spokespersons and salespeople.

Another possible future development is that more articles and chapters such as this one will appear within the field of language education, in which experienced presenters carry out research, write, publish, and present on presenting, so that it is no longer necessary to keep borrowing from other fields. Eventually, being able to give effective presentations in our field will be accepted as a distinct sub-set of knowledge, skills, and competencies, which would lead to fewer sub-standard presentations, and more positive, professional presentations instead.

Discussion Questions

1. Do you prefer to present your work in writing or orally to an audience? Give reasons for your preferred mode of presenting your work.

2. As a presenter, would you describe yourself as "confident" or "lacking confidence"? If you are a confident presenter, from where does that confidence come? If you lack confidence, how could that be built up?

3. How would you weigh up the costs and benefits of being able to present your work to a live audience effectively and engagingly?

4. How aware are you of the paralinguistic messages sent to you from the person or people in front of you? What kinds of signals, cues, or clues do you pick up on, and what do they tell you about your audience?

References

Abercrombie, D. (1968). Paralanguage. *International Journal of Language & Communication Disorders*, 3(1), 55–59.

Austin, J. L. (1962). *How to do things with words*. Cambridge, MA: Harvard University Press.

Cohen, L. L., Greco, L., & Martin, S. (2013). Presenting your research. In M. J. Prinstein (Ed.), *The portable mentor: Expert guide to a successful career in psychology* (133–143). New York, NY: Springer.

Finlay, L. (2002). Negotiating the swamp: The opportunity and challenge of reflexivity in research practice. *Qualitative Research*, 2(2), 209–230.

Harper, D. (2012). *Online etymological dictionary*. Retrieved from: http://www.etymonline.com/

Polit, D. F., & Beck, C. T. (2003). *Nursing research: Principles and methods*. Philadelphia, PA: Lippincott Williams & Wilkins.

Openwetware. *How to present your research well*. Retrieved from: http://openwetware.org/wiki/How_to_present_your_research_well

Vitae. *Presenting your research*. Retrieved from: http://www.vitae.ac.uk/researchers/1297/Presenting-your-research-.html

CHAPTER 34

Publishing Your Research

Paul Kei Matsuda

INTRODUCTION

Writing for publication is like a conversation – much like those hallway conversations we have with our colleagues about our shared professional interests. It is a way of discussing what we know, what we do not know, what issues or problems we face as professionals, and what new information or insights we need in order to address those issues and problems. One of the major differences between casual conversations among colleagues and writing for publication is that, in the latter, the knowledge creation and sharing processes need to be more systematic and thorough in order to meet the standard of evidence expected for the particular publication outlet. Another important difference is that published writing needs to speak to a broader group of readers who have developed a shared understanding of everything that has been said and done about the topic – at least as far as the readers of the particular publication are concerned.

To publish our research successfully, then, we need to know what research questions have already been addressed as well as what research questions remain (content knowledge), how to answer research questions through data collection and analysis (methodological knowledge), and how best to communicate the information (genre knowledge). These types of knowledge will help us develop a manuscript, but to publish the manuscript successfully, we also need to know how to choose appropriate outlets for our research and to navigate through the submission process (procedural knowledge). This chapter focuses on the last category, the knowledge of the submission process, with a focus on one of the most common forms of research publications in language teaching: journal articles.

BACKGROUND: WHY PUBLISH?

Language teachers and researchers seek to publish for various reasons. The most important reason of all is to contribute to the development of a professional knowledge base. The knowledge base will help enhance our collective understanding of the nature of language, learning, and teaching, as well as of learners and teachers, and the institutional and societal conditions that surround us all. It will in turn help us develop new and better ways of teaching while avoiding reinventing the wheel. Indirectly, writing for publication can benefit language teachers because it requires us to keep up with developments in the field, giving us reasons to keep reading widely.

There are other, more practical reasons. For some, research publication is an important aspect of career advancement, as many institutions use publications as the most tangible evidence of professional development (Curry and Lillis, 2004; Flowerdew, 1999). Writing for publication is associated with institutional prestige, especially in higher education. Because research output is being used as a criterion for institutional ranking, many institutions – even those that have traditionally been teaching focused – have come to require research publications for hiring, promotion, and tenure decisions.

Although it is important to recognize the role of research publication as a tool for career advancement, excessive utilitarianism has promoted publication for publication's sake, creating problems for individuals and for the entire profession (Leki, 2003; Matsuda, 2003). Too often, novice researchers who are eager to publish their work focus on perfecting their methods, following genre conventions, and editing language; these are all important considerations, but they are not sufficient conditions for a publishable manuscript. In contrast, successful publications have a clear focus on raising new questions or providing new insights that help move the conversation forward – or at least they provide new data in support of existing claims that have not been widely accepted (Berkenkotter and Huckin, 1995). Researchers who attempt to publish for its own sake often fail unless they give enough attention to the real goal of writing for publication: contributing new knowledge to the community of knowledgeable peers.

PRACTICAL APPLICATIONS

CHOOSING AN APPROPRIATE JOURNAL

The choice of appropriate journal often depends on both etic and emic perspectives. The etic perspective reflects the values of disciplinary outsiders – i.e., the criteria established by institutions without regards to field-specific considerations. In contrast, the emic perspective reflects the values and practices of the members of the field.

THE ETIC PERSPECTIVE

In many countries, the pressure to publish for career advancement is also accompanied by the imperative to publish in prestigious journals. Traditionally, journals were considered well established if they are edited by internationally recognized experts in the field; if manuscripts are peer-reviewed by experts; if the journal has a large circulation; and if they have a relatively low acceptance rate. While the first two criteria – the involvements of the recognized experts in the field – continue to remain salient, the latter two criteria have become less relevant. With the shift from print to electronic publications, the circulation of the journal – measured by individual subscriptions – has become irrelevant, as readers access individual articles by downloading them directly from the publisher or through libraries. The acceptance rate has always been problematic as a measure of the quality of the journal because it varies with the size of the field and the number of journals that are available in the field. With the growing pressure to publish, more researchers from a growing number of countries and regions have begun to submit manuscripts and, as a result, the acceptance rates for many journals in language-related fields have become severely deflated.

More recently, governments and institutions in many countries – especially Europe and Asia – have come to rely on citation indices – databases of articles published in scholarly journals – as a way of assessing the quality of publications. Currently, one of the most influential citation indices in language-related fields is the Social Science Citation Index developed by the Institute of Scientific Information (which is now part of Thomson Scientific). Being included in a citation index means that the journal has met certain criteria, such as the number of issues per year, having a peer review system, and so on. In addition, the database can be used to estimate the impact of the journal by calculating the Impact Factor. The Impact Factor is based on the average number of times that individual articles published in any given journal are cited in other articles that are included in the database during a certain period of time.

Citation indices and the Impact Factor provide convenient ways of assessing the prestige of the journal – and, by association, of the articles that are accepted for publication in those journals. This is an important function because it is difficult, if not impossible, to assess the relative worth of knowledge contributions to the field for those who are not knowledgeable members of the field. It is important to keep in mind, however, that these etic measures do not necessarily mirror the emic perceptions of the knowledgeable members of the field about the quality or the real impact of any given article or journal.

THE EMIC PERSPECTIVE

A more important – though often neglected – consideration is the match between the insights that the author has to share and the audience who can benefit from them. The choice of publication venue can make or break the odds of getting published because what is new knowledge to one group of readers may be common knowledge to another. Different journals also have different inclinations towards certain topics, theoretical perspectives, or methodological approaches. It is important to read the guidelines for authors carefully and to study previously published articles in the journal to understand the expectations of the audience.

Here are a few questions to consider as you choose the journal:

- Does the journal publish articles on the topic of your manuscript?
- If not, can you explain why the topic is important for the readers of the journal to consider?
- Does the journal publish articles that use theoretical framework or methodological approaches that are similar to the ones used in your manuscript?
- Does the journal reach the right audience who will likely benefit from the knowledge and insights that your manuscript provides?
- Does your manuscript cite relevant sources from the journal?

If you believe the manuscript is appropriate for several journals, create a priority list. Ideally, the priority should be based primarily on the fit between insights your manuscript can offer and the needs of the audience for the journals. In reality, the criteria also include what happens to be valued by your institution, which will be determining the worth of the publication based partially on the prestige of the journal.

AVOIDING PUBLICATION MILLS

In recent years, the number of journals in language-related fields has increased considerably. Unfortunately, many venture businesses have learned that they can turn academic publishing into business opportunities by capitalizing on the academics' desire to publish. While many publishers invest the time and effort necessary in establishing the academic network that provides quality control, others seem to focus on creating the appearance of legitimacy. Some publishers contact just about everyone who has presented a conference paper or written a thesis on a relevant topic, asking them to serve as editors, editorial board members, reviewers, and contributors. While many of these publishers are "legitimate businesses" (to the extent that they seek profit without engaging in illegal activities), they are not necessarily respectable academic outlets. Publishing in those venues may not help – or may even harm – the author's professional profile or career prospect.

Here are additional questions that may help you evaluate the quality of a journal:

- Is the journal edited by well-established members of the field?
- Does the journal have editorial board members who are well established in the field?
- Does the journal have an editorial review process that involves reviewers who are experts on the topic?
- Does the journal regularly include articles by authors who are well-established members of the field?
- Are articles in the journal cited frequently and widely in other reputable journals?

These questions are only suggestive; not all quality journals meet all the criteria – especially at their inception. In the end, you have to decide which journal is more suitable for your own professional goals. If you are not sure, you may wish to consult colleagues and mentors who are more knowledgeable about the dynamics of publishing in the field.

SUBMITTING YOUR MANUSCRIPT

Once you have chosen the journal, carefully review the editorial policy, including the guidelines for manuscript preparation and the submission procedure. If the journal asks authors to prepare manuscripts in APA style, follow the guidelines in the *Publication Manual of the American Psychological Association* (American Psychological Association, 2009) carefully. Unless otherwise specified, use the latest edition. Do not use published articles as examples of how to format citations. Many publishers have their in-house style, and they will change the style to suit their own guidelines during the production process. Editors and reviewers, however, usually expect the authors to follow the style specified in the guide to authors.

If a cover letter is required, simply state your request to consider the attached manuscript (and mention the manuscript title) and provide your full contact information, including your name, institution, mailing address, phone number, fax number, and email address. For article submissions, it is not necessary to explain the content of the manuscript or its significance. Keep it simple.

For journal articles, multiple submissions are not allowed. A manuscript can be submitted only to one journal at a time, and it cannot be submitted to another journal until it has been rejected or withdrawn. Editors do often find out about multiple submissions because they or editorial board members often read manuscripts for other journals in the same field. Since manuscript reviewers are not being paid for their work, it is important not to abuse their good will.

WAITING FOR THE RESPONSE

After the manuscript is submitted, the editor (who should be an expert in the field) usually conducts a preliminary review to see if it fits the scope and general expectations for the journal. It is then sent out to several reviewers for assessment and feedback. The journal's editorial board members usually serve as reviewers, but most journals also rely on outside reviewers who have expertise in the particular topic of the manuscript. The review may take three months or longer depending on the journal's policy and the availability of appropriate reviewers. The reviews are returned to the editor, who then compiles them and makes the decision.

What if the journal editors do not acknowledge your submission or provide review results promptly? Although it is rare, it does sometimes happen. If you do not receive acknowledgments within a week or so, you can contact the editor to see if the manuscript has arrived safely. If you do not receive the review results within three months – or a time period specified in the guide to authors – wait for another week or so and then contact the editor. In any case, the communication should be professional and polite, giving the editor the benefit of the doubt. It is possible that one of the reviewers went missing in action, or that the editor got sick. Instead of accusing the editor (for example, "It has been three months and you have failed to send me the review results as promised!"), politely request an update (for example, "Would you be able to update me on the status of my manuscript, which I submitted on December 3?") If, however, you do not hear from the editor after a few attempts, it is appropriate to send the editor a letter of withdrawal and send your manuscript to another journal. (I personally would not feel obliged to wait for the editor's response in such a case.)

THE INITIAL DECISION

In general, editors' decisions fall under the following categories: a) accept as is; b) accept with revision; c) revise and resubmit; or d) reject. It is rare for manuscripts to be accepted as is, although it does happen. Even when a manuscript is rejected, it does not necessarily mean that the manuscript is fundamentally flawed. It may mean that the manuscript does not fit the scope of the journal, or that the journal has published too many articles on the same topic and is seeking to diversify its coverage. In those cases, the author can send the manuscript to another journal that might be a better fit. Once the manuscript has been rejected, it cannot be resubmitted to the same journal. It would be best not to quarrel with the editor's decision but to simply thank the editor and move on gracefully.

Even if the manuscript is rejected, do not discard your work just yet. Review your manuscript and reviewer comments to see if it might stand a chance with another journal. If you are not sure, ask a knowledgeable mentor or peer to take a look at your manuscript and the reviewer comments. Most qualified submissions fall under the category of revise and resubmit. This category allows the editor to provide the author with a chance to revise without the commitment to accept the manuscript. The editor and reviewers usually provide detailed comments to help improve the manuscript. Some novice researchers are disappointed when they are told to revise and resubmit, but they should be encouraged; it is a sign that the manuscript has a potential of being published if revised appropriately.

In responding to the comments from the editor or the reviewers, it is best to avoid reacting to the comments and suggestions. If the comments upset you, do not try to respond or revise immediately; instead, set the manuscript aside until you are level-headed. When you are ready, read each comment carefully and address each of them thoroughly. When you send the revised manuscript to the editor, it is useful to write a cover letter summarizing all the comments and explaining how you addressed each point. Some journal editors specifically instruct authors to provide the explanations, but many do not; provide item-by-item explanations anyway. In some cases, you may disagree with the comments; if so, you can try to explain why you decided not to revise as suggested. Keep in mind, however, that the reviewers' concerns may represent the perspective of other readers. Even if you believe the reviewer misunderstood your intentions, it is useful to consider why the misunderstanding may have happened, and to adjust the wording to avoid future misunderstandings.

When you resubmit the revised manuscript, the editor may make the decision to accept the manuscript – with or without additional revisions – or send it out for another round of reviews. If it is not accepted, the manuscript will probably be rejected; it is rare for the manuscripts to receive the second chance for revise and resubmit, although it does happen sometimes. If your manuscript is finally rejected, do not contest the decision. It is usually not appropriate to submit the revised version of a rejected manuscript to the same journal, but if you have revised the manuscript so completely that it appears to be a different manuscript, you might ask the editor if they would consider it as a new submission. This is also rare, but it does happen from time to time.

Once the manuscript is accepted, it will be copyedited. Some editors ask the author to review the copyedited manuscript before sending it to production. Based on the copyedited manuscript, the page proof – a typeset document that looks almost exactly like the published text – is produced. In many cases, the editor will ask the author to review the page proof for typesetting errors. Major changes are not permitted at this stage, and if extensive changes are made (especially those that affect pagination), authors may be charged to cover the expenses.

AFTER ACCEPTANCE

At some point during the production process, the publisher will ask you to sign a contract stipulating your agreement to have your work published in the journal. Read the terms of the contract carefully. Most academic journals in language-related fields do not offer honoraria or royalty payments to the authors or reviewers. It is not unusual for publishers to require the author to transfer the copyrights to the publisher. This practice is customary, and it facilitates the process of granting permissions to reprint or to quote extensively. It also makes it possible for publishers to sell the journal to another publisher without the complex process of negotiating with all of the authors. The author can usually request the publisher for the permission to reprint the article in another publication with proper acknowledgment. Depending on the publisher, the author may also be able to make part or all of the article available online. Check with the publisher for guidelines about sharing your work.

Increasingly, publishers offer the option of open access contract – even for journals that are not open access by default. The open access contract allows the author to pay a fee to the publisher in exchange for making the article accessible online to anyone for free. This option is made available for authors who have been funded by their governments or other agencies that require authors to make the outcomes of funded research open access.

The whole production cycle – from acceptance to publication – may take anywhere from a few months to over a year. If there is a large backlog of accepted articles, it may take even longer before the article is finally published. The production cycle for edited books tends to take longer.

Once the article is out, some authors promote their work by posting announcements on social media as well as their own blogs and professional websites. While it is not necessary, it can increase the chance of being noticed by potential readers who do not access the journal regularly.

Finally, take the time to celebrate your success in writing for publication. Cheers!

Discussion Questions

1. What motivates you to write for publication? Do you seek to publish out of institutional pressure? For your own career advancement? To contribute new ideas or perspectives to the field? To question or challenge the status quo? Or something else altogether?

2. Sometimes people have an inaccurate understanding of the evaluation criteria being used by their own institutions. Describe the publication expectations at your institution using concrete evidence – for example, contracts, job descriptions, department manuals,

evaluation forms, etc. To what extent do they match your assumptions about publication requirements? Are there any discrepancies? How does this information affect your own strategy for writing for publication?

3. Create a list of journals that publish articles on one of the topics you are interested in. Which ones would be more highly valued by your institution and why? Which ones are considered more prestigious among researchers and teachers in the field and why? Do your answers to these two questions match or are there discrepancies?

4. Have you received a solicitation email from a publisher or journal editor encouraging you to submit your manuscript? Using the set of questions provided under the section on avoiding publication mills, evaluate the quality of the journal. Based on your assessment, do you consider it to be a respectable journal?

References

American Psychological Association. (2009). *Publication Manual of the American Psychological Association* (6th ed.). Washington, DC: Author.

Berkenkotter, C., & Huckin, T. (1995). *Genre knowledge in disciplinary communication: Cognition, culture, power.* Hillsdale, NJ: Erlbaum.

Curry, M. J., & Lillis, T. M. (2004). Multilingual scholars and the imperative to publish in English: Negotiating interests, demands, and rewards. *TESOL Quarterly*, 38(4), 663–688.

Flowerdew, J. (1999). Problems in writing for scholarly publication in English: The case of Hong Kong. *Journal of Second Language Writing*, 8(3), 243–264.

Matsuda, P. K. (2003). Coming to voice: Publishing as a graduate student. In C. P. Casanave & S. Vandrick (Eds.), *Writing for publication: Behind the scenes in language education* (pp. 39–51). Mahwah, NJ: Lawrence Erlbaum Associates.

Leki, I. (2003). Tangled webs: Complexities of professional writing. In C. P. Casanave & S. Vandrick (Eds.), *Writing for scholarly publication: Behind the scenes in language education* (pp. 103–112). Mahwah, NJ: Lawrence Erlbaum Associates.

SECTION 4

RESEARCH CONTEXTS

This final Section 4 is about research contexts. It consists of two chapters, one about using research for language-program evaluation, and the other comparing language teacher research across six continents.

Chapter 35 is about using research for language-program evaluation. The chapter begins by discussing the differences between the notions of research methods and program evaluation. The chapter then turns to contextual factors that may influence the choices of research strategies. After exploring key issues that are involved choosing research methods, the authors survey the language-program evaluation literature. Their discussion of example evaluations highlights the notions of triangulation and logic models, and argues for the value of contextually relevant research methods in language-program evaluation.

Chapter 36 summarizes language teacher research across six continents including 68 studies conducted in Europe, the Americas, Asia, the Middle East, Australia/New Zealand, and Africa. All of the teacher researchers were systematically reflecting on their own teaching practices, but they addressed a wide range of topics and issues. This summary considers the methods used, the results, key teacher reflections, and the types of author (predominantly university level, but also including a number of elementary, middle, high school, and two private school teacher researchers).

Editors' Preview Questions

1. How does research in the context of language-program evaluation differ from research in other contexts? Do you think that program evaluation research could include a variety of research types? How so? To what degree to you think language-program evaluation

research can only be interpreted with reference to the particular program where the research was conducted? (see Chapter 35)

2. How does research in different parts of the world vary in terms of how it is conducted and interpreted? What similarities are there in research methods around the world? (see Chapter 36).

3. In what context might you find yourself doing research? What are the special characteristics of that context that would make research easy for you? Difficult? Important?

CHAPTER 35

Using Research in Language-program Evaluation

Janet Orr and Deon Edwards-Kerr

INTRODUCTION

In this chapter, we discuss key issues in using research in language-program evaluation. We will focus on the role of contextual factors in shaping the use of research strategies, taking as our starting point the link between research and program evaluation. We will then examine the key issues involved in the choice of research methods, followed by a discussion of the language-program evaluation literature. Our exemplars aim to provide practical applications of how contextual factors shape the use of the research strategies in conceptualizing, developing, and conducting evaluation in language-education programs.

Research methods form the basis for answering questions about program impact and the efficacy of program design, development, and implementation within particular settings (Alderson and Beretta, 1992). However, while most research-based studies set out to objectively prove or disprove a concept, analyze a problem, or confirm a hypothesis, program evaluation seeks to concretely answer the questions of diverse stakeholders to inform decision-making. Program evaluation also has the distinction of being the main vehicle used by policy-makers, language-education practitioners and funding bodies to verify outcomes and ensure greater accountability in language education interventions.

Research methods create opportunities to find out about program processes and products. Social, cultural, and political factors embedded in particular contexts can be both constraining and enabling in achieving desired evaluation outcomes. Therefore, the choice of research strategy is not an afterthought, but is central to the design of the evaluation.

BACKGROUND

The preceding chapters have highlighted the pragmatic use of research methods. Pragmatism is a key feature of program evaluation in any field: in this chapter, we support Beretta's view that, "evaluation is applied research and must confront the real world"

(1986: 146). Contention with "the real world" makes the contexts of the language-program evaluation a central factor in the choice of research methods, the process of conducting the evaluation, and the product of the evaluation and how it is presented.

Understanding contextual factors sheds light on the identities of the audience and participants and their willingness to accept the evaluation process and evidence. Importantly, the context of the evaluation is also inextricably linked to the purpose. Upfront clarification of the *purpose* of the evaluation must therefore be made alongside selection of research methods. As program evaluators, we take as our starting point what the evaluation outcomes will be used for, since multiple audiences may have different expectations. These expectations are linked to the audiences' sense of identity and relationship to the program and its evaluation. For example, policy-makers will want to know whether a bilingual program has impacted language learning among immigrants, and in what ways. Evaluators will have to provide them with hard evidence of effect size generated from robust experimental and quasi-experimental studies. Practitioners and educators, on the other hand, will want information about how teaching strategies are working to influence success in the classroom. They will want to know specifically, how they might go about improving teaching and learning in their classrooms. For this audience, evidence of effective practice is important and evaluators will need to present accounts of teaching strategies from multiple sources. Getting it right requires significant skills in the selection of an evaluation approach, weighing the merits of different approaches that may not match textbook models. Our practical applications below illustrate these points.

Research methods do not magically resolve these issues; in fact, they are part of the struggle with "the real world." Nevertheless, research is the means through which credible evidence is provided from a program evaluation. What do we mean by credible evidence? Across all research paradigms, credible evidence has become synonymous with validity. Although validity means different things in quantitative and qualitative research paradigms, educational researchers are all too aware of the need to show consistency and logic in data collection and analysis. The high-stakes nature of language-program evaluation makes the question of validity paramount as stakeholders routinely ask, "Are the data collection methods valid?" or, " Can we draw significant conclusions from the evidence of outcomes?" In other words, what guarantee can evaluators provide that the evidence of program outcomes or impact is based on sound research design and practice?

However, validity considerations for the multiple methods often employed in program evaluation are always a work in progress. We agree with Beretta (1986) that the usability and the use of language-program evaluations make external validity crucial. In terms of quantitative research, external validity would implicate the representativeness of the study and likelihood of generalizing from one context to another. However, in language-program evaluation – where contextual factors may differ significantly – the participants, and the resolute need to shape teaching and learning around the needs of students, render attempts at generalization problematic. The solution to this has been that language-program evaluations – as well as other forms of evaluation – have grown up as sites for the use of multiple research methods.

Research on this Topic

Language-program evaluation in the early nineteenth century focused on curriculum implementation and effectiveness (Kiely and Rea-Dickins, 2005). It guided decision-making about what was taught and what instructional techniques were used. Today, program evaluation has shifted to a more multi-dimensional examination of program effectiveness through the collection of data from multiple sources. This shift is aligned with a greater focus in educational policy on accountability and standards and the need for evidence about the worth and value of language programs. For instance, language-program evaluation today often focuses on accountability especially in K-12 schools enrolling large numbers of English Language Learners (ELL) in the United States. The monitoring of Adequate Yearly Progress (AYP), based on the National Assessment of Educational Progress (NAEP) or on state assessments, measures growth toward academic standards in a subject area. In this respect, the policy context in education is shaping the purpose and the audience of program evaluation, and, consequently how research strategies are employed.

Although second and foreign language education programs emphasize authentic teaching and learning through communicative/experiential approaches, much of the evaluation of such programs has been based on using standardized test scores as the means for evaluating program outcomes (Beretta, 1986). As the types of questions being asked shifted from strictly achievement outcomes to issues of quality in the teaching and learning process – focusing particularly on the social, cultural, and political contexts of language education programs (Lynch, 1996) – it became necessary to broaden the use of research strategies to include qualitative approaches, allowing evaluators to answer questions about implementation integrity in specific program contexts.

Moreover, language education programs through their very nature generate large amounts of complex data that require multiple methods for collection and analyses. That is, the nature of evaluation and the context of programs demand the use of research strategies that are both robust enough to produce credible results as well as flexible enough to accommodate contextual data. For example, systematic literature reviews (Willig, 1985; Slavin and Cheung, 2005) of the impact of bilingual programs point to differences in research strategies as the basis for contradictory conclusions on efficacy of such programs. In fact, in relation to bilingual education, Slavin and Cheung (2005: 275) argue for the use of qualitative and quantitative research strategies to "illuminate the conditions under which native language instruction maybe beneficial." This recognition of contextual conditions is an important consideration for evaluators in conceptualizing the research design that will underpin program evaluation.

Lynch's (1996) context-adaptive model is particularly useful in this respect to help evaluators think about aspects of program evaluation contexts that are relevant for shaping the research design, and for reporting on the evaluation. The combination of questions to be answered, the identification of and addressing key contextual issues – such as target audience(s), goals of the evaluation, and the social and political contexts – are crucial in helping evaluators to decide on whether a quantitative or qualitative approach, or a combination of both, is appropriate. Specifically, Lynch (1996: 10) makes a cogent argument for the use of multiple methods as the iterative process embedded in such an approach, "… strengthens research in applied linguistics by opening up the field to different types of knowledge and knowledge validation …"

Attention to context is not new; prior to Lynch, authors such as, Greene, Caracelli, and Graham (1989) outlined a conceptual framework for the use of mixed-methods program evaluation. They too emphasized the program evaluation context as essential to the purpose and application of mixed-methods design. It has been suggested that addressing contextual issues through appropriate articulation of research methodology will "develop greater explanatory power" of the evaluation, (Kiely and Rea-Dickins, 2005). In this way, the evaluators have reasonable basis for attribution. Attribution is particularly important in program evaluation as evaluators attempt to identify effective strategies linked with outcomes; with these links substantiated through the research process and context, evaluators have greater claim to external validity. In other words, the chances of extrapolating the findings identified that can be replicated by other interventions or in other contexts can create the basis for building future language program successes.

Practical Applications

Each evaluation design is unique, to respond to questions posed, the context of the program, and the stakeholders. Following are two applications of strategies used in diverse language-program evaluations.

Triangulating Language Teaching Strategies in a Creole-Speaking Context

An evaluation of the national curriculum in Jamaica aimed to assess the implementation of constructivist (i.e., based on the belief that learning occurs as learners are actively involved in a process of meaning and knowledge construction as opposed to passively receiving information) teaching strategies in primary literacy, English language in secondary schools, and modern languages at both levels. The outcomes of the evaluation would be used to inform policy and practice. While the vast majority of the population speaks Creole, English is the official language and is taught as a discrete subject in upper primary and secondary schools. Although supported by research, the bilingual character of language in Jamaica is unacknowledged in the mainstream.

The evaluation included the administration of survey instruments to primary and secondary teachers targeting their knowledge and use of constructivist strategies in language education. Teachers' responses were overwhelmingly in favor of constructivist approaches and positive about regular use of such methods. However, systematic observation of language classrooms, interviews with teachers and principals, analysis of national assessment results, and students' surveys revealed a different reality. For example, systematic observations showed that teachers mostly used traditional "chalk and talk" rather than the communicative approach to language teaching that would allow students to experiment with various forms of language. Students indicated that teaching was largely didactic with emphasis on right and wrong ways of speaking and using English. Moreover, secondary students felt that their home-language, Creole was marginalized in the classroom.

The dilemma for evaluators was how to reconcile these varying perspectives on the status of implementation of the teaching strategies. Unlike research studies, program evaluation cannot tolerate loose ends and there is a strong need to come up with definite and concrete answers quickly. The use of multiple methods allowed the evaluators to triangulate (i.e., check for consistency of evidence across different sources of data) the diverse views of several stakeholders. That is, survey methods were used in conjunction with interviews and systematic observations to juxtapose the perspectives of teachers, students, and principals.

A socio-cultural narrative analysis of the data helped the evaluators to examine how each stakeholder was dually committed to English as the language of instruction, as well as, Creole which constitutes their cultural identities and social interaction. For example, teachers by definition ought to be seen to be enabling the development of critical English language skills among students, ensuring that these become a part of the way they relate to the world. However, both teachers and students use Creole in their daily interactions, such that, they have a double-consciousness of language use. Although the use of Creole is minimized in the classroom, it is largely used for social interaction, so that English language skills are not always fully formed among students. One consequence of this is that the outcomes of national assessments in English Language are often poor. The effect of this is that principals with their own commitments to English Language teaching, Creole-speaking and raising student performance emphasized the need for drill and practice in English instructions as the means of passing examinations.

Although there were several contentious views about the status of the implementation of the national curriculum in English language, the use of multiple research methods (i.e., surveys, observations and interviews) in this program evaluation helped the evaluators to show that there was a critical gap between classroom practice and everyday language use that undermined effective implementation of constructivist teaching strategies in English language.

USING A LOGIC MODEL TO LINK OUTCOMES IN VARIED CONTEXTS

A donor provides grants to ten organizations supporting immigrant education. The donor's aim is to maximize immigrant student potential to ultimately access higher education by directing resources to programs that have proven effective in improving student learning and raising academic performance. He or she requested an evaluation of the endeavors of funded organizations to impact immigrant education in order to guide the donor in selecting future targets.

The evaluators work began with standard research practices including a review of documents about the programs supported by donor funds, the design of a sampling plan, the development of data collection methodology and instruments, and a data collection schedule. Data collection included minutes from network meetings, a staff implementation survey, stakeholder phone interviews, parent/community and student focus groups, and an interview with each of the organizations administrators.

Each organization in the network of funded entities focuses its services on different aspects of immigrant student life, so the next step in the evaluation process was to create a collective hypothesis that identified what educational success looks like for an immigrant student. A visioning activity brought forth unique views through the eyes of the diverse service providers, as each based their contributions on best practices and research literature in their sphere of work. Services provided by the organizations included counseling, tutoring, and mentoring immigrant students; curriculum development, parent language, literacy and championing training; professional development for teachers; and advocacy services. These perspectives were amalgamated into a vision that identified the collective impact for all funded programs anticipated.

The next step in this evaluation process was to establish a connection between the actions carried out by the organizations with the expected results of the donor. The development of a logic model seemed ideal as it "contributes to clarity about a sequence of interactive relationships" (Knowlton and Phillips, 2009). The process allows individual programs to map their path toward achieving the collective impact/outcome – producing a theory of change for each organization as well as one for the whole network. The product of logic model development is a graphic series of *if-then* statements that show the trajectory of a program through its activities, outputs, to its outcome.

In this case, the data collected provided a draft logic model which linked the donor-supported resources used for activities to the outputs the activities produced and their outcomes. Through these outcomes, we observe changes that indicate an impact – in this example, the desired impact – on the subject. The network of organizations observed how their actions contributed to change for immigrant students as and, as a result, were able to develop a supportive network with a common goal.

Logic models (e.g., Figure 35.1 overleaf) are built either horizontally or vertically, but non-linear models are also used to display relationships among project elements and are especially useful to observe feedback loops as organizations change. Displays – what logic models look like – can vary tremendously across different evaluations as they convey the complexity of organizations and the creativeness of the stakeholders. The purpose of logic models is to link activities and strategies that result in the development of a theory of how change occurs to reach specified outputs and goals. The results they demonstrate feed back into the research knowledge base.

Figure 35.1 Example Logic Model

CONCLUSIONS

Kiely and Rea-Dickins' (2005: 289) suggestion that, as evaluators, we are involved in a process of "learning through evaluation as well as learning from evaluation" highlights the extent to which research in program evaluation is as much about knowing as it is about making known – for example, language program structures and processes, the nuances of teaching strategies and how these are linked to the context and the participants, the overall program effectiveness. The exemplars above highlight this discursive relationship between the evaluation contexts, the research strategies, and the conduct of an evaluation.

Emerging trends in language-program evaluation make the need for contextually relevant research strategies even more fundamental to presenting credible evidence of program success and impact. For example, research-based indicators of instructional effectiveness are being used to judge performance levels in classrooms and to identify teachers' strengths and weakness. However, quantitative indicators on their own are insufficient to enable reliable conclusions about teacher effectiveness; evaluators must then combine these with systematic observations and structured interviews.

Similarly, increased focus on accountability in education has facilitated a shift from instructional objectives as the basis for evaluation toward utilizing more universally recognized student performance standards or frameworks that identify specific student competence – such as those produced by Teachers of English to Speakers of Other Languages (TESOL), World-class Instructional Design and Assessment (WIDA), and the Common European Framework of Reference for languages (CEFR). Often the standards are linked to instruments – such as ACCESS for ELLs, EGRA (Early Grade Reading Assessment) – that allow evaluators to quantify student progress. However, evaluators must also consider the social, economic and cultural conditions which frame both students' and teachers' everyday realities, as well as schools' pedagogical practices and philosophy, and their institutional and organizational arrangements, not just as caveats but as essential to creating understanding of how performance is framed and enabled in particular situations.

What is certain is that as innovations in research strategies have developed, these have, in turn, generated the evolution and growth of language-program evaluation, and the synergy between both has created a validation effect.

Discussion Questions

1. Explain the difference between research questions and evaluation questions?
2. How are the results of evaluations used versus the results of research studies?
3. Triangulation is used to verify facts or actions from different perspectives. As an evaluator, how do you weigh responses when they are divergent?
4. What are the implications of a logic model that uses a hypothesis to state the desired impact versus a researched-based outcome?
5. What do stakeholders contribute to the evaluation process?
6. How can language standards or language teaching standards be used in the program evaluation process?

References

Alderson, J. C., & Beretta, A. (1992). *Evaluating second language education*. Cambridge: Cambridge University Press.

Beretta, A. (1986). Toward a methodology of ESL program evaluation. *TESOL Quarterly*, 20(1), 144–155.

Greene, J. C., Caracelli, V. J., & Graham, W. F. (1989). Toward a conceptual framework for mixed method evaluation designs. *Education Evaluation and Policy Analysis*, 11(3), 255–274.

Kiely, R., & Rea-Dickins, P. (2005). *Program evaluation in language education*. Hampshire, UK: Palgrave McMillan.

Knowlton, L. W., & Phillips, C. C. (2009). *The logic model guidebook: Better Strategies for great results*. Thousand Oaks, CA: Sage.

Lynch, B. (1996). *Language program evaluation*. Cambridge: Cambridge University Press.

Slavin, R. E., & Cheung, A. (2005). A Synthesis of Research on Language of Reading Instruction for English Language Learners. *Review of Educational Research*, 75(2), 247–284.

Willig, A. C. (1985). A meta-analysis of selected studies on the effectiveness of bilingual education. *Review of Educational Research*, 55(3), 269–317.

CHAPTER 36

"It's like crossing a desert": An Oasis of Language Teacher Research Across Six Continents

Thomas S. C. Farrell

INTRODUCTION

Although Austin (1995: 182) has said that teachers conducting research can be "like crossing the desert," this chapter outlines and discusses an "oasis" of language teacher research that was conducted across six continents, 68 studies in all, carried out in Europe, the Americas, Asia, the Middle East, Australia/New Zealand, and Africa.

BACKGROUND

Language teachers are best suited to carry out research in their own classrooms because they know their context better than researchers who probably work and live in a different setting (Freeman, (1998). This has not always been the case, however, as throughout their careers language teachers have experienced research as something that is conducted on them by others. More often than not, the results of such research never get back to the teachers or to the institutions that hosted the outside researchers in the first place. Thus language teachers must be at the center of any research that is conducted in their context if it is to be meaningful to their practice (Freeman, 1998).

RESEARCH ON THIS TOPIC

TESOL's *Language Teacher Research* series was an initiative developed (by this author) with Freeman's comments in mind so that language teachers could have a forum not only to carry out research in their own context, but also to share the results of this teacher-generated research. What is distinctive about this series is that all the reported studies document how language teachers systematically reflected on their own practice. Because the range of topics in language teaching that teacher researchers can focus on is practically unlimited, all 68 chapters across the six continents were organized around a template to help authors and readers compare across chapters and volumes, by looking at aspects such as the research issue, background literature, procedures, results, and reflection explained as below.

PRACTICAL APPLICATIONS

This section outlines the oasis of existing language teacher research in terms of research topic/issue, methods used, results, reflections, and who carried out the research.

TEACHER RESEARCH IN EUROPE

Language teacher research in Europe (Borg, 2006) outlines and discusses research conducted by language teachers at different levels, many in a university setting (66% of participants), to secondary/high school setting (33% of participants), and covers 12 issues/topics, only three of which were similarly related to language teacher education. All the others were very different in focus. Table 36.1 gives a summary of the topics, the methods used in each study, the results of the studies, the authors' reflections, and the type of author.

Most issues in Europe centered on improving student learning in some way, such as finding ways of improving both the motivation and the speaking and listening skills of the engineering students on a language course, while one teacher education issue focused on better preparing learner teachers about how to do research. In addition, the most common research methods used by the participants were qualitative in nature, such as journals, questionnaires, observations, and samples of student work.

TOPIC/ISSUE	METHOD	RESULT	REFLECTION	AUTHOR
professional development for primary EFL teachers	field notes, journals	teachers motivated to do classroom research	teacher-heavy workloads and lack of time obstacles to teacher research	university
ethnic minority students writing skills at university	formative & summative data, phone interviews	noted improvements to student writing	problems with attention to detail of research design	university
secondary school learners' reflections about learning	interviews, written narratives, learner self-assessment	learners' positive attitude towards learning English	differences between views of success and importance of learning foreign language	high school
design & implement an effective literature-based English course	questionnaires, observations, test scores	literature-based learning improved autonomy and motivation of students	level of student interest in literature important for student success	high school

(continued overleaf)

TOPIC/ISSUE	METHOD	RESULT	REFLECTION	AUTHOR
(ctd.)				
research methods for learner-teachers	questionnaires, interviews, students' written/oral work	student-teachers developed research identity	challenge to develop a researcher identity	university
improve speaking & listening skills	mini-projects, pre-post-test scores, students' written/oral work	proficiency levels in speaking and listening improved	engaging in teacher research rewarding, time consuming	university
local & national action research implementation	intrapersonal journal writing, group discussions with teachers	national and local methods combined	AR methodology and importance of teacher collaboration	university
support for linguistically weaker students mixed-level ESP course	study groups, performance and evaluation data	participation of all students improved	importance of collegial collaboration	university
language teachers use when setting up tasks	audio recordings of language lessons	3 functions for teacher language: teaching, structuring, rapport-enhancing	analyzing samples of teacher language helps	university
active vs. passive participants in class discussions	questionnaires, learners' self-assessments, teaching journal	increased awareness of 'other' perspectives on oral participation	sharing between teacher and students very important	high school
pre-service course based on Multiple Intelligence theory	observations, trainees' work, end of course evaluations	MI theory can be productively applied in teacher education contexts	takes time for students to adjust to MI	university
intercultural communicative competence	interaction journals and emails	interaction journals stimulate intercultural learning	teachers important role managing and monitoring learning environments	high school

Table 36.1 Language Teacher Research in Europe

TEACHER RESEARCH IN THE AMERICAS

Language teacher research in the Americas (McGarrell, 2007) outlines and discusses a diverse range of research from both North (Canada and USA) and South America (for example, Brazil, Colombia, and Jamaica), with most conducted in a university setting and only two by practicing classroom teachers. Table 36.2 summarizes the Americas' topics, methods of research, the results, the author(s) reflection, and the type of author(s).

TOPIC/ISSUE	METHOD	RESULT	REFLECTION	AUTHOR
raise test scores reading & writing	survey, questionnaires, interviews	drafts not seen as necessity in writing tasks	not enough critical thinking	university
training pre-service teachers in teacher-feedback	survey, open-ended questions	commented inappropriately on content	with training, can learn how to comment on more than surface errors	university
films for language learning	student questionnaires	students appreciate cultural aspects of learning from films	films stimulate discussion best when students can identify with the themes	university
preparing ESL students for interactions in university	observation of students' oral discourse, interviews, teacher journal	students valued opportunities for critical inquiry	importance of teacher collaboration with ESL students	university
students problems on tests	student responses, two tests	students discovered overall purpose of articles read	tests should engage students in activities that allow them to show what they know	university
listening to stories to increase vocabulary	testing & scores of ESL students after listening to a story	reading aloud assists vocabulary gains	importance of developing curriculum to suit students' needs	elementary school
communicative techniques & writing development	observations, collaborative research sessions	students' writing improved	reflective collaboration helpful for innovative teaching approaches	university
preservice teachers resistance to using English outside class	attitude survey, focus group	students' feared loss of self-identity when using English outside class	continue to a bilingual approach to teaching	university
preservice teachers awareness of sociocultural aspects of TEFL	teaching journals, critical incident reports, videotaped classes, questionnaires	began to critique beliefs about sociocultural factors	approach helped teacher educator become more informed about teaching	university
teaching vocabulary to middle-school ESL students	sustained silent reading in class, group discussion	Spanish L1 students had the most trouble with English words of Germanic origin	importance of collecting and analyzing data about own students	middle school

(continued overleaf)

(ctd.)				
TOPIC/ISSUE	**METHOD**	**RESULT**	**REFLECTION**	**AUTHOR**
use of discourse markers	corpus linguistics (frequency counts, posterior analysis)	non-native speakers use far fewer discourse markers and conversational hedges	realization of the value of research	university
metacognition to improve English learning	exam scores, discussions, self-evaluations	no significant increase between those trained in metacognition or not	training process may be a longer-term investment	university

Table 36.2 Language Teacher Research in the Americas

Similar to Europe, most of the topics in the Americas focused on improving student learning of some sort, covering such issues as improving writing, vocabulary, listening, and better use of strategies. The researchers tended to use qualitative methods exclusively, such as survey examples of their students' work and questionnaires as well as teacher and student journals, and only one study utilized both quantitative and qualitative methods.

TEACHER RESEARCH IN ASIA

Language teacher research in Asia (Farrell, 2006) presents research that was conducted by language teachers at all levels, but mostly in a university setting and only one from high school and one from a private language school. The countries represented cover both north and south Asia. Table 36.3 summarizes Asia's topics, methods of research, the results, the author(s) reflection, and the type of author.

The topics in Asia tended to focus on the learner, learning, and how learning can become more autonomous; understanding student dependence on the teacher; creating a self-access language learning center in a high school; and developing project-based learning. Only two chapters were devoted to research on language teacher education. The researchers tended to use interviews, observations, and questionnaires as their preferred mode of data collection and as in the other volumes.

TEACHER RESEARCH IN THE MIDDLE EAST

Language teacher research in the Middle East (Coombe and Barlow, 2007) presents research that was conducted mostly by English language teacher educators in a university setting and just one high school teacher and one language training development officer. Table 36.4 summarizes the Middle East's topics, methods of research, the results, the author(s) reflection, and the type of author.

The focus of most of the research in the Middle East was on improving student performance in some way and especially in or around the writing class. Just as in the other volumes, the researchers tended to use qualitative methods such as interviews and questionnaires as their preferred mode of data collection, and two used both quantitative and qualitative methods.

TOPIC/ISSUE	METHOD	RESULTS	REFLECTION	AUTHOR
improve writing	teach genre	students' writing improved	continue using genre	university
expert and non-expert teachers learning teaching methodology	diaries, lesson plans, observations, interviews	non-expert teachers used surface approaches, experts applied concepts beyond the course	teachers need regular opportunities to reflect	university
learner autonomy in English classes	observations, interviews	independent work does not always mean independent learning	teachers should 'step back' during independent work	university
what do student teachers learn?	pre-course and post-course concept maps	students showed more detail in answers, but lack complexity	reflection with concept maps useful	university
teacher-dependent students	interviews	exam-oriented curriculum largely to blame for dependence	critical assessment of role of teacher	university
impact of self-access language learning centers	questionnaires, implementation of self-access center	hours spent voluntarily at center indication of usefulness of program	diverse learning preferences and needs served in centers	high school
improve ESL students' listening	questionnaires, implementation of process-oriented lessons	used more cognitive and meta-cognitive strategies	students developed greater self-awareness as learners	university
conflict between language and content	analysis of lectures, student evaluations	students' differing language abilities caused instructor to re-evaluate methods	most appropriate methodology is one that best suits students' abilities	university
balance between language learning and testing	student survey, curriculum revision	students wanted more TOEFL test instruction	importance of curriculum review, consult stakeholders	university
teacher & student impressions of lessons	learning logs – teacher reflections, course evaluations	students focused on process and content	teacher learned about impressions students develop about lessons	university
implementing Project Based Learning	PBL program, class discussions, observations	success dependent on appropriate planning, implementation, and assessment	use materials appropriate to linguistic abilities & interests of students	university
willingness to communicate in L2	teaching journal, tape-recorded lessons, peer observation	comprehension and participation better when content familiar	need to increase student extrinsic motivation	private school

Table 36.3 Language Teacher Research in Asia

TOPIC/ISSUE	METHOD	RESULTS	REFLECTION	AUTHOR
language learning anxiety	questionnaires, interviews, statistical analysis	causes of anxiety were peers, the language teacher, and instructional materials	language listening labs to reduce anxiety	high school
course evaluations	evaluation forms, statistical analysis	not many students able to comprehend all questions on evaluation form	translate evaluation form into students' native language	university
spelling errors	spelling activity scores	1 in 5 words misspelled at intermediate level	raise learners' awareness of graphological differences between Arabic & English	university
native English speakers & non-native speaker teachers	student essays	students definite preference for native speaking teachers	make students aware of qualities of all teachers	university
male & female students inside & outside class	survey, analysis	students see benefits of working in mixed groups – prepares them for workplace dynamics	students given more opportunities to work with opposite gender	university
exam-driven curriculum	questionnaires, interviews	exam-driven curriculum not good for facilitated learning	students want to communicate in English in authentic, occupational context	language development officer
learning contracts	questionnaires, learning contracts	students took more responsibility for learning	learning contracts positively affect motivation	university
improve students' thinking	six-lesson model to reframe thinking	model helped students plan & organize thoughts better	teachers need to promote thinking time	university
best practices in teaching	interviews, analysis	good teaching includes effective organization, link between theory & practice	some improvisation in addition to well-planned lessons	university
peer feedback on students' writing	pre/post tests, writing samples	improvement in students' writing	peer feedback good	university
students repeating same level of English class	class observation, group & individual interviews, questionnaire	70% of multiple repeaters passed course during the research project	understanding of linguistic needs of failing students crucial	university
computer assisted learning (CAL)	online surveys	students enjoyed CAL, found it useful	CAL activities need to be integrated into class content	university

Table 36.4 Language Teacher Research in the Middle East

TEACHER RESEARCH IN AUSTRALIA/NEW ZEALAND

Language teacher research in Australia/New Zealand (Burns and Burton, 2008) outlines and discusses research that was conducted mostly by English language teacher educators in a university setting and just one high school teacher and one language training development officer. Table 36.5 summarizes Australia/New Zealand's topics, methods of research, the results, the author(s) reflection, and the type of author.

Although the topics covered in Australia/New Zealand were diverse, they tended to focus on culture, the concept of authenticity, and the design of curriculum for specific audiences such as a study of the responses of students of cross-cultural parentage who speak one or more non-English heritage language, the effect of local cultural norms on students' development of English as an additional language (EAL), and how students retain new vocabulary items. Again, like all the other volumes, the Australia/New Zealand researchers tended to use qualitative research methods such as action research as their preferred mode of data collection, and one used a combination of qualitative and quantitative methods.

TOPIC/ISSUE	METHOD	RESULTS	REFLECTION	AUTHOR
immersion programs	reflective writing, interviews	most students had positive response	provide opportunity to talk to locals and host family	university
authenticity of EAP texts	recorded authentic lectures	students want explicit written outlines with lectures	students need to be taught how to adopt more reflective stances on course content	university
authentic models for teaching ESL conversation skills	pre/post tests, survey, reflective journal	listening to home-made cassettes helpful	need for clear wording in student surveys	university
retaining new vocabulary items	student reflections, interviews, video-recorded lessons	repetition, focusing, & turn-taking all had positive effects on recall new vocabulary	greater awareness of role of interaction in lessons	university
success in international exams	questionnaires, interviews, statistical analysis	higher-scoring students reported more frequent use of strategies related to all four skills	teaching test strategies in addition to the regular curriculum beneficial	International Consultant
mixed-parentage students & non-English heritage languages	40-page survey	those whose parental languages were non-English assessed literacy skill three times lower than with one English speaking parent	ask students more questions about their native languages and cultures	university

(continued overleaf)

(ctd.)

TOPIC/ISSUE	METHOD	RESULTS	REFLECTION	AUTHOR
multi-level, immigrant language classes	implementation of new curriculum	peer assistance met with unwillingness	quality of personal reflective practice enhanced	university
EAP course for discipline-specific students	implementation of EAP course, students' written work, survey	students asked for more models of critical language in English	importance of reflection on and evaluation of curriculum	private
reconciling researcher & practitioner identities	reflections on practice, email correspondence	teaching practice far less valued than research in academia	both identities equally useful and important	university
native speaking teachers' perceptions of non-native speakers	interviews	interviewed non-English native speaking teachers did not see themselves as victims	cultural awakening of researcher	university
course to improve literacy for deaf students	implementation of and ESL course for deaf students	creating maxims designed for deaf students helped to keep the course beneficial	importance of making tacit understandings of teachers explicit	university
teaching text comprehension strategies	teaching strategy skills, student samples of work	students became less teacher-dependent	must become more adaptable to classroom issues	university

Table 36.5 Language Teacher Research in Australia and New Zealand

TEACHER RESEARCH IN AFRICA

Language Teacher Research in Africa (Makalela, 2009) outlines and discusses research that was conducted by a diverse group of language educators from university professors, to ESL teacher and teacher trainers. Table 36.6 summarizes Africa's topics, methods of research, the results, the author(s) reflection, and the type of author.

Topics covered in Africa ranged from research on the challenges faced by English Communication students with isiXhosa language background to the use of debate to afford students autonomy and critical thinking skills required at a university level; how a local language can be used as a resource, not an impediment, in teaching English pronunciation; and naturalized spelling errors in the writing of university students. Although the majority of researchers in this volume tended to qualitative research methods as their preferred mode of data collection, three out of the eight studies used a combination of qualitative and quantitative methods.

TOPIC/ISSUE	METHOD	RESULT	REFLECTION	AUTHOR
difficulties with English academic writing conventions	audio recording, writing protocols, focused group discussions, interviews	neither code-translation of academic concepts nor reliance on dictionary is helpful for students	directly intervene in compositions	university
debate to develop oral English proficiency	self-reflective enquiry	teachers' and peers' feedback and assessment successfully built into the assessment of the debates	look at practical constraints of learner communication preferences	university
corrective feedback in L2 student writing	quasi-experimental, pre-, during, and post-feedback writing	comparison of pre- and post-intervention feedback writing favored post-feedback writing	focus on immediate writing needs of the learners	university
spelling errors in the writing of university students	writing tests, dictation test, questionnaires	more errors seen in de-contextualized dictation test	need for strategies of teaching spelling at secondary school levels	university
acquisition of English vocabulary	COBUILD pattern grammar series	challenges with students recalling lexical items for use due to inadequate lexical knowledge and failure to make use of lexical information	precise presentation of lexical information, and shifts in meaning	university
text genre and process writing drills	ethnography and quasi-experimental design	level of uptake on process writing very low	assumptions of process writing not met in culture that has different orientation for organization of ideas	university
local language as resource in teaching English pronunciation	corrective feedback, post-feedback pronunciation task	improved pronunciation skills & positive attitudes toward English pronunciation	teachers decide what to concentrate on	university

Table 36.6 Language Teacher Research in Africa

Conclusion

A common theme across the six continents and 68 studies is how teachers can improve student performance in various aspects of language learning, with the majority of researchers using some kind of qualitative research methods as their preferred mode of data collection, with only seven out of 68 studies (or ten percent) using some form of quantitative research methods. Most of the research seemed to have been conducted in university settings in each region, although Asia seemed to produce more research with the high or middle school system. This result could likely be because people working in university settings are given more time and funding, and are also expected to complete research regularly, whereas secondary or middle school teachers are not. Given the result of this cross analysis that across all six continents practicing ESL teachers seem to be grossly underrepresented, it may be necessary for international organizations such as TESOL and IATEFL to provide more support for these teachers to systematically reflect on their own practices.

Discussion Questions

1. Why do you think that most of the research conducted across the six continents reported on in this chapter was conducted at the university level?

2. Most of the topics of research conducted across the six continents were about improving student performance in some manner. What topic(s) of research would you like to research and why?

3. Look at each of the topics in each of the six continents in this chapter (try to get each volume cited in the references below). Which topic would you like to replicate and why?

References

Austin, T. (1995). Teacher as researcher: A synonym for professionalism. *Journal of Teacher Education*, 48(5), 179–192.

Borg, S. (Ed.). (2006). *Language teacher research in Europe*. Alexandria, VA: TESOL.

Burns, A., & Burton, J. (Eds.) (2008). *Language teacher research in Australia & New Zealand*. Alexandria, VA: TESOL.

Coombe, C., & Barlow, L. (Eds.) (2007). *Language teacher research in the Middle East*. Alexandria, VA: TESOL.

Farrell, T. S. C. (Ed). (2006). *Language teacher research in Asia*. Alexandria, VA: TESOL

Freeman, D. (1998). How to see: The challenges of integrating teaching and research in your own classroom. *The English Connection* 2, 6–8.

Makalela, L. (Ed.) (2009). *Language teacher research in Africa*. Alexandria, VA: TESOL.

McGarrell, H. M. (Ed.). (2007). *Language teacher research in the Americas*. Alexandria, VA: TESOL.

Index

Abercrombie, David 269
action research 30–1, 63, 92–3, 99–104, 105
　challenges in the ELT field 104
　conceptualisations of 100–1
　criticisms and constraints 100
　demonstration 93
　elements of 99
　features of the approach 99–100
　forms of 101
　influence of complexity theory 103
　influence of dynamic systems theory 103
　influential concepts 100
　member checks 101
　models of 102
　practical applications 102–3
　praxis concept 100
　processes 102–3
　research on this topic 101–2
　self-reflexivity 101
　triangulation 101
Africa, language teacher research 296–7
allusion, in image-nuclear news stories 136
American Council of Teachers of Foreign Languages (ACTFL) 212
Americas, language teacher research 290–2
Analysis of Covariance (ANCOVA) 256, 259
Analysis of Variance (ANOVA) 48, 58, 255, 256, 258–9
analytic rubrics 239, 240, 241, 244
Asia, language teacher research 292, 293
Australia, language teacher research 295–6
autobiographic interviews 211

autoethnography 63, 64, 155, 157–61
　considerations and challenges 159–61
　criticisms 159–61
　ethical considerations 161
　future developments 161
　stages and steps in narrative research 158–9
axiological layer of consciousness 70, 71, 74

Bacon, Francis 71
Bank of English corpus 120
behaviorism 232, 233
Belmont Report (1979) 184
beneficence principle 177, 178, 184
bivariate Pearson correlations 256, 257–8
Brew, Angela 3
British National Corpus 119

Cambridge International Corpus 123
Cambridge Learners' Corpus (CLC) 122, 123
case study, definition 112
case-study research 63, 72–3, 112–17
　advantages of 112–13
　application in language education 112–13
　conducting case-study research 114–17
　crucial elements 114–17
　definition of a case study 112
　development in SLA and L2 education 113–14
　example (Anna) 112–13, 114
　outcomes 117
　practical applications 114–17
　research on this topic 114
　scope of 113–14
　types of cases 112
catalytic validity of critical research 96

Chaudron, Craig 28
chi-square test 48, 58, 256, 257
Chomsky, Noam 233
citation indices 274
clarification technique 81–3
classroom discourse, conversation analysis 130–1
classroom discourse analysis 137
cluster sampling 201, 202
Collins Birmingham University International Language Database (COBUILD) 120
commensurability legitimation 80
communicative competence concept 134–5
Communicative Language Teaching movement 149
complexity theory 103
concordancer programs 123–4
concurrent introspection 248
confounding variables 56, 219
consent forms 177
constructionism 3
constructivist teaching strategies 284–5
context, language teacher research across six continents 288–98
context-adaptive model 283
control variables 56
convenience sampling 202
convergence technique 80, 81–3
conversation analysis 48, 63, 127–32, 137
　agnostic stance toward social categories and identities 129
　co-construction of language 129
　definition 127–8
　future directions 131–2
　history of development 128
　practical applications 130–1
　research approach 128
　research on this topic 129–30

299

conversation analysis (*cont.*)
  student-initiated research 131–2
  transcripts 127–8
  understanding classroom discourse 130–1
  use of naturalistic data 128–9
conversion legitimation 80
corpus-assisted discourse analysis 137
Corpus of Contemporary American English (COCA) 119, 121, 122, 123
corpus research 119–25
  areas for further development 124–5
  concordancer programs 123–4
  corpora used in language teaching and research 119
  corpus-based research areas 120–2
  definition of corpus linguistics 119
  development of learner dictionaries 120
  doing corpus research 123–4
  formulaic expressions 120
  grammar 121
  learner corpora 122
  lists of commonly used words 120
  phraseology studies 120
  practical applications 122–4
  register 121–2
  using corpora in the classroom 119, 122–3
  vocabulary 120
correlation (statistical procedure) 58, 257–8
correlational research designs 57, 58
Cramer's V coefficient 256, 257
Creole speakers in Jamaica, evaluation of English language teaching 284–5
critical approaches to classroom research 31–2
critical discourse analysis 74, 93–4, 136
  demonstration 93–4
critical ethnography 94–5, 152–3
  demonstration 94–5
critical research 89–96
  action research 92–3
  catalytic validity 96
  critical discourse analysis 93–4
  critical ethnography 94–5

critical theory 90
deciding on a methodology 92–5
developing a critical research question 91–2
distinction from other approaches 90
ideology critique 95
importance of the critical agenda 96
introduction in language education and TESOL 89–90
practical applications 91–5
research on this topic 90
starting with a critical agenda 91
critical strategies 73–4
critical theory 90
critiquing the research of others 11–17
  approach to 11–12
  checklist for assessing research 13–15
  critical approach to reading research 15–17
  definitions of research 12–13
  importance of context 12
  practical applications 13–17
  "reading against" a text 15–17
  research on this topic 12–13
  views on who should conduct research 12–13
cross-cultural communications 137–8
cross-tabulations 257
cultural (intercultural) competence 149

data-driven learning (DDL) 119, 123
data elicitation methodologies 231
Davies, Mark 121, 122
delayed retrospection 248
dependent variables 56, 254
diary studies 235, 247–51
  analysis of data 248, 250
  as a research procedure 247–8
  concurrent introspection 248
  critiques 250–1
  delayed retrospection 248
  features of 247
  immediate retrospection 248
  in mixed methods studies 250
  introspection 247–8

  issue of selective recording 248
  methodology 250–1
  methods of recording journal entries 250
  practical applications 249–51
  research on this topic 248–9
  role in language teaching and learning 247
  stimulated recall 248
  think-aloud procedures 248
  use of computer analysis 250
  value of a language-learning journal 249–50
  value of a teaching journal 249–50
dictionaries, development of learner dictionaries 120
digital environments, research ethics 181
directional hypothesis 193
discourse analysis 74, 134–8
  classroom discourse analysis 137
  communicative competence concept 134–5
  conversation analysis 137
  corpus-assisted discourse analysis 137
  critical discourse analysis 136
  cross-cultural communications 137–8
  features of 134
  future developments 138
  genre analysis 135–6
  history of development 134–5
  identity research 136–7
  image-nuclear news stories 136
  Japanese discourse conventions 135, 137–8
  multimodal discourse analysis 136, 138
  non-linguistic behavior 134, 135
  online communities 136–7
  practical applications 137–8
  pragmatics 135
  research on this topic 135–7
  social and cultural setting 134–5
  social media 137
  structure of discourse 135
  use of allusion 136
  use of ethnographic data 135–6
  using interviews 211

divergence technique 80–2
dynamic systems theory 103

Education Resources Information Center (ERIC) Digests 43, 45
effect size and statistical significance 59, 259
elaboration technique 81–3
emic perspective 146, 154, 273, 274
epistemological perspective 70–1
ethics in research 176–81
  anonymity 177
  approach to ethical decision-making 181
  aspects of 176
  beneficence principle 177
  confidentiality 177
  considerations relating to human subjects 183–4
  definition 176
  ethical clearance for research projects 176–7
  ethical criteria 177
  "ethics of care" model 178
  ethnographic research 152
  informed consent of research participants 177, 181
  informed consent with unequal power dynamics 179–80
  justice principle 177
  language research 177
  language research in multilingual and multicultural settings 180–1
  macroethical framework 177–8
  microethical framework 178
  narrative inquiry 161
  ongoing review of ethical practice 181
  practical applications 179–81
  qualitative research 65
  questionnaire research 222–3
  research on the topic 177–8
  researching digital environments 181
  respect for persons 177
  risk/benefit ratio 177
  tensions and dilemmas 177–8
  virtue ethics theory 178
  see also human subjects review
ethnographic data, use in discourse analysis 135–6

ethnographic interviews 211
ethnography 63, 64, 146–53
  application in educational contexts 148–9
  carrying out ethnographic research 149–52
  coherence for an outside audience 148
  critical ethnography 94–5
  critical turn in ethnography 152–3
  definition of ethnographic research 146
  describing research as "ethnographic" 149–50
  development of the ethnographic perspective 146
  emic perspective 146
  ethical issues in ethnographic research 152
  evaluating ethnographic research 147–8
  features of ethnographic studies 72–3, 146–8
  history of development 146
  macro perspective 147
  member checking 147–8
  micro perspective 147
  practical applications 149–52
  reflexivity 148, 149
  research on this topic 148–9
  thick description 146–7
  widespread use as research methodology 152–3
  see also autoethnography
etic perspective 146, 154, 273–4
Europe, language teacher research 289–90
ex post facto research designs 57, 58
Exact Test 256, 257
exemplification technique 81–3
experimental strategies 70, 71–2
expert sampling 202
external validity of quantitative research 56–7, 282

factor analysis (statistical procedure) 58
Finlay, Linda 267
focus groups 224–9
  analysis of data 226
  as a research method 227

  benefits of 225–6
  characteristics 225
  combining with other methods 229
  definitions 224–5
  focus group practice 228–9
  key issues 226–7
  limitations 226
  nature of focus group research 224
  participant interaction aspect 226–7
  practical applications 227–9
  reporting of methodology 227
  research implementation challenges 229
  research on this topic 226–7
formulaic expressions 120
Freeman, Donald xiv, 288
French learner corpora 122
funding see research funding and grants

Gardner's social-cultural model of motivation 39, 40
Garfinkel, Harold 128
Geertz, Clifford 64
generalizability of quantitative research 56–7
genre analysis 135–6
Goffman, Erving 128
grammar, corpus-based research 121
grants see research funding and grants
grounded theory 72–3, 214

Harris, Zellig 134
Hawthorne Effect 57
Heath, Shirley Brice 64
hermeneutic model of knowledge 70, 71
hermeneutic utility of language 69–70
heterogeneity/diversity sampling 202
holistic rubrics 238, 239, 240–1
human subjects review 183–7
  beneficence principle 184
  ethical considerations 183–4
  formal review processes 185–7
  guidelines for good practice 184
  justice principle 184
  macroethical principles 184, 185
  microethical principles 184–5
  ongoing review of ethical guidelines 187

human subjects review (cont.)
  practical applications 185–7
  research ethics committees 185–7
  research on this topic 185
  respect for persons 184
  respect for the rights of individuals 183–4
  review boards 185–7
  see also ethics in research
hypotheses 192, 193
hypothesis testing 253

identity research, discourse analysis 136–7
ideology critique 95
illocutionary aspect of a presentation 269
image-nuclear news stories 136
immediate retrospection 248
Impact Factor for a journal 274
independent variables 56
informed consent of research participants 177, 181
  with unequal power dynamics 179–80
inside-out legitimation 80
Institute of Scientific Information 274
integrated research designs 74–5
interaction technique 81–3
internal validity of quantitative research 56–7
International Corpus of Learner English (ICLE) 122
International English Language Testing System (IELTS) 212
interpretative strategies 72–3, 74
intervening variables 56
interviews 209–14
  analysis methods 214
  as a research topic 212–13, 214
  autobiographic interviews 211
  decision to interview 213–14
  discourse analysis 211
  ethnographic interviews 210, 211
  future directions 214
  generic features 209
  grounded theory method of analysis 214
  instrument view 212–13, 214
  introspective research method 234–5

  language biographies 211
  life history interviews 210, 211
  longitudinal interview studies 210–11
  memoirs (interview type) 211
  narrative interviews 211
  Observer's Paradox 211
  oral proficiency interviews (OPIs) 211–12
  participants 209
  practical applications 213–14
  protocols 210
  qualitative interviews 210–11
  representation in the research report 214
  research on this topic 209–13
  role in language research 209
  social practice view 212–13, 214
  sociolinguistic interviews 211–12
  standardized survey interviews 209–10
  theoretical perspectives 212–13, 214
  variationist sociolinguistics 211
introspection 247–8
introspective research methods 231–6
  choice of appropriate method 235–6
  data elicitation methodologies 231
  diary studies 235
  exemplary studies 236
  goal of 231–2
  history of development 232
  influence of behaviorism 233
  interviews 234–5
  practical applications 235–6
  research on this topic 232–5
  retrospection 234
  retrospective study (self-revelation) 234
  role in language research 231–2
  self-observation 234
  self-report 233–4
  self-revelation 234
  stimulated recall 234
  talk alouds (self-report) 233–4
  think alouds (self-observation) 234
  underlying assumptions 236
  use in language research 232–5
  variety of types and uses 235–6
  verbal reporting 233–4

Jamaica, evaluation of English language teaching for Creole speakers 284–5
Japanese discourse conventions 135, 137–8
Jefferson, Gail 128
journal publication see publishing your research
justice principle 177, 184

Labov, William 211
language biographies 211
language-program evaluation 281–6
  accountability and standards 283, 286
  constructivist teaching strategies 284–5
  context-adaptive model 283
  credible evidence 282, 286
  emerging trends 286
  influence of findings 281
  practical applications 284–6
  pragmatic use of research methods 281–2
  purpose of 281–2
  qualitative approaches 283
  research focus 282–3
  research on this topic 282–3
  research strategies 283, 286
  role of contextual factors 281–2, 283–6
  selection of an evaluation approach 281–2
  triangulating language teaching strategies in a Creole-speaking context 284–5
  use of multiple research methods 282, 283
  using a logic model to link outcomes in varied contexts 285–6
  validity considerations 282, 283
language teacher research
  across six continents 288–98
  common theme across six continents 298
  importance of teacher research 288–9
  in Africa 296–7
  in Asia 292, 293
  in Australia/New Zealand 295–6
  in Europe 289–90

in the Americas 290–2
in the Middle East 292, 294
Language Teacher Research series 288–98
practical applications 289–97
see also teacher research
legitimation, nine subtypes of 80, 82–3
Lewin, Kurt 100
life history interviews 210, 211
linguistic ethnography 63
literature review 42–4, 169–74
benefits for a research study 169–73
creating a research niche 169, 171–2
definition 169
identifying a gap in the literature 171–2
practical dos and don'ts 174
purposes of 169–71
role in a research study 169
structure of 170–1
locutionary speech acts 269
logic models, linking outcomes in varied contexts 285–6
Louvain Corpus of Native English Conversation (LOCNEC) 122
Louvain Corpus of Native English Essays (LOCNESS) 122
Louvain International Database of Spoken English Interlanguage (LINDSEI) 122

Marx, Karl 11
member checking/validation 63, 101, 147–8
memoirs (interview type) 211
Merton, Robert 225, 227
metaphors, assumptions underlying 69
methodology *see* research methodology choice
Michigan Corpus of Academic Spoken English (MICASE) 119, 122
Michigan Corpus of Upper-level Student Papers (MICUSP) 119, 122
Middle East, language teacher research 292, 294

mixed methods research (MMR) xiii, 31, 46, 63, 66, 74–5, 78–83
definition 78, 79
distinction from other research methods 78, 79
legitimation of MMR 79–83
nine subtypes of legitimation 80, 82–3
practical applications 79–82
research on this topic 79
research questions 194, 196
six practical techniques to enhance MMR studies 80–3
types of 78–9
use of diary studies 250
use of focus groups 229
modal instance sampling 202
moderator variables 56
motivation, Gardner's social-cultural model 39, 40
multimodal discourse analysis 136, 138
multiple research methods, use in language-program evaluation 282, 283
multiple validities legitimation 80

narrative inquiry 48, 63, 73, 155–61
applications in education 156
autoethnography 155, 157–8
characteristics in ELL 156–7
characteristics of 155–6
considerations and challenges 159–61
criticisms 159–61
ethical considerations 161
future developments 161
practical applications 158–61
range of applications 156
research on this topic 156–8
stages and steps in narrative research 158–9
narrative interviews 211
naturalistic paradigms 68
New Zealand, language teacher research 295–6
non-directional hypothesis 193
non-linguistic behavior 134, 135
nonprobability sampling 199, 200, 202–3
nonproportional quota sampling 202

nonproportional random stratified sampling 201
noun-noun sequences 121
null hypothesis 59, 193
null hypothesis significance testing (NHST) 59

Observer's Paradox 211
one-group pre-test – post-test design 57–8
one-shot case study 57
online communities, discourse analysis 136–7
online questionnaire development programs 222
ontological perspective 69–70
OpenWetWare wiki website 268
oral presentation of research *see* presenting your research
oral proficiency interviews (OPIs) 211–12

paradigmatic mixing legitimation 80
paralanguage 268–9
perlocutionary aspect of a presentation 269
phenomenological studies 73
phi coefficient 256, 257
phraseology studies 120
political legitimation 80
positivist paradigms 68
postpositive paradigms 68
power relations in language learning 73–4
pragmatic strategies 74–5, 135, 281–2
praxis concept 100
pre-experimental designs 57–8
presenting your research 265–70
advantages of oral presentation 266
definitions of "present" 265–6
feedback from the audience 267, 268
illocutionary aspect of a presentation 269
importance of effective presentation 267–8
importance of presenting well 265–6
levels of speech acts 269

presenting your research (*cont.*)
  locutionary speech acts 269
  negative effects of bad presentation 268
  non-verbal messages from the audience 268–9
  oral presentation skills 266–8
  paralinguistic signals from the audience 268–9
  perlocutionary aspect of a presentation 269
  practical applications 268–9
  presentation training for researchers 269–70
  reflexivity in research 267
  research on this topic 267–8
  taking account of the audience 266–7, 268–9
  use of visual support 267–8
  Vitae organization 266
  ways of presenting research 265
  weighing costs and benefits 267, 268
  see also publishing your research
pre-test – post-test control group design 58
primary sources 43
primary trait rubrics 238, 239, 241
probability sampling 199, 200–2
program evaluation *see* language-program evaluation
proportional quota sampling 202–3
proportional random stratified sampling 201
publishing your research 266, 272–7
  after acceptance 277
  avoiding publication mills 274–5
  career advancement tool 273
  choosing an appropriate journal 273–5
  citation indices 274
  content knowledge 272
  contracts 277
  copyright and permissions 277
  editor's initial decision on your manuscript 276–8
  emic perspective 273, 274
  etic perspective 273–4
  factors in successful publication 272
  genre knowledge 272
  guidelines for manuscript preparation 275
  Impact Factor for a journal 274
  journal submission process 272, 273–7
  knowledge sharing process 272
  methodological knowledge 272
  online access 277
  open access contracts 277
  procedural knowledge 272
  production cycle timescale 277
  professional knowledge base 272–3
  promotion using social media 277
  reasons for publishing 272–3
  revising and resubmitting your manuscript 276–7
  Social Science Citation Index 274
  submitting your manuscript 275
  waiting for the response 275–6
purposive sampling 202–3

qualitative research xiii, 31, 46, 61–6
  approaches to 63–4
  background 62–4
  characteristics of 61–2
  definitions 61
  development of 62–3
  ethical challenges 65
  focus of 61
  future need for 66
  growth of mixed methods 66
  holistic aspect 62
  inductive aspect 62
  interviews 210–11
  language-program evaluation 283
  local situatedness 62
  methodologies 63–4
  participant-orientation 62
  practical applications 65
  quantitative–qualitative debate 29–30, 31
  range of research methods 64–5
  relevance to language teaching and learning 64–5
  research on this topic 64–5
  research questions 193, 195–6
  researcher sensitivity 62
  respondent/member validation 63
  rigour and reliability issues 66
  thick description 64
  triangulation 63
quantitative research xiii, 31, 46, 55–60
  definition 55
  external validity 56–7
  focus of 55–7
  generalizability 56–7
  internal validity 56–7
  issues for teachers to consider 55–9
  null hypothesis significance testing (NHST) 59
  practical applications 59
  purposes of 55
  quantitative–qualitative debate 29–30, 31
  range of research designs 57–8
  replication research 140–4
  research on this topic 57–9
  research questions 193, 194–5
  statistical significance and effect size 59
  statistical tests 58–9
  types of variables 56
quasi-experimental designs 48, 57, 58
questionnaires 217–23
  administering 222
  advantages and disadvantages of using 218
  analyzing 222
  design considerations 219–21
  designing and formatting a questionnaire 219
  ethical principles of questionnaire research 222–3
  features of 217–18
  feedback 221
  length of 220
  online questionnaire development programs 222
  open/closed format for questions 220
  piloting 221
  practical applications 219–22
  purpose of 217–18
  qualities of good questionnaires 218–19
  question order and grouping 220–1
  question types 220

reasons for doing questionnaire
  research 218
 research on this topic 218–19
 response rate 221
 role in ELT research 217
 sample size 221
 writing good survey items 221–2
 see also survey research

random sampling techniques 201–2
rating scales *see* rubrics
reflexivity in research 267
 in ethnographic research 148, 149
register, corpus-based research 121–2
regression (statistical procedure) 48, 58, 256
replication research 40–1, 140–4
 approximate (partial) replication 141
 argument for repeating previous studies 140–3
 challenges for researchers 143–4
 conceptual (constructive) replication 141
 distinction from follow-up or extension studies 141–2
 practical applications 143–4
 research on this topic 142–3
 role in scientific methodology 142–3
 role in validation of previous findings 142–3
 scarcity in applied linguistic research 140–3
 sources of possible replication research studies 143
 types of replication studies 141
reporting findings *see* presenting your research; publishing your research
research, definitions xiv, 12–13, 27–8, 39
research design 42
 for quantitative research 57–8
research funding and grants 19–26
 annotated model of a successful grant application 22–5
 checklist for research applications 25
 features of a good application 25–6

making a convincing case 20–1
 practical applications 20–5
 sources of funding and grants 19–20
 the need to secure funding 19
 writing a grant application 19–20
research in the language classroom 27–32
 action research 30–1
 approaches to 31–2
 critical approaches 31–2
 definitions of research 27–8
 mixed methods research 31
 practical applications 30–1
 quantitative–qualitative debate 29–30, 31
 reasons for undertaking 28–9
 research on this topic 29–30
 role of students 31–2
 why it is important 28–9
research literacy xiv–xv
research methodology choice 46–51
 eight steps to use in decision making 48–51
 influence of research type 48
 learning about new methods 51
 mixed methods research 46
 narrowing the range of options 46–8
 practical applications 48–51
 proliferation of research methods xiii–xiv
 qualitative research methods 46
 quantitative research methods 46
 range of research methods 47–8
 research on this topic 47–8
research niche creation 169, 171–2
research paradigms in second language research 68–75
 assumptions underlying metaphor 69–70
 axiological layer of consciousness 70, 71, 73–4
 case studies 72–3
 critical discourse analysis 74
 critical strategies 73–4
 epistemological perspective 70–1
 ethnographic studies 72–3
 experimental strategies 71–2
 gaining knowledge of the language learner 70, 71

grounded theory 72–3
 hermeneutic model of knowledge 73–5
 hermeneutic utility of language 69–70
 integrated research designs 74–5
 interpretative strategies 72–3, 74
 methodological perspectives 70–1
 mixed methods approach 74–5
 narrative research 73
 naturalistic paradigms 68
 nature of language and the second language learner 69–70
 nature of the research paradigm 68
 ontological perspective 69–70
 perspectives 69–71
 phenomenological studies 73
 positivist paradigms 68
 postpositive paradigms 68
 power relations in language learning 73–4
 pragmatic strategies 74–5
 re-storying 73
 stereotypes 74
 strategies 71–5
 symbolic interactionism 69–70
 tripartite hermeneutic model of knowledge 70, 71
 types of 68
research problem
 components 41–2
 identifying a research problem 39–40
 sources of 40–1
research project
 checklist for framing and defining 44
 components of a research problem 41–2
 framing and defining 39–44
 identifying a research problem 39–40
 influence on quality of results 44
 literature review 42–4
 nature of a research project 39–40
 nature of research 39
 replication of previous research 40–1
 research design 42
 research on framing and defining 42–3

research project (*cont.*)
　significance of the research problem 42–3
　sources of research problems 40–1
research questions (RQs) 190–6
　categories of 190
　challenge of developing good RQs 190–3
　developing a critical research question 91–2
　examples of well- and poorly-written RQs 194–6
　features of effective RQs 196
　hypotheses relating to 192
　in mixed methods research studies 190, 193, 194, 196
　in qualitative research 190
　in quantitative research 190
　influence on study design 191–2
　location in the manuscript 191
　number per study 191–2
　order in the study 193
　practical applications 194–6
　qualitative RQs 193, 195–6
　qualities of good RQs 194
　quantitative RQs 193, 194–5
　research on this topic 193–4
　roadmap analogy 190, 196
　role in the research design 57
　sources of 191
research type, influence on research method used 48
respect
　for persons 184
　for the rights of individuals 183–4
respondent validation 63
re-storying 73
retrospection 234
rubrics 238–45
　advantages and disadvantages of different types 240–1
　analytic rubrics 239, 240, 241, 244
　approaches to rubric construction 242–3
　appropriateness for a given research use 241–2
　automated scoring systems 244
　choice of 241–2
　definition of a rubric 238
　holistic rubrics 238, 239, 240–1

issues in scoring language performance 244
　practical applications 243–4
　primary trait rubrics 238, 239, 241
　raters 238
　research on this topic 242–3
　role in language performance assessment 240, 244–5
　types of 238–40
Ryle, Gilbert 64

Sacks, Harvey 128
sample legitimation 80
sampling 198–204
　and statistical procedures 203
　categories of 199
　definition 198
　generalization and sample representativeness 198, 199–200
　methodologies used in language research 203–4
　nonprobability sampling 199–200, 202–3
　practical applications 200–3
　probability sampling 199–200, 200–2
　purpose of using samples 198
　random sampling techniques 201–2
　research on this topic 199–200
　sample representativeness 198, 199–200, 203
　sample size 203
　sampling methods and implications 199–203
Schegloff, Emanuel 128
scholarship 3–4, 5
secondary sources 43
self-observation 234
self-reflexivity 101
self-report 232, 233–4
self-revelation 234
sequential legitimation 80
simple random sample (SRS) 201
snowball sampling 202
social-cultural model of motivation (Gardner) 39, 40
social media, discourse analysis 137
Social Science Citation Index 274
sociolinguistic interviews 211–12
Spanish learner corpora 122

speech acts, levels of 269
standards for student competence 283, 286
static-group comparison 57–8
statistical analysis of data 253–60
　Analysis of Covariance (ANCOVA) 256, 259
　Analysis of Variance (ANOVA) 255, 256, 258–9
　bivariate Pearson correlations 256, 257–8
　chi-square test 256, 257
　consideration in research planning 259–60
　correlations 256, 257–8
　Cramer's V coefficient 256, 257
　criteria for effective use 259–60
　cross-tabulations 257
　effect size procedures 259
　Exact Test 256, 257
　hypothesis testing 253
　identifying and measuring variables 254
　importance of data accuracy 253
　phi coefficient 256, 257
　practical applications 255–9
　preparing data for statistical analysis 254–5
　research on this topic 254–5
　screening data for statistical analysis 255
　selecting appropriate statistical tests 255–9
　Statistical Package for the Social Sciences (SPSS) 254
　statistical significance 59, 253, 259
　t-tests 256, 258
　tests used in language studies 58–9
　see also sampling
Statistical Package for the Social Sciences (SPSS) 254
statistical significance 59, 253, 259
stereotypes 74
stimulated recall 234, 236, 248
storytelling *see* narrative inquiry
stratified random sampling 201
student-initiated research 131–2
students, role in language classroom research 31–2
subject selection issues 56–7

survey interviews 209–10
Survey Monkey 222
Survey Select 222
symbolic interactionism 69–70
systematic sampling 201

t-tests 48, 58, 256, 258
talk alouds (self-report) 233–4
teacher research 3–9, 105–10
    and action research 105
    approaches to research 3
    as part of formal study programs 106
    as scholarship 3–4, 5
    barriers to 6–9, 107–8
    benefits of doing research 6
    challenges of 110
    components of 3–5
    constructionist approach 3
    definition 105
    facilitators of teacher research 109–10
    foreign/second language classroom research 5–6
    methodologies 105
    motivations for 6, 8–9, 28–9
    origins of 105–6
    practical applications 4–5, 6, 108–10
    practical manuals 106
    publications in language education 106
    relevance and role for teachers 107–8
    research on teacher engagement 5–6
    research on this topic 106–8
    role of teaching practice 4–5
    school leader perspective 109
    teacher as researcher 6
    teacher researcher perspective 108
    views on who should conduct research 12–13
    see also language teacher research
TESOL, critical research 89–96
thick description 64, 146–7
thin description 146
think-aloud procedures 234, 248
triangulation 63, 101
tripartite hermeneutic model of knowledge 70, 71
true experimental designs 57, 58
typical case sampling 202

variables, types of 56
variationist sociolinguistics 211
verbal reporting 233–4
virtue ethics theory 178
Vitae organization 266
vocabulary, corpus-based research 120

weakness minimization legitimation 80
word lists 120

Notes